Treating Sex Offenders

Treating Sex Offenders
An introduction to sex offender treatment programmes

Sarah Brown

WILLAN
PUBLISHING

Published by

Willan Publishing
Culmcott House
Mill Street, Uffculme
Cullompton, Devon
EX15 3AT, UK
Tel: +44(0)1884 840337
Fax: +44(0)1884 840251
e-mail: info@willanpublishing.co.uk
Website: www.willanpublishing.co.uk

Published simultaneously in the USA and Canada by

Willan Publishing
c/o ISBS, 920 NE 58th Ave, Suite 300,
Portland, Oregon 97213-3786, USA
Tel: +001(0)503 287 3093
Fax: +001(0)503 280 8832
e-mail: info@isbs.com
Website: www.isbs.com

First published 2005

ISBN 1-84392-122-7 (paperback)
ISBN 1-84392-123-5 (hardback)

British Library Cataloguing-in-Publication Data

A catalogue record for this book is available from the British Library

Project managed by Deer Park Productions, Tavistock, Devon
Typeset by TW Typesetting, Plymouth, Devon
Printed and bound by TJ International Ltd, Trecerus Industrial Estate, Padstow, Cornwall

In memory of Sam and Eileen Holwill

Contents

Acknowledgements   xi

1 Introduction   1
The extent of the problem   2
Sex offenders: who are they?   5
Criminal justice response   12

2 Development/history of sex offender treatment programmes   17
Early treatment for sex offenders   17
'Nothing works'   19
Behavioural therapy for sex offenders   20
'Something works'   24
'What works?'   27
Cognitive-behavioural treatment for sex offenders   33

3 Current use of cognitive-behavioural sex offender treatment   41
Why treat?   41
Current use of sex offender treatment   45
Canada   45
USA   51
UK and Ireland   54
Australia   70
New Zealand   75
Europe and the rest of the world   78

4 Theoretical underpinnings of programmes   80
Developmental theories   80
Hall and Hirschman's quadripartite model   81
Marshall and Barbaree's integrated theory   82
Situational theories   84
Finkelhor's integrated theory of child sexual abuse   85
Maintenance theories   87
Wolf's multi-factor model of deviant sexuality   87
Recent theoretical developments   90
Ward and Siegert's 'pathways model'   90

5   **Treatment ethos and effects on staff**   95
    Treatment ethos and therapeutic context   95
    Treatment staff: problems of working with sex offenders   103

6   **Cognitive-behavioural sex offender treatment goals**   114
    Offence-specific treatment goals   116
       Denial and minimization   116
       Cognitive distortions/cognitive restructuring   120
       Victim empathy   128
       Sexual arousal/sexual fantasy   135
    Non-offence-specific treatment goals   139
    Relapse prevention   141

7   **Are programmes effective? Part 1: Difficulties in evaluating
    programmes**   151
    Design   153
       Experimental design/randomized control trials   153
       Quasi-experimental designs   158
       Within-treatment studies   163
       Cost-benefit analysis   165
    Outcome measures   166
       Recidivism   166
       Personal and clinical characteristics   175
    Generic evaluation problems   179
       Treatment characteristics   179
       Offender characteristics   182
       Drop-outs   183
       Statistical power   185

8   **Are programmes effective? Part 2: Research evidence**   191
       North America   192
       UK and Ireland   202
       Australia   205
       New Zealand   206
    Meta-analyses   208
    Conclusions   214

9   **Are programmes effective? Part 3: What works?**   217
    Cost benefit   217
    What works, with whom?   219
       Treatment drop-outs   220
       Treatment compliance   221
       Offender characteristics   222
       Treatment characteristics   227

Group cohesion   230
Therapist characteristics   230
Why does it work?   232

10 Conclusion / the future of sex offender treatment   235

References   247
Index   277

Acknowledgements

A book such as this, which is based almost entirely on the literature, clearly owes a great deal to the efforts of all those who have published their work. Thus, I am indebted to all the authors whose work is included in this book. In addition, I would like to thank all the family, friends and colleagues who have provided support and encouragement throughout the completion of this work. Particular thanks are due to Dr Clare Wood for her enthusiastic reading of draft chapters and subsequent helpful comments and to Steve for his continued love and support.

Chapter 1

Introduction

Over the last two decades, the problem of sexual offending has received widespread public, media and political attention. In fact, Sampson (1994: xi) argued that 'public concern about sexual crime has become panic'. Media reporting has created the image that there has been a dramatic increase in sexual crime and that women and children face a constant and continued threat of attack. Sexual offenders are despised perhaps more than any other type of offender; so much so, that:

> The equation of sexual offender and monster is now firmly part of the public psyche. 'Monster' and 'beast' are common euphemisms for sex offenders in the prison system.
>
> (Sampson 1994: 43)

This has been supported by politicians who were keen to play the law and order card, and calls for tougher sentences for sex offenders have largely gone unopposed (Sampson 1994). The result has been a more punitive criminal justice response, enforced by a recent flurry of rushed legislative changes; for example, in England and Wales at least ten statutes affecting sex offenders have been introduced since 1991. Such an approach is not isolated to England and Wales, for example:

> Sexual abuse in North America is epidemic and the criminal justice system response to it is, for the most part, more reflexive, fear-driven, and irrational than it is practical.
>
> (Freeman-Longo and Blanchard 1998, cited in Laws 2000b: 30)

During the 1980s, sexual offending emerged as a major social problem, although it was not a new phenomenon (see Calder (1999) for a brief history of child sexual abuse, and Silverman and Wilson (2002) for a short history of sexual offending). A persistent feminist campaign coupled with high levels of media attention was largely responsible for increasing public awareness and concern. The picture the media continues to portray is one of widespread sexual offending where women and children (although male victims are increasingly being recognized) are at a constant risk, despite the fact that sex offences comprise only a small proportion of all recorded crimes. Approximately 4.7 per cent of those convicted in the US are convicted of sex-related offences (Greenfield 1997, cited in Burdon and Gallagher 2002), which at the end of 1999 was approximately 296,100 offenders (Bureau of Justice Statistics 2001, cited in Burdon and Gallagher 2002). However, these figures do not include sex offenders who are most recently convicted of non-sex related offences. In England and Wales, sexual offences comprise less than one per cent of all recorded crimes. However, there has been an increase in the number of recorded sex crimes from 21,000 in 1980–1; 29,000 in 1990–1; 37,300 in 2000–1 to 52,000 in 2003–4[1] (Home Office 1991; 1995; 2001a; 2004). From 1986 to 1996, the increase in recorded sexual offences averaged around 10 per cent per year (Home Office 2004). In 2003–4, the half a million recorded sexual offences comprised 26,709 indecent assaults on a female, 1,942 incidents of gross indecency with a child, 13,247 rapes (93 per cent of which were rapes of a female), and 4,070 indecent assaults on a male. Recorded sexual offences in 2003–4 increased by 7 per cent from the previous year to account for 5 per cent of all recorded violent crimes and 0.9 per cent of all recorded crime (Home Office 2004). A combination of the growth in recorded sexual offences and an increase in media attention to these crimes has led to the impression that sexual offences are becoming more common. However, some of the increase in recorded offences is likely to be attributable to an increasing number of offences being reported to and recorded by the police, rather than an increase in the actual number of offences (Home Office 1995).

The extent of the problem

A wide range of behaviours are officially classified as sexual offences but treatment work (and hence this book) generally focuses on those who offend against either those who did not, or those who could not, give

---

[1] Changes in police recording practice introduced in 2001 have inflated the numbers of crimes in police statistics, in particular for violent offences (including sexual offences). The introduction of the National Crime Recording Standard (NCRS) had the effect of increasing the number of recorded crimes.

their consent (e.g. offences of child sexual abuse, rape and exhibition-ism). It is important to note that sex offending is a legal definition; strictly speaking a sex offender is someone who has been sanctioned by law for a sexual offence, although more widely the term is used (and will be employed in tyhis book) to define those who engage in sexual behav-iours that are illegal, whether or not they have been officially sanctioned for these offences. Paedophile on the other hand, a term that is often used interchangeably with sex offender (and child molester), is a *clinical* definition of a specific group of people who may engage in adult–child sexual behaviour. The fourth edition of the *Diagnostic and Statistical Manual of Mental Disorders (DSM-IV)* (American Psychiatric Association 1994) classifies paedophilia within a broader category of paraphilias (sexual disorders in which there are strong, recurring sexually stimulat-ing urges, fantasies or behaviours usually involving (a) objects other than humans; (b) humiliation or pain for the partner or self; (c) children or other non-consenting partners). Specifically paedophilia is diagnosed if: (a) for six months or more, a person has had such fantasies or behaviours involving children below the age of puberty; (b) these fantasies/behaviours result in clinically meaningful difficulties or distress at work, in social contexts, or in other major areas of functioning; (c) the person is 16 years or older, and is at least five years older than the child or children. There are many problems with this definition (and the DSM-IV classifications of paraphilias in general, for example, see McConaghy (1999b)) and in using it to clinically diagnose paedophiles. Perhaps most important is the need for clinically meaningful difficulties or distress, which may not be exhibited in many of those who have fantasies, and/or engage in sexual behaviour with children and the need for these fantasies (which clearly cannot be observed) to be reported to the clinician. Crucially in terms of this discussion, it can be seen that not all sex offences (even all those committed against children) are likely to be committed by clinically diagnosed paedophiles (or even those without such formal diagnosis, but who would meet these criteria), even though many refer to all those who sexually offend against children as paedophiles. Although many argue that all clinically diagnosed paedophiles are sex offenders, this does not necessarily follow, as it is possible that someone could experience fantasies and urges that they do not act upon. In this book, to avoid confusion, the term paedophile will only be used if it was used to classify offenders by the authors of the original publication being cited.

It is difficult to accurately assess the scale of the problem of sexual offending for a number of reasons: societal denial, the secrecy of the offence, the consequences of disclosure for the victim, and the lack of a standard definition and methodology (see Calder 1999; for a more detailed discussions see Goldman and Padayachi (2000); Hulme (2004);

Sampson (1994)). Thus, estimates of the incidence (estimates of the number of new cases in a given period of time) and prevalence (estimates of the proportion of a population that has been affected by the phenomenon) are unreliable and provide a confused picture. For example, Safafino (1981, cited in Goldman and Padayachi 2000) estimated that 336,200 sex offences were committed against children each year in the USA, which varied considerably from the estimate of 44,700 by the National Centre on Child Sexual Abuse and Neglect (NCCAN 1981, cited in Goldman and Padayachi 2000). Rind, Tromovitch and Bauserman (1998, cited in Goldman and Padayachi 2000) reported that estimates of the prevalence of abuse ranged for males from 3 to 37 per cent, with a mean estimate of 17 per cent; and for females ranged from 8 to 71 per cent with a mean of 28 per cent.

Despite this confusion, numerous studies (there are fewer prevalence than incidence studies of child sexual abuse (Goldman and Padayachi 2000)) suggest the problem is significant and larger than we would like to believe.

> Depending on the definitions used, surveys have yielded widely differing statistics of adults' recollections of sexual abuse as children [prevalence], but even the lowest estimates suggest that at least ten per cent of the population has been involved in some childhood encounter.
>
> (West 1996: 53)

For example, Finkelhor (1994) summarized the data from 19 surveys of American adults investigating their experiences of sexual abuse as children. He reported that considerable evidence existed that at least 20 per cent of women and 5 to 10 per cent of men experienced some form of child sexual abuse, although the rates were lower for people born before World War II. There was no evidence that the rates of abuse had increased dramatically in generations born after the war, nor that race or socioeconomic circumstances influenced the likelihood of abuse. However, the studies did show that children who experienced parental inadequacy, unavailability, conflict, harsh punishment, and emotional deprivation had an increased risk of abuse. Davies (1998) estimated that current prevalence studies of child sexual abuse would include 1,500,000 girls and 520,000 boys in the UK (where there were approximately 11.9 million children aged 0–15 (Census 2001; 2003)). Similarly, the lowest estimates suggest that 10 per cent of women have been adult victims of sexual offences (Sampson 1994). For example, Koss (1993) reported that approximately 10 to 25 per cent of all American women are raped or sexually assaulted as adults. As some of these individuals may have been victimized as both children and adults, and no reliable figures are available for sexual assaults against adult males, it is not possible to accurately estimate a lifetime prevalence rate. Yet, it is clear that a considerable proportion of the population will be the victim of at least one sexual offence during their lifetime.

It is difficult to use these data to estimate the number of sexual offenders, as some of these victims may suffer abuse from a number of different offenders and some offenders may be responsible for the victimization of many individuals. However, the problem is not confined, as the media image of sex offenders often depicts, to a handful of 'sick monsters'. Indeed, Davies (1998) extrapolated that there are 1.1 million sex offenders who have victimized children in the UK (which has a total population of approximately 58.8 million (Census 2001; 2003)). Furthermore, Marshall (1997) revealed that by the time they were 40, 1 in 90 men born in 1953 in England and Wales (at least 165,000 men) had been convicted of a serious sexual offence (e.g. rape, incest, gross indecency) against a child; 1 in 60 had been convicted of a sexual offence, which included less serious offences. When this is considered with Abel et al.'s (1987) finding that their sample of sex offenders committed an average of 380 crimes during their lifetimes (although bear in mind that this sample is unlikely to be representative of all sex offenders), or that offenders report an average of six years of undetected offending prior to arrest (Elliott et al. 1995), it is clear that the scale of the problem is considerable.

Dealing effectively with this issue, though, is problematic as Percy and Mayhew (1997) reported that there are 15 times more unreported sex offenders than reported ones. For example, only 18 per cent of the rapes that were reported to the British Crime Survey had been reported to the police (Myhill and Allen 2002) and only 8 per cent of reported rapes led to a conviction (Cowling 1998). As well as making intervention difficult, the large number of unidentified offenders means that evidence about sex offenders is essentially biased, as it is based on identified/convicted offenders.

Sex offenders: who are they?

The image of sex offenders portrayed by the media is of lonely, isolated men who offend in this way because they are 'evil', 'sick' or 'mad' and ultimately different in some way from the 'normal' members of society. This impression is encapsulated by the following *Daily Mail* headline 'Sex Monster Free Soon' (Rose and Wright 1999) and is not confined to tabloid newspapers. In 1997, the *Guardian* contained a lengthy, supposedly well-researched and well-informed article entitled 'Monsters with Human Faces' (Birkett 1997). This image is mirrored by popular culture in best-selling novels and hit movies, such as *The Silence of the Lambs*, *Se7en* and Patricia Cornwell's *Kay Scarpetta* novels. These works of fiction imply links to real life cases and portray serial killers (often with sexual motives) as 'evil' loners who were born 'bad' and thus were driven to commit the most heinous crimes, and who, ultimately, have no hope of rehabilitation.

The pervasive and enduring nature of this image perhaps lies in the impression that as a society, we find it easier to believe crimes with motives we find hard to comprehend are carried out by 'abnormal' individuals living at the fringes of our communities. A corollary of this is that we find it easy to believe, and gain comfort from the idea, that these offenders can be readily identified by some 'abnormal' characteristic(s) that sets them apart from the 'normal' population. Indeed, for many years a large number of research studies attempted to identify such characteristics. However, these studies have shown that:

> There is no personality profile that differentiates sexual abusers from nonabusers, nor is there any battery of psychological tests that will identify if an individual is or is not a sexual offender.
>
> (Groth and Oliveri 1989: 316)

Furthermore, research suggests that sex offenders are a highly heterogeneous population distributed throughout socioeconomic groups (Howard League 1985; West 1996), although more sex offenders from lower socioeconomic groups are processed by the Criminal Justice System (Howard League 1985). The majority is not mentally ill in the sense that they suffer from psychiatrically diagnosable conditions (Barker and Morgan 1993; Simon 2000), and many of those who are apprehended have no previous convictions for sexual or non-sexual offences (Quinsey *et al.* 1995; West 1996). In truth, 'the available research suggests greater similarities than differences between sexual offenders and other people' (Marshall 1996b: 322).

It could be argued that Marshall's 'other people' should more accurately be described as 'other men', given that most research studies and criminal statistics suggest that the vast majority of sex offenders are male. More recent work (for example Elliott 1993; 1998), however, highlights the hidden nature of women's sexual offending, and suggests the problem is more widespread than was previously believed (for reviews of the limited literature on female perpetrators of child abuse, see Atkinson (1996); Grayston and De Luca (1999)). Yet, estimates of the extent of sexual abuse conducted by female offenders vary widely. For example, Duncan and Williams (1998) contrasted the 1 per cent estimate of Groth (1979) to the 24 per cent estimate of Finkelhor and Russell (1984). In Finkelhor's (1994) review of studies, 90 per cent of the perpetrators were male. Until recently (for example, see Lewis and Stanley (2000); Nathan and Ward (2002)), there have been few studies investigating the characteristics of female sex offenders; thus, there is limited knowledge about this group of offenders.

'Other men' implies, as does the media image, that all sex offenders are adults; however, a significant proportion of sexual offences are committed by juveniles or adolescents. For example, arrest statistics and victim surveys indicate that approximately 30 to 50 per cent of incidents of child sexual abuse and 20 per cent of all rapes are carried out by adolescents (Brown *et al.* 1984 and Deisher *et al.* 1982, cited in Davis and Leitenberg 1987). Furthermore, approximately half of adult sex offenders report an onset of sexual offending during adolescence (Gebhard *et al.* 1965; Groth *et al.* 1982; Smith 1984; Abel *et al.* 1985; Becker and Abel 1985, all cited in Davis and Leitenberg 1987). Davis and Leitenberg (1987) reviewed the research on characteristics of adolescent sex offenders, their offences and victims and found that in the majority of cases (nearly two-thirds), the victims were children younger than the perpetrators and were acquaintances or relatives. Furthermore, Shaw *et al.* (2000) found that there were no differences in the type of abuse committed by adults or juveniles on children. Abuse conducted by juveniles, like that conducted by adults, was characterized by 'themes of secrecy, dominance, coercion, threat and force' (p. 1598). Moreover, the sexual acts of the juvenile offenders were 'advanced beyond those expected for the age' and 'often included oral and vaginal intercourse and forcible penetration of the anus or vagina with fingers or other objects' (ibid). Victims of both adult and juvenile abusers experienced the same level of difficulties, and emotional and behavioural problems.

One consequence of the media image of sex offenders is that when thinking about sexual offences, we tend to imagine the most violent predatory crimes. However, sexual offending encompasses a wide range of behaviours from exposure to penetration, enacted using force that varies from subtle coercion through to overt physical violence. As West (1996: 51–2) highlighted, 'only a small minority of sexual attacks involve homicidal violence, significant injury, sexual mutilation or even gross brutality'. Furthermore, as Cowburn and Dominelli (2001: 403) point out, there are

> two images – the dangerous beast and the harmless, largely incompetent and misunderstood dirty old man . . . In this context, there is no stereotype that relates to the abuser who offends against children for whom he has a responsibility of care.

Yet, most offences are carried out by someone known to and/or trusted by the victim in private locations (Smith 1989; Kelly *et al.* 1991; Elliott *et al.* 1995; Simon 2000; Fieldman and Crespi 2002; Myhill and Allen 2002). Research and published statistics consistently show that children and adults are much more likely to be abused by people they know, despite the focus on 'stranger-danger' in the media and the fears of the public. For example, Finkelhor's (1994) review of 19 studies (referred to previously) found that 70 to 90 per cent of abuse was conducted by someone known to the child, with family members constituting one-third to one-half of those who offended against girls, and 10 to 20 per cent of those who offended against boys. Similarly, Myhill and Allen (2002) found that only 8 per cent of the rapes of women that were reported to the British Crime Survey were committed by strangers. Forty-five per cent were committed by current partners, 11 per cent by ex-partners, 10 per cent by other intimates, 11 per cent by dates and 16 per cent by acquaintances.

The 'evil monster' image and recent media coverage suggests that all sex offenders have an enduring high risk of sexual recidivism. For example, the New York Governor, George Pataki was cited as saying '. . . studies have shown that sex offenders are more likely to repeat their crime than any other crime' (Zgoba *et al.* 2003: 135). In reality however, 'not all sex offenders are high risk. In fact, most sex offenders are never convicted of another sexual crime' (Hanson and Bussière 1996). Although average rates of recidivism mask a great deal of variation between offenders with some offenders displaying high rates of recidivism (and many very low rates of recidivism), on average the sexual recidivism rate for untreated sex offenders is approximately 15 per cent over a five-year follow up period and 20 per cent over a 10-year follow up period (Hanson and Bussière 1998; Hanson and Thornton 2000). Even studies with long follow up periods and thorough searches for reoffences, rarely calculate recidivism rates in excess of 40 per cent (Hanson and Bussière 1996). Furthermore, the risk of reoffence for sex offenders is not higher than other groups of offenders. This is illustrated clearly by the two-year rates of recidivism of offenders released in 1998 from prisons in England and Wales (Home Office 2001b). The average reconviction rate for adult male prisoners was 55 per cent. The highest recidivism rates were found for the offences of burglary (75 per cent) and theft and handling (74 per cent). Medium recidivism rates were found for violent offences (43 per cent), drug offences (39 per cent) and for fraud and forgery (37 per cent). In contrast, one of the lowest rates of recidivism (1890), and a rate well below the average rate (18 per cent) was exhibited by sex offenders. Furthermore, over a 15 to 30-year follow up period of offenders released from prisons in Canada, non-sexual criminals had an overall (any offence) recidivism rate of 83 per cent, compared to 62 per cent for sexual criminals. However, while the average risk of reconviction for sex offenders is low, it is a persistent one (Soothill and Gibbens 1978; Gibbens *et al.* 1981; Hanson *et al.* 1993; Cann *et al.* 2004). For example, in a 21-year follow up study of 419 sex offenders released from English and Welsh prisons in 1979 (Cann *et al.* 2004), 43 men (10 per cent) offended within a two year period; 66 men (16 per cent) within five years; 84 men (20 per cent) within 10 years; and 103 men (25 per cent) within a 21 year period (22 per cent were reconvicted of a violent offence and 62 per cent a general offence in this 21-year period). Thus, 5 per cent of the offenders (19 men, or one-fifth of those who sexually reoffended) were reconvicted for the first time more than ten years after being released from prison (note that this does not mean that they did not reoffend before this time; only that they were not convicted before this time).

These average rates of recidivism mask variations in risk levels between different groups of offenders. Studies have consistently shown that exhibitionists have the highest recidivism rates; followed in turn by extra-familial offenders (many but not all studies suggest that offenders who exclusively abuse boys or those who abuse both boys and girls have higher recidivism rates than extra-familial offenders who exclusively abuse girls); with the lowest reconviction rates being found among familial abusers. For example, Marshall and Barbaree (1990b) reported recidivism rates of between 41 and 71 per cent for exhibitionists; 13 to 40 per cent for offenders who abused boys outwith the family; 10 to 29 per cent for those who abused girls outwith the family; 4 to 10 per cent for incest offenders; and 7 to 35 per cent for rapists.

These categories (and the media image of sex offenders) give the impression that sex offenders are 'specialist' offenders; that is, that they only commit sexual offences, and furthermore that they only commit certain types of sexual offences (e.g. commit incest exclusively, or rape adult women only). However, there is little empirical evidence to support these views (Simon 2000). Some studies (e.g. Abel *et al.* 1987; Elliott *et al.* 1995) have shown that around one-fifth of those abusing children abused both boys and girls; and approximately a quarter of such offenders offended both within and outwith the family. These findings are contentious though, with Marshall and Barbaree (1990b) arguing that such offending patterns are restricted to highly deviant samples of offenders. Indeed, some studies (e.g. Beech *et al.* 1998; Marshall and Eccles 1991) have reported much lower rates of varied sexual offending patterns. Although there is disagreement about the rates of such offending patterns, it is clear that some offenders, at least, commit a range of sexual offences. Furthermore, rates of recidivism of non-sexual offences (for example see the rates reported in the evaluation literature discussed in Chapter 8 and Cann *et al.* (2004) discussed above) reveal that many sex offenders commit other violent and non-violent crimes (for a more detailed discussion of the evidence showing that sex offenders are not 'specialized' offenders, mentally disordered or unusually dangerous, see Simon (2000)). However, there is some evidence to suggest variation between offender groups, with rapists having more general criminal careers and some child sex abusers more specialist ones (Motiuk and Brown 1996). Interestingly, Simon argues that the problems that are seen to be characteristic of sex offenders (e.g. denial, cognitive distortion, lack of empathy, low self-esteem; see Chapter 6) are also characteristic of other offenders. Thus, he argues that sex offenders are not a distinct group of offenders. This conclusion is not supported, however, by the research of Hanson and his colleagues (Hanson *et al.* 1995; Hanson and Bussière 1996) which suggests that sex offenders do differ from non-sexual criminals.

Research has consistently revealed that a number of factors, such as number of previous convictions, offence type (discussed earlier), age and marital status are strong predictors of risk (Furby *et al.* 1989; Hanson *et al.* 1993; Bélanger and Earls 1996; Grubin and Wingate 1996; Hanson and Bussière 1996). Those with previous convictions for sexual offences display higher rates of sexual recidivism than do those with no or fewer convictions, while older and married (or those in stable relationships) offenders have lower levels of risk than do younger, unmarried ones. Factors not related to sexual recidivism, somewhat surprisingly, are age of victim(s), history of exhibitionism, history of sexual victimization, poor relationship with mother, poor relationship with father, alcohol or drug use, previous non-sexual convictions, education level or IQ, and scores on a range of metal health, personality and psychometric tests (Hanson *et al.* 1995). Thus, factors that have shown the greatest predictive value are static factors, i.e. those that are not likely to change. This creates problems when risk assessments, based on these static factors, are made to determine detention and/or release from detention (for a more detailed discussions, see Hanson 1998; Harris *et al.* 1998). For example, in many of the risk assessment tools that are based on these static factors, the only thing an offender can do to reduce their risk score is to get married and wait until he or she becomes older, and this is only likely to have a limited impact on the overall score. Consequently, offenders detained on the basis of such static risk assessment measures are not likely to be released, as their risk assessment is not likely to improve.

Recently more attention has been given to dynamic risk factors, i.e. those that can change (for example, see Hanson *et al.* 1993; Proulx *et al.* 1997; Hanson and Bussière 1998; Hanson and Harris 2000; Hudson *et al.* 2002). These studies have produced mixed findings. Some have shown no link between treatment completion and recidivism (Hanson *et al.* 1993), while others have shown that the completion of treatment is linked to a lower risk of recidivism. Yet, this may be as much, or even more, to do with the characteristics of the men who complete treatment than the actual treatment programmes themselves (Hanson and Bussière

1998). Treatment completion was the only dynamic variable that Hanson and Bussière identified in their review of 61 studies that was linked to recidivism. However, Hanson and Harris (2000, see also Hanson 1998) interviewe[d] [comm]unity supervision officers in Canada and reported that offenders [who reo]ffended had poor social supports, attitudes tolerant of sexual off[ending,] antisocial lifestyles, difficulties cooperating with supervision an[d] [poor] self-management skills. In addition, although not a factor th[at can b]e applied generally to determine recidivism (as overall mood b[etween] recidivists and non-recidivists was similar), in the offender[s previ]ously described, factors such as low self-esteem, distress and an[ger play]ed a role as acute risk variables; that is, they were present imme[diately b]efore reoffending. How these factors could be incorporated [into r]isk assessment that determined release from detention, howe[ver, is n]ot clear. Furthermore, research is needed to validate the findin[gs of H]anson and Harris and to assess whether these factors could be use[d to in]tervene before offenders reoffend.

Although Hanson *et al.* (1995) showed no link between prior sexual victimization and sexual recidivism, there is a pervasive view that sex offenders were sexually abused as children and furthermore, that this abuse led to the development of deviant sexual behaviour (for more detailed discussions of this issue, see Federoff and Moran (1997); Glasser *et al.* (2001)). Federoff and Moran (1997) argued that this 'myth' is enduring because it has face validity and stems from a claim by Groth (1979) that 40 per cent of a sample of sex offenders reported child sexual victimization. However, Federoff and Moran highlighted a number of weaknesses of this study and crucially they pointed out that 60 per cent of the sample (clearly the majority) did not report a history of child sexual abuse. Many including Federoff and Moran have also argued that as the majority of victims are female and the majority of perpetrators male, this cycle of abuse hypothesis is fundamentally flawed. Research generally reveals a rate of sexual victimization in sex offenders of between 20 to 30 per cent (Hanson and Salter 1988; Freund *et al.* 1990, both cited in Glasser *et al.* 2001); thus, there is not a simple link between sexual victimization and sexual offending. However, some have argued that sex offenders who have been sexually victimized may be different from those without such a history of victimization; for example, they may be more highly deviant and have a greater likelihood of psychological disturbance (for example, see Hanson and Salter 1988, cited in Glasser *et al.* 2001).

Finally, some empirical evidence questions the extent to which sexual offending behaviours are 'abnormal'; that is, they are only evident in a tiny minority of the population. Thirty-five per cent of the college males investigated by Malamuth (1981) admitted that they would rape if they could be assured of not being caught/punished. With only 8 per cent of rapes resulting in a conviction, it is of course unlikely that they would be caught/punished. Goodman and Zellman (1984) reported that the majority of high school males they studied thought that date rape was 'acceptable' and 28 per cent of college males investigated by Rapaport and Burkhart (1984) reported that they had engaged in sexually coercive behaviour. Furthermore, Laws (1994, cited in Cowburn and Dominelli 2001) found that the literature relating to self-report surveys and phallometric testing was unable to clearly distinguish between the convicted rapist and the 'normal' male. When considering offences against children, Brier and Runtz (1989) observed that 21 per cent of the college males they surveyed reported some sexual attraction to children and 7 per cent said there was some likelihood that they would abuse if they thought they would not be caught/punished. In addition, 10 per cent of males interviewed by Finkelhor and Lewis (1998) admitted sexually abusing a child as did 3 per cent of the college males surveyed by Fromuth *et al.* (1991).

What these data reveal is that the image of sex offenders as identifiable 'abnormal' adults who offend against strangers in a particularly predatory and violent manner is flawed. Some, particularly those arguing from a feminist perspective, point out that: 'an alternative interpretation of the data presented above is that sexually violent behaviour by men is endemic in our society, but only some get caught' (Cowburn and Dominelli 2001: 410). Despite this, the image of the predatory 'evil' stranger is remarkably persistent and informs public fears. More worryingly, this image also seems to have driven social policy and criminal justice legislation.

Criminal justice response

In the last decade, 'the danger to children from sexual offenders has become a matter of obsessive public concern' (West 1996: 52), and 'those who perpetrate such crimes are hated and despised more than almost any other offender' (Sampson 1994: xi). 'Yet, media coverage has few suggestions as to what should be done with sex offenders other than excluding them from a particular locale' (Cowburn and Dominelli 2001: 406). One result of these responses has been a wave of legislative changes that have toughened penalties, lengthened sentences and more recently required increased monitoring of offenders in the community (Freeman-Longo 1996).

For example, in the UK during the 1980s, concern was expressed that the police and the courts were not taking a severe enough view of rape. In 1986, the Court of Appeal made a guideline judgement (*R. v. Billam* 1986) that led to an increase in the length of custodial sentences.

Offenders also received more severe punishments; that is, they were much more likely to receive a custodial sentence. Consequently, the proportion of convicted sex offenders receiving immediate custodial sentences in England and Wales rose from 20 per cent in 1979, to 33 per cent in 1989 (Barker and Morgan 1993) and 44 per cent in 1993 (Home Office 1995). This had an effect on the prison population: in 1980, 4.7 per cent of sentenced male prisoners in custody were convicted of a sexual offence, whereas this figure had risen to 7.5 per cent in 1989 (Home Office 1995). Between 1979 and 1990, the number of sex offenders in prison doubled from 1,500 to 3,166, with two thirds (2,006) of those in prison in 1990 serving sentences of four or more years (Clark 1993). These trends reflect public demand, encouraged by the tabloid press (Soothill and Walby 1991; Kitzinger 1999) and by government policy of tough punishment (Sampson 1994).

This pattern has continued and even escalated in the 1990s, where at least 10 pieces of legislation were introduced that had an impact on the criminal justice response to sex offenders. These acts have toughened and enhanced existing criminal justice policy, for example by providing for automatic life sentences and extended supervision; and also introduced a range of more innovative measures, such as registration, sex offender orders and offences of sexual grooming, which are designed to increase community protection. The speed at which many of these acts were introduced, however, highlights the reactive nature of this legislation and it appears that little thought has been given to the way in which each new piece of legislation impacts on, and sometimes conflicts with, the existing provision. Furthermore:

> Many of the more recent legislative actions appear to be the result of emotional public responses to violent crime rather than based upon fact and research that these laws will make a difference in the frequency of a particular crime.
>
> (Freeman-Longo 1996: 96)

During this time public rhetoric has demanded, and legislation has increasingly enforced, a more punitive response to sex offenders. However, throughout this period the rehabilitative approach of providing cognitive-behavioural treatment programmes, which has been virtually ignored or unnoticed by politicians, the media and the public alike, has developed significantly. This is despite the fact that: 'sentencers operate within the philosophical and practical constraints of a system to which the specific treatment needs of sex offenders are often subsumed' (Henham 1998: 77).

In his opening address to a conference on the sentencing of sex offenders, Kenneth Baker, the then Home Secretary (UK), expressed the

Government's belief that the best approach was to view criminal sentences as a continuum; part in custody and part in the community (Bradley and Lamplugh 1992, cited in Henham 1998). It can be argued that policy which combines punishment with rehabilitation, as well as reflecting public attitudes (Brown 1999), is in keeping with such an approach. When employed in both custodial and community settings, sex offender treatment is able to combine a punitive and rehabilitative approach and, if effective, increase public safety. Public and media attitudes of 'just lock them up and throw away the key' are prevalent but this is not realistic given the available resources and nature of most criminal justice systems. Prisons in the US and UK are overcrowded and sentencing structures allow almost all sex offenders to return to the community following incarceration, typically after serving only a proportion of their original sentences. Reliance on incarceration ignores the fact that many sex offenders present a relatively low risk of reoffending and furthermore, that it is ineffective with many groups of criminals including sex offenders (Chapter 2).

So despite a trend towards more punitive action, rehabilitative intervention for sex offenders – cognitive-behavioural treatment – has gradually developed and expanded. This approach will be described and evaluated in this book. Introduced in North America, this intervention has experienced remarkable expansion in recent years (see Chapter 2).

> While it remains true that most of the well-developed and established programs are in North America (United States and Canada) . . . similar programs have appeared with increasing frequency over the past 10 years in the United Kingdom, the Netherlands, Australia, and New Zealand. Furthermore, it is evident that both Western . . . and Eastern Europe . . . as well as South Africa . . . and Bermuda . . . are developing treatment for sexual offenders.
>
> (Marshall *et al.* 1998: 477)

Programmes are also being developed for increasingly diverse populations (Marshall *et al.* 1998). Yet, despite this expansion and apparent diversity, most programmes adopt a cognitive-behavioural approach that is guided by the principles of relapse prevention (Marshall *et al.* 1998; see Chapters 3, 4 and 6). Thus, in practice:

> The beliefs, attitudes, and perceptions of sexual offenders are being challenged using a supportive but firm approach that respects the dignity of the client while offering alternative, more prosocial views of the offence and the victims.
>
> (Marshall *et al.* 1998: 477; see Chapter 5)

Although the use of cognitive-behavioural treatment programmes is increasing, there is still considerable debate surrounding the effectiveness of this form of intervention (see Chapter 8). Some authors (for example Furby *et al.* 1989; Quinsey *et al.* 1993) have reached negative conclusions about the efficacy of these programmes. However, many of the programmes investigated by these researchers employed treatment techniques and approaches that are now obsolete (Marshall and Pithers 1994). In addition, critics of cognitive-behavioural treatment programmes (for example Quinsey *et al.* 1993; McPherson *et al.* 1994) have argued that the use of poor methodology has led to research that has failed to demonstrate conclusively that these treatment programmes are effective. However, given the reality of social science research and the nature of these programmes, it is unlikely that researchers will ever be able to demonstrate conclusively the efficacy of this form of treatment (see Chapter 7). Rather, over time and with an increasing number of studies, trends and patterns will be discerned that suggest programmes are effective. In fact, a large number of studies published in the 1990s do just this, leading Peebles (1999: 278) to conclude:

> Overall, a compelling body of scientific literature is accumulating to show that untreated men convicted of sex crimes tend to reoffend sooner and at a greater rate than men who have undergone treatment.

However, Marshall and Eccles (1991: 87) point out that 'not all forms are effective and not all applications of all forms are effective. We are not uniformly effective with all offender types . . .' (see Chapter 9). Thus, sex offender treatment should not be used in isolation and other ways of preventing sexual offending should be developed, with more attention given to primary and secondary prevention interventions (see Chapter 10).

The purpose of this book, then, is to provide an overview of cognitive-behavioural sex offender treatment programmes, based on the findings of the published literature. The discussion begins in Chapter 2 by describing the development of cognitive-behavioural programmes in the context of the 'What works?' evaluation literature. In Chapter 3, an outline of the current use of these programmes in Canada, the USA, the UK, Australia and New Zealand will be provided. The theoretical underpinnings and the therapeutic approach/ethos of this form of intervention will be described in Chapters 4 and 5 respectively. In addition, the effects of this work on treatment practitioners will be examined in Chapter 5. Cognitive-behavioural programmes will be explored in more detail in Chapter 6 with a description and evaluation of the range of treatment goals. The next three chapters focus on the evaluation of this treatment, with Chapter 7 exploring the methodological difficulties of programme evaluation. In Chapter 8, the outcome literature will be assessed, grouped by county of origin (North America, UK, Australia, New Zealand) followed by meta-analyses, to determine whether these programmes are effective or not. In Chapter 9 the same literature will be reviewed to determine what treatment works and with whom it works. Finally, Chapter 10 will draw together the findings from the previous chapters and examine cognitive-behavioural treatment in the wider context of public protection and sex offence prevention.

Chapter 2

Development/history of sex offender treatment programmes

Intervention or treatment efforts with sex offenders and other offenders within the criminal justice and mental health systems are not new. Wood *et al.* (2000) argue that there have been three distinct approaches to the treatment of sex offenders over the last 60 years. The first period involved insight-oriented, psychoanalytic therapy or humanistic treatment delivered to sex offenders detained in the USA under 'sexual psychopath' legislation. The use of behavioural therapy constituted the second approach, which gave way to the third, and current approach, using cognitive-behavioural treatment. These developments have generally mirrored those used with other groups of offenders, where it can be argued that there have been three fundamental shifts in treatment or intervention philosophy throughout this time period, from 'nothing works', to 'something works', to 'what works?'. This chapter will chart the development of sex offender treatment across these three approaches and will discuss the shifts in general treatment/intervention philosophy that have occurred as sex offender programmes evolved.

Early treatment for sex offenders

Beginning in the late 1930s, many states in the USA enacted 'sexual psychopath' legislation, which provided for the involuntary civil commitment of sexual offenders. By the 1960s, more than half the states had enacted such statutes, which were directed at 'psychopathic personalities', 'sexually dangerous persons', 'psychopathic offenders' but most commonly 'sexual psychopaths'. Regardless of the exact term used, the statutes were directed towards offenders who were thought to be

17

dangerous to society, because of a combination of psychopathic and sexually deviant behaviour, and who fell between mental health and criminal justice provision. Although these offenders were recognized as not being mentally ill, they were not considered 'normal', and determinate sentences were not felt to be effective for this group of assumed dangerous offenders. Thus, the statutes allowed the indeterminate civil commitment of offenders, in lieu of a criminal sentence, until they had been 'cured' or were no longer considered dangerous. Although it could be argued that the main aim of the legislation was to protect society from these individuals, there was also a clear rehabilitative aspect with the belief that therapy could bring about a change in behaviour, or a 'cure' for the 'condition'. Similar legislation, the Sexual Psychopath Act, was enacted in Canada in 1948, which required the identification and treatment of dangerous sexual offenders.

It is difficult to identify what constituted treatment under the provision of this legislation. Wood et al. (2000) argue that the Atascadero programme (Frisbie 1958; 1969; Frisbie and Dondi 1965, cited in Wood et al. 2000) provided a well-documented example, although the 'treatment' was still not clear from these publications. It seems that in a generally permissive environment, staff varied widely in their level of competence and were inconsistent in their 'treatment' approach. Much 'treatment' was directed by other patients and it is inferred that psychoanalysis was a main component of 'treatment'. Many patients were released after around 18 months with no consideration given to progress or 'cure', and patients could be released simply to free up a bed. An evaluation of the programme revealed that 20 per cent (385 out of 1,921 patients released between 1954 and 1960) of the sample reoffended. However, this study was poorly designed with no comparison group or reliable data about the level of risk of these patients. Thus, it is difficult to draw conclusions about the efficacy of these programmes. From the description of the 'treatment', however, it would be a surprise if it had much impact on patients' behaviour. Laws and Marshall (2003) point out that although some early reports of treatment outcome from this period showed reductions in recidivism, later evaluations of the same programmes, with longer follow-up periods, indicated that treated offenders had higher reoffence rates than untreated offenders. Thus, Harris, Rice and Quinsey (1998: 94) concluded that the results from humanistic and psychodynamic treatment evaluations were 'quite discouraging'.

During the 1970s and 1980s most 'sexual psychopath' statutes were repealed or disused, or in the case of Canada replaced by newer legislation, in large part as a result of studies showing poor treatment outcome, but also because of a number of difficulties with the legislation. Crucially, the definitions employed by the statutes and the identification of offenders based on these definitions was problematic, which resulted in the legislation being applied inconsistently. A change in attitudes may also have played a part in this process. Offenders who had been viewed as 'sick' individuals who were unable to control their behaviour, were later seen as being responsible for their actions, and hence, were deemed 'bad' rather than 'ill'. Furthermore, therapeutic optimism had given way to therapeutic pessimism, in large part because of the 'nothing works' literature.

'Nothing works'

In the 1970s, the rehabilitative approach suffered a major setback due to the frequently cited conclusion of Martinson (1974) that 'nothing works'. Although Martinson's review is most commonly cited, he was not the only one to draw such conclusions. Following reviews of hundreds of studies, Bailey (1966), Robinson and Smith (1971), Logan (1972), Lipton *et al.* (1975) and Brody (1976) all concluded that data, even that which suggested a positive treatment outcome, did not indicate that correctional intervention was effective, although many of these findings have been disputed (for example, see Andrews and Bonta 1994). To be fair, the 'nothing works' conclusion attributed to Martinson (1974) is actually an oversimplification of the findings of his review, where serious methodological weaknesses in the evaluations repeatedly impeded accurate interpretations of intervention effectiveness. Thornton (1987) re-examined the studies reviewed by Lipton *et al.* (1975) (on which Martinson's paper was based) and found that only 38 out of the 231 studies reviewed used recidivism as a variable, an experimental design involving matching or randomization to treatment and control groups (see Chapter 7) and thus, were classified by Lipton *et al.* (1975) as methodologically acceptable (their 'A' category). Furthermore, although Martinson's (1974) review was generally not favourable to the interventions he and his colleagues reviewed, he never actually concluded that 'nothing works'. In fact, he reported (p. 49):

> It is just possible that some of our treatment programs are working to some extent, but that our research is so bad that it is incapable of telling.
>
> Having entered this very serious caveat, I am bound to say that these data . . . give us very little reason to hope that we have in fact found a sure way of reducing recidivism through rehabilitation. This is not to say that we found no instances of success or partial success; it is only to say that these instances have been isolated, producing no clear pattern to indicate the efficacy of any particular method of treatment.

Thornton (1987) argued from his re-examination of the studies reviewed by Lipton *et al.* that the negative conclusion that nothing works was unwarranted. He pointed out that 16 of the 38 (nearly half) classified as methodologically acceptable showed treatment effects in favour of the intervention. Only one study showed a significant disadvantage of treatment. Moreover, Thornton revealed that the interventions evaluated by the majority of these 38 studies were 'psychological therapies' (e.g. counselling, intensive casework, psychotherapy or a therapeutic milieu) and thus, a small subset of all treatment interventions. Hence, a negative conclusion based on these 38 studies (which Thornton argued was not warranted by the fact that half showed a positive outcome) would state that 'psychological therapies' did not work, not that 'nothing works'.

Despite this, Martinson's (1979) subsequent more positive analysis, and the conflicting reports that concluded that some interventions were effective (Hood 1967; Palmer 1975; Quay 1977), the 'nothing works' doctrine held sway for many years, particularly with respect to social policy. Andrews and Bonta (1994) and Laws (2000b) argued that the 'nothing works' position was due to political currents within the criminological profession and was taken by 'antipsychological criminologists'. Cooke and Philip (2000) suggest that conflicting ideologies encouraged the acceptance of the 'nothing works' doctrine. Left-wing 'critical criminology' espoused that social rather than individual/psychological forces were the causes of crime; hence, individual therapy could do nothing to impact on crime. Right-wing 'just deserts' views promoted punishment rather than rehabilitation, despite the fact that much of the rehabilitation berated by the 'nothing works' doctrine was undertaken in conjunction with punishment, i.e. in institutional or prison settings. Although evaluation methodology has generally improved since Martinson's review, methodological issues still cloud the conclusions of evaluation research. Many have reached similar conclusions to Martinson regarding sex offender treatment programmes. Yet, the literature regarding the general effectiveness of interventions has over time become more positive.

Behavioural therapy for sex offenders

The claims of 'nothing works' did little to dampen the zeal of some to develop programmes for sex offenders. Although legislative approaches shifted away from therapy and rehabilitation, in favour of determinate punitive sentences, proponents of sex offender intervention argued (and continue to argue) that intervention was still necessary (and perhaps even more necessary) as sex offenders would eventually, and usually, be released back into the community. In fact, fixed-term prison sentences made this much more likely, as although most were eventually released into the community under the previous legislation, there was the possibility of continued detention if the offender was deemed not to have been 'cured', or was determined to be a continued danger to the community. Moreover, release into the community under determinate punitive sentencing is determined solely by the length of the sentence, rather than on assessments of risk or likely future behaviour. Nevertheless, the 'nothing works' research, and in particular the failure of the humanistic and psychotherapeutic approaches to sex offender treatment (and in correctional treatment more generally), was not ignored, and so the 1970s saw a shift away from these ineffective approaches towards behavioural methods of treatment. This shift was not isolated to sex offender treatment, and reflected a general shift in psychology towards behaviourism and the development of behavioural techniques to an increasing range of problematic behaviours. (See Laws and Marshall (2003) for a more detailed account of the development of behaviourism and its impact on sex offender treatment.)

Behaviourism stresses the role of external, environmental factors in shaping behaviour. Behaviourists focus only on behaviours that can be observed and recorded accurately, and hence, ignore thoughts or mediating variables that can only be assumed, as direct recording of them is impossible. The theories of behaviourism stress the importance of positive and negative reinforcement and punishment in shaping behaviour, whereby behaviour followed by something perceived as positive is likely to be repeated, and behaviour followed by something perceived as negative is less likely to be repeated, particularly if this is consistent over time. In a number of studies, behaviourists showed how reinforcement could be used to manipulate behaviour. Although it is now acknowledged that behaviourist methods and techniques involve cognitive processes (such as memory), the principles of behaviourism (for example reward and punishment) are still widely supported, particularly in the criminal justice arena, and have become very influential.

Early behavioural therapy focused on reducing deviant arousal. This was believed to be sufficient to bring about an end to deviant sexual behaviour (see for example Bond and Evans 1967), as it seemed to be assumed that 'normal' arousal would develop naturally once the deviant arousal had been extinguished. This approach was not at all new: Laws and Marshall (2003) point out that attempts at changing sexual arousal, using what would today be termed behavioural therapy, were reported as far back as the late 1880s. Furthermore, they showed that early theorists, namely Binet and Norman, had argued in the late 1800s and early 1900s that sexual deviancy was a learned response reinforced by masturbation to deviant fantasies. These ideas are still considered important aspects in the development of sexual offending behaviour, although current theories incorporate these ideas with a wide range of other factors. McGuire *et al.*'s (1965) theorizing was broadly similar to those of early theorists, but perhaps provided the impetus for the development of behavioural treatments with sex offenders (see Laws and Marshall 2003).

Behaviour therapy involves a range of techniques based on the principle that behaviours followed by positive experiences are likely to be repeated and behaviours followed by negative experiences are less likely to be repeated. For example, aversion therapy involves the pairing of the target problematic behaviour (e.g. arousal to pictures of children or non-consenting, violent acts of sex with adults) with negative stimuli, for example nausea (achieved by the injection of nausea-inducing substances), electric shock, unpleasant odours, boredom, and shame or embarrassment. Other techniques (see Wood *et al.* 2000; Laws and Marshall 2003; Marshall and Laws 2003, for more detailed discussion of the range of techniques applied to sex offenders) involve pairing positive stimuli with non-deviant arousal, often quite soon after the pairing of negative stimuli with deviant arousal (e.g. in orgasmic or masturbatory reconditioning); or the pairing of deviant fantasies or thoughts with imagined distressing consequences (covert sensitization).

Kelly (1982) argued that behavioural techniques were successful at reducing deviant arousal in paedophiles, but there is little to support arguments that they produced long-term changes in arousal in paedophiles or those demonstrating other forms of deviant arousal. Moreover, there is limited evidence that these techniques produced a change or cessation in deviant behaviour (see Quinsey and Earls 1990; Laws and Marshall 2003), i.e. that changes in arousal led to changes in behaviour. The failure of these simplistic approaches lies not so much in the behavioural therapy itself, which has proved to be effective for a variety of problematic behaviours and had some impact on deviant arousal, but rather in the theory behind the causes of deviant sexual behaviour. Early theories (see Chapter 5 for a more detailed discussion on theory) focused on single, simple causes. The principles of behaviourism determined that psychologists should only be concerned with behaviours that could be measured and observed; thus, thoughts and cognitions that could only be inferred and not directly observed were ignored (despite the fact that some behavioural techniques involve fantasy and imagined events which clearly involve unobservable thoughts (Wood *et al.* 2000)). Furthermore, there seemed to be a widespread belief that deviant sexual behaviour was primarily driven by biological sexual drives. However, empirical evidence and arguments from new groups of theorists (perhaps most notably from feminists) revealed the complex nature of sexual deviancy, which is driven by a range of factors including those that cannot be directly observed, such as attitudes towards women and children, beliefs of sexual entitlement, and issues of power and control, to name but a few. Moreover, it could be argued that deviant arousal is not, in itself, a sufficient cause for the development of deviant behaviour. Thus, intervention methods focusing only on this aspect are likely to fail; no matter what treatment approach is used.

Gradually, sex offender treatment providers recognized the complexity of the deviant behaviour and other elements were added to basic behavioural programmes. Firstly, attempts were made not only to reduce deviant arousal, but also to increase non-deviant arousal, e.g. by using masturbatory reconditioning. Laws and Marshall (1991) suggested that evidence for the effectiveness of these techniques was weak, although much of this was due to the limited nature of the research. In addition to the more theoretically based behaviour techniques, some began to add other elements to behavioural programmes to form what some have since termed augmented behavioural treatment programmes. For example, in 1971, Marshall argued that as well as reducing deviant arousal, it was also necessary to enhance appropriate sexual arousal, and to provide social skills training to make appropriate sexual encounters more feasible. These ideas led to a programme that included social skills training and sex education alongside more traditional behavioural techniques (Marshall and Williams 1975). Throughout the 1970s, the range of factors incorporated into behavioural treatments was expanded. Marshall and his colleagues (see Marshall 1996a) expanded programmes to include enhancing self-esteem, reducing hostility and anger, training in controlled drinking, and teaching offenders to use their leisure time more constructively. By the late 1970s, Abel *et al.* (1978) had added components on assertiveness, sexual dysfunction and gender role behaviour, and by 1980 had also incorporated empathy enhancement (Murphy *et al.* 1980), forming what could arguably be described as one of the first cognitive-behavioural treatment programmes for sex offenders.

Development in sex offender treatment at this time was rapid and clearly developed on the basis that something could be done to change the behaviour of sex offenders. Yet, evidence for the efficacy of these treatments was scarce. In a review of published sex offender evaluations, which mostly included behavioural and augmented behavioural programmes (and humanistic and psychoanalytic programmes), Furby *et al.* (1989) concluded that there was no evidence to suggest that sex offender programmes to date had been effective in reducing recidivism. Ironically, the ensuing debate mirrored the debate that had arisen from the Martinson's 'nothing works' paper, published 15 years earlier. Furby *et al.* concluded, in arguably a similar vein to Martinson, that the methodology employed by evaluative studies was so poor that there was a lack of clear evidence providing support for the efficacy of sex offender treatment; yet, many used Furby and colleagues' conclusion as evidence that sex offender treatment was ineffective, in effect that 'nothing worked' with sex offenders. However, by the time of the publication of Furby and colleagues' paper, the overriding view in the more general field of correctional intervention was that 'something works'.

'Something works'

The late 1970s and 1980s saw a shift in attitude from 'nothing works' to 'something works'. The impetus for this shift is generally attributed to Gendreau and Ross (Gendreau and Ross 1979; Ross and Gendreau 1980; Gendreau 1981), although these were not the only researchers at this time drawing more positive conclusions about the effectiveness of correctional interventions. Interestingly, in 1979, Martinson himself conceded that some programmes work. Gendreau and Ross produced updated literature reviews, showing that out of 95 experimental or quasi-experimental studies (which methodologically produce more re-liable and valid data, see Chapter 7) published between 1973 and 1978, 86 per cent reported positive outcomes. Furthermore, they pointed out that offender/treatment interactions, which had previously been dis-missed as showing that treatment did not work, were important considerations and in fact showed that treatment did indeed work for some offenders. At this time proponents of the 'something works' doctrine argued that the methodological weaknesses of studies showing positive outcomes also applied to studies revealing negative outcomes; a factor they argued the 'nothing works' proponents ignored, by applying methodological criticism most fervently to studies showing positive outcomes (see Andrews and Bonta 1994).

The reviews discussed thus far involved the reviewers collating relevant studies from which they drew conclusions about effectiveness. This method is open to bias, as the conclusions are clearly influenced by the reviewers' values and beliefs about methodology (and perhaps about correctional treatment and intervention). In the mid 1980s, a relatively new method of review, the meta-analysis, was used in the evaluation of correctional 'treatment'. This approach requires the calculation of a standard statistic, the effect size, from all the studies reviewed (see Chapter 7 for more information). To a large extent, a meta-analysis is only as good as the studies involved; however, adjustments can be made for variation in the methodological rigor of studies and extraneous variables can be statistically controlled for. Studies hampered by small sample sizes can be collated together and the biases or problems of individual studies tend to be averaged out. Hence, the overall treatment effects across the range of studies become more evident. 'Meta-analysis has the advantage, therefore, of revealing broad patterns of findings in a body of research with much more clarity and consistency than traditional research review techniques' (Lipsey 1995: 66).

Lösel (1995) reviewed the 13 meta-analyses on offender 'treatment' that had been published to date, which in total reviewed over 500 studies (many of these analyses, however, involved overlapping samples of studies). All of these studies revealed a positive mean effect size, ranging from 0.05 to 0.36. Although generally used to show that treatment works, some of these mean effect sizes are small. Yet, these effect sizes are averages, so clearly some poorer interventions with smaller or negative effect sizes balanced out the effects of the better interventions with larger, positive effect sizes. Furthermore, Marshall and McGuire (2003) argue that the effect sizes of some treatments for medical disorders are very small, yet the treatment is considered both effective and worthy. Lipsey (1989; 1995) conducted what is widely believed to be the most comprehensive meta-analysis of correction 'treatment' efficacy, reviewing over 400 studies with control groups published in English since 1950, representing over 40,000 participants. Sixty-four per cent of these studies showed favourable treatment results. Lipsey assumed a 50 per cent recidivism rate for the control groups and argued that the average effect size meant that the treatment groups would have a recidivism rate of 45 per cent. Thus, correctional 'treatment' produced a 10 per cent reduction in recidivism, which Lipsey (1995) argued was on a par with treatment viewed as significant in medical interventions. Furthermore, this finding is statistically significant and remained of the same magnitude when statistical corrections were made to account for the variations in methodology, and when only the best, methodologically robust, studies were included in the analysis. Thus, it seems that meta-analysis research supports the reviews of Ross and Gendreau, providing irrefutable evidence for the 'something works' argument, and with it sealing the demise of the 'nothing works' doctrine.

The meta-analysis studies, however, are not without their critics, who raise doubt about the conclusions of this research. Lösel (1995) pointed out that approximately 80 per cent of the studies included in the 13 meta-analyses he reviewed referred to juvenile delinquency. Indeed, Lipsey's study, which is considered the most comprehensive study, and hence, is most often used to show support for correctional intervention, investigated 'treatment' for juvenile delinquents, aged 12 to 21. Thus, while these analyses may provide evidence for efficacy of interventions with juvenile delinquents, they provide much less support for interventions with adult offenders. Only one of the 13 analyses reviewed by Lösel (1995) focused solely on adult offenders. This study, which was conducted by Lösel and his colleagues, reviewed 18 evaluations of treatment in social-therapeutic prisons, and found an average effect size of 0.11. Although this demonstrates a positive treatment effect, the treatment reviewed in this analysis is not comparable to many other correctional interventions. Consequently, the meta-analytic studies provide little support for the broad range of interventions used for adult offenders; yet interestingly, Lipsey's study is often quoted by reviewers of adult interventions as providing evidence that 'something works'.

Larzelere *et al.* (2004) raise doubts about the conclusions of these meta-analytic studies, mainly because of the poor methodology of the studies included in the reviews, although they also question the conclusions of efficacy given what they consider to be the small average effect sizes. Larzelere and colleagues argue that the studies included in the reviews are rendered unreliable and invalid because of bias in the selection of the treatment and control groups (see Chapter 7 for more information). To support this argument, they point out that the very few studies that employ randomization to control and treatment groups (a technique that eliminates selection bias) have very small treatment effects, which are in fact very close to 0 (which would indicate that the treatment had no effect). The techniques of meta-analysis can control for some methodological weaknesses, but it is difficult to argue that selection bias could adequately be controlled for statistically, if virtually all studies included in the meta-analytic review demonstrate this problem. Yet, for many reasons that are discussed in more details in Chapter 7, it is very difficult to routinely employ randomized designs in evaluations of interventions with offenders. Thus, it is unlikely that this issue will be resolved conclusively and many will continue to debate the effectiveness of offender treatment based on the level of importance, if it is considered at all, they give to the issue of selection bias.

It should also be pointed out that the vast majority of studies included in the meta-analytic reviews are North American based, and are published in English; thus, the generalizability of the findings can be questioned. In addition, it is a widespread belief that there is a publication bias towards studies showing positive treatment outcome. However, Hanson *et al.* (2002) reveal a bias in the opposite direction, with unpublished studies showing the greatest treatment effects, and Redondo *et al.* (1996, cited in Vennard *et al.* 1997) found no significant difference between the treatment effects of published and non-published studies. Hence, the existence of a publication bias has not been demonstrated conclusively.

Another problem with meta-analytic studies is that the evaluations reviewed cover a wide range of intervention/treatment techniques. Furthermore, these vary in the overriding theoretical perspective used, ranging from those working to increase the deterrence effect, those focusing on the principles of punishment, to those aiming towards rehabilitation. In addition, some are conducted in institutional settings, others in the community; some intervene with the offender/delinquent only, while others focus on the family, or a range of other people significant in the lives of the offender/delinquent. Lipsey's (1995: 66) study included 'every treatment found in the eligible research literature that was targeted on delinquency reduction'. Therefore, while the meta-analytic reviews show that intervening in some way can be effective, they do not provide support for any one technique. As a result, the acknowledgement that 'something works' was quickly replaced by the question 'what works?'.

'What works?'

Despite the problems discussed previously, the meta-analytic research of programme effectiveness is generally cited as evidence supporting the claim that correctional interventions work, or at least that some of these interventions work. For example, on using this literature, McGuire (2000) estimated that the impact of evidence-based programmes would be around a 10 per cent reduction in recidivism. Although the 'something works' conclusion is obviously more positive than the 'nothing works' conclusion, it is not particularly helpful to treatment staff and policy makers who clearly need to know exactly what works, what can be improved on, what should be abandoned as ineffective, and what is worth investing in. Fortunately, meta-analytic research has been able to answer some of these questions.

Interestingly, given political and public rhetoric regarding the use of imprisonment and other punitive approaches, meta-analytic research consistently shows that these punishment-based interventions are poor at reducing recidivism (for example, see Gendreau et al. 2000). In fact, some studies show that these approaches actually increase recidivism. For example, Lipsey (1992, cited in McGuire and Priestley 1995) found that punitive approaches on average actually increased recidivism in juvenile delinquents by 25 per cent, compared to controls. The issue of the efficacy of incapacitation, though, is complex (for a fuller discussion of this issue, see McGuire and Priestley (1995)). Yet, McGuire and Priestly argued that all the evidence suggests that incapacitation is an ineffective strategy. However, as Andrews and Bonta (1994) pointed out, when incapacitation is compared to no intervention or an intervention based in the community, recidivism rates are compared for the time at risk in the community only, and the period when no offences were committed during imprisonment is ignored. Thus, evaluations are based on post-programme effects on recidivism, with in-programme incapacitation effects being neglected.

This makes comparability across interventions based in the community and those based in institutions extremely difficult. However, in their discussion of the efficacy of imprisonment, McGuire and Priestley (1995) reasoned that the rate of imprisonment would have to rise significantly, and to proportions that would be difficult to fund and justify ethically, before it would have a significant impact on the overall crime rate. So, imprisonment seems to have an incapacitative effect that has a significant impact only if huge numbers of offenders are imprisoned for long periods of time.

As well as punishment, other more therapeutic approaches have consistently been revealed as ineffective. Classical psychotherapy, psychodynamic and counselling-based approaches have a limited impact on reoffence rates, although they can be effective in many other areas of psychological intervention. For example, Grendreau (1993, cited in Laws 2000b) identified traditional psychodynamic or non-directive, person-centred therapies as ineffective treatments for offenders. Furthermore, programmes that emphasized a 'talking' cure, a good relationship with the client as a primary goal, unravelling the unconscious mind and gaining insight, fostering positive self-regard, self-actualization through self-discovery, externalizing blame to parents and society, and ventilating anger were also revealed to be ineffective by Gendreau. In addition, medical intervention, that is the use of medication or other approaches such as dietary change, is very unlikely to have a lasting impact on recidivism rates (McGuire and Priestley 1995). That is not to say that medical intervention should be ignored completely, as it may have an important role to play, but only as part of a more comprehensive programme of intervention.

The conclusions discussed thus far can more accurately be described as what does not work; however, the 'what works' literature has also reported some consistent findings that are more akin to its title. The treatment approach that is constantly revealed as the most promising in terms of reducing recidivism is the cognitive-behavioural approach (for a review see Vennard et al. 1997); however, there is a lack of consensus over what this approach encompasses, which raises some concern about the validity of these findings. Nevertheless, Lösel (1995: 91) stated in his review of 13 meta-analytic studies that 'it is mostly cognitive-behavioural, skill-orientated and multi-modal programmes that yield the best effects'.

As well as identifying the treatment approach that is the most effective, the meta-analytic research has also revealed important programme characteristics that discriminate the more effective programmes from the least effective programmes. For example, controlling for methodological concerns, Lipsey (1989) found that the following variables were associated with reduced recidivism: longer duration of treatment and more meaningful contact (except for the institutional contact provided by institutional care); 'treatments' that were focused and structured; services provided outwith formal correctional settings and institutions; 'treatment' for higher-risk cases; 'treatment' that focused on non-individual characteristics, e.g. interventions with families; and 'treatment' under the influence of an evaluator. Lipsey concluded that, with a few exceptions, the best treatments were those identified as the most 'clinically relevant' by the Carleton University Group (Andrews *et al.* 1990; Andrews, Zinger *et al.* 1990). This group (see also Andrews and Bonta 1994; Cooke and Philip 2000) identified four principles consistent with the psychology of crime and with the requirement of clinical relevance. These are the principles of risk, need, responsivity and professional discretion.

The risk principle, which is 'so obvious that it hardly needs to be stated, and so subtle that it needs to be developed very carefully' (Andrews 1989: 6), proposes that the level of risk presented by an individual determine the level of treatment or intervention. Thus, 'higher levels of service should be allocated to the higher risk cases. On the obvious side, "If it ain't broke, don't try to fix it."' (p. 6). Andrews pointed out that the issue of risk is often misunderstood. Many often assume that the 'good' post-treatment functioning of low-risk individuals reveals the success of the treatment; yet, it is likely that these individuals would have had 'good' functioning without the treatment. Thus the resources used to provide the treatment produce very little additional benefit, and it could be argued, are wasted. On the other hand, the 'poor' post-treatment functioning of high-risk individuals is seen as evidence that treatment is ineffective; yet, although the functioning may be 'poor', it could be significantly better than it would have been without the treatment, which would indicate that the intervention is effective. This provides a good illustration of why, when evaluating treatments or interventions, it is important to compare a group of individuals who complete the treatment to a group who do not complete the treatment (see Chapter 7), rather than just examining the outcome of the treatment group. Andrews reasoned that another aspect of this principle is that the least severe sentence that can be applied that will have an impact on recidivism, should be applied, for example, by giving low-risk offenders non-custodial sentences.

The determination that treatment or intervention services should be targeted to the criminogenic needs of each individual offender is the need principle. It is important that criminogenic needs are precisely identified, as Andrews (1989: 8) pointed out: 'if recidivism reflects antisocial thinking, don't target self-esteem, target antisocial thinking. If recidivism reflects difficulties in keeping a job, don't target getting a job, target keeping a job'. Criminogenic needs are the factors of a person's characteristics, thoughts, behaviour and lifestyle that lead to his or her antisocial or criminal behaviour. Mostly these are dynamic factors that can be changed, although some factors are more amenable to change than others. The needs that Andrews (p. 8) suggested as promising targets for change are: changing antisocial attitudes and feelings; reducing antisocial peer associations; promoting familial affection, communication, monitoring and supervision; promoting identification and association with anticriminal role models; increasing self-control, self-management and problem-solving skills; replacing the skills of lying, stealing and aggression with more prosocial alternatives; reducing chemical dependencies; shifting the rewards and costs for criminal and non-criminal activities in familial, academic, vocational, recreational and other behavioural settings, so that non-criminal alternatives are favoured; providing the chronically psychiatrically troubled with low-pressure, sheltered living arrangements; changing other attributes of clients and their circumstances that, through individualized assessments of risk and need, have been linked reasonably with criminal conduct; and ensuring that the client is able to recognize risky situations and has a concrete and well-rehearsed plan for dealing with those situations.

> The risk principle assists in deciding who might profit most from intensive rehabilitative programming. The need principle suggests the appropriate targets of change for effective rehabilitation. Responsivity has to do with the selection of the appropriate modes and styles of service.
>
> (Andrews 1989: 9)

Hence, the responsivity principle determines that the mode and style of treatment is matched to individuals' abilities, skills and learning styles. For example, using a treatment involving a great deal of time discussing complex theoretical models is clearly not going to be effective with individuals who have learning difficulties, poor educational backgrounds, or perhaps, who simply are not used to this style of explanation.

Finally, the principle of professional discretion determines that:

> The professional reviews risk, need, and responsivity for a particular case under particular circumstances, and makes the decision that best reflects ethical, humanitarian, legal, and effectiveness considerations. Principles of treatment, no matter how solid the research base, must be applied by an informed and sensitive professional.
>
> (Andrews 1989: 11)

The fact that these principles seem to be important in effective treatment is a reasonably robust finding. Andrews and his colleagues (Andrews *et al.* 1990; Andrews, Zinger *et al.* 1990) found that interventions that adhered to these principles produced the largest mean treatment effect sizes (0.30) compared to those that were inappropriate, i.e. did not follow the principles (−0.06) and those where the treatment was unspecified (0.13). Similarly, Gendreau and Groggin (1996, cited in Cooke and Philip 2000) obtained the average effect sizes of 0.25, −0.03 and −0.13, respectively, for the same treatment groupings. Andrews and Ross (1994, cited in Cooke and Philip 2000) replicated findings for the need and responsivity principle, but not for the risk principle; however, the concept of risk is problematic. In order for this research to be reliable and valid, researchers need to be using the same levels of risk in categorizing high- and low-risk offenders. It is difficult to see how this can be done reliably when researchers use a variety of risk assessment tools and the studies included in meta-analytic research cover a broad range of offenders and offending behaviours. Furthermore, the dichotomy of high and low risk is rather simplistic and may mask complex relationships between risk and effectiveness. It could also be agued that in many, if not most instances, 'high-risk' actually refers to medium-risk offenders as many treatment programmes routinely select out the most problematic offenders. For example, in sex offender treatment programmes, offenders with high levels of denial are often excluded. Thus a programme that does this, but claims to treat high-risk offenders, is not treating the most risky. The risk principle, therefore, is one that needs more careful analysis and research.

There is a growing consensus that treatment integrity must also be tackled if programmes are to be effective (Cooke and Philip 2000). Cooke and Philip argue that this should be another principle of successful treatment outcome and show that meta-analytic reviews have demonstrated that the quality of treatment delivery is critical. Treatment integrity means that the programme is delivered as it was intended and continues to be delivered in that manner. Although this sounds obvious, it is not as easy to apply in practice as it sounds, and has only been given serious consideration since the late 1980s and early 1990s. Hollin (1995: 197) identified three broad processes that can militate against treatment integrity. These are programme drift, programme reversal and programme non-compliance.

Programme drift is 'characterized by the gradual shift over time of the aim of the programme' (p. 197), which may, for example, occur when too much emphasis is placed on day-to-day administrative and management issues, to the detriment of long-term therapeutic goals. Programme reversal occurs when some factor or factors work in opposition to the aims and goals of the treatment. Hollin noted that this was illustrated by Schlichter and Horan's (1981) account of a self-control programme for young offenders. Although the young offenders were trained to control their anger and aggression, some staff modelled aggressive behaviour in response to angry provocation, and others encouraged the expression of 'pent up' anger. Thus, the young offenders were given conflicting information, which may have been confusing and counterproductive. When practitioners decide for some reason, however well intentioned, to change or omit parts of the programme, this starts a process of change, particularly when new staff are trained to the 'adapted' programme, that Hollin likened to a game of Chinese Whispers. Over time, the programme changes so that it bears little resemblance to the programme that was originally designed and implemented. Although programme change and development should be encouraged, the problem with programme non-compliance is that it takes place in an unmanaged and uncoordinated way. Although the changes instigated by staff may be effective and well meaning, they are not necessarily shared by all staff and when introduced in an *ad hoc* way, not evaluated effectively. Thus programme change should be managed within an ongoing strategy of continued monitoring, evaluation and development, managed in such a way to encourage and support input from all programme staff.

Cooke and Philip (2000) describe a large number of factors that can enhance treatment integrity. These are designing programmes according to an empirically validated theoretical framework; developing a comprehensive treatment manual; developing and maintaining a strong institutional commitment; and ensuring the treatment is well resourced. There are also a number of factors relating to programme staff. The success of treatment can depend on: staff selection; the skills and characteristics of those who are selected; the skills and abilities of the programme leader; the quality and style of staff training; the support and supervision provided to staff; and the support to the programme provided by non-programme staff, which particularly applies in institutional settings. Finally, treatment integrity can be enhanced and maintained through continued monitoring and evaluation.

The impact of the findings of the meta-analytic research and the principles of effective treatment outlined earlier cannot be underestimated and have led to a general shift towards evidence-based practice, and towards programme accreditation (UK) or registration and/or licensing (North America). For example, in the UK, the 'what works' principles were originally applied in a piecemeal way until 1996. From then onwards, a system of accreditation was developed by HM Prison Service and applied to the National Probation Service from 1999. The process of accreditation is supervized by the Correctional Services Accreditation Panel (previously called the Joint Prison/Probation Service Accreditation Panel), which oversees and regulates the quality of both programme design and delivery in terms of adherence to 'what works' principles of best practice (for more information see the annual Reports of this panel and audit Reports of accredited programmes, which are published on the Home Office website). In summary, to be accredited a programme must demonstrate that it: has a clear model of change backed by research; selects offenders who need to change and whose risk is likely to be reduced by the programme; targets dynamic risk factors; targets a range of risk areas; uses methods that have been proven effective; is skills orientated; matches participants' learning styles and abilities; encourages engagement and motivation; has continuity of programmes and services; has ongoing monitoring and evaluation (Home Office National Probation Directorate 2001).

> The shift from the 'nothing works' doctrine (Martinson 1974) to 'what works?' (McGuire 1995) has profoundly influenced the policies of HM Prison Service over the last decade with a shift in emphasis from the containment of prisoners to the rehabilitation of prisoners.
> (Friendship and Thornton 2001: 285)

This extract clearly indicates the impact of the gradual change from the negative views of the 1970s to the more positive, evidence-based approaches of the 1990s and 2000s. Although the development of sex offender treatment programmes has continued throughout this period, the findings of the meta-analytic research have had some impact, encouraging evidence-based practice and providing more support for cognitive-behavioural approaches, the development of which are described below.

Cognitive-behavioural treatment for sex offenders

As discussed previously, the cognitive-behavioural approach developed initially from behavioural therapy. Gradually, however, it was recognized that these early therapies were too simplistic and a multi-modal approach within behavioural therapy was adopted. Consequently, in the 1970s and 1980s, corresponding with a general shift in psychology from a behavioural to a cognitive approach, the scope of these programmes was broadened to include cognitive processes (for a more detailed discussion see Marshall and Laws 2003).

> The term, 'cognitive' as used here, refers to an individual's internal processes, including the justifications, perceptions and judgements used by the sex offender to rationalize his child molestation behaviour. Clinically, a child molester's cognitive distortions appear to allow the offender to justify his ongoing sexual abuse of children without anxiety, guilt and loss of self-esteem that would usually

result from an individual committing behaviours contrary to the norms of his society.

(Abel *et al.* 1989: 137)

Surprisingly, given the more recent focus on evidence-based practice, the shift from behavioural to cognitive approaches, as Marshall and Laws (2003) highlight, had more to do with the changing beliefs in psychology at the time, rather than the emergence of empirical evidence demonstrating the value of cognitive techniques. Despite this, cognitive elements have gradually been expanded in sex offender treatment programmes to the point where behavioural elements have been relegated to a small, supportive part of broadly cognitive-based programmes (see Chapter 3). This can be seen particularly in the UK where, compared to programmes in North America and New Zealand, the behavioural element is barely noticeable and is very much overshadowed by cognitive elements.

The cognitive-behavioural approach developed from an integration of behavioural and cognitive traditions to stress the complexity of the relationships between thoughts, feelings and behaviour, and the interplay between the individual and the environment. Initially researchers and theorists pointed out that behavioural theories relied on implicit cognitive elements, such as memory and other thought processes. This recognition and key theories, such as social learning theory, which although based on behaviourism stressed the importance of cognitive processes such as modelling and observation, gradually led to a greater integration between the two traditions. This integration can clearly be seen in forensic psychology, where traditionally social explanations of crime and behaviour could be incorporated and combined with traditionally psychological, or individual explanations. Thus, although the environment is recognized as an important factor in the shaping of behaviour, crucially it is also recognized that its impact is mediated by thoughts, feelings and, more fundamentally, by perceptions of environment factors. Importantly, since it is believed that behaviours are learned, albeit subtly, and not necessarily consciously, over long periods, it is thought that behaviours can be unlearned and new behaviours learned. This premise of course determines that change is possible and hence, that interventions are possible, and even necessary to bring about that change.

The shift from behavioural to cognitive-behavioural approaches in sex offender treatment developed in two ways. The first occurred rapidly in North America with treatment practitioners adding more cognitive components to what had originally been behavioural programmes. Eventually most programmes explored and attempted to change attitudes towards sexual behaviour and sexually deviant behaviour; attitudes towards women and children and sexual entitlement; cognitive-distortions (or thoughts and attitudes encouraging sexually deviant behaviour); offence cycles or offence chains including thoughts and behaviours leading to sexually deviant behaviour; empathy; self-esteem; and social skills (see Chapter 6 for a more detailed discussion of key cognitive-behavioural treatment goals).

Marshall and Laws (2003: 97) assert that the change from behavioural to cognitive was so rapid in psychology that by the end of the 1970s 'strict behaviorists had become members of an endangered species'. Indeed, as Abel and Blanchard (1974, cited in Marshall and Laws 2003) emphasized, the early programmes' focus on fantasy meant that in reality many programmes originally referred to as behavioural, were actually cognitive-behavioural, as fantasy is clearly a cognitive process. Marshall (1996a) argued that Abel played a seminal role in the development of cognitive-behavioural treatment for sex offenders, encouraging others to adopt his approach and expand the range of treatment components in frequent conference presentations and publications describing his methods. Marshall's contribution to the development of this approach cannot be ignored either, with his many publications, some of which included descriptions of his treatment approaches, performing a similar function to Abel's work. Gradually, others adopted the broader approaches of Abel and Marshall and many added their own elements, so that the cognitive-behavioural approach spread throughout North America.

The other way in which cognitive-behavioural programmes were developed can be illustrated by the introduction of sex offender programmes to the prison service of England and Wales (see Chapter 3 for a more detailed discussion of the development of treatment programmes in the UK). Here, once a decision had been taken at a political level to introduce sex offender treatment programmes, a focus on evidence-based practice led to a review of the 'what works?' literature, which determined that cognitive-behavioural programmes were the most effective programmes (generally and with sex offenders). Thus, the new initiative was introduced with programmes being modelled on the most promising programmes from North America, incorporating the more general findings and principles from the 'what works?' literature.

The introduction of relapse-prevention strategies to sex offender treatment programmes was argued by Marhsall (1996a: 180) to be '[w]ithout doubt, the most important development in the 1980s'. Although some treatment providers had attempted to develop relapse-prevention type strategies, it was not until Pithers et al. (1983) extended the relapse-prevention model, originally developed in the area of addiction by Marlatt (1982; see also Marlatt and Gordon 1985), that relapse-prevention became a key element, if not a central part, of most cognitive-behavioural programmes (see also Pithers et al. 1988; Laws

1989; 1995; Marques and Nelson 1989; Pithers 1990; 1991). The main aim of this approach was to encourage and support the maintenance of treatment-induced abstinence (see Chapter 6 for a more detailed description).

Following the addition of relapse-prevention techniques, there have been no major significant additions to the cognitive-behavioural programmes, although evaluation research and theoretical developments have led to a gradual improvement and refining of these core components (see Chapter 6). Although the majority of cognitive-behavioural programmes tend to have the same core components, programmes also have idiosyncratic elements, for example drama therapy, to such an extent that the current treatment approach, although most often referred to as cognitive-behavioural, is more truly a multi-modal approach (see also Vennard *et al.* 1997).

By the end of the 1980s, the core elements of sex offender cognitive-behavioural programmes had been established. The major development in the 1990s was a dramatic expansion in the number of treatment programmes, the expansion of sex offender treatment provision on a global scale, and a general increase in interest in the area. The number of sex offender treatment programmes has increased substantially, both in North America and significantly in many others countries (e.g. the UK, Australia, New Zealand). From a handful of programmes in the 1970s, the provision has expanded to such an extent that the Safer Society Program and Press identified more than 1,700 programmes in North America treating those with sexual behavioural problems in 1994 (Freeman-Longo *et al.* 1995). In addition, programmes have become a more integral part of the criminal justice and mental health provisions in a variety of countries. For example, provision in England and Wales has expanded from a small number of programmes developed on an *ad hoc* basis in the early 1980s, to provision that is now a key element of sex offender intervention in both HM Prison Service and in the community, via the National Probation Service (see Chapter 3 for more details).

Marshall and Laws (2003) provide some interesting examples of the growth of the field in a relatively short period of time. They report that the first conference on behavioural or cognitive-behavioural sex offender issues was held in 1975. A symposium on treatment issues was attended by ten people, whereas in 2000, more than 1,600 attended the Association for the Treatment of Sexual Abusers (ATSA) conference in the USA. With the development and expansion of treatment to many other countries, and the fact that many would be unable or unwilling to attend such a conference, this figure is likely to be a fraction of those who currently practise in sex offender treatment in some form, i.e. as treatment providers, researchers or trainers. Furthermore, there has been a huge growth in research in the area and an associated rapid increase in the number of publications, made more prominent by the introduction of two specific journals: ATSA's *Sexual Abuse: A Journal of Research and Treatment*, first issued in 1995 (although this had evolved from *The Annals of Sex Research* which was first published in 1988), and NOTA's (the National Organization for the Treatment of Abusers, based in the UK) *Journal of Sexual Aggression*, with its first edition published in 1994.

Sex offender treatment was initially developed with adult sex offenders; however, programmes have been developed for other groups of offenders, most notably with juveniles and offenders with learning difficulties, and to a lesser extent with female sex offenders. Although it is not possible to chart the developments of treatment provision in this publication in detail, key developments will be summarized, starting with juvenile offenders.

As discussed in the opening chapter, a significant proportion of adult offenders report an onset of deviant thoughts and arousals in their teenage years. Moreover, a significant proportion of sexual offences are committed by juveniles or adolescents. Thus, many have argued for the need to target intervention at this group of offenders, or at those yet to become offenders, who are starting to develop high-risk behaviours and cognitions. Yet, as Bourke and Donohue (1996) pointed out, it was not until the late 1970s that sex crimes committed by adolescents were considered worthy of serious investigation (see Groth 1977). Marshall and Laws (2003) state that Groth's (1983) adult offender programme, which was adapted for juveniles, became the model for intervention with this group of offenders (see Groth and Lorendo 1981). Most likely because of this adaptation from an adult programme, juvenile treatment programmes often contain the same core elements as adult cognitive-behavioural programmes (for a review see Bourke and Donohue 1996; Tarolla *et al.* 2002); however, juvenile programmes often contain other elements such as interventions focused at the family and peer relations, and they are more accurately termed multi-systemic treatment rather than cognitive-behavioural (for more detailed discussion of juvenile sex offender treatment see Rich (2003)). Descriptions of juvenile treatment programmes can be found in Marshall *et al.*'s (1998) book. The rapid expansion of treatment programmes for juvenile sex offenders in North America is evidenced by the increase from nine programmes in 1982 to 645 in 1989 (Knopp 1982; Knopp and Stevenson 1989). Yet, to date only one controlled evaluation using a comparison group had been conducted on juvenile sex offender treatment provision (see Borduin *et al.* 1990), which was of a multi-systemic programme. Despite the development of treatment for this group of offenders, its use is generally more sporadic and less integrated into criminal justice and mental health services than treatment for adult sex offenders, and in some areas, provision for this group of offenders is poor.

Marshall and Laws (2003) note that treatment programmes for female sex offenders began to emerge in the 1980s. Literature surrounding female offenders is still scarce, certainly when compared to male offenders and even juvenile offenders (for more information on female sex offenders see the following two books: Elliott (1993); Saradjian (1996)). As discussed in the previous chapter, there is a great deal of debate surrounding the extent of sexual abuse committed by women. However, regardless of the true extent of this behaviour, the fact remains that very few women are convicted of sexual abuse. Hence, the identified need for treatment programmes for women offenders is rather limited, and group programmes are difficult as female offenders are geographically widely spread. This may account for the fact that there is very little literature discussing cognitive-behavioural treatment for women sex offenders and no published controlled/comparison treatment evaluation studies.

As Marshall and Laws (2003) report, treatment for offenders (usually adult men) with learning difficulties (or the developmentally or intellectually disabled) emerged around the same time period as the increased interest in, and awareness of, female sex offenders. In 1983, Murphy *et al.* discussed treatment issues with intellectually disabled sex offenders and by 1987, Knopp and Lackey (1987) detailed 40 treatment programmes for this group of offenders. Early programmes were outlined by Griffiths and colleagues (Griffiths *et al.* 1985; Griffiths *et al.* 1989) and a more recent description is provided by Coleman and Haaven (1998). Recently, in the UK, Lindsay and her colleagues have developed a programme, based on cognitive therapy and social skills training, that has produced promising outcome data (Lindsay and Smith 1998; Lindsay, Neilson *et al.* 1998; Lindsay, Marshall *et al.* 1998; Lindsay 2002; Lindsay *et al.* 2002). As with the provision for juvenile offenders, although there are now a substantial number of programmes for intellectually disabled offenders, evaluation of these programmes is poor. Barron *et al.* (2002) found that there were no controlled, comparison group evaluation studies. Furthermore Barron and colleagues noted that there were still 'significant areas of deficit in service provision and a number of unanswered questions about appropriate disposal and management' (p. 460).

Following the development of programmes for the specific groups of offenders described above, there has been a general spread in programme diversity, with programmes catering for an ever-wider range of subgroups of offenders. For example, in Marshall *et al.*'s (1998) publication, programmes for deaf, aboriginal, professional, clergy, and Hispanic sex offenders are described. No doubt this is a small selection of the full range of programmes now being provided for specific subgroups of offenders.

Interestingly, this chapter ends where it began, with treatment in the USA having moved full circle with the re-emergence of civil commitment laws. As Prentky and Burgess (2000, cited in Marshall and Laws 2003) argue, sexual predator laws are introduced (or reintroduced) in the United States following a certain level of public outcry. The laws are then legally challenged and repealed or disused, only to be reintroduced again, in slightly modified form, when public outcry peaks again. Surprisingly, given the history of this type of legislation in the USA, and although not specifically for sex offenders, legislation has been proposed in the UK that would provide for the detention (i.e. civil commitment) of dangerous offenders with personality disorders. The proposal would allow for the indefinite detention of individuals who are assessed as having a personality disorder and of being at risk of committing violent (including sexually violent) offences until such time, following treatment, that they are determined 'safe' for return to the community. It is proposed to allow for the detention of such individuals regardless of whether the individual has committed an offence or not. Although this has yet to be enacted in the UK, 14 states in the USA have enacted Sexually Violent Persons laws. Legislation in Canada also allows for the indeterminate detention of 'dangerous' offenders, which includes sex offenders (for a more detailed review of this and other legislation aimed at 'dangerous' offenders, see John Howard Society of Alberta (1999)).

Clearly, such legislation places an emphasis on the treatment of detained individuals; otherwise, they would have to be detained for the rest of their lives (unless one assumes that personality disorders and risk of violent behaviour significantly reduces with age). In 2000, Marques *et al.* reported that the programme they devised and evaluated in previous years for California's Sex Offender Treatment and Evaluation Project was currently being revised to treat sex offenders committed under the new sexual predator laws, a procedure no doubt being completed by many more treatment providers. As Marshall and Laws (2003) point out, it is not yet possible to determine the effect that the Sexually Violent Persons laws will have in the USA, or indeed in the UK, if the current proposals are enacted into legislation. However, without a clear way to determine the accuracy of risk assessments and the effects of treatment on treatment completers, there is a limited hope of release for those who are committed under such legislation. The prospect of release is reduced further with the reliance on static risk factors (which do not change) in risk assessments and little current knowledge of the impact of dynamic factors on assessments of risk (although research is currently increasing in this area, see for example Hanson and Harris (2000); Hudson *et al.* (2002)). If individuals are detained on the basis of static risk factors and reassessed on the basis of the same static risk factors, then their determined level of risk will never decrease to a level that allows for their release. Thus, this type of legislation is controversial, yet to date it has sustained all legal challenges in the USA.

So, it seems likely that this form of indeterminate legislation will become more widespread and yet again those determined to be 'dangerous' offenders, particularly sexually (and violently) dangerous offenders, will be treated differently and separately from the rest of the offender population. This might suggest that sex offender treatment has progressed little from the 1930s when this form of legislation was first introduced; however, this would be an oversimplification, as the context in which this 'new' legislation is introduced has changed enormously, as has treatment provision generally and more specifically for sex offenders. Evidence-based practice, or work based on the 'what works?' literature, has become standard practice and so it is much more likely that the treatment delivered under the 'new' legislation will be monitored and evaluated much more effectively than was the case previously. Hence, it should also follow (although this issue is hotly debated, see Chapter 8) that the treatment offered under the 'new' legislation will be more effective. Often informed by the 'what works?' literature, treatment programmes have developed so much that programmes delivered as part of the early legislation bear very little resemblance to current cognitive-behavioural, multi-modal approaches. Similarly, the place of sex offender treatment within the context of criminal justice and mental health provision has improved. This provision is now considered an important part of all aspects of criminal justice and mental health policy, rather than treatment provided only for those detained under 'sexual predator' legislation. This can be seen more clearly in the next chapter, where the current provision and policy will be summarized and compared across a number of countries.

Chapter 3

Current use of cognitive-behavioural sex offender treatment

Chapter 2 charted the development of cognitive-behavioural treatment for sex offenders in the context of the development of correctional interventions for offenders more generally. As can be seen from this discussion, an early therapeutic and rehabilitative optimism gave way to therapeutic and rehabilitative pessimism, as it was felt by many that 'nothing works'. However, gradually research has encouraged a return to the more optimistic view of rehabilitation, although it can be argued that the current optimism is more realistic and focused. It is now acknowledged that treatment requires a great deal of effort (on behalf of the treatment providers and receivers) over sustained periods, and that although it may work for some, it may not work for all. Furthermore, it is accepted that a single treatment cannot hope to be effective for all offenders and that adjustments must be made to account for need, risk and responsivity, in a manner than ensures sustained treatment integrity. This more positive approach has led to the general acceptance of sex offender treatment as an important aspect of criminal justice and mental health provision in a range of countries. The current provision, and development of this provision in countries outwith North America, will be summarized in this chapter, following a brief discussion of why it is now commonly believed that sex offender treatment is a vital part of social, criminal justice and mental health policy.

Why treat?

Given the small percentage of sex offenders sanctioned by the custodial and non-custodial elements of the Criminal Justice System, and the level of resources required to provide sex offender treatment programmes, it seems pertinent to question the use of sex offender treatment programmes. Abel (1994: 531) argued that:

> To object to the development of programs to diagnose and treat adolescent and adult sexual aggressives is like sticking one's head in the sand hoping that if we do not confront the cause, sexual violence will just go away.

Given that the majority of sex offenders either remain in the community or return to the community after serving a determinate custodial sentence (McPherson *et al.* 1994; Williams 1996b), the most frequent and vehement response to this question is that we should treat these offenders in order to reduce victimization and hence, human suffering (Groth and Oliveri 1989; Perkins 1990; Marshall 1992; Lewis and Perkins 1996).

> To the extent that there is social support for treating sex offenders, it is not because society thinks incarcerated offenders have the right to decent mental health services to improve their outlook on life. Society supports treatment for this population, precisely because sex offences are reprehensible and repetitive and because there is a prevailing belief that there is at least some possibility that specialized treatment might enable sex offenders to refrain from further abuse of innocent women and children.
>
> (Pithers 1997: 35)

In addition, Lancaster (1996) pointed out that information gathered during treatment regarding offenders' methods and modes of offending, can help in the protection of children generally.

Some commentators (Perkins 1987; Marshall 1992; Kaul 1993) have noted that sex offender treatment is also cost effective (see also Chapter 9). Williams (1996b) argued that in financial terms alone, over a one-year period, preventing as few as 40 sex offenders from reoffending would pay for the continuation of the Canadian programme and would obviously reduce the suffering of potential victims. In addition, a few authors support a more humanitarian argument that offenders should be helped to change (Groth and Oliveri 1989; Ward 2002a; Ward and Stewart 2003) and live as free and satisfying lives as possible (Lewis and Perkins 1996).

Many have argued that imprisonment seems to be ineffective in reducing recidivism in this group of offenders (Taylor 1981; Groth and Oliveri 1989; Kosky 1989; Lewis and Perkins 1996) and Kelly (1995) contended that custody serves to make offenders go to greater lengths to avoid conviction. Renvoize (1993) reasoned that as perpetrators have often been offending for long periods of time, a short period of imprisonment is unlikely to have an impact on their behaviour. These arguments, however, have been contested. The Howard League (1985) were keen to make the point that most sex offenders do not reoffend and Kaul (1993: 209) stated that:

> The majority of sex offenders are not reconvicted irrespective of any intervention they may have received. However, it is unclear whether punishment (custodial or otherwise) that they may have received following their conviction had any role to play in the prevention of further offending behaviour.

Soothill and Gibbens (1978), however, found that men who were accused of sexual offences but who had been found not guilty by the courts, had higher rates of recidivism than convicted and incarcerated offenders, which suggests that imprisonment does have an impact on recidivism.

These arguments, however, imply that a choice should be made between the use of imprisonment (and more traditional sentences) or treatment. No matter how effective incarceration is, it will inevitably fail to deter all offenders. Similarly, treatment cannot hope to be 100 per cent effective and so both approaches should be used to maximize the number of offenders who are deterred from reoffending. Furthermore, there are a number of reasons to suggest a combination of the two approaches may be the most effective response.

Marshall et al. (1993: 442) suggested that 'very few people, sex offenders included, voluntarily change their behaviour, attitudes and beliefs, unless there is an advantage'. Thus, they argued that imprisonment (or the threat of it) offers a leverage to engage offenders in the treatment process and that, 'any time in prison which does not involve therapy is a waste for the sex offender and results in a risk to the community' (p. 444). In support of this, Chaffin (1994) showed that a group of prosecuted juvenile offenders attended a sex offender programme more regularly and obtained better progress and victim empathy ratings than did a group who had attended juvenile court but escaped prosecution. Marshall et al. (1993) also pointed out that incarceration protects society while the offenders are undergoing treatment and remain a risk to the community. Finally, it can also be argued that sex offenders should be punished (Marshall et al. 1993) as this sends out a clear message to victims and the rest of society that this behaviour will not be tolerated.

Having argued that treatment should be provided alongside the punishment of imprisonment, it should also be noted that in order to maximize treatment effectiveness and to reach as many offenders as possible, treatment should also be available in the community. Three main reasons underpin this conclusion. Firstly, many sex offenders do not receive custodial sentences: Sampson (1994) noted that only about one third of convicted sex offenders were sentenced to immediate custody. Thus, if treatment were only available in a custodial setting, only about one third of convicted sex offenders would be able to receive treatment. Secondly, if treatment is available in the community, outside the Criminal Justice System, sex offenders or potential sex offenders may chose to attend treatment on a voluntary basis. Although it seems counter-intuitive that sex offenders would volunteer to attend treatment, the Nood Clinic in Brussels found that its number of self-referrals increased from 3 to 30 per cent when it decided to end cooperation with the police (*Guardian*, 12 July 1991, cited in Sampson 1994). Furthermore, the Stop It Now! Vermont helpline received calls from 99 self-identified abusers (15 per cent of the total calls to the helpline) in a four-year period (Tabachnick and Dawson 2000), despite the mandatory requirement in the USA for staff to officially report all previously undisclosed offences. Forty per cent of over 1,300 calls, from July 2002 to January 2004, to a similar helpline in the UK and Ireland were received from those concerned about their own behaviour (Kemshall *et al.* 2004). Finally, for offenders who do receive treatment in prison, the potential benefits of this treatment may be reinforced and strengthened by continued aftercare and/or booster treatment sessions in the community (Marshall and Eccles 1991; Marshall *et al.* 1993).

In summary, then, it would appear that treatment should be provided, alongside more traditional, punitive responses, in both custodial and non-custodial settings to maximize the number of offenders who are deterred from reoffending. However, it should also be pointed out that this approach will have a limited impact as few offenders will be exposed to treatment (McCall 1993). This is because conviction rates are low and there are many problems in reliably identifying potential offenders. As Sparks and Baron (1985: 2, cited in McCall 1993) argued:

> Even if the mental health and criminal justice systems could be improved to provide increased conviction and effective rehabilitation, it is likely that we would identify, detain, and treat only a small proportion of the offenders or potential offenders. We would not eliminate sexual violence. We must still find ways of intervening to alter the conditions in our community that continue to *produce* offenders.

Thus, there seem to be many sound reasons for offering treatment in a range of settings both as part of the criminal justice provision and also outwith this provision. The extent to which current policy in a range of countries fits this model will now be discussed in more detail.

Current use of sex offender treatment

Canada

As Canada (and the USA) led the development of sex offender treatment, the development of treatment in Canada is described in the previous chapter. However, a clearer and more detailed picture of the development in Canada can be found in the following two surveys: Borzecki and Wormith (1987) and Wormith and Hanson (1992). In 1992, treatment was provided annually for 1,500 offenders using behavioural, cognitive-behavioural and psychodynamic approaches. At this time, the duration of programmes ranged from three to 36 months, with between one to 33 hours of treatment per week. Since 1992, provision in Canada has developed such that it currently provides a good model that could, and perhaps should, be adopted elsewhere. Evaluation and research are key elements of this provision (for the range of publications, see the Forum of Corrections Research, access via the Correctional Service of Canada's website) and consequently programmes are based on the best-evidence literature. It is not possible to describe all the programmes in detail here but a summary of the provision will be provided later with references to publications that provide greater depth. Information about Canadian policy and practice in general can be found in Gordon and Porporino (1990), Lundström (2002) and Williams (1996b). An overview of the Canadian approach to treatment in custodial and community settings is provided by Marshall and Eccles (1996).

The Correctional Service of Canada (CSC) is a single organization (although it is split into five administrative regions) that manages offenders in both custodial and community settings; thus, there are strong links between treatment in custodial and community settings, and there is a smooth transition from custody to community supervision. The CSC has three levels of management: *National*, which is often referred to as Federal; *Regional*; and *Institutional and Parole Offices*. As well as managing Federal penitentiaries, the CSC also has two Regional Psychiatric Centers for male offenders, which are jointly hospitals and prisons and two Regional Centers that are stand alone units within other penitentiaries. Thus, provision for offenders with mental health problems is contained within a single-service provision, rather than being split between criminal justice and mental health arenas, as is the case in most other jurisdictions.

In 1994, the CSC created the first Corporate Advisor Sex Offender Programme, which was established to help guide and structure the Service's work with sex offenders. This was replaced with a committee of Correctional Service clinical, research and administrative staff who were tasked to develop the basic infrastructure of a cohesive sex offender strategy. The committee produced a statement of principles, standards for delivery of services, assessment and treatment guidelines, and evaluation and accountability guidelines (Williams 1996a). The result of this work is a standardized provision using the cognitive-behavioural approach.

Following the introduction of a system for programme accreditation in the UK, and using this as a model, a similar system was introduced to the CSC (see Lundström 2002; Correctional Service of Canada 2003). This process was initiated in 1997, when accreditation procedures in HM Prison Service, the Scottish Prison Service, the American Correctional Association and other processes were studied. The best elements of these systems of accreditation were synthesized to form the CSC accreditation process that was introduced in 1997. There are two types of accreditation panels: an International Expert Panel who are responsible for overseeing the accreditation process; and several International Accreditation Panels who review accreditation applications. Building on the work of HM Prison Service of England and Wales, the CSC identified eight criteria which programmes must address for accreditation: explicit empirically-based model of change; target criminogenic need; effective methods; skill orientated; responsivity; programme intensity; continuity of care; ongoing monitoring and evaluation. Programmes should have a well-developed programme manual, a training manual, research and evaluation reports, awareness materials for offenders and staff, and a cost-benefit analysis. Programmes must be re-accredited every five years and successfully perform during site accreditation visits, which are designed to inspire staff commitment to reintegration goals, restrain the tendency for programme drift, encourage the adoption of best practices from one region to the next, and help standardize programmes delivered across different locations.

When an individual is convicted of an offence, the process of assessing his or her range of needs begins immediately and a sentence management plan is formulated. When an offender is sentenced to two or more years' imprisonment, he or she is sent to a Federal Prison. On incarceration, offenders in many of the regions are sent to a centralized reception facility to go through an assessment process before moving to their 'home' institution (for example, see Malcolm 1996). Sex offenders taking part in treatment programmes are housed separately from other offenders to enable them to concentrate on the treatment. Unusually, these programmes accept all offenders including those who deny the offence. Sex offenders who do not comply with their sentence management plan are not eligible for parole until they have completed virtually their entire sentence.

The CSC provides a range of sex offender programmes and if necessary, individual treatment. Programmes for offenders with high-intensity needs are delivered by specialist staff, such as psychologists, while programmes in some prisons may be delivered by correctional officers who have a social sciences degree and who receive appropriate training. With the introduction of the accreditation procedures, and using the approach adopted in the UK, a process of programme rationalization has begun in the CSC where a range of accredited programmes will be delivered in a variety of establishments throughout Canada. This system will more fully formalize and consistently structure, across the five CSC regions, a provision that is already well designed.

Programmes available in Federal Prisons in Canada provide treatment for a range of offender needs. For example, (for more detailed descriptions see Barbaree *et al.* 1998; Lundström 2002) in the CSC region of Ontario (which is the best described in publications in English), the Kingston Penitentiary Sex Offender Programme treats maximum-security offenders, while the Warkworth Sexual Behaviour Clinic (established in 1989) works with medium-security offenders. In 1991, a programme was established at Bath Penitentiary, which was originally a minimum-security establishment that has since (in 1995) been recategorized as medium-security. Thus, this programme deals with offenders who have moved down from higher security levels, many of whom have received treatment in other programmes, and works with low- to moderate-risk sex offenders. Provision for minimum-security offenders was then established in the Pittsburg and Frontenac Penitentiaries, where work is conducted with low-risk sex offenders placed directly into minimum-security after assessment. In addition, every minimum-security institution offers a relapse-prevention programme. From 1990 to 1992, community-based programmes were established in Toronto, Hamilton, Ottawa and Kingston, and later numerous other programmes and services were provided in smaller communities in Ontario. Thus, treatment provision is available throughout the sentence in custodial, special hospital (for those with mental health issues) and community settings. The range of treatment provision and its flexibility allows for treatment to be fitted together throughout the length of the sentence to best accommodate offenders' needs and risk, according to the 'what works?' literature. This flexibility can be seen more clearly in the brief programme descriptions provided below.

The Regional Treatment Centre Sex Offender Programme (RTCSOP) is the oldest continuously running sex offender treatment programme offered by the CSC. It was designed by Marshall and Williams and introduced in 1973 (see Di Fazio *et al.* 2001; Lundström 2002). Aubut *et al.* (1998) described a programme operating in a similar environment in a different region of the CSC. There are very few admission criteria for the RTCSOP in Ontario, which accepts offenders with low intellectual capacity, reading and writing disabilities, psychosis controlled by medication, those with manageable medical conditions and those who deny their offences. Admissions to the programme are made in rank order of eligibility for statutory release dates for those serving finite sentences, and parole eligibility and sentence commencement dates for those serving life or indeterminate sentences. There are three components to this programme: group therapy, individual therapy and milieu therapy.

The intensive programme takes seven months to complete on a groupwork basis, and also includes an individual therapy programme for sex offenders who present high treatment needs and a high risk of reoffending. A three- to five-month individual therapy programme is also available for special needs inmates, such as those with learning difficulties, major mental disorder in remission or stabilized through medication, and for those who are very disruptive or unable to cope with treatment in group settings. This programme is also offered to offenders who, having completed the intensive programme are considered to be in need of follow up treatment. The residential nature of the programme is a key element and the milieu therapy takes place when nursing staff spend at least two hours per shift on the unit discussing issues with clients and reinforcing treatment messages.

The programme uses a cognitive-behavioural approach and has five key components: disclosure of offence, victim awareness, relapse prevention, social skills and human sexuality. In addition, as offenders enter the programme, they are assigned a psychologist and a prime nurse whom they see at least once a week. Issues discussed at these meetings include: history taking and an examination and understanding of why the offence(s) took place, development of a list of problem areas and treatment procedures aimed at reducing the likelihood of repeat offending. Other areas of discussion are self-esteem, anxiety, relationships, dealing with rejection, sexual problems, fantasies, deviant arousal (sexual responding to children or violence), impulsivity, anger control and relapse prevention.

The Warkworth programme, modelled on programmes set up elsewhere by Marshall and Barbaree, is described in more detail by Barbaree *et al.* (1998) and Seto (1999). It is a cognitive-behavioural programme that has three stages. *Stage one* works on developing compliance and motivation for behavioural change, by encouraging acceptance of responsibility for sexual crimes and reducing denial, minimization and cognitive distortion, and increasing awareness of victim harm and developing empathy. In *stage two* the main aim is to achieve behaviour change by exploring behavioural chains and developing awareness of antecedents and precursors to offences, developing a relapse-prevention plan, eliminating deviant sexual arousal, and finding community supports and resources. The implementation of the relapse-prevention plan forms the final stage of the programme. Stages one and two are completed in institutional settings, while *stage three* of the programme takes place in the community, with the assistance of a community clinician and parole officer. There are three versions of the programme for offenders with different sentence lengths and at different stages in their sentence. The full prerelease programme is completed in sessions lasting three hours a day, conducted five days a week for five months. The long-term programme takes place over a period of eight months with weekly sessions focusing on stage one of the programme, while the advance programme focuses on stage two and sessions are held four days a week over a four-month period.

The Bath Programme was developed and directed by Marshall and is described in more detail by Barbaree *et al.* (1998). This programme provided two levels of treatment: for those initially assessed as low or low to moderate risk; and those assessed as moderate risk or above. The low-risk programme is run using an open format, meaning that each offender proceeds at his own pace, with a new offender taking his place when the offender has finished treatment. This means that the offenders attending the programme are at different stages in the treatment process. Typically these groups have 10 to 12 participants who take part in two three-hour sessions per week for a minimum of three months. The treatment targets are reducing denial, minimization, cognitive distortions and pro-offending attitudes, increasing victim empathy and self-esteem, working on relationship issues and producing relapse-prevention plans. Although following essentially the same treatment programme with the same treatment targets, treatment for offenders with moderate risk levels or above is conducted at a more extensive and intensive level, with a closed group format (all participants start and finish at the same time), typically with eight to 10 offenders completing three three-hour sessions each week for four months.

The programmes described thus far are located in institutional settings, although the latter stages of some are completed in the community. Eccles and Walker (1998) described a community-based programme in the Ontario region of the CSC. Offenders begin the treatment process in the community with an assessment, which takes two to three half days to complete. High-risk offenders may be recommended for institutional treatment, and very low-risk offenders may be passed over in favour of allocating places to those who are a greater risk. Thus, moderate-risk offenders are the most suitable for this treatment provision. Most offenders begin treatment in a group setting: female and adolescent offenders and offenders with learning difficulties are not allocated to groups, as there are usually insufficient numbers and so treatment is conducted on an individual basis.

Treatment groups meet once per week for two hours per session. Two types of groups are provided: *closed groups* which take 15 to 20 weeks to

49

complete; and *open groups* which have indefinite periods of completion that are dependent of each offender's progress. The closed group is used for offenders who have not received treatment before, and occasionally for offenders who need the structure of this format. The open group contains offenders who have completed other sex offender treatment programmes, e.g. in federal or provincial prisons, and offenders who are felt not to need the full closed group programme. The programme utilizes cognitive-behavioural and relapse-prevention approaches to cover the following issues: acceptance of responsibility for all sexual offending; understanding of the impact of the offending on the victim and others; the offence chain; thinking errors associated with offending; warning signs leading to offending; consequences associated with decisions to offend or not to offend; building a support network; and developing a relapse-prevention plan. After the end of formal involvement with offenders, staff may continue to meet with offenders periodically for follow up sessions, for example contact with moderate to high-risk cases takes places every two to three months. Staff also make themselves available to provide support to offenders who request it post-treatment and follow up.

Canada has a large aboriginal population, who are particularly prevalent in some regions of the CSC. Programmes specifically designed for aboriginal sex offenders have been developed and are provided where this is appropriate. Such provision is described by Ellerby and Stonechild (1998) and Williams (1997). There is insufficient space here to explain this programme in more detail, except to say that it blends the more traditional goals and methods of cognitive-behavioural programmes with concepts and contexts that are more in keeping with traditional aboriginal cultures and values. Such an approach is important to ensure that the 'what works?' need and responsivity principles are adhered to; however, as yet there is no published evaluation of this provision.

As can be seen from this description, the CSC provides an excellent range of services that caters for a range of offender groups. However, provision for female and adolescent offenders is less well established than treatment for adult male offenders, although it is possible for these offenders to receive treatment, albeit on an individual rather than a group basis. Similarly, provision for offenders with learning difficulties is not well established in the full range of settings, although as with female offenders this is largely a result of the difficulty in providing provision for a small number of offenders who are geographically spread. These problems aside, the programmes described here provide treatment for offenders with varying risk levels in both custodial and community settings. Furthermore, these programmes have a similar set of core elements so treatment programmes 'map' onto one another, which allows offenders to progress from one programme to another with ease. Many of these programmes have published evaluations, which are summarized in Chapter 8.

USA

Like Canada, the development of sex offender treatment in the USA has been discussed in the previous chapter. However, the state structure of criminal justice and mental health provision the USA (as compared to the national structure of this provision in Canada) and the number of states in the USA, makes it impossible to provide a summary of the full range of treatment provided in this country. Each state has its own legislation and policy, as well as its own correctional model and facilities, and its own health care provision. Despite this, sex offender treatment using a broadly similar model of treatment is provided in many states, although it is not clear if it is delivered in every state and it is difficult to assess the proportion of offenders that receive treatment (Gallagher *et al.* 1999).

In 1994, there were 90 prison-based treatment programmes for sex offenders and 710 in total throughout the US (Freeman-Longo *et al.* 1995), which was a 139 per cent increase over the number of programmes in 1986. Although the majority of these programmes reported that they used a cognitive-behavioural approach, so few of these programmes have published treatment descriptions that it is difficult to assess just how similar these programmes are. And although many US programmes led the way with Canada in the development and improvement of treatment provision, it should not be assumed that all programmes in the US are this advanced, or that provision is equal in all states.

Unlike the other countries discussed in this chapter, where the majority of treatment programmes are delivered in criminal justice areas, the US has a greater number and greater variety of treatment providers, ranging from correctional services, to faith organizations, to local community groups, to mental health establishments. This issue has raised concern among some who have worried about the quality of treatment provided by such a range of organizations, and so many states have introduced, or are in the process of introducing, licensing arrangements, to ensure a minimum standard of quality of all sex offender treatment provision (for a brief discussion of such arrangements, see Jensen and Jewell-Jensen (1998)). In addition, minimum standards of care policies such as that produced by Coleman *et al.* (2000) have been adopted (guidelines for the development of new programmes were outlined by Schlank 1999).

A recent survey by the Colorado Department of Corrections (West *et al.* 2000) found that 39 of the 43 states that responded to the survey offered treatment programmes to incarcerated offenders, including a structure of programmes in West Virginia that were under review for standardization across all state institutions. In addition, Maine was considering the introduction of a programme and Idaho was in the early stages of developing such provision. Of the programmes in the 39 states, 20 (and two more states were developing such programmes) were provided in therapeutic communities and were highly structured residential programmes. The variety of provision and the difficulty in summarizing US treatment is revealed by the fact that sex offender populations ranged from 161 offenders in North Dakota to 25,398 in Texas. Programme capacity ranged from 70 sex offenders in Vermont, with a total sex offender population of 362, to 1,100 in Michigan, which had a total sex offender population of 9,756, and 1,200 in Pennsylvania, with a total sex offender population of 6,931. Of the 34 states that reported information about the duration of the programme, 28 states provided programmes that took a year or more to complete, 19 conducted up to three years of treatment, and the programmes of eight states took more than three years to complete. North Dakota provided treatment for up to five years, and recent changes in the Arizona programme also provided for treatment for up to five years. In Massachusetts, inmates were eligible to begin treatment when they were within six years of their earliest projected release date; once in the programme, inmates remained active until release. All reporting states used a cognitive-behavioural approach with relapse prevention as the focus of treatment; however, programme structures, materials, sequence, complexity and intensity varied a great deal (see the report for the programme details provided by each state). Despite this variety, there were a number of common elements: assessment, orientation to treatment, education or psychoeducation, cognitive-behavioural group therapy, intensive treatment (group or residential), transition into the community and aftercare. However, only 14 states reported having a system for monitoring programme effectiveness and seven provided evaluation data.

Given the number of sex offender treatment programmes in the USA, there are few detailed descriptions of these programmes (although the number of these has increased in recent years), and even fewer descriptions of statewide policies or provisions (for a description of provision in Vermont, see Lundström (2002)). A range of US programmes provided in both prison and community settings and for a range of offenders are described in Marshall et al.'s (1998) book; the Twin Rivers programme delivered in a medium-security prison in Washington State is described by Gordon and Hover; the Portland Sexual Abuse Clinic, a community-based programme in Oregon, is discussed by Maletzky and Steinhauser; the Joseph J. Peters Institute Intervention

Programmes, Philadelphia, Pennsylvania are described by Pessin *et al.*; and the Massachusetts Treatment Center for Sexually Dangerous Persons is described by Schartz and Canfield. In addition, the treatment of female offenders, in Minneapolis, Minnesota, is described by Matthews; learning disabled offenders, in Greenfield, Massachusettes, by Coleman and Haaven; deaf offenders, in Harrison, Virginia, by Dennis and Baker; clergy offenders, in New York, by Kelly; professional offenders, in Atlanta, by Abel *et al.*; and juvenile offenders, in South Pasadena, California, by Johnson. Finally, the treatment of American Indian sex offenders in South Dakota is described by Ertz; Hispanic offenders in Arlington, Virginia by Moro; and inner-city African-American and Latino youth in New York by Jones *et al.*. In addition, the Sexual Predator Treatment Programme of Kansas is described by DesLauriers and Gardner (1999) and the Minnesota Sex Offender Programme by Schlank *et al.* (1999).

These chapters clearly reveal the diversity of provision in the USA, the high standards of many programmes, and the innovative approaches with sub-groups of offenders, although few of these programmes have published robust evaluation data (see Chapter 8). Further descriptions of US programmes can be obtained from the evaluation literature, particularly for treatment programmes where evaluation has been a key feature of the treatment provision. For example, the programme in Atascadero State Hospital in California has been described by Marques and her collegues (Marques, Day *et al.* 1989; Marques *et al.* 1993; 1994; Marques *et al.* 2000), and Vermont's programmes have been described by a number of researchers (Pithers *et al.* 1989; Pithers 1994; Gordon and Nicholaichuk 1996; Nicholaichuk 1996; McGrath *et al.* 2003; Nicholaichuk *et al.* 2000).

This brief outline has shown that programmes in the USA are more diverse than programmes in other countries, although the majority have the same core elements as the Canadian programmes. Treatment providers in the USA have been keen to deliver programmes to a range of offenders and thus, programmes have been described for some groups of offenders that are not specifically catered for in other countries. However, the descriptions of such programmes emanate from a single treatment provider, and therefore it is not possible to ascertain the extent to which these programmes are unique, or whether a similar provision is proved throughout the state or in other states. Because of the nature of the programme descriptions (i.e. they focus on individual programmes rather than delivery in a region or state) it is not possible to see if, or how, regional or state provision caters for offenders with different levels of risk, or different types of sentence. However, the range of provision outlined in the programme descriptions suggests that offenders with different levels of treatment needs are catered for, at least in some areas. The greatest weakness in the US provision is the lack of evaluation research. Only a small number of US programmes have been evaluated (see Chapter 8), which is a tiny percentage of all programmes, given the number of programmes being delivered. The adoption of accreditation and licensing systems may improve this situation if evaluation and monitoring are key criteria.

UK and Ireland

Development of sex offender treatment in the UK

Compared to the USA and Canada, the UK and Ireland were slow to introduce and develop cognitive-behavioural treatment for sex offenders. In the mid 1980s, work developed in the UK on an *ad hoc*, piecemeal basis (Barker and Morgan 1991; HM Inspectorate of Probation 1991; Thornton 1991; Wyre and Tate 1995). A small number of practitioners became interested in the treatment of sex offenders and gained expertise as they introduced this approach to their work in prisons and the Probation Service (for an example of an early probation treatment programme, see Eldridge and Gibbs (1987)). Ray Wyre, who began his work in the Prison Service and developed his knowledge by working with practitioners in the USA, has been particularly influential in the development of these programmes. He co-founded the Gracewell Clinic, which was the first residential treatment centre to be located in the UK. As well as providing treatment to sex offenders, this establishment was also responsible for training the majority of the early practitioners in this field. As these workers became recognized experts, they in turn trained other colleagues in treatment techniques. This led to a situation in the UK where most treatment programmes adopted a remarkably similar ethos and employed comparable methods: broadly speaking using a cognitive-behavioural approach. Later, as programmes were introduced throughout a service because of policy change, the provision was developed using the research and evaluation literature, which further ensured the similarity of approach and the continuation of cognitive-behavioural programmes.

Residential treatment programmes

As discussed previously, the Gracewell Clinic was influential in the development of treatment programmes for sex offenders in the UK; however, it has had a troubled history. Founded in 1988 with private funding, it was the only residential treatment centre in the UK. Yet it often received criticism from the media and members of the local community, who were unhappy that the centre was situated in a residential area within close proximity to schools, particularly as offenders were not 'locked in' the facility. Following a public campaign, the centre was closed in 1994 (see Wyre and Tate 1995). Shortly after this, the STEP evaluation (Beckett *et al.* 1994) was published, which demonstrated that the clinic was successful in its treatment efforts with offenders. Furthermore, the clinic was effective with high-risk offenders, in contrast with most of the other community programmes that were evaluated by the STEP team. Sixty per cent of the sample from Gracewell who were categorized as high deviance offenders reached a normal profile at post-treatment testing and follow up data showed that none of these men had been reconvicted within two years.

The Lucy Faithful Foundation, supported with governmental funding, took over the work of the Gracewell Clinic and made plans to open another residential clinic; however, this proved to be extremely difficult. High-profile public campaigns in a number of places thwarted attempts to obtain planning permission (see Eldridge and Wyre 1998; Brown 1999). Eventually, 18 months after the closure of Gracewell, a new clinic was opened in a hospital setting in Epsom, Surrey in August 1995. The programme, described by Eldridge and Wyre (1998), was primarily a cognitive-behavioural programme; however, drama and art therapy were also used to access feelings in more interactive ways. The Lucy Faithful Foundation programme was improved and developed on the basis of the findings of the STEP evaluation. Offenders began with a four-week residential assessment. If assessed as suitable, offenders continued to the full-time programme which took between six and 12 months to complete. The programme followed a rolling format, so offenders could join at any stage. Sessions included structured module groupwork, individual therapy and a more informal evening and weekend residential programme. The programme was modified over time, but eventually included four core elements: victim awareness and empathy development; the role of fantasy in offending patterns; sexuality and relationships; and assertiveness and anger management.

In 2002, residential treatment in the UK suffered another set back when the Lucy Faithful clinic was closed and the country was again without residential provision for sex offenders. An attempt to move the clinic from Epsom to Silverlands in Surrey was met with such determined local opposition that it was eventually dropped and the clinic was closed as the land on which it had been based was sold by the Government (BBC News 2002).

Despite this setback, progress within the Criminal Justice System has been more positive. Barker and Morgan (1993: 2) noted that there was: 'an increasing demand, driven by the 1991 [Criminal Justice] Act, for programmes to address sexual offending, in both the custodial and the non-custodial context'. Thus, since the introduction of this Act, the use of sex offender treatment programmes has expanded within both the Prison and Probation Services, as is discussed below.

Development of programmes within the Prison Service

In June 1991, Kenneth Baker, the then Home Secretary, announced a coordinated approach to the assessment and treatment of sex offenders: the Sex Offender Treatment Programme (SOTP). This was targeted at those who were serving sentences of four or more years (and who were willing to cooperate), which in 1990 included 63 per cent of the incarcerated sex offender population (Crighton 1995). The aim of the SOTP is to address offending behaviour, help to stop offending and resolve psychological problems, leading to a more satisfying offence-free life. For more detailed information of this programme see Beech *et al.* (1998), Grubin and Thornton (1994), and Mann and Thornton (1998).

The SOTP was established nationally in 1992 in 17 establishments. It was centrally designed (and has since been centrally refined) and, as mentioned in the previous chapter, it adhered to the principles determined by the 'what works?' literature. Furthermore, monitoring for treatment integrity and ongoing evaluation was established as an integral part of the programme. Thus, in a departure from the previous *ad hoc* development of sex offender treatment programmes, the pattern for evidence-based, 'what works?', practice was established in this arena, which was later also incorporated in the community-based treatment provision (as will be discussed in more detail later).

Sex offenders are assessed, over a two-month period, in units in a number of high-security prisons that have been designated as assessment centres. A decision is then made as to whether treatment is needed, and the level of such treatment, if it is felt necessary (Grubin and Thornton 1994). Treatment is provided in a large number of prisons by a variety of staff, including prison officers, prison-based probation officers, prison education staff and psychologists (see Mann and Thornton (1998), for a more detailed description of the operation of such an approach) who attend a training programme to enable them to carry out this work (Sabor 1992). Initially, it was not possible to treat all convicted sex offenders, therefore offenders were categorized as low, medium, or high priority, based on a combination of offence severity and risk of reoffending (Grubin and Thornton 1994). By 2002, all sex offenders were assessed for suitability and willingness to attend, and all suitable candidates would be offered a place, where this was practical (Home Office Communication Directorate 2002). Offenders are still assessed for risk (among other things) in order to provide the most suitable treatment and to develop appropriate sentence plans.

This treatment provision has gradually been expanded throughout England and Wales, and by 1998, the SOTP was running in 25 establishments (including young offender institutions), ranging from highest to lowest security establishments, with 24 of these providing the core programme, and nine offering a booster programme to reinforce work undertaken earlier in the sentence (Beech *et al.* 1998; HM Inspectorate of Probation 1998; Mann and Thornton 1998). Furthermore, by 1998, the programme had become available for those serving sentences of less than four years, but not for those serving less than two years. This was due to the lengthy process of assessing offenders for treatment and then transferring them to prisons where the programme was provided (Beech *et al.* 1998; HM Inspectorate of Probation 1998). However, this policy was further revised to allow provision for all those who could complete a programme during their period of imprisonment (Home Office Communication Directorate 2002). Participation in the programme is voluntary but some categories of prisoner are not eligible: those who are mentally ill, of low intelligence, with extreme personality disorders (e.g. with PCL-R scores above 30) or who are serious suicide risks (Calder 1999). Currently the provision is only available to male sex offenders. This is largely a result of the small number of female offenders and the difficulty of providing group programmes (as the SOTP is delivered) for a very small number of geographically dispersed offenders.

In 1998–9, 605 eligible sex offenders completed programmes (Howarth 1999), compared to 284 in 1992–3, 554 in 1994–5 and 565 in 1995–6 (Mann and Thornton 1998). Furthermore, in 1995–6, 33 offenders completed the Booster Programme (see below), which rose to 108 in 1996–7. In 2002–3 the number of sex offender treatment programme completions was 1,046 (HM Prison Service 2004), although this information is not broken down into the type of programme completed. It has been estimated that a quarter of all incarcerated sex offenders attended the programme(s), which was half of those serving sentences long enough to allow them to complete the treatment (HM Inspectorate of Probation 1998). Mann and Thornton (1998) reported that about 1,400 male sex offenders are received into prison each year with sentences of two or more years, and with half of these agreeing to treatment, the demand for the Core Programme is between 700 and 1,400 places per annum.

Spencer (1998) described how sex offender treatment programmes were introduced to the Scottish Prison Service. A group programme for a few offenders began on an *ad hoc* basic in 1992. More significantly, however, following three days of training from Bill Marshall, the STOP programme was developed and introduced into a refurbished wing specifically for sex offenders, in January 1993. The aims of the STOP programme are to engender acceptance of personal responsibility, address the consequences of offending behaviour for both self and victims, and develop personal strategies that will assist the exercising of self-control and avoid situations that are likely to lead to reoffending. This provision is designed for offenders convicted of offences against either adults or children (or both), and priority is given to those determined to be of the highest risk of recidivism. Like the programmes in the English and Welsh Service, the STOP programme is delivered by a range of staff, such as prison officers and social workers who are provided with training (for more detail on this training, see Spencer (1998; 2002)).

The STOP programme has three components: Assessment, Groupwork Programme and Maintenance Programme (for more detailed information, see Spencer (1998)). As its name suggests the assessment component assesses the men using interviews and psychometric tests and begins the process of challenging denial. The groupwork programme is delivered in two, 40-session phases with a break in the middle. Groups of eight to 10 offenders meet twice a week for approximately two and a half hours. The first phase focuses on cognitive restructuring, consent, responsibility, cycles of offending and victim empathy; while the second phase continues the exploration of the offenders' cycles of offending and uses module work to examine other areas, all of which forms the basis of the development of relapse-prevention plans. The maintenance component incorporates a mix of two or three offender groups: higher risk offenders who are graduates of the previously described components, low-risk offenders who only complete the maintenance component; and more unusually high-risk offenders who have problems integrating into the groupwork programme, who begin with the maintenance programme as a bridge to enable future admission to the core programme.

This provision is unusual as it is delivered in a prison where at least 85 per cent of the prison population of about 200 inmates are sexual offenders (Spencer 1998), which allows for a culture that supports the work. It was intended that about one third of the sex offenders should be attending the programme, with one third being graduates of the programme and encouraging the remaining third to enter the programme. Thus, over a three- to four-year cycle all sex offender inmates would have the opportunity to complete the STOP programme. From the introduction of the programme to 2000, 185 prisoners started the programme and nine prisoners repeated the programme: 140 completed the programme (Spencer 2002). Sex offender provision was later introduced in other Scottish prisons and a national policy is under consideration (see the report of the review group on the future management of sex offenders: Spencer (2002)).

Development of programmes within the Probation Service

Although sex offenders formed only a small population, estimated to be between 3 and 10 per cent of the Probation Service of England and Wales's caseload, in 1993 it was estimated that only 13 probation services were not providing a formal treatment programme for sex offenders

(Barker and Morgan 1993). However, only three of the 63 programmes that were being provided by 43 probation services had been running for more than five years, and 29 were established between two and five years prior to Barker and Morgan's survey. Thus, Barker and Morgan concluded: 'it is clear that most probation services have recently begun to give sex offenders a higher priority than was previously the case' (p. iv). By the time of an Association of Chief Officers of Probation (ACOP) survey in 1995, the number of programmes had increased to 109, providing 1,907 places per year, with only seven probation areas having no such provision (HM Inspectorate of Probation 1998).

Barker and Morgan (1993) and HM Inspectorate of Probation (1998) found that the majority of programmes provided by the Probation Service utilized a cognitive-behavioural approach. However, most programmes examined by Fisher and her STEP (Sex Offender Treatment Evaluation Project) colleagues (1995) did not contain a behavioural element. In addition, little evidence was found that programme participants had acquired any formal relapse-prevention skills. However, by 1995, this situation was seen to have improved greatly by HM Inspectorate of Probation (1998).

The form and duration of treatment varied considerably (Barker and Morgan 1993; Beckett 1998; HM Inspectorate of Probation 1998) with three main approaches being adopted: (1) short-term, one- or two-week programmes (often used for assessment); (2) mid-length programmes, meeting for a couple of hours on a weekly or fortnightly basis for two to six months; (3) long-term programmes, meeting weekly or fortnightly for a year or more (Barker and Morgan 1993). There was consensus among workers that short-term courses were likely to achieve little beyond starting the treatment process, and consequently there was a trend for probation services to use a combination of approaches.

Approximately one third of the programmes surveyed by Barker and Morgan (1993) restricted intake to offenders who had victimized children. In some areas, this policy was implemented because the Probation Service provided treatment in conjunction with the NSPCC, which was only able to fund work with those who had abused children. Thus, provision was poor for rapists and also for female sexual offenders (Fisher and Beech 1999). In the past, training had often been provided in a piecemeal manner, although most areas had either written, or were in the process of writing, training strategies to deal with this problem (Barker and Morgan 1993). Much of the work relied on the enthusiasm and commitment of individual probation officers: only 15 of the 43 probation areas had given this work status as part of job descriptions (Barker and Morgan 1993). By 1995, however, 52 per cent of probation services had created specialist probation posts to manage and deliver treatment for sex offenders (Beckett 1998).

As can be seen, the provision of treatment for sex offenders in the UK changed enormously throughout the 1990s. Key developments have continued to take place since 2000, and these are discussed below with a description of the current provision in the UK and Ireland.

Current sex offender treatment in the UK

In 2002, a foreword by the Director-General of HM Prison Service of England and Wales and the National Director of the National Probation Service of England and Wales (Home Office 2002: 2) stated that:

> We are committed to ensuring that the assessment, treatment and management of sex offenders is co-ordinated seamlessly, from pre-sentence reports, through any period of custody to release and supervision in the community or a non-custodial sentence, where the court may direct programme attendance.

These two services are currently being combined into a single national service (the approach used in Canada and New Zealand): the National Offender Management Service (NOMS) should ensure that the commitment described above can be achieved more easily. In the past, treatment programmes were developed by the separate services, but in 2002, a commitment was made to jointly develop future programmes (Home Office 2002). Furthermore, as discussed in Chapter 2, in order to ensure the quality of the treatment provision a system of accreditation was developed by HM Prison Service, introduced in 1996 and applied to the National Probation Service of England and Wales in 1999. Audits review six key areas of the provision: institutional support, selection and training of staff, selections and initial assessment of participants, products, quality of delivery, and communication with aftercare agencies (Mann and Thornton 1998). In addition, the accreditation panel advises on development and ensures that the programmes are kept up to date with best practice developments. Since the introduction of this accreditation process, a number of programmes have been accredited, which are delivered in either custodial or community settings.

> The . . . treatment programmes are not mutually exclusive. Prisoners are not expected to choose between addressing their offending behaviour in custody or in the community. Ideally, a prisoner will attend a programme in prison and build on the treatment gains following release by attending a probation programme.
>
> (Home Office 2002: 4)

Sentence length and time on licence will determine the treatment plan. The range of treatment provision in England and Wales is outlined below and described in a little more detail in the following two publications: Home Office (2002) and Home Office Communication Directorate (2002).

The Scottish Prison Service has recently reviewed its provision for sex offenders and it has also introduced a system of accreditation. Links with community provision are not as well coordinated in Scotland as they are in England and Wales, but this issue has been identified as a weakness and there are plans for improvement. The provision for Scotland is also summarized later and is discussed in more detail by Spencer (1998; 2002).

Possibly because of the conflict in Northern Ireland and the small numbers of offenders due to the size of the area, there is currently limited provision for sex offenders in Northern Ireland, although the SOTP (from England and Wales) is available in two prisons. In the Republic of Ireland, sex offender treatment programmes are provided, albeit in a less centralized, monitored and evaluated form (Lundström 2002). Currently there is no system of accreditation, but the provision is under review. In 2000, a Steering Committee was established by the Irish Prison Service to develop a multi-disciplinary sex offender programme and a research consultant was appointed to introduce this initiative using best-practice evidence. There is very little sex offender treatment provision in the community in Ireland and there are poor links between custodial and community services (Lundström 2002). Although this situation may change in the future, it will take a while to develop the range of services to match the provision currently available elsewhere.

Treatment in custodial settings

A range of accredited sex offender treatment programmes is provided in 27 establishments in England and Wales, which are audited annually. Generally, treatment sessions run for two to two and a half hours, two to five times per week. Treatment is delivered in a groupwork context with, on average, eight inmates and three treatment staff. At the end of each course, each offender's progress is reviewed. Each establishment has a resettlement manager whose role it is to communicate offenders' progress to probation officers/case managers.

To ensure the maximum availability of treatment provision and the flexibility needed to account for the risk and need principles, HM Prison Service has developed a range of programmes that are designed to 'fit' together, so that the most suitable package of treatment is completed by each offender depending on his level of risk, sentence length and treatment need. These programmes are designed to address issues that are common to all offenders no matter what the age and gender of, and their relationship to, their victims, based on the 'what works?' literature. The provision is currently available for male offenders only, but work is in progress to develop programmes for female offenders (Home Office 2002). There are currently five programmes (described in the following publications: Home Office (2002); Home Office Communication Directorate (2002)), each of which will be described briefly. All the programmes use a range of methods, such as group discussion, role-play and skills practice.

The Core Programme (CP) is the basic and original programme, although in 2000, version three of this programme was introduced (and accredited in March 2000). The programme is revised periodically following the principles of evidence-based practice (see Mann and Thornton (1998) for a discussion of the keys changes made to each version of the core programme). This programme is designed for medium-risk offenders with IQs of 80 or above. The course has 90 sessions, taking six to eight months to complete, with three to four sessions a week. The CP addresses a range of offending behaviours: challenging thinking patterns; developing an understanding of the victim's point of view; understanding who is affected by sexual offending; developing an understanding of risk; and developing strategies to live without reoffending.

The Adapted Programme (AP) (accredited in March 1998) is based on the CP but it is adapted for offenders who have difficulty with the language and literacy skills required in the CP, for those with IQs below 80 and for those who cannot read or write (the assessing prison psychologist has some discretion in deciding who should complete the CP or AP). The AP has 85 sessions, delivered three to four times a week, for six to eight months. Although broadly similar, the AP has slightly different goals to the CP: increasing sexual knowledge; modifying thinking patterns; developing an ability to recognize risk factors; and generating strategies to avoid offending.

In the previous two courses, offenders all start and end at the same time; however, in the Rolling Programme (RP) (accredited October 2001) offenders (with IQs of 80 or above) join and leave the programme as appropriate. Sessions depend on the individual treatment needs of the offenders in the programme and the average length of treatment is three to four months, with three sessions per week. The RP addresses the same range of content as the CP and has two target groups: low risk and low deviancy offenders; and high risk offenders who have already completed the CP (and possibly the EP, see below).

Offenders (with IQs of 80 or above) who successfully complete the CP and/or RP who could still benefit from additional work can complete the Extended Programme (EP), which was accredited in February 2002. This programme takes six months to complete, with three sessions per week and 74 sessions in total. The goals of the programme are to work with thinking styles related to offending; manage offence-related emotional states; develop skills to successfully manage intimate relationships; understand the role of offence-related sexual fantasy; and develop skills to manage this.

Finally, the Booster Programme (BP), accredited in March 1996, is designed for those who have 'successfully' completed the CP, RP or EP who are within 18 months of release. This programme has 35 sessions, delivered over a two- to three-month period with three sessions per week. As its name suggests, this programme reviews the work from the CP or RP and further, it allows participants to plan and prepare for release in more detail. This provision is currently being revised with a view to providing more support in maintaining change for prisoners with long sentences.

This national approach and the 'pick and mix' nature of this provision is an innovative solution to the difficulty of providing group programmes to offenders with differing levels of risk and sentence lengths. Furthermore, according to Mann and Thornton (1998: 48), the SOTP has five aspects that make it unusual in comparison to other programmes:

(1) its multi-site implementation (operating in over 25 establishments; Mann and Thornton stated that they believed it to be the largest offender treatment programme in the world);

(2) its commitment to systematic evaluation guided by its own short-term evaluations and other research information;

(3) the use of lay therapists to deliver treatment;

(4) the emphasis on therapeutic style as well as programme content;

(5) the system of annual accreditation.

The recent development of many of these programmes means that robust evaluation data is scarce, although some evaluation data is available and is discussed in Chapter 8.

In the Scottish Prison Service all prisoners serving sentences of over four years are assessed as part of their sentence-management process and those identified as having committed a sexual offence, or an offence with a sexual element, are automatically referred for specialist assessment for suitability for sex offender intervention programmes. The STOP programme, described previously, was revised and developed by the English and Welsh Prison Service, and received accreditation in 2001. It is 160 hours in length and delivered over nine to 12 months in two Scottish prisons: Peterhead and Barlinie. This programme is designed for low-, medium- and high-risk offenders, with high-risk offenders being expected to complete follow-on work. From 2000 to 2002, 62 prisoners completed this programme at Peterhead and 11 at Barlinnie.

An adapted programme (ASTOP) is also available in the Scottish Prison Service for offenders with lower than average intelligence levels, low verbal ability or poor social skills. This was developed by HM Prison Service and introduced to the Scottish Prison Service in 2001. It is also available in two establishments: Peterhead and Polmont, and has the same number of sessions and time period as the STOP programme. The treatment goals are to increase sexual knowledge; modify offence justifying thinking; develop the ability to recognize feelings in themselves and others; gain an understanding of victim harm; and teach relapse-prevention skills. From 2001 to 2002, seven prisoners completed this programme in each of the two establishments providing the programme.

A 20-hour programme delivered once a week over a 14-week period is also available in the Scottish Prison Service. This is targeted at prisoners who have difficulties forming and maintaining relationships. It aims to develop self-awareness, improve understanding of intimate relationships and show how to develop and maintain these effectively and constructively. The Service also provides a Sex Offender Awareness Programme (SOAP) in Peterhead Prison. This provision is designed for offenders who have significant levels of denial that preclude them from participation in other programmes. The aim of SOAP is to raise awareness of the issues surrounding sexual offending; lower the risk of future offending; challenge attitudes towards men, women and children and also attitudes to society; challenge denial; increase the likelihood of engaging in future offence-specific work; and increase the likelihood of future self control.

The Service is also developing an extended STOP programme (ESTOP) directed at medium- and high-risk offenders who have completed the STOP programme. The treatment goals are to change dysfunctional schemas, improve emotional management, learn to control deviant sexual fantasy, improve attachment style and intimacy skills, and increase sophistication of relapse-prevention plans. A rolling programme (RSTOP) is also planned for low-risk and low-deviancy offenders, those who have attended the STOP programme and need further work, and those who have completed STOP but because of their long sentences could benefit from a booster programme later in their sentence. This programme is similar in nature to the STOP programme but is delivered in a rolling format like the RP described above. This programme will have eight modules delivered over a four-month period. A version of the STOP programme is also being developed for young offenders (YSTOP) and although there is currently no provision for female offenders, recommendations have been made to provide services for these offenders.

The Scottish Prison Service is gradually developing a provision on a par with the English and Welsh provision, and thus, shares the same strengths. Its SOAP programme is quite innovative and the provision in other areas of the UK and Ireland would benefit from the introduction of a similar programme, as currently offenders in those areas with high levels of denial are excluded from treatment provision, despite the fact that they probably form a high-risk group of offenders (see Chapter 6 for a discussion of this issue). Research and evaluation was neglected for many years by the Scottish Prison Service but with the introduction of accreditation and the development of a wider range of programmes, this issue has been addressed. To date, however, there is no robust evaluation data for the Scottish provision, although data is currently being collected.

In 1994, a programme was introduced in Arbour Hill Prison in Ireland using the manual designed for use in English and Welsh prisons (for the original SOTP described earlier). This programme is described in more detail by Murphy (1998) and as it is based on the SOTP will not be discussed further here. In 2000, the updated manual was utilized and the programme was introduced in Curragh Prison. As with the English and Welsh SOTP, the programme is delivered by psychologists, Probation and Welfare Service officers, who complete a training programme. In 1998, a research project evaluating the programme in Arbour Hill was started and is discussed in Chapter 8. The SOTP is also delivered in two prisons in Northern Ireland. Although there are no evaluations that are specific to Northern Ireland, evaluations of the SOTP have been published and are discussed in Chapter 8.

Treatment in community settings

With the introduction of programme accreditation in the Probation Service in 1999, the Probation Service (England and Wales) opted to rationalize its treatment provision into three groupwork programmes (GPs) (described by the Home Office (2002)). The three GPs were selected from the existing provision that had demonstrated some level of effectiveness, and gained accreditation in 2000 and 2001. As with the SOTP, the three GPs, which are described here, were developed according to the 'what works?', evidence-based literature. Each area of the Probation Service has been allocated one of the accredited programmes: London, Wales, West Midlands and East Midlands regions deliver the C-SOGP; East of England, South East and South West regions deliver the TV-SOGP; and North East, North West, Yorkshire and Humberside regions deliver the N-SOGP. This model allows the programmes to be compared and, thus, provides for a more robust evaluation. Evaluation of the GPs is an integral part of the provision and a comparison study is expected within five years of the start of delivery of the Northumbria programme, which began in early 2002. It is possible that following evaluation, the best programme will be adopted as the single community-based provision in England and Wales.

In each probation area, a treatment manager is responsible for assessing offenders and assigning them to treatment, which is currently available for adult males with IQs of 80 or above. As with the SOTP, the programmes are designed for all offence types (offences against children or adults, contact and non-contact offences). Thus, there remains poor provision for female sex offenders, who account for less than 1 per cent of the caseload, and for offenders with learning difficulties. The community programmes are designed to have sufficient flexibility to allow access at different points in the delivery of each programme, which enables the maximum of offenders to attend the programme whose sentences will begin and end at different times and last for different lengths of time. Community provision is also designed to cater for offenders with varying levels of previous treatment, including offenders who have had no previous treatment, e.g. offenders not sentenced to custody, or sentenced to short custodial periods that did not provide sufficient time for the completion of a custodial programme.

The first programme, C-SOGP, was originally developed in the West Midlands and was accredited in September 2000. It has three main components. The first is a 50-hour induction component that is the point of entry into the programme. It is a closed group (all members start and end at the same time) beginning with a full week of attendance, followed by a two and a half-hour session on a weekly basis for 10 weeks. In this component, offenders are encouraged to identify patterns in their offending, take greater personal responsibility for their offending and reduce minimization in the accounts of their offending. Following the completion of the induction component, offenders assessed as medium or high risk or high deviancy complete the long-term therapy component, which takes 190 hours to complete over 76 weekly sessions. The component has six modules and offenders can join at the start of any module (other than victim empathy). The six modules challenge distorted thinking; identify maladaptive relationships styles and core beliefs; teach new skills to improve self-management; improve understanding of the role of deviant fantasy; develop victim empathy; introduce relapse-prevention skills and new lifestyle goals.

Offenders who are assessed as low risk and/or low deviancy during the induction component go on to complete the relapse-prevention component, which takes 50 hours to complete over 20 weeks. This is a rolling programme component, so offenders can join at any session and continue for 20 weeks. Offenders who have made treatment gains during the successful completion of custodial programmes and who are assessed as low or medium risk and low deviancy may enter the C-SOGP in the relapse-prevention component. This component challenges cognitive distortions, develops victim empathy, enhances relapse-prevention skills and encourages lifestyle change.

Developed originally in the Thames Valley region (see Beckett 1998; Bates *et al.* 2004), the TV-SOGP was accredited in March 2001. This programme has five main components: low-deviancy offenders complete the foundation, victim-empathy and relapse-prevention blocks; high-deviance offenders complete the full 160-hour programme. Successful SOTP completers can enter the programme at the start of any block. The 60-hour foundation block is the main point of entry into the programme. This closed group block takes place over two full weeks and tackles offence details; attitudes towards the offence; identifying offence patterns; and the role of deviant sexual thoughts. The programme has a closed-group, 16-hour victim empathy block with eight twice-weekly two-hour sessions, taken after the foundation block. Offenders work on perspective taking and relate this to victim perspectives of sexual abuse. The 40-hour life skills block of 20 sessions, each lasting two hours, is delivered once or twice a week as a closed group. It addresses problem recognition and solving skills, coping skills, relationship skills and other non-offence-specific factors which may contribute to an individual's offending. The relapse-prevention block of 44 hours is delivered in weekly two-hour sessions. Ideally, offenders start at the beginning of this block, but it is possible to join in later sessions. This block focuses on learning and practising strategies for leading a more satisfying life without sex offending. Unusually, the TV-SOGP also has a 36-hour partners' programme, which is for female partners who intend to continue their relationships with their offender partners.

N-SOGP, which was accredited in October 2001, is the third programme and was originally designed in Northumbria. This programme has two components: core programme and relapse prevention. Offenders assessed as high risk and/or high deviancy will attend the core programme followed by the relapse-prevention programme; whereas low-risk and/or low-deviancy offenders will normally complete individual work followed by the relapse-prevention programme. The 144 hour, core programme is delivered in four blocks of eight weeks, with four and a half-hour weekly sessions. Offenders can join at the start of any block. The sessions combine 'personal' work, where individuals present their work to the group for challenge, and 'thematic' work, which involves the whole group in structured exercises. Personal work includes 'my offence', cycle of offending, what's changed and risk factors. Thematic exercises cover the links between sexual fantasy and deviance; cognitive distortions; victim empathy; risk awareness and management; problem solving and social skills. The relapse-prevention block is a closed-group block with 12 weekly three-hour sessions where offenders identify new prosocial ways of behaving and the positive feelings associated with an offence-free lifestyle are reinforced. Each member leaves this programme with an individual relapse-prevention plan.

This rationalization of programme delivery in the community is an innovative approach. Furthermore, the joining of the Prison and Probation Services into one national service (NOMS) should enable a more coordinated approach with greater links between prison and community treatment, and allow for a more harmonized release to community supervision following a period of incarceration. The recency of these developments means that it is not yet possible to gauge their impact. Similarly, as the community programmes are newly accredited, there is limited evaluation evidence to date; however, there is some evaluation data for the West Midlands programme (prior to accreditation) and some early findings from the TV-SOGP, which are discussed in Chapter 8.

In Scotland, sex offender treatment provision in the community is much more variable than it is in England and Wales. Currently there is no centrally organized provision as there is in England and Wales, nor is there a standardized approach adopted by each of the local authorities in Scotland. Not all areas in Scotland deliver personal change programmes and so depending on the area of release, offenders receive variable supervision, management and intervention. Although there has been an increase in the availability of sex offender programmes in the community, there are still significant gaps in the provision. This lack of consistency has been noted and a more centralized approach that integrates with the custodial provision is recommended (see Spencer 2002). As discussed previously, work is needed to establish more fully community provision in Ireland and Northern Ireland.

There remains no community residential provision in the UK. However, in September 2004, the Government announced plans to open an unspecified number of 25-bed residential centres throughout England and Wales (BBC News 2004). Given the persistent and determined opposition to previous residential projects, quite how the Government believes that these plans can be achieved is not understood, or explained in any detail. According to the BBC News report, Paul Goggins, the Home Office Minster, admitted that it was a 'tricky challenge', but stated: 'if we can get the balance right, if we explain, if we can reassure people, then we will overall make our society a safer place to live'. It remains to be seen whether this approach will be successful, but previous attempts and the fact that public and media opinion regarding sex offenders has changed little in recent years would suggest otherwise. No dates or locations have been published for these plans, and given the difficulties in obtaining planning permission, it is likely to take a while before any news residential centres open.

Treatment outwith the criminal justice services

Work with sex offenders is also undertaken within the National Health Service, Social Services and to a lesser extent by charitable organizations, such as the NSPCC and Barnados, who provide services mostly for juvenile offenders (Fisher and Beech 1999). The focus of work by Social Service departments is child protection, yet some social workers are involved in working with families and work on programmes that are provided by other agencies (Fisher and Beech 1999).

In the National Health Service, sex offenders receive treatment from psychiatrists, psychologists and other specialists, but the range of treatment approaches is eclectic, and there are few if any comprehensive treatment programmes (Grubin and Thornton 1994: 56). Sex offenders are only eligible for admission to Regional Secure Units (RSUs) and special hospitals if they are assessed as being mentally disordered, and the numbers tend to be relatively low (Fisher and Beech 1999). According to Fisher and Beech (1999), staff tend to view many of these offenders sympathetically, believing that the offence occurred as a result of the mental illness and that controlling the mental illness will also control the sexual offending; however, these authors argue that this is not always the case. Another group of offenders, those with psychopathic personality disorders, are regarded as difficult, if not impossible to treat, and there has been a great reluctance to admit them to RSUs (Fisher and Beech 1999). Fisher et al. (1998: 192) report that psychiatrists in Britain display a 'good deal of ambivalence' towards sex offenders, which has a negative impact on the quality of work with this group of patients.

Given that there are very few sex offenders detained in an RSU at any one time, many of whom are poorly motivated to engage with treatment processes, the type of work that can be undertaken is restricted, although it is not uncommon for staff to provide group therapy for in-patient sex offenders (Fisher, Grubin et al. 1998). However, sex offenders are more common in high-security hospitals, where it is estimated they are nearly half of all offender patients (Fisher, Grubin et al. 1998). Despite this, Fisher and colleagues describe how the focus of treatment in these special hospitals has been the mental illness, perhaps with the addition of some non-specific psychotherapy or sex education. This approach does not appear to be effective and there was some recognition in the late 1990s that cognitive-behavioural treatment programmes would be beneficial in these environments, although there are many complexities involved in providing such a provision there (see Fisher, Grubin et al. 1998). The majority of sex offenders seen by RSU staff are outpatients referred for assessment and treatment. Treatment is provided in short-term groups using the cognitive-behavioural approach (Fisher and Beech 1999). The outpatient provision of one RSU is briefly described by Fisher,

Grubin et al. (1998). Recently the increase in cognitive-behavioural work with sex offenders outside the mental health provision has led to an increase in the development of programmes in mental health settings, yet to date there is no published evaluation data.

As can be seen from the above outline, the provision for sex offenders in the UK is strongest in the criminal justice arena, and particularly in England and Wales, where treatment provision now models criminal justice provision in Canada. Prison Service programmes in Scotland are close to mirroring provision in England and Wales and some Scottish programmes (SOAP and YSTOP) could be adopted elsewhere. However, community treatment and links between custodial and community settings could be enhanced. Treatment in Northern Ireland and Ireland needs further development. Treatment for sex offenders outwith the criminal justice arena could be improved: residential centres are needed and treatment in mental health settings could be developed further. Furthermore, practices for ongoing evaluation and monitoring in these settings are needed. Finally, the main area of focus to date has been adult male offenders, and consequently, there is very little provision for female and juvenile offenders.

Australia

Like the UK, Australia was slow to develop sex offender treatment programmes, but unlike the UK, progress in this area still appears to be slow, perhaps because of a lack of political commitment in Australia that has been present in the UK since 1991. Cook et al. (2001) discuss a number of reasons why prison has been the preferred sentencing response for sex offenders and treatment approached reluctantly in Australia, such that 'treatment for sex offenders remains a somewhat unaccepted course of action in the criminal justice response to such offending behaviour' (Department of Human Services, cited in Cook et al. 2001: 71). These reasons are based around societal and community objections (as many do not accept that treatment is appropriate or effective) and criminal justice system problems. Obstacles in the criminal justice system centre on resource issues: namely a lack of resources and overcrowding in an environment where scarce resources are being demanded for 'get tough' policies, such that few, if any, resources are left for treatment provision which is seen as unwarranted and a 'soft option'.

Despite these obstacles, treatment programmes have been implemented in Australia and, furthermore, developments have mostly (particularly in more recent years) been based on the 'what works?' literature. However, unlike in Canada and the UK, a system of accreditation has not been introduced. In May 2004, Lievore's (2004) Report incorporating a review of current provision was published, and this has been used to produce the summary of Australia's treatment provision discussed here.

Currently, all but three Australian Correction Service departments – Northern Territory, Southern Australia and Tasmania – have sex offender treatment programmes in custodial and community settings, although there is a programme in Southern Australia for paedophiles, which is provided by a non-correction service agency. Lievore (2004) reported that the Correctional Services in the Northern Territory and Tasmania were lobbying for funding to develop programmes and that the implementation of two new programmes was planned by the Southern Australian Department for Correctional Services. Although the Australian Capital Territory Correctional Services provide treatment for adults and juveniles, they have yet to finalize their rehabilitation programme, and so details of treatment provision were not available. In most of the jurisdictions that provide treatment, convicted sex offenders are offered the opportunity to complete treatment provided that they are eligible: offenders are usually excluded if they deny the offence, have a psychiatric diagnosis, or learning/intellectual difficulties (although programmes are provided for offenders with intellectual difficulties in some jurisdictions). Most commonly, treatment is provided by Correction Service facilities, but it may also be provided by health care agencies and community-based organizations. As is the model in other countries, treatment in Australia is usually provided in groups, although it may be provided on an individual basis to deal with issues that are not suitable for discussion in group contexts, such as deviant fantasy and arousal.

Programme staff assess each offender's risk of sexual recidivism, treatment needs and cognitive capacity to participate in the programme. Most jurisdictions have a range of programmes, so that high-risk offenders are most likely to be placed first in prison-based programmes, and then in community-based programmes; while lower-risk offenders may be placed only in programmes provided in community settings.

New South Wales

The New South Wales Department of Corrective Services provides treatment on a voluntary basis to male rapists, child molesters and offenders whose crimes are sexually motivated. The Custody-Based Intensive Treatment programme (CUBIT) is delivered by a multi-disciplinary staff team (i.e. psychologists and custodial, welfare and education staff), in a self-contained unit in Long Bay Correctional Centre. The high-intensity programme takes approximately 10 months to complete and the moderate intensity programme, eight months. The programme is delivered in process groups, which address topics such as denial, cognitive distortions and victimization; and issues groups, which focus on knowledge and skills that are required to complete treatment goals, for example arousal and anger management, relationships and communication. There is also an adapted version of CUBIT for special needs offenders with literacy and borderline intellectual problems that takes approximately 12 months to complete.

A CUBIT Out Reach programme (CORE), delivered by psychologists, is provided for low-risk, low-treatment needs offenders. This non-residential programme targets the same treatment goals as CUBIT, although the process and issues groups are combined. It is delivered via two half-day sessions per week over a five-month period. The Custodial Maintenance Programme, attended by offenders who have completed CUBIT or CORE, maintains and reinforces treatment goals and focuses on relapse-prevention issues that are specific to each individual. In addition, Forensic Psychological Services provide post-release follow-up services.

The City Branch of the Forensic Psychological Services provides two community-based programmes: maintenance and treatment. The *maintenance programme* is designed for offenders who have completed treatment programmes elsewhere, to reinforce and maintain treatment goals and to further develop and adapt relapse-prevention plans. Depending on the level of intensity of treatment needed, offenders meet for a weekly or fortnightly/monthly two-hour session, for at least six months. Designed for low-risk, low- to moderate-needs offenders who do not receive custodial sentences, or who were unable to attend treatment in prison, the *treatment programme* is delivered in two weekly half-day sessions for a period of six months, or one weekly half-day session for a year.

Victoria

In Victoria the sex offender strategy was designed by the Public Correctional Enterprise (CORE) and is delivered in publicly managed prisons (Ararat Prison) and community-based Correctional Services (Carlton Community Correctional Services, Melbourne). The programme, which is aimed at rapists and child molesters, or offenders whose crimes contain a sexual element, is delivered by a multi-disciplinary staff team. Offenders' participation is voluntary, but in some instances, the parole board may mandate treatment. Programmes are available at four levels and are also provided for special needs offenders.

The *level one* Skills Programme, which addresses general offence issues such as aggressive behaviour, gender attitudes, social skills, adult relationships, practical living skills, drug and alcohol awareness, assertiveness and stress management, can be completed by all offenders. Sex offenders must complete the first four modules before they can progress to other programmes, although completion of all other components is desirable. At *level two*, the Management and Intervention Programme is designed for offenders serving short sentences, or sentences in the community, or who are repeating treatment. The target of this programme is to develop a relapse-prevention plan. Offenders who complete the programme in prison attend four sessions a week for four months, while offenders completing the programme in the community attend one session a week for six months.

The Wimmera Treatment Unit at Ararat Prison houses a residential unit providing the *level three* Intensive Sex Offender Programme. After a one-month assessment period, offenders complete an eight-month programme. Only two groups of 12 offenders complete the programme concurrently. The programme goals are to build on skills developed in the previous levels of treatment, develop insight into offending behaviours, develop victim empathy, teach sexual fantasy management and produce relapse-prevention plans. At *level four*, offenders who have completed programmes at levels two and three complete their treatment with a Maintenance Group. With the aim of implementing offenders' relapse-prevention plans, the groups, which can be prison or community based, are delivered in fortnightly meetings.

Queensland

Four types of programme are delivered to offenders with functional levels of literacy and intellectual ability by the Queensland Department of Correctional Services. The Preparation for Intervention Programme (PIP) is designed for offenders who have long sentences that preclude them from taking part in other programmes and prepares them for the Sexual Offender Treatment Programme (SOTP). It is completed early in the sentence by offenders who have considerable levels of cognitive distortions, but who are willing to attend treatment. In addition to regular individual sessions, the programme comprises 30 group sessions that are delivered over a 15-week period. Sex offenders who commit offences against adults and children, and who are eligible for parole within six to 18 months, are entitled to complete the SOTP. To provide maximum flexibility and individualized treatment, this is a semi-structured, group-based programme that is self-paced and, therefore, open-ended in terms of duration. It usually takes between eight to 18 months to complete, depending on the seriousness of the offence and the offender's level of commitment and honesty. The SOTP is based on the relapse-prevention model and requires seven hours of weekly group contact.

The Indigenous Sex Offender Treatment Programme (ISOTP) is delivered in a dedicated unit at the Townsville Correctional Centre (for more detailed information on this programme, see Lees (2001)), and a

73

second programme was due to start in Capricornia Correctional Centre in Rockhampton. This programme is adapted to take account of the different cultural experiences and needs of aboriginal and Torres Strait Island offenders. It is aimed at serious offenders and is delivered in three weekly group sessions over a period of 12 months. The programme has one cultural module and three intervention modules. The former module identifies indigenous history and the impact of colonization and offenders complete a life review of their family and community. In the latter modules participants are encouraged to: disclose their offending and take responsibility for it; identify the antecedents and consequences of offending; challenge their thinking patterns that develop and maintain offending behaviour; recognize the situations that increase risk of future offending; and develop relapse-prevention plans. The Sex Offender Intervention Programme (SOIP) aims to establish community support for offenders, increase behavioural management skills, and apply relapse-prevention techniques, over 30 two-hour sessions.

Treatment in community settings is also provided in Queensland, although not in the form of a comprehensive programme and thus, is aimed at low-risk/low-needs offenders. Like PIP, one of the objectives of this programme is to establish community support. Comprising two components, Intervention Programme and Maintenance Programme, the treatment takes 58 hours to complete. The former programme addresses a range of issues, such as denial, victim empathy, risk factors and recognizing risk in 14 three- to five-hour weekly sessions. The Maintenance Programme provides feedback on relapse-prevention plans in six fortnightly two-hour sessions.

Western Australia

In Western Australia, high-risk offenders complete the Intensive Programme, which is delivered in therapeutic communities in Casuarina Prison and Bunbury Regional Prison, which are maximum-security establishments. The programme is delivered in groups for six hours a day, three days a week, for a six-month period. In addition, individual counselling is provided. As its name suggests the Medium Programme targets medium-risk offenders over a 16-week period. It is available in regional prisons and is delivered in twice weekly, six-hour group sessions. Based in Greenough Regional Prison, the Indigenous Medium Programme is an adaptation of the Medium Programme for indigenous offenders. For more detailed information about this programme see Davies (1999) and for a discussion of issues surrounding the treatment of Australian Aborigines in Western Australia, see Cull (1998). When there are sufficient numbers in metropolitan prisons to warrant a group, the Intellectually Disabled Programme is delivered for medium-risk offenders with learning and literacy difficulties. This is another adaptation of the Medium Programme and hence, has the same treatment goals; however, work addressing social skills, relationships and sexuality is also included.

Community programmes are also available in Western Australia. A Maintenance Programme, involving fortnightly, open-ended meetings, is designed for offenders who have completed prison-based programmes, but who need additional work. It focuses on the daily management of behaviour. The Community-Based Programme (available in Perth and Bunbury) and the Community-Based Intellectually Disabled Programme (available in Perth) are both intended for low- to medium-risk offenders who have a community-based order. Sessions are three hours in length and the programmes take six months to complete, covering four core modules: relapse prevention, victim empathy, sexuality, relationships and anger management.

As can be seen from the above discussion, Australia has a range of cognitive-behavioural sex offender treatment programmes, provided in both custodial and community settings. However, although evidence-based and similar to programmes delivered in other countries, many of these programmes are less intensive than those of other jurisdictions. There is also variation in the provision offered across different states and territories. Nevertheless, provision exists in some states and territories for sex offenders with learning difficulties and for indigenous offenders; however, there is a lack of provision for female sex offenders, and scarce provision for juvenile offenders. Published evaluations of the programmes outlined above are particularly scare in Australia (see Chapter 8).

New Zealand

In 1989, the New Zealand Department of Justice decided to set up a unit to house and treat convicted child molesters (Hudson et al. 1995). Hudson and colleagues argued that this decision was made for practical reasons: there was concern that incarcerated offenders were not being treated, which required a specialized unit, and for safety reasons other treatment options should not be considered until the efficacy of treatment had been established. Three other factors also played a part in this decision (Bakker et al. 1998; Hudson et al. 1998). These were concerns regarding the recidivism rates of child molesters, the Psychological Service of the Department of Justice's commitment to reduce reoffending, and a growing optimism about the value of cognitive-behavioural sex offender treatment programmes. Thus, the new unit, Kia Marama (a Māori name meaning 'let there be light and insight') was established in Rolleston Prison in Christchurch with a strong commitment to evaluation (see Chapter 8) and dissemination of knowledge (see Hudson *et al.* 1995; Bakker *et al.* 1998; Hudson *et al.* 1998). When it was established, it was the first facility of its type in the world (New Zealand Department of Corrections 2004a).

The Kia Marama unit contains 60 self-contained rooms in a grass compound that is surrounded by a five-meter perimeter fence, with a staff ratio of 1:10. Prison officers try to maintain an environment that is conducive to therapeutic gains while conducting their custodial duties. Officers are assigned to therapy groups and are encouraged to provide support to offenders, as well as monitoring the therapeutic progress of the therapy group members. Only men convicted of child sexual offences are housed in the unit. In the first three years of operation, 238 offenders were released as graduates of the programme (Bakker *et al.* 1998) and by July 2004, over 700 men had completed the programme (New Zealand Department of Corrections 2004a).

While in the unit, men complete a treatment programme that was devised by Marshall, who trained the first group of staff. The programme begins with a two-week assessment period and ends with a two-week reassessment period. The main treatment programme, delivered over 29 weeks (33 with assessment periods included), is delivered primarily in group sessions: individual sessions are provided, but only to enable a resident to participate in the main group sessions. Groups usually have eight to 10 offenders and one therapist, and meet for three two and a half-hour sessions per week. The unit has a full-time member of staff, the reintegration coordinator, who is responsible for liaison between the residents, community agencies and significant others, in the release of offenders back to their local communities. In addition, a Kia Marama follow-up support group meets released offenders on a monthly basis, usually for a period of nine to 12 months. Furthermore, within the first month of release, offenders are encouraged to meet with those they have nominated to support them in their reintegration into the community, and their probation officers who are responsible for their supervision.

The programme is split into a number of modules (this programme is described by Hudson and his colleagues in 1992 and 1995, and descriptions differ slightly, presumably as a result of programme development: the later description is summarized here): *Norm Building* (six sessions), where group rules are established and personal details are disclosed; *Understanding your Offending* (17 sessions), where offence preconditions are disclosed, factors contributing to offending are identified, own experiences of abuse are disclosed, and dysfunctional cognitions challenged; *Arousal Reconditioning* (six sessions), where covert sensitization and masturbatory reconditioning techniques are employed; *Victim Impact and Empathy* (12 sessions), where the impact of offending on the victim is identified, victim accounts are read, videos portraying victim experiences played, a discussion with an abuse survivor is held, an 'autobiography' from the offender's own victim written, and role-plays between self and victim conducted; *Mood Management* (12 sessions), where the cognitive model of mood is explained, mood emotions associated with offending are identified, and physiological, cognitive and behavioural skills to manage these moods are developed; *Relationship Skills* (12 sessions), where intimacy and sexuality are discussed, and skills for establishing and maintaining intimate relationships are identified; *Relapse Prevention* (12 sessions), where the relapse chain is described, skills to manage relapse prevention are identified, support people are identified, and a personal statement presented (for more detail on these modules, see Bakker *et al*. 1998; Hudson *et al*. 1998).

Te Piriti, meaning 'the bridge', was established in May 1994 (for more detailed information about this programme, see Larsen *et al*. 1998; Nathan *et al*. 2003). It was developed using Kia Marama as a model, but with the treatment programme adapted to place treatment in a Māori cultural context to improve provision for Māori sex offenders (although non-Māori sex offenders are not excluded from Te Piriti). Like Kia Marama, but based in Aukland Prison (Paremoremo), the unit is a 60-bed stand-alone unit for men who have committed offences against children. The Te Piriti treatment programme takes approximately 40 weeks to complete, with groups meeting for three two and half-hour sessions per week. Like its forerunner, the programme begins and ends with assessment sessions. Although the core treatment is founded on the Kia Marama model, and so will not be described again here, this programme was innovative in its blending of Māori cultural values and beliefs within this framework (see Larsen *et al*. 1998; Nathan *et al*. 2003). So, although they are similar, the two programmes have key differences, one of which is clearly highlighted in the management of release to the community (described previously for Kia Marama). Part of the release plans in Te Piriti is the holding of a *whanau hui* (family meeting) to provide information to the family about the offender's pattern of offending, which empowers the *whanau* to support the offender following release (New Zealand Department of Corrections 2004b).

Although these two programmes are excellent examples of treatment provision, with evidence-based treatment programmes, thorough assessment procedures, good evaluation and dissemination practice, and well thought out release to community strategies, the provision is only available to male sex offenders who offend against children. The provision of treatment for Māori offenders is clearly a positive intervention; however, there is currently no specific provision for sex offenders with learning difficulties, or for female or juvenile sex offenders.

Europe and the rest of the world

Published accounts of cognitive-behavioural sex offender treatment programmes written in English tend to be focused in the countries discussed earlier; however, this does not mean that they are the only countries to provide treatment for sex offenders. In Europe, provision ranges from countries like the UK with a range of programmes and legislation for sex offenders, to countries that claim not to have a sex offender problem or extensive sex offender population (for a discussion of sex offender treatment in Europe, see Frenken (1999)). The European Union (EU) is currently attempting to draft an EU policy on sex offenders and sexual offences, but the diversity of responses to this issue across EU member countries will make this a difficult policy to draft, and furthermore, to negotiate agreement upon. Many European countries provide treatment that has psychoanalysis as its main treatment approach. As these programme are not, strictly speaking, cognitive-behavioural programmes, they have not been discussed here; however, there are many similarities in the treatment provided within these two approaches. Similar diversity in responses to sex offenders can be seen throughout the rest of the world, but the use of sex offender treatment, and in particular, cognitive-behavioural treatment, is being introduced in more and more jurisdictions.

This discussion has argued that sex offender treatment should be provided in both custodial, residential and community settings, and it can be seen that such intervention is indeed provided by the majority of the countries included in this review. It is encouraging to note that ongoing monitoring (in the form of accreditation or licensing) and evaluation is becoming a key aspect of the treatment provision in an increasing number of countries; as is the dissemination of evidence-based practice, which can easily be seen in the increasing range and quality of materials provided in criminal justice/corrections websites, and the incorporation of this literature in programme design and development.

There are a number of similarities across the range of provision that has been described, which is to be expected with the widespread adoption of evidence-based practice. Most programmes provide treatment in groups, and many jurisdictions provide a range of treatment programmes for offenders with differing levels of risk and treatment need. There are also similarities in the gaps in provision. Some jurisdictions provide programmes for offenders with learning difficulties, but provision for this group is generally poorer than provision for offenders with no such difficulties. In addition, cognitive-behavioural programmes for female and juvenile offenders are scarce. It is also the case that the bulk of treatment is provided for convicted sex offenders within criminal justice/corrections settings, which means offenders outwith this arena are neglected.

The majority of programmes target very similar treatment goals, with most addressing the key issues of responsibility and denial, cognitions, victim empathy, relapse prevention, and social and relationship skills, which will be described in more detail in Chapter 6. Key differences lie in the extent to which programmes provide individual work/therapy, and discuss and attempt to modify sexual arousal and fantasy. There seems to be no clear model for programme duration and intensity, even when programmes designed for offenders with similar risks and treatment needs are compared; however, there are very few 'short' programmes, lasting no longer than a few weeks or months, yet there are also few 'long-term' programmes, which last longer than a year. In some countries, however, offenders who are required to complete the full range of programmes will be involved in treatment for a considerable period. What is most striking from the treatment descriptions is the similarity of the treatment approach, which will be discussed in more detail in the next two chapters.

Chapter 4

Theoretical underpinnings of programmes

There are many mono-causal theories of sexual offending: biological theories suggest biological factors such as brain abnormalities or hormonal imbalances; developmental (or psychological) explanations range from those of a psychoanalytic nature to conditioning or learning theories; structural theories take account of the social context of sexual offending; and family explanations emphasize dysfunctional roles, relationships and behaviours within families that cause or maintain abuse (for reviews of these theories see Lanyon 1986; Marshall and Barbaree 1989; Barker and Morgan 1991; Sampson 1994; Epps 1996; Hall 1996; Lewis and Perkins 1996; Calder 1999). However, mono-causal explanations of sexual offending have generally been replaced by integrated theories (otherwise referred to as multi-causal, multi-modal or eclectic approaches) because the mono-causal theories tended to be mutually exclusive (Marshall and Barbaree 1990a), were often population specific, based on data difficult to replicate in other settings, or proposed causal sequences of behaviours that did not allow for alternatives (Hall 1996). Despite this, mono-causal explanations are by no means redundant, as integrated theories tend to combine many mono-causal explanations. Such integrated explanations have tended to adopt one of two approaches in explaining the aetiology of sexual offending: developmental and situational.

Developmental theories

The first approach integrates mono-causal theories and tends to be developmental in nature, arguing that there are many factors, often acting in combination, that lead to the commission of the first offence. Two such theories, which are the most influential and will be described briefly below, were developed in the early 1990s by Hall and Hirschman (1991; 1992) and Marshall and Barbaree (1990a).

Hall and Hirschman's quadripartite model

The quadripartite model was first developed to explain rape (Hall and Hirschman 1991), but was later extended to explain child sexual abuse (Hall and Hirschman 1992). Ward (2001) points out that the model has not been empirically tested, although Hall (1996) discusses the clinical use of the model. This model suggests that someone commits an act of rape or child sexual abuse because of four vulnerability factors and the presence of opportunity or other situational factors. The vulnerability factors are: physiological sexual arousal, distorted cognitions that act to justify sexual aggression, affective dyscontrol (or lack of emotional regulation), and personality problems. It is suggested that offending will occur when the presence of these vulnerability factors exceeds a threshold and the opportunity for the offence (e.g. the presence of a victim) exists. According to Ward (2001), a key aspect of this model is that while each of these factors will contribute to sexual aggression, one factor is prominent and constitutes the primary motive that 'pushes' an individual over the offence threshold. Hall and Hirshman (1991) argued that synergistic interactions between the vulnerability factors may occur, such that the intensity of one affects the intensity of one or all the other factors. Ward (2001) argues that the 'critical threshold' element of this theory is unique and explains how long-term vulnerability factors interact with situational variables to produce sexual offending.

Another strength of this model, which, in Ward's opinion makes it superior to Marshall and Barbaree's model (see below), is its ability to construct an offender typology. From this typology different treatment plans can be devised. With each of the four vulnerability factors taking priority, four subtypes of offenders are described. The first is characterized by deviant sexual arousal and represents the classic preferential offender who commits a large number of offences. Treatment for this subtype of offender should focus on reducing deviant arousal. The second subtype (distorted cognitions) may misinterpret women and children's behaviour as revealing sexual intent. These offenders may have good planning and self-regulatory skills, e.g. incest offenders. Thus, therapy must challenge cognitive distortions and offenders' beliefs of sexual entitlement. Situational offenders, who are characterized by impulsive and unplanned behaviours as well as susceptibility to respond to negative affective states, form the third subtype. Treatment for these offenders would revolve around learning to control affective states. The final subtype is defined by developmentally related personality problems, which affect individuals' ability to function effectively in the world and establish intimate relationships.

Although Ward (2001) praises many elements of the model, he also argues that it has a number of significant weaknesses. According to Ward, it fails to specify the mechanisms that generate the vulnerability factors or discuss how these are interrelated. Ward states that the four vulnerability factors overlap to some degree (e.g. cognitive elements are involved in sexual preferences and fantasy) and the synergistic relationships between these factors is vague, needing more detail to clarify how one factor intensifies other factors. In addition, the 'personality problems' vulnerability factor is not clearly described. Ward argues further that the model is not unified in that it actually consists of a number of submodels that each explains sexual offending. In addition, the model does not explain why an individual chooses to offend against a child or an adult. Although Ward praises the notion of the critical threshold the concept has problems, in that it is not possible to identify where the critical threshold is, whether this level is consistent across offenders, or how this idea may be used to prevent sexual offending.

Marshall and Barbaree's integrated theory

The integrated theory was developed as a general theory of sexual deviance (Marshall and Barbaree 1990a). Ward (2002b) points out that, like the quadripartite model, this theory has not been systematically evaluated, but its clinical utility has been reviewed by Marshall *et al.* (1999). In this publication, Marshall and colleagues update the theory, although its basic form is unchanged (Ward and Siegert 2002). The integrated theory proposes that the presence of vulnerabilities, which develop as a result of adverse early developmental experiences, leave offenders unprepared to deal with the surge of hormones at puberty, and unable to understand the emotional world. As a result, the offender inappropriately satisfies their emotional and sexual needs in deviant ways. This theory suggests that sexual offending occurs because of an individual's sex and aggression drives becoming fused as these functions share the same structure in the brain.

> Biological inheritance confers upon males a ready capacity to sexually aggress which must be overcome by appropriate training to instil social inhibitions toward such behaviour. Variations in hormonal functions may make this task more or less difficult. Poor parenting, particularly the use of inconsistent and harsh discipline in the absence of love, typically fails to instil these constraints and

may even serve to facilitate the fusion of sex and aggression rather than separate these two tendencies. Socio-cultural attitudes may negatively interact with poor parenting to enhance the likelihood of sexual offending, if these cultural beliefs express traditional patriarchal views. The young male whose childhood experiences have ill-prepared him for a pro-social life may readily accept these views to bolster his sense of masculinity. If such a male gets intoxicated or angry or feels stressed, and he finds himself in circumstances where he is not known or thinks that he can get away with his offending, then such a male is likely to sexually offend depending on whether he is aroused at the time or not.

(Marshall and Barbaree 1990a: 270–1)

This theory does a good job in combining the range of factors, psychological, biological, social, cultural and situational, that have been linked to sexual offending and Ward (2002b) praises the model on a number of grounds. He argues that the focus on resilience and psychological vulnerability gives the theory an advantage over other theories and clarifies how developmental adversity contributes to sexual offending. The theory, Ward states, has resulted in developments and research in previously neglected areas such as intimacy deficits and furthermore, it explains causal mechanisms, such as attachment style, maladaptive beliefs and self-regulatory style. Ward also notes a degree of specificity in this theory that is absent in many other theories.

As well as these strengths, Ward also highlights a number of conceptual weaknesses. The theory's focus on disinhibition, in Ward's opinion, seriously limits the scope of the theory as other possible offence pathways are ignored, and empirical evidence (Hudson *et al.* 1999) suggests that only a small number of sex offenders have significant problems with self-regulation. Furthermore, the general nature of the theory means that it cannot account for issues related to the different types of sexual offences. While the theory is able to explain offenders who develop their sexual offending behaviour early (i.e. adolescence), it does not account for offenders who begin offending as adults. Ward also argues that the focus on aggression is a mistake, as it is not a central characteristic of all offences (e.g. child abuse, although it may be more central to rape) and the notion that sex and aggression become 'fused' is ambiguous and has several distinct meanings that lead to separate offence pathways. Finally, Ward suggests that although the theory has low self-esteem as a central component, there are theoretical and empirical reasons to believe that sex offenders have a range of self-esteem disturbances. In addition, the theory suggests that offenders become disinhibited, for example through the consumption of alcohol or

83

as a result of stress, before they offend; however, this does not account for the ongoing nature of sexual grooming and offence planning, that has been shown to be a critical part of many offenders' behaviour (Craven *et al.*, under review). Furthermore, this may encourage offenders to provide excuses for their behaviour, which is discouraged in cognitive-behavioural programmes (see Chapter 5). It is also not clear from this theory why offenders engage in one type of sexual aggression (e.g. child abuse) over another (e.g. rape).

To some extent Hall and Hirshman's model and Marshall and Barbaree's theory have been influential in the development of cognitive-behavioural sex offender treatment programmes, although it should be noted that both were developed after the basic components of cognitive-behavioural treatment had been established (see Chapter 2). Moreover, developmental explanations have had a limited impact, as these factors are not the main source of concern in cognitive-behavioural treatment programmes (see Chapter 5). Although Hall and Hirschman's model suggests different treatment strategies for offenders with different offending pathways, this issue has tended to be overlooked in current treatment provision, as the structure of treatment has moved towards accredited programmes that are delivered to all offenders (with the exception of adjustment for offenders with learning difficulties, or cultural differences). Given the principle of treatment need and its link to programme effectiveness, as discussed in Chapter 2, this is surprising. As Ward points out, the greatest impact of Marhsall and Barbaree's theory in the delivery of treatment has been the development of work on previously neglected areas such as intimacy deficits and on other causal mechanisms such as attachment style, maladaptive beliefs and self-regulatory management, which are often incorporated into treatment programmes.

Situational theories

The second theoretical approach is less developmental and more situational. It focuses on the context and setting associated with the commission of an offence, and assumes that a number of factors or conditions must be present before the offence can take place, and further, that the removal of any of one these conditions will prevent the offence. For example, Schwartz (1995) argued that sex offenders must have a motive for the offence (e.g. sexual arousal, anger, lack of power, fear of women, or distorted attitudes) and a releaser that allows the offender to engage in the behaviour (e.g. lack of empathy, stress, cognitive distortions, substance abuse, peer pressure, pornography, psychosis or brain damage). Similar in principle, Finkelhor's model (1984; 1986) is used extensively in cognitive-behavioural treatment (in the UK at least) and so will be described in more detail here.

Finkelhor's integrated theory of child sexual abuse

Finkelhor's model (1984; 1986) was the first integrated or multi-factorial model, and as such was groundbreaking. Yet according to Ward and Hudson (2001) it has never been systematically evaluated, although Howells (1994) reviewed the empirical basis for the model and its clinical utility. The model was designed to explain child sexual abuse only and has been extremely influential in the treatment of sex offenders in the UK.

Finkelhor argued that factors contributing to child sexual abuse could be grouped into four preconditions, each of which must be present if the offence is to take place. The first of these is *motivation*, where the offender is motivated to abuse because either sexual contact with a child satisfies emotional needs (emotional congruence), the child represents a source of sexual gratification for the abuser (sexual arousal), or alternative sources of sexual gratification are not available or are less satisfying (blockage). *Overcoming internal inhibitions* is the second precondition; here the offender must overcome internal inhibitors that act against his or her motivation to abuse (disinhibition). These inhibitors can be overcome by minimizing or denying the negative effects of the abuse on the child, by justifying the behaviour, or by using disinhibitors, such as alcohol and drugs. In the third precondition, offenders must *overcome external inhibitors* protecting children from abuse. Thus, offenders groom and manipulate situations so that they are able to be alone with the child. Finally, the offender must *overcome the victim's resistance*. As well as the more obvious method of overt, physical force, offenders also use very subtle, covert methods of 'force'. Perpetrators may be able to identify children who are 'good' potential targets and children may be 'groomed' (where trust is developed, secrets are kept and sexual behaviours gradually introduced) for the offence over long periods of time. Although Finkelhor did not use the term 'grooming' himself, others have subsequently used this term to explain his model.

The model provided a clear framework for the study of child abusers and led to clear treatment goals (Ward and Hudson 2001). However, Ward and Hudson argue that the richness of the model is also its Achilles' heel, as it has many theoretical possibilities, overlapping constructs and a rich array of vulnerability factors that require empirical support. The precondition model also has a number of other problems: it was developed on the basis of little empirical research and there are a number of common-sense assumptions, not all of which are supported by the research and some are not tested; the model is primarily descriptive rather than causal; and it is naïve to assume that offenders are 'blocked', as many offenders have active adult relationships when they abuse. In addition, Ward and Hudson argue that the incorporation of theories and constructs from different traditions leads to inconsistency and incoherence; it is not explained why emotional congruence or blockage are expressed in a sexually abusive manner; there are multiple causal models embedded in one theory; distinctions between key constructs are unsustainable (e.g. blockage and emotional congruence) and there is a failure to consider other self-regulatory problems. Furthermore, the fact that different offenders might use different strategies to overcome external inhibitors and the victims' resistance is not considered.

Ward criticizes the pre-condition model because he claims that there would be an internal conflict between the first and second pre-conditions and that in Finkelhor's model an offender would not overcome this conflict and would not offend. He argues that you cannot be sexually motivated to abuse while your internal inhibitors are in place; i.e. internal inhibitors suppress sexual deviancy, and hence there is no progression to an offence. However, Finkelhor argued that disinhibition alone is not a source of motivation but the reason motivation is 'unleashed'. Finkelhor proposed that child sexual abuse cannot adequately be explained by the simple fact that an adult is sexually aroused by a child. Instead, this arousal may be negated through alternative sources of sexual gratification, or as a result of inhibitory mechanisms, such as adherence to social controls. For example, Finkelhor suggests that it seems unlikely that an individual who has no prior motive to sexually abuse children will be encouraged to do so due to a loss of inhibitions. Similarly, if an individual is totally inhibited from any form of adult-child sexual activity, neither arousal nor emotional congruence will trigger a sexual interaction with a child.

Despite these problems, Finkelhor's model has been influential in the treatment of sex offenders. Although there are other models that explain the development of 'motivation' to sexually offend, the model's strengths lie in the other three preconditions. The model operates at a high level of generality (Calder 1999) and perhaps it is because of this, and its simplicity, that it is used in treatment programmes, often in conjunction with Wolf's (1985) model. Although the model was designed to explain child sexual abuse, at the level of generality used in treatment programmes, it can also be used to explain other sexual offences. Indeed, the model is often explained to sex offenders, as it allows their offences to be examined in detail, and it can be used to teach offenders that their behaviour did not 'just happen', rather that they consciously manipulated people and events to enable the commission of the offending behaviours (Lancaster 1996). Thus, responsibility for the offence(s) is firmly located with the offender, which fits in with the ethos of cognitive-behavioural treatment (as discussed in the next chapter). Furthermore, the fact that all four preconditions need to be met for an offence to occur provides a simple model of desistance, where offend ers remove at least one of the preconditions to avoid future offending. Quite simply this could be avoiding being alone with a child, which maintains external inhibitions and eliminates the likelihood that the offender will be able to overcome the child's resistance. In this way, Finkelhor's model links well to the development of relapse-prevention plans, which is perhaps another reason why it is used in treatment programmes.

Hence, in treatment offenders are asked to locate their behaviours in each of the four preconditions. Some programmes start with the last precondition, overcoming resistance, and work back to the motivation for the offence, as offenders find it more difficult to identify (or accept) their motivation for the offence(s) than they do to identify behaviours in the other three preconditions. Once the preconditions have been identi-fied and examined in detail, offenders are taught that the removal of any one of these preconditions will eliminate future offending. The ways in which these preconditions can be removed are then explored in more detail, and although only one precondition needs to be eliminated, programmes work towards eliminating all four.

Maintenance theories

Feldman (1977) distinguished between factors that lead to the initial offence and factors that maintain the behaviour in the current environ-ment. The theories and models described thus far, with the possible exception of Finkelhor's, focus on the development of sexual offending and less on how this behaviour is maintained following the first offence. Although it attempts to explain the factors that lead to the commission of the first offence, the major strength of Wolf's (1985) model, and its key difference in comparison to other models and theories, is its ability to explain the maintenance of offending behaviour.

Wolf's multi-factor model of deviant sexuality

Wolf (1985) postulated that an early history of physical or emotional abuse, sexualization or neglect leads to the development of a type of personality that predisposes individuals to develop deviant sexual interests. Abuse, he argued, results in the development of poor self-esteem and a belief that adult men have power over weaker people. In addition, disinhibitors, such as alcohol, drugs and pornography, disrupt normal social controls against deviance. Wolf argued that offenders learn that sex and sexual fantasy feel good and offer an escape from uncomfortable feelings of powerlessness and vulnerability. Masturbation to these deviant fantasies positively reinforces associations with deviant sexual behaviour, increasing its attractiveness. Thus, these ideas are similar to those later theorized by Marshall and Barbaree.

Wolf argued further that these factors operate in the following cyclic way. An event (or events) triggers feelings of inadequacy and powerless-ness, and perpetrators withdraw into deviant sexual fantasies. These fantasies build into the planning of offences, and the grooming and manipulating of events to facilitate the commission of the offence. Following the offence, offenders experience feelings of guilt and discom-fort, which are alleviated by distorted thinking that rationalizes and/or minimizes the abuse. These perpetrators have an underlying awareness that they have done something shameful, which further damages self-esteem and makes them more vulnerable to start the cycle again. Over time, and after a number of offences, the cycle is developed and maintained by increasingly distorted thinking and positive feelings associated with sexual release. Thus, 'sex' serves both sexual and non-sexual needs, especially the need for power and control.

It has become increasingly common to view sexual offending as an addictive behaviour, which is similar in nature to addiction to other substances or behaviours, such as alcohol, drugs or gambling (for more detail on addiction models of sexual offending see Carnes (1983; 1990); Herman (1988)). This viewpoint has been responsible for the introduc-tion and development of relapse-prevention techniques in sex offender programmes (see Pithers et al. 1983; Laws 1989; 1995; Marques and Nelson 1989; Pithers 1990; 1991). Wolf's (1985) cyclic model fits very well with this approach. It is perhaps because of this, the fact that it is easy for treatment providers and offenders to understand, and the way in which it can be applied to many different types of sexual offences, that it (or the general principles of it) continues to be used in treatment programmes. This is despite the fact that the model has received no direct empirical validation.

In treatment, this theory is explained to offenders, so that they are able to identify their own patterns of offending. Many programmes encour-age offenders to identify their offending cycles (see for example Calder (1999) and Laws (1995)) or, with less emphasis on Wolf's theory, and more emphasis on relapse-prevention models (see Chapter 6), offence chains (for example, see Laws 1995). Once cycles (or chains) have been identified and explored in detail, offenders are encouraged to identify ways in which their cycles can be broken (or the chain could have been broken). This is usually combined with a relapse-prevention approach, in which it is stressed that it is easier to break a cycle at the stage of feeling stressed and/or inadequate than it is to break it at the stage of being alone with a child. Offenders are also taught to identify and plan a number of strategies that can be employed at a variety of stages throughout the cycle (chain), to ensure continued abstinence from offending.

It can be seen from these theoretical examples that different explanations focus on different stages of offending behaviour: some focus on factors leading to the initial offence; others on factors existing at the time of the offence; and others on factors that maintain the behaviour. Marshall and Barbaree's (1990a) theory and Hall and Hirschman's (1991; 1992) model are developmental in their outlook, focusing on the factors that impact throughout an individual's life leading them to perpetrate a sexual offence. Schwartz (1995) and Finkelhor (1984; 1986), on the other hand, focused on the conditions that existed at the time of the offence and while factors contained in the developmental explanations may be present (e.g. in the list of motivations or releasers) they are given less emphasis. Other theories (e.g. Wolf 1985) focus on factors that maintain offending behaviour and thus, those that should be eliminated in order to ensure that the offender desists from offending again. The fact that different theoretical explanations focus on different stages of the offending process is rarely made explicit. This results in a confused theoretical position where practitioners are forced to use an amalgamation of these explanations.

Ward and Hudson (1998a) argued that a failure to coordinate and integrate theory building has resulted in this *ad hoc* proliferation of theories that often overlap and ignore each other's existence. They argued further that there has been a general failure to distinguish between levels of theory, with explanations currently being offered at three levels: integrated approaches, which ultimately aim to develop a comprehensive theory of sexual offending (such as Hall and Hirschman's quadripartite model and Marshall and Barbaree's integrated theory); middle-level theories, the mono-causal theories described at the beginning of this chapter; and micro-models that focus on building descriptive models, such as of the offence chain or relapse process (see for example Pithers 1990; Ward, Louden *et al.* 1995, and Chapter 6). Ward and Hudson (1998a) believe theory construction at these three levels should be encouraged, but that a coordinated approach should be developed within the meta-theoretical framework they describe.

Another problem with current theoretical explanations is that some theorists attempt to describe all types of sexual offending (although this is rarely made explicit), while others focus on one type of sexual offence (for example, rape or incest). Marshall and Barbaree's (1990a) integrated theory encompassed all types of sexual offending (although its focus on aggression may make it most applicable to rape), whereas Finkelhor's

(1984; 1986) model focused on child sexual abuse. This is also a problem with mono-causal theories; for example, family explanations obviously focus on offending within the family (incest perpetrated by biological and/or step-parents); whereas biological and psychodynamic explanations are not offence specific. However, the limits of each theory are rarely specifically noted, and few publications (with the exception of Laws and O'Donohue (1997)) attempt to describe the theory relating to each type of offence. Thus, there would appear to be some confusion or conflict as to whether or not a single, comprehensive theory can explain all types of sexual offending, although this has yet to be debated openly in the literature.

Recent theoretical developments

The theories and models discussed thus far are now rather dated, with Hall and Hirschman's model being the latest theoretical offering in 1991 and 1992. Since then, there has been very little theoretical debate in the literature, and as Ward has pointed out, little empirical work to test these theories and models. As discussed above, in 1998, Ward and Hudson argued that sex offending theory needed further attention as the previous strategy of proliferation and neglect was inefficient and wasteful, where interesting ideas were not fully developed or were inadvertently duplicated. Consequently, theorists and researchers were unaware of exploratory gaps or ignored fruitful avenues of enquiry in a fragmented and uncoordinated theoretical landscape. Since then Ward, often in conjunction with his colleagues, has published extensively in this area in an effort to improve this situation. Despite these publications, theoretical debate is still limited, as few have responded to these articles, although with the length of time it takes for articles to be processed for publication, it may be that it is too early to see these replies.

Ward and Hudson (2001) and Ward (2001; 2002b) began by assessing what they argued were the three most influential theories and models (the integrated theory, quadripartite model and the preconditions model) and then moved to 'knitting' these theories and models together to form a new more comprehensive theory that hopefully avoided the weaknesses of the separate theories and models, but incorporated their strengths. Ward and Siegert (2002) called the ensuing theory of child sexual abuse the pathways model.

Ward and Siegert's 'pathways model'

Although the original theories and models addressed a range of sexual offending behaviours, Ward and Siegert (2002) chose to develop a model only for child sexual abuse. The reason for this is not clear, but perhaps it is because they believe that it is not possible to develop a single model that adequately explains all sexual offending. The 'pathways model' is based on the dysfunction of four psychological mechanisms (a mechanism is a set of psychological processes that cause specific outcomes or effects): intimacy deficits, sexual arousal, emotional regulation and cognitive distortions (deviant sexual scripts). Ward and Siegert argue that all of these psychological mechanisms are involved in the development of child sexual abuse; that is, every sexual offence against a child involves the presence of these mechanisms. In addition, they provide empirical evidence to support the presence of these mechanisms. Like the quadripartite model, the pathways model produces a typology of offenders, as Ward and Siegert argue that in each offender one of the psychological mechanisms will be more important than the other three (creating four subtypes); or in some offenders, all the mechanisms will be fairly evenly balanced (the fifth subtype). In this model, each pathway has its own unique array of causes. The model also attempts to identify situational triggers, which might interact with an individual's vulnerability to offend, so that an offence actually occurs. Thus, vulnerability factors and situational or opportunity factors are needed for offences to occur.

Ward and Siegert's model (see also Drake and Ward 2003) identifies 'intimacy deficits' as the first etiological pathway in child sexual abuse, where offenders who possess normal sexual scripts offend only at certain times, for example if their preferred partner is unavailable, as they have deficits in intimacy and social skills. The primary causal factor within this pathway is insecure attachment styles and subsequent problems establishing satisfactory relationships with adults. Individuals in the second pathway, 'deviant sexual scripts', have subtle distortions in their sexual scripts, such as seeking sex in inappropriate situations (e.g. when angry), having preferences for inappropriate partners (e.g. children) or engaging in inappropriate harmful activities (e.g. sadism). These dysfunctions interact with dysfunctional relationship schemas. These scripts may result from early and inappropriate sexual experiences, victimization issues or deviant learning. The third pathway identifies individuals with normal sexual scripts, but dysfunctional mechanisms in some aspect of the 'emotional regulation' system, such as problems identifying emotions, an inability to use social support in times of stress or an inability to control anger. Thus, the primary causal mechanisms are defects in emotional and behavioural control, or the inappropriate use of sex as a coping strategy. The fourth pathway, 'antisocial cognitions' (cognitive distortions), contains individuals who have normal sexual scripts but pro-criminal attitudes and beliefs, which may be further facilitated by patriarchal views towards women and children and a sense of their own superiority. The final group of offenders, in the 'multiple dysfunction' pathway, will have developed deviant sexual scripts and exhibit pronounced flaws in the other psychological mechanisms. Thus, they constitute 'pure' paedophiles. It is not possible to give an account here that reflects the detail of Ward and Siegert's (2002) work, which contains empirical support for their claims and many examples in each of the pathways. In addition, Drake and Ward (2003) explain the different treatment requirements of offenders from each of the five pathways.

Ward and Siegert argue that a good theory should be able to describe the development, onset and maintenance of behaviour, yet the focus of the pathways model appears to be concerned with the development and onset of child sexual abuse. Although, Ward and Hudson (2001) criticize Finkelhor for not discussing the different styles of offenders in overcoming inhibitors and the victims' resistance, this is also omitted from the pathways model. The model is also less able to describe the maintenance of sexual behaviour. Ward and Siegert (2002) devote just one paragraph to this issue. They point out that the act of sexually abusing a child may alter or distort offenders' sexual scripts. In addition, they state that although continuation is likely to be related to vulnerability factors, it should not be assumed. Yet, it is anticipated that maintenance is likely to be linked to positive and negative reinforcers that will be a function of the vulnerability factors. Clearly, this element of the model needs more attention and detail. However, these weaknesses can be overcome to some extent (less so in terms of maintenance) if the pathways model is combined with Ward and Hudson's (1998b) self-regulation model (see also Drake and Ward (2003), which describes how this model can be linked to treatment), which gives an indication of the different styles of offending and ways of gaining access to victims.

The 'self-regulation model' (Ward and Hudson 1998b) is described by Ward and his colleague as a micro-level theory, and places offenders in four categories: *avoidance-passive*; *avoidance-active*; *approach-automatic* (or approach-passive); and *approach explicit* (or approach-active). Avoidance-passive offenders wish to avoid offending but fail to do so, perhaps because they lack coping skills or through disinhibition. These offenders are impulsive and use covert planning in their offences. Avoidance-active offenders wish to avoid offending but use inappropriate and ineffective strategies. For example, an offender may believe that he or she will offend less if they masturbate to fantasies, rather than acting them out; however, this inadvertently reinforces deviant desires and thus increases the likelihood of reoffending. Approach-automatic offenders wish to continue offending; however, their goals are not under control and they respond most to situational factors. Thus, offences tend to be planned, but only in a basic manner. Finally, approach-explicit offenders are those who wish to offend and consciously and explicitly plan their offences. These offenders are likely to believe that their behaviour is legitimate.

The pathways model has also recently been linked to risk assessment (Beech and Ward 2004), which further increases the utility of the model, although as Ward and Siegert (2002) themselves argue, the model needs rigorous empirical validation and further development through debate with other professionals and the incorporation of research findings. Bickley and Beech (2002) found that the self-regulation model could be reliably employed to classify child sexual abusers, with inter-rater agreement in more than 80 per cent of the 87 offenders assessed. Furthermore, differences in psychometric data and offence characteristics across the two group distinctions – approach versus avoidance and active versus passive – provided support for the validity of the model. However, Marshall and Serran (2000) have questioned the extent to which all offenders engage in some kind of planning, arguing that there is little evidence to support the assumption that all sex offenders do this. Marshall and Serran question the categorizations made by Hudson *et al.* (1999) and are particularly sceptical of the categorization of implicit planning, arguing that some offenders simply take advantage of situations as they unexpectedly arise. Thus, more work is needed to investigate the extent to which offenders do plan, and if they do the differences in the styles of planning across offender groups. In addition, validation studies are required for the pathways model. A model is also needed for other offences, such as rape and exhibitionism.

The pathways model provides a comprehensive and complex picture of the causes of child sexual abuse; yet, it is most easy to apply the model retrospectively, i.e. once an offender has been identified and assessed, the offender's pathway can be identified and an associated treatment plan developed. It is less clear whether the model can be used to identify offenders at an early stage in their pathway before such time that they actually commit an offence (this is also a problem with most other theories). Furthermore, the model's use in terms of preventing sexual abuse is questionable. For example, although insecure attachments are identified as a causal factor, for child sexual abuse to be the outcome, these act in combination with many other factors. So, even if it were possible to identify all those who suffer insecure attachments, it would be difficult to identify those that would go on to offend. As will be discussed in Chapter 10, most current interventions take place once at least one offence has taken place, which on its own is not the most effective strategy of reducing sexual offending.

Nevertheless, these two models and other more recent work on micro-level theory (see Chapter 6) have vastly improved the theoretical underpinnings of cognitive-behavioural programmes (despite the fact that the basic framework for these programmes was developed long before this work). Although it is too early to assess the impact of this work on treatment programmes, it would be surprising if this work had no impact on treatment, particularly when accreditation and licensing procedures require treatment providers to document the theoretical basis and model of change for their programme(s). However, these latest models are more complex than some of the early models and so, although they may be used to development treatment plans and improve treatment programmes, it is conceivable that the more simplistic models of Finkelhor and Wolf (or the basic principles of these ideas) will be explained to offenders in treatment, as these can be easily and quickly understood and applied to relapse-prevention plans. Furthermore, although the pathways model suggests different treatment programmes for offenders in each of the pathways, the trend in treatment has been towards programmes that treat all offenders (including non-child sexual offences, which of course are not explained in the pathways model) and strictly follow programme manuals.

This issue is discussed by Drake and Ward (2003) where, not surprisingly, they question the use of manuals and the 'one programme fits all' model. Instead, they suggest a formulation-based approach where treatment is tailored to each individual offender, based on a thorough assessment of the offender's psychological vulnerabilities and problems. As well as maintaining treatment integrity, manuals and standard programmes for all offenders have been adopted as this provides the easiest method of treating a range of offenders across wide geographical areas, particularly when groupwork is the preferred method of delivery. Thus, it seems unlikely that treatment will be offered on a wholly individual, formulation basis. However, the pathways model has four key psychological mechanisms, which apply to all offenders but to a different degree, so perhaps it is possible to produce a modular programme based on these four mechanisms that allows offenders to complete as much or as little treatment in each of these key areas as they need. This would allow some adjustment for individual treatment needs, while still allowing for the delivery of group pro-grammes that cater for a range of offenders.

Chapter 5

Treatment ethos and effects on staff

The theories and models underpinning cognitive-behavioural sex offender treatment programmes were discussed in the previous chapter; yet, it is not possible from these alone to ascertain the ethos and context of these programmes. For, as well as deriving from the specific sex offending theories described in the previous chapter, the context and ethos of treatment is also derived from the cognitive and behavioural approaches that are outlined in Chapter 2. Hence, the underlying approaches and principles of treatment are described below. As will be seen, some of these principles are difficult for treatment providers to apply and this, in conjunction with a variety of other factors, means that the work can have a range of effects on staff. As these can have an impact on treatment integrity and programme drift, these effects are discussed in the second half of this chapter.

Treatment ethos and therapeutic context

The term 'treatment' implies a medical model of sex offending, but the following statement by Marshall *et al.* (1993: 442) more accurately reflects the views of most sex-offender treatment providers.

> We do not believe that sex offenders have either a disease or a congenital defect which renders their sexual behaviour outside their control. Child molesters and rapists typically carefully plan their offences to maximize the probability that they can enact their desired behaviour while minimizing the possibility of detection, apprehension and punishment. It is clear that the majority of sex

offenders fantasize about what they are going to do prior to offending and many make explicit plans to offend. They know what they are doing; they know it is a criminal offence; and they expect to be punished if caught.

In fact, some providers prefer not to use the term 'treatment' at all. This is part of the reason for the programme in Scotland being called STOP, rather than SOTP, as those responsible for the development of STOP did not wish to use the term treatment programme (TP) (see Spencer 1998). A similar case is put forward by Lundström (2002: 17) with reference to provision in Ireland.

> Throughout this document the Sex Offender Programme provided in Ireland is not called a 'Treatment' programme as is the case in many other jurisdictions. This strategy was adopted for the following reason given very eloquently by a member of Specialist Services.
>
> *'Treatment' of sex offenders implies an illness. If you refer to 'treatment' of sex offenders you collude with a lot of their defence – 'I only did this because I was ill and if you cured me I wouldn't do it again. Therefore I am an ill person, therefore I am not really responsible'. Whereas, challenging the behaviour of sex offenders or the re-education of sex offenders is a more appropriate name for the programme. In using 'treatment' the offender can apply a passive approach and say it is the therapist's job to 'cure' him. And if I do re-offend, it is your fault because you did not 'cure' me.*

As is clear from the above comment, according to the preferred approach (and cognitive-behavioural theory), offenders are seen as being responsible for their own behaviour, and intervention programmes encourage offenders to recognize and accept this. However:

> One of the difficulties in treating these men is to have those who were abused understand the role their victimization may have played in the etiology and maintenance of their offending, while at the same time having them understand that they still made the choice to offend.
>
> (Marshall 1996b: 321)

Generally, cognitive-behavioural programmes spend little time assessing the developmental causes of each offender's behaviour; rather, they start from the principle that others may have experienced similar developmental problems to the offender, but did not offend. Thus, as Marshall argued above, an offender is seen to have made a choice to offend, no matter what his or her personal history, and programmes start from the point that regardless of what has happened prior to the start of treatment, offenders can now choose, with the help of the treatment programme, not to offend. Offenders with issues that may be linked to their offending behaviour, such as previous victimization, alcohol and drug dependency, may be offered the opportunity to attend other programmes to deal with these issues. This allows the focus of the sex offender programme to remain on personal responsibility for offending without allowing the offender any excuses for his or her behaviour, yet at the same time, the offender is given the opportunity to deal with issues that they feel make it difficult for them to accept this responsibility.

The term 'treatment' implies a passive process: something that is done to the offender. Yet, as can be seen from the previous discussion, cognitive-behavioural treatment is an active process, which requires an offender to accept their behaviour and, more importantly, to accept that he or she was an active participant in this behaviour, e.g. that it did not just happen, that it was planned. Furthermore, offenders are expected to work to change their thinking styles and lifestyles to avoid reoffending. Clearly, this is not something that can be done 'to' an offender without their active engagement: thus, there has been some debate about whether offenders should attend programmes voluntarily or be mandated to attend (for a review of coercion and treatment, see Burdon and Gallagher (2002)). Many argue that treatment should be voluntary, as there is no point in requiring an offender to attend treatment if they refuse to fully engage in the treatment process. Others have argued that most offenders would not engage in this process at all unless there was some coercion, at least for them to attend treatment. Consequently, many believe that coercion or mandated treatment forces offenders into treatment (and to remain in treatment), in the hope that treatment will initiate some change in their behaviour.

In reality, the fact that sexual offending is an illegal behaviour that is sanctioned by criminal justice, correction and mental health systems means that coercion into treatment is inevitable. For example, in the UK, imprisoned sex offenders complete treatment on a 'voluntary' basis, yet offenders also know that they will be viewed more positively by professionals if they complete treatment, which may have implications for their release and the number of sanctions or restrictions placed upon them. Furthermore, offenders will be continually encouraged to attend treatment by a range of professionals. In some jurisdictions, where treatment is completed in special units, offenders can be motivated to complete treatment, so that they have the opportunity to be housed in these units with other sex offenders, and away from the mainstream prison population, where sex offenders are perceived and treated very negatively. Offenders may also be coerced into treatment by family and friends and there may be internal cognitive processes, such as guilt, that encourage the completion of treatment. Thus, few offenders enter treatment on a truly voluntary basis and this seems unlikely to change. However, perhaps somewhat ironically, it is not possible to coerce or mandate an offender to take treatment seriously, to fully engage in the process of treatment, or to embark upon the process of change: thus, inevitably they do this voluntarily.

Given the context of treatment, it is widely acknowledged, and has been acknowledged for some time, that cognitive-behavioural treatment programmes cannot 'cure' sex offenders. As McPherson *et al.* (1994: 41) stated:

> Many professionals now believe that it may be unrealistic to expect that treatment can 'cure' sex offenders, in the sense that it can totally eliminate the deviant sexual desires of all sex offenders. Rather a more realistic goal of treatment is training or educating offenders on how to control their deviant behaviours, and it is unlikely to be effective with all offenders. This approach to treatment involves lower expectations and viewing the treatment and supervision of sex offenders as a long-term process.

As a long-term process, treatment programmes should be followed by continued long-term contact with offenders, whether in the form of 'booster' treatment sessions, direct supervision, or relapse-prevention treatment (McPherson *et al.* 1994). In addition, it is important that offenders have a source of support available to them indefinitely, for example via drop-in centres or telephone help-lines, so that they are able to obtain help if they feel they are likely to reoffend. However, such provision is extremely limited. For example, McPherson and colleagues found that few programmes included aftercare. In their survey, only one-third of programme providers said that they provided some form of long-term provision and this ranged from 'check-ins' to prolonged therapy. Whilst the provision of booster programmes and/or treatment in both custodial and community settings for high-risk/high-need offenders has improved so that it now forms a key component of treatment provision in many jurisdictions (see Chapter 3), the provision of long-term aftercare is still lacking in most jurisdictions. Even though some offenders may be involved in treatment for many years, there is still very little support once they have exhausted the range of treatment programmes that are provided. Long-term support groups, drop-in centres or telephone help-lines (as McPherson and colleagues suggest) are still extremely rare.

Similarly, once offenders have completed treatment and/or served their sentence, it is very unlikely that they will be reassessed, or 'booster' programmes suggested, unless they come into contact with the criminal justice system again through the commission of another crime, or behaviour that would induce suspicion that they were about to commit another crime. In fact, the resources do not exist for such provision, which would fall outside the remit of the criminal justice system, since the offender would have completed his or her sentence. If public protection is the main goal of treatment, then this issue needs to be addressed. Even the strongest supporters of the effectiveness of sex offender treatment would question its effectiveness on a long-term basis and recognize that the impact of any form of intervention reduces over time (for a more detailed discussion of the impact of treatment over time see Barbaree (1997)). It is possible that such an intervention could be incorporated into an existing provision. For example, in the UK sex offenders are required to register their names and addresses under the Sex Offenders Act (1997) and, as part of the implementation of this legislation, they may be assessed and monitored by the police over a prolonged period of time. Currently, however, the importance given to treatment in these assessments is unclear. Yet, it seems unlikely that the police would suggest that offenders should attend 'booster' treatment sessions (or that the resources exist for this), or that the police would have the appropriate training to assess which offenders may be in need of such sessions. This is despite the fact that the requirements of this Act are perhaps the best source of long-term contact and support for this group of offenders.

As can be seen in Chapter 3, groupwork is the most common method of programme delivery. A number of reasons have been cited for this method (for an outline see Beech and Fordham 1997). According to treatment officials surveyed by McPherson *et al.* (1994), the group approach was considered to be more common because it was harder for offenders to deceive other offenders, and because group sessions provided role models of individuals who were succeeding. In addition, it was argued that peer confrontation and support played a key role in changing deeply rooted patterns of thinking and fulfilling needs. Glaser and Frosh (1993) suggested that groupwork was the most appropriate method as it breaks down the secrecy inherent in sexual offending. Furthermore, Behroozi (1992) suggested that confrontation from other offenders, rather than treatment providers, can be seen as being more credible and more effective, which helps offenders reduce their levels of denial and increase acceptance of their problems. Cook *et al.* (1991: 239) stated:

> The objectives of the group have been to facilitate discussion of mutual problems, reduce feelings of isolation and abnormality, confront members with the effects of their behaviour on victims, to

provide strategies for the management of sexual feelings, and to promote the development of wider social contacts as part of the process of disengaging from the group.

Groups also provide a supportive environment for offenders that include appropriate models of social relationships. Beech and Fordham (1997) argued that this structure also provides opportunities for peer discussion, to share problems, to experience being valued, to help others and to improve self-esteem, empathic responding and social skills. Furthermore, they suggested that when many sex offenders are isolated, have low self-esteem, poor social skills and little experience of being valued, the importance of these opportunities should not be underestimated, and can be an important aspect of the process of change. Yet, the impact of the range of factors emanating from supportive group environments has been neglected in the evaluation literature.

Despite these positive aspects, it is possible that groupwork encourages offenders to set up networks, that post-treatment may encourage offending, or lead to the formation of offending rings or groups. Hanson (2000) points out that among non-sex-offending criminals, one of the strongest predictors of recidivism is association with other offenders (Gendreau et al. cited in Hanson (2000)). Furthermore, offenders may enjoy listening to other offenders' accounts of their offending, learn new techniques and ways or offending, or develop new sexual fantasies. Treatment staff try to reduce the likelihood of these outcomes; for example, many groups, particularly those in community settings, have rules that ban offenders from seeing one another outside the treatment environment, and staff are vigilant to try to ensure that offenders are not becoming aroused during accounts of offending behaviour. In addition, the discussion of some issues, such as sexual fantasy, is reserved for individual rather than group treatment work (or not included at all in programmes where groupwork is the sole method of treatment delivery). However, there is very little research examining the impact of the group environment on treatment effectiveness (see Chapters 7 and 9) and, although it is generally assumed that the positive effects of groupwork outweigh the negative, there is very little empirical investigation into this issue.

Working with sex offenders can be very challenging, because cultural scripts make it easy to despise these men for what they have done. Indeed, some 'therapeutic' approaches for this group of offenders have been based on a confrontational approach and some argue that sex offenders must be confronted about their behaviour in treatment/ therapy (see Salter 1988). However, the term 'confrontation' is used in a confusing manner as it covers a continuum of behaviours and treatment styles. For example, therapists can be encouraged to confront sex offenders about their behaviour, or to adopt a confrontational approach throughout the whole of the treatment process. It is possible to do the former in a supportive environment, although the term 'challenge' more accurately reflects the nature of the interaction in such an environment, and 'challenges' of behaviour or of attitudes, thoughts and beliefs that encourage sexual offending are a key part of most cognitive-behavioural treatment programmes.

Nevertheless, most respected practitioners and treatment providers strongly discourage a more general 'confrontational' approach because 'if treatment providers fail to respect the human dignity of clients, regardless of the deplorable nature of their client's conduct, the likelihood of significant change is greatly diminished' (Pithers 1997: 36). Marshall and Serran (2000) argue that a confrontational style does not model empathy and is likely to reduce clients' self-confidence, which is likely to impede therapeutic change (Marshall et al. 1997). At the same time, though, Marshall (1996b) argues that to avoid confrontation altogether is just as much a failure as an excessively confrontational style, as the therapist colludes with the offender and does not challenge any of the offender's statements. Thus, what is actually being discouraged is not any form of confrontation, as this is inevitable in programmes that challenge behaviour, but an environment in which 'emotional invective and personal denigration in the guise of confrontation' (Pithers 1997: 37) is used, as this is 'more likely to promote anger and distrust than personal change'.

Although the use of a general confrontational style has been discouraged for many years, it is only more recently that literature has been published that provides empirical and/or theoretical support of this view. Pithers (1997) detailed some quite shocking examples of how 'confrontational' drama therapy denigrated clients, which resulted in injunctive hearings in the federal district court (in Vermont, USA). More positively, Kear-Colwell and her colleagues (Kear-Colwell and Pollock 1997; Kear-Colwell and Boer 2000) provide theoretical support for the use of non-confrontational approaches and, encouragingly, there are now research findings that show that therapists using confrontational styles are less effective in engendering change in their clients than those using a supportive therapeutic style, which features empathy, warmth and directive and rewarding behaviours (Marshall, Serran et al. 2003; Serran et al. 2003). See Chapter 9 for a more detailed discussion of this evidence.

Hence, the general approach adopted by most cognitive-behavioural programme therapists is described by Marshall (1996b). He pointed out that although they have committed sexual offences, most sex offenders engage in many pro-social activities and hence are not 'monsters', a fact that is so often ignored, particularly by the media. Marshall argued that these men should be respected and yet their behaviour should not be condoned.

> It seems to me that we can, and should, have both compassion for Fred [sex offender] as a person and repugnance for his offensive behaviour. It is quite possible for a genuinely compassionate person, as all therapists should be, to hold these two conceptualizations ... simultaneously. (p. 319)

Thus, Marshall argues that therapists should adopt a style that:

> Involves forming a relationship with clients that is respectful of their dignity, engenders trust, displays empathy for them, and accepts them as persons while not accepting their offensive behaviours. It reinforces small changes and involves some degree of self-disclosure by the therapist.

Such an approach, he argues, provides an empathic model for these offenders and a model for supportive interaction with others. More simply, Pithers (1997: 35) stated that:

> ethical treatment providers differentiate the actor from the act ... [and] view sexual assault as profoundly unacceptable but perceive abusers as people capable of creating meaningful change in their beliefs and behaviors.

Adopting such a therapeutic approach is not a simple task. It constantly requires practitioners to tread a difficult path between many conflicting positions, for example, respecting the offender while despising the behaviour. Rogers and Dickey (1991: 59) highlighted another area of conflict and suggested a strategy for clinicians.

> Clinicians may wish to openly acknowledge their own conflicted roles in attempting to serve both the needs of the offender and the community. On one hand, clinicians try to develop a trusting therapeutic relationship, while on the other, they carefully monitor offenders (particularly those under probation or parole) for non-compliance or recidivism. Without a frank acknowledgement of these dual roles, clinicians run the risk of modelling deception to offenders but expecting honesty in return.

The difficulties involved in working with sex offenders are discussed in more detail in the next section.

Treatment staff: problems of working with sex offenders

Working with sex offenders, particularly in an environment where detailed descriptions of sexual offences are discussed, is not easy. As Blyth and Milner (1990: 197) stated:

> In sociological terms child abuse is an excellent illustration of 'dirty work'. Hughes' (1958) 'dirty work' includes those activities which have to be done but are nevertheless distasteful in the doing and those which ought not to be done but unfortunately seem unavoidable.

As Glaser and Frosh (1993) pointed out, each of the words 'child', 'sexual' and 'abuse' evoke strong emotional responses. 'Sexuality arouses excitement, embarrassment, confusion, or inhibition in most adults; this is complicated for professionals by the additional factor of having to deal with a child's experiences' (p. 166). Thus, this work requires staff to examine their personal attitudes, behaviour and relationships in a way that does not apply with other types of offence-based work (HM Inspectorate of Probation 1991).

In addition, the work creates a tension, which Lea *et al.* (1999) term the 'professional-personal dialectic', between the need to develop a professional relationship with the sex offender, while at the same time negotiating the desire not to develop a relationship because of the offender's abhorrent criminal behaviour. This tension is made more difficult by the extremely negative media and public response to this group of offenders. Thus, professionals, who have to display tolerance and understanding of sex offenders, have to place themselves in an attitudinal context that is at odds with the intolerant, negative attitudes of society (and even of their colleagues). Furthermore, they risk attracting a courtesy stigma because others may perceive them to have sympathy for sex offenders. Lea *et al.* (1999) reported that professionals found it more difficult to negotiate the professional-personal dialectic when salient features of the case evoked personal feelings (for example when the victim had similar characteristics to close family members), when the case was particularly violent or damaging to the victim, the victim died or thought he or she was going to die, the victim was severely traumatized, or the victim was very young or old. The difficulties of this work are acknowledged by many working in the field and warnings are given about the dangers if these issues are overlooked.

> We recognize that: working with sex offenders is difficult and emotionally demanding, that there can at times be a personal cost to

103

individuals working in this area. . . . Work with child sex offenders can be harrowing and traumatic to the hardest of officers, social workers and managers. The nature of the offences raises issues of personal sexuality, victimization and vulnerability. These dangers should *not* be underestimated.

(Strathclyde Regional Council, Social Work Department and the Scottish Prison Service 1995: 7)

Any interaction with sexual offenders may induce complex feelings in members of the treatment team. Frequently, powerful feelings of revulsion and anger occur when hearing of distasteful acts committed by the offender. If staff are not adequately supervized and supported, it is possible that these strong, induced feelings may cause actions to be taken which are counterproductive to the progress of therapy, at the professional level and, if unrecognized, may give rise to some significant stress symptoms at the personal level.

(Lewis and Perkins 1996: 258)

Abel (1983: 283–250) states 'one cannot ignore the very personal impact of working day in day out with rapists and potential rapists. The recounting and exploring of the details of such violent fantasies and atrocious acts in effect serve to surround the therapist in an emotional world of violence on top of violence. If the work force to prevent sexual violence is to be effective with its difficult task, we must be aware of the high "burn-out" of personnel and provide staff training and staff development that can maintain that work force'.

(Farrenkopf 1992: 217–18)

Despite this awareness, there have been only a few studies exploring the effects of this work on practitioners. Garrison (1992) noted that the work can be extremely stressful and that Staffordshire practitioners complained of being over-stretched. These workers felt that they had insufficient time to process and evaluate the enormous amount of written work demanded by the treatment programme and that there was not enough time to prepare programme materials.

West (1996: 238) highlighted another stressor: 'namely that of carrying the burden of a patient's potential as if his whole future behaviour depended solely on one's intervention'. This issue was also noted by Lea *et al.*'s (1999) respondents who described the stress of working with a group of offenders who were seen to be highly dangerous, a categorization that applied to all offenders, as all offenders, even the relatively harmless, were seen as being capable of upgrading their crimes to very serious offences. This stress was further enhanced by the notion that all sex offenders have a poor prognosis. These two ideas work together to increase the perception or potential that an offender will one day commit a serious crime, that somehow the professional will have some responsibility for. Clearly, this increases the stress of working with this group of offenders, although to cope with this, some professionals reported being realistic in their expectations and goals, for example by seeing any reduction in victimization as a success.

The attitudes of colleagues who do not support the provision of treatment programmes for sex offenders can add to the stress felt by practitioners. In Barlinnie Prison (Glasgow), there was a feeling that sex offenders were receiving more than their fair share of resources (HMP Barlinie unpublished). Here, and in other prisons, sex offenders were seen as 'beasties' (or 'nonces') and it was felt that it was futile to try to work with these men. Consequently, staff working on treatment programmes received a hostile response from their colleagues; for example, by being nicknamed 'beastmasters'. In the Probation Service too, there was some disquiet that this work was in conflict with the original values of the Service (advise, assist, befriend) and that it was a specialist area of work, which was not part of the basic knowledge of probation officers (Garrison 1992).

Kearns (1995) argued that staff working with sex offenders can become isolated from those working with different client groups; furthermore, that the work climate can discourage discussion of the negative aspects of the work and that staff working with offenders can be discouraged from discussing these issues if there is a lack of support from friends and colleagues. These difficulties were noted in the professionals (police officers, social workers, assistant psychologists, probation officers and prison officers) interviewed by Lea *et al.* (1999), where a quarter claimed that they felt unable to report their stress because the institutions for which they worked did not acknowledge the potential negative impact of working with sex offenders. Thus, they felt that they would be seen as being unable to cope or not cut out for the job.

Ellerby (1998, cited in Ennis and Horne 2003) conducted a study with the largest sample of sex offender treatment providers – 683 in total – and provided further support for Kearn's claims. Ellerby found that higher levels of distress and burnout were reported in treatment staff who had limited opportunities for supervision and consultation, while those who had more opportunities for such support reported higher levels of personal accomplishment in their work. Ennis and Horne (2003) examined the responses of 59 mental health professionals involved in work with sex offenders and also found that perception of peer support was a predictor of psychological distress and post-traumatic stress disorder symptoms (PTSD), with increased support being linked to fewer symptoms. However, Ellerby (1997, cited in Shelby *et al.* 2001) found that treatment providers received little or no support from the community, correctional system or colleagues who do not treat sex offenders. Ninety per cent of respondents reported negative responses to their work and only 47 per cent reported positive reactions. Furthermore, 71 per cent felt that they had to justify their work.

The fact that most abusers are male invokes feelings that may be dependent on the gender of the worker (Glaser and Frosh 1993). Men may feel a sense of collective guilt or defensiveness; women may feel isolated and vulnerable, exhibiting more paranoia and vigilance in their daily lives and perhaps expressing constant concern over their children's safety (HM Inspectorate of Probation 1991; Farrenkopf 1992; Glaser and Frosh 1993). HMP Barlinnie (unpublished) suggested that work with sex offenders can be more stressful for women than men. They noted that women needed to be extremely aware of themselves in terms of what they wear and how men treat them. A large proportion of offenders found it hard to take part in programmes without bullying women in positions of power and had problems reacting to women in a non-sexual way. These men tended to refute anything a woman said if it was not backed up by a man, and they tried to isolate women and eliminate them from the conversation. Women felt that they needed to challenge these behaviours themselves without reinforcing stereotypes and relying on men. Crighton (1995) noted that offenders may use offensive and explicit language that may be intended to embarrass women tutors. Consequently, women found these groups very stressful. Despite these problems, the professionals interviewed by Lea et al. (1999) thought that gender was useful in obtaining different things from offenders. Women felt that their involvement in treatment was important in inhibiting male collusion, facilitating confession through the offender being attracted to the female interviewer, and challenging offenders' views of women as powerless. For men, gender was a means of identifying with offenders and encouraging 'men's talk' about sexual behaviour. All those interviewed by Lea and colleagues advocated the use of mixed gendered treatment teams to maximize the effectiveness of intervention.

In addition, there is the possibility that workers may have been abused themselves. Turner (1992, cited in Mann and Thornton 1998) noted that unresolved issues from such abuse came to the fore in programme tutors with a history of abuse, as a result of work on the SOTP (HM Prison Service, England and Wales). For this reason, Glaser and Frosh (1993) argued that it was important for institutions to provide emotionally supportive supervision arrangements. However, the HM Inspectorate of Probation (1991) noted that supervisors and managers were not always as aware of this as they should be. Edmunds (1997, cited in Scheela 2001) suggested that therapists who were abuse victims were at an increased risk of burnout compared to therapists with no such history of abuse.

A further source of stress noted by Lea and colleagues was the offenders' persistent denial and minimization, which caused considerable frustration. Crighton (1995) noted that programme tutors (UK SOTP) faced practical and ethical difficulties in preserving offenders' confidentiality and that there were dangers when offenders sought tacit support for their behaviour through sophisticated collusive strategies. In addition, he reported that sometimes offenders could develop inappropriate fixations towards tutors, and other studies have shown that treatment staff have received threats to personal safety. Fifty-one per cent of the sample studied by Jackson *et al.* (1997, cited in Shelby *et al.* 2001) reported verbal or physical assaults by clients and 84 per cent of the women questioned by Ellerby (1997, cited in Shelby *et al.* 2001) stated that their sex offender clients had violated their personal boundaries.

Lea *et al.* (1999) noted that training and experience played an important role in professionals' ability to work with sex offenders. Interestingly, they noted that separating the offender from the act, which is the approach encouraged by Marshall and Pithers (discussed earlier in this chapter), enabled professionals to work with offenders without the intrusion of their feelings about the sex offences committed. This, in turn, seemed to engender a personal resolve about their work with sex offenders. Despite this, all the professionals interviewed by Lea and colleagues reported that the work was, at times, stressful and suggested a number of strategies to cope with this, which included taking a break from working with sex offenders, undertaking further training and developing a network of support.

Turner (1992, cited in Mann and Thornton 1998) studied 82 SOTP tutors working in 16 English and Welsh prisons and described the ways in which working on the SOTP affected tutors' personal and emotional lives. One third said that their intimate relationships had been affected by the work. Some reported that they felt that they had to protect their partners from the details of the work, while others found that they were preoccupied with programme issues to such an extent that it affected their personal relationships, and a minority reported loss of interest in sex and even sexual impotence. Two-fifths of those who had children reported negative effects on their parenting. Some felt self-conscious about their own behaviour with their children and some said that they were unable to play with children in a physical way or to bathe them, while others reported being overprotective towards their children. Some tutors had started to worry that they were 'turning into an abuser', as they were thinking about child sexual abuse so much. As discussed earlier, in tutors who had been abused, unresolved issues from that experience came to the fore as a result of work on the SOTP. These findings were mirrored by Ellerby (1997, cited in Shelby *et al.* 2001) who found that treatment staff had become more concerned about family safety, more cautious in personal relationships and generally felt more unsafe. Similarly, Jackson *et al.* (1997, cited in Shelby *et al.* 2001) reported that respondents were more concerned about the safety of children and more vigilant of strangers.

Other problems were also described by the SOTP tutors studied by Turner (1992, cited in Mann and Thornton 1998). Some said that they wanted to avoid certain offenders and many reported being angry with the sex offenders, without knowing how to deal with this anger. Anxious to avoid collusion, tutors distanced themselves, both physically and psychologically, from group members. Some tutors found the progress of work slow and groupwork difficult and as a result lost self-confidence because they felt they were ineffective tutors. In contrast to the findings of Lea *et al.* (1999), Turner found that experience and training seemed to be unrelated to adverse effects. In order to deal with these problems, Mann and Thornton (1998) described how the SOTP introduced two strategies: forewarning tutors of the potential difficulties that they would experience and introducing a system of independent personal support. However, Mann and Thornton gave no indication of whether these strategies were effective.

A detailed study examining the effects of working with sex offenders was conducted by Farrenkopf (1992). The findings from this study are based on questionnaires completed by 24 health therapists who worked with criminal and sex offender clients in Oregon. Over half (54 per cent) reported a shift in their perspective, with diminished hopes and expectations for the offenders, and a more pessimistic outlook regarding the potential for client change. In addition, they became more cynical and objective, and less liberal or naïve. Two-fifths (42 per cent) experienced a hardening or dulling of emotions and some loss of humour. They felt rising anger and frustration and had become more confrontational and less tolerant of others. Frustration with the correctional system, or society, and disillusionment with an inconsistent justice system was felt by 38 per cent of the respondents. Just under a third (29 per cent) felt they had become hyper-vigilant and suspicious of others, and consequently were more protective of their families' personal safety. Some, especially female therapists, reported that they saw potential abusers everywhere, and some women even reported nightmares. Generalized high stress, exhaustion, depression or 'burnout' were reported by a quarter of the sample.

From these findings, Farrenkopf (1992) identified a number of distinct phases in working with sex offenders. The first, 'shock', is characterized by feelings of fear and vulnerability, where some practitioners are overwhelmed by the prevalence of abuse in society. This initial reaction is followed by a phase of professional 'mission', where workers have zeal for treatment effectiveness. Farrenkopf argued that this phase lasts for one to five years, during which therapists engage in emotional repression and desensitization. These repressed feelings emerge in the next phase, which is one of 'anger'. 'The therapist becomes less allied with the offender client and identifies more with the victim and society at large' (p. 221). During this phase, client guilt is assumed and self-reports are devalued. This can result in a sense of resentment and thoughts of the futility of treatment: the 'erosion amplified' stage. Therapists in this stage reported feelings of depression and exhaustion, while a quarter reported 'burnout'. One fifth of the practitioners stopped working with sex offenders. Some managed to regain work motivation: the alternative to 'erosion', 'regain motivation' stage, by adopting a more detached attitude, where expectations were lowered. Important coping strategies identified by these therapists were diversifying work areas and/or decreasing work with sex offenders. A quarter said that attitude adjustment, which would mean a realistic detachment from client outcome or client change, was essential. Finally, 38 per cent said there was a lack of support systems available to those working with this difficult group of clients.

Using the Maslach Burnout Inventory (MBI), Shelby et al. (2001) examined burnout in 86 US licensed mental health providers who treated sex offenders in custodial settings (43 per cent of the sample), in community settings (51 per cent) or in both settings (6 per cent). Compared to MBI norm data, Shelby and colleagues's sample reported higher levels of emotional exhaustion (EE), depersonalization (DP) and personal accomplishment (PA). Thus, although they reported increased negative effects of their work (EE and DP), they also had effects that were more positive in term of accomplishment (PA). In comparison with social service workers, however, the sample reported higher levels of EE and DP only. In contrast to Farrrenkopf's findings, there was no difference in burnout levels of men compared to women. Neither were there differences in the number of years of experience or the percentage of clients who were sex offenders. However, those in inpatient/prison facilities reported higher levels of EE, DP and PA than those in outpatient facilities. It is difficult to assess whether this difference was due to the more difficult nature of the clients sentenced to custody or inpatient treatment, or to factors associated with custodial/inpatient environments.

In contrast to the findings of Farrenkopf and Shelby and colleagues, Ennis and Horne (2003) found that, on average, their 59 respondents reported low levels of general psychological distress and PTSD symptomalogy, although three (5 per cent) met the DSM-IV criteria for PTSD diagnosis, and Ennis and Horne did not include a comparison group. However, Edmunds (1997, cited in Shelby et al. 2001) discovered that 29 per cent of their respondents experienced an increase in emotional, psychological and physical symptoms associated with burnout, while more than half reported increased fatigue and frustration and one third cited increased cynicism, sleep disturbances and irritability. Like Shelby and colleagues, Ennis and Horne did not find a relationship with the number of hours worked with sex offenders and therapist distress. They suggested that these findings could be explained if a number of their respondents had attained Farrenkopf's 'adaptation phase', although more research would be needed to confirm this.

In contrast to much of the previously discussed literature, Scheela (2001) found that sex offender therapists working in an outpatient Sexual Abuse Treatment (SAT) in the US described their experiences as positive and rewarding, although they did acknowledge the challenges of the work. Scheela noted that positive effects of working with sex offenders had been noted in other studies, although the focus had generally been on the negative effects. Satisfaction came from a sense of mission (Jackson *et al.* 1997), making a difference in people's lives (Freeman-Longo 1997; Jackson *et al.* 1997; Rich 1997, all cited in Scheela 2001), witnessing change and growth in sex offenders and their families (Freeman-Longo 1997; Jackson *et al.* 1997) and the development of empathy and compassion (Farrenkopf 1992; Ellerby 1997). The 17 therapists interviewed by Scheela reported that the main reasons their work was a positive experience were team support, feedback, supervision and group decision making. The SAT was also well supported by local professionals, such as attorneys, judges, social workers and other correction professionals. It is noticeable that these factors suggest that the SAT is located in a strong supportive environment, which has been noted as a protective factor against stress in many of the other studies discussed previously. This may account for the more positive accounts of these therapists, compared to other groups. The SAT therapists noted that it was important not to take offenders' problems, behaviours, choices and treatment outcomes personally and they stressed the importance of the philosophy of separating the offender from the offending, which has been discussed previously. They also described a great satisfaction from seeing offenders change and suggested that the diversity of their work may also contribute to their positive feelings.

The therapists interviewed by Scheela also noted the negative effects of sex offender work, which were similar to those outlined in other studies: negative impacts of the system, such as lack of funding and mandated reporting of previously undisclosed offences, which was seen as the 'antithesis of a therapeutic relationship'; negative societal attitudes of sex offenders; worry about offenders reoffending, of reprisals from disgruntled offenders, and of being sued; feeling desensitized and hardened to abuse or conversely, feeling more vulnerable; and being suspicious of others' intentions. Thus, it is hard to tell if the more positive findings of Scheela's research happened because of a real difference in the feelings of the SAT therapists compared to other groups of treatment providers, or whether it is Scheela's emphasis on the positive aspects of the work, compared to the negative focus of most of the other studies, that accounts for this difference, an issue which Scheela herself debates. Perhaps it is a combination of both. From Scheela's account, it seems that the SAT staff work in a particularly supportive environment, which may account for some of the differences in staff well-being and positive feelings.

Brown and Blount (1999) investigated the reported stress of a neglected group of treatment staff: treatment managers. They interviewed 21 SOTP managers (HM Prison Service England and Wales), who often have more limited face-to-face contact with sex offenders than programme tutors, but have other pressures not experienced by programme tutors. Brown and Blount found that there was considerable variability in reported stressors, but the most frequently cited, by about one-third of the sample, were members of the team not pulling their weight, tutors not appreciating the importance of supervision, a lack of clear policy guidelines, a lack of understanding from governors and a general lack of support. Four (19 per cent) treatment managers scored zero on the General Health Questionnaire but 43 per cent scored three or more, which represents a critical threshold for psychological distress. Managers reported that they had no facility to offload their concerns and were isolated.

Brown and Blount identified three clusters of factors experienced by treatment managers: those related to aspects of the job itself; those to do with relationships with others; and those linked to more personal concerns and home relationships. The number of years of experience as a treatment manager was linked to concern with a particular set of stressors. The least experienced managers (less than two years) were most concerned with personal safety and home relationship issues. They had less confidence in the support of their governors than more experienced managers, and they were worried that staff were resisting supervision. With increased years' experience (two to four years), there was a shift in concern to challenges to their role and authority, workload and taking work home; and eventually (five years or more) to concern with the strategic challenges of policy and organization. Brown and Blount argued that this shift reflects similar changes in treatment therapists, such as those described by Farrenkopf (1992). To reduce stress in treatment managers, Brown and Blount suggested mentoring new managers, better communication and support from governors, clearer policy directives, and model guidance on achieving annual accreditation.

Clearly, then, working with sex offenders is a difficult task. Yet, it is not obvious from the research, which very rarely compares sex offender therapists with other workers, whether the stresses suffered by the former group are greatly in excess of the latter. The stressors experienced by different groups of workers are patently very different, but how these differ in terms of overall stress levels is difficult to assess. Most of the studies discussed have focused more on the negative aspects of the work, despite the fact that many therapists continue to work with sex offenders for many years, which suggests that they do not find the negative effects of the work overwhelming.

Research to date has highlighted the array of problems, and to a lesser extent the positive effects of doing this work; however, there has been little focus on the personality characteristics that may make people more or less suitable for this work, or the effectiveness of the variety of strategies that can be employed to reduce the stressors. Many suggest that therapists/tutors should only undertake sex offender treatment work for a short period of time to avoid burnout, but this has implications for programme delivery, as there would be a high turnover of staff, which would mean that most tutors would have relatively little treatment experience and the demands on resources to continually train new staff would be high. Yet, there are many examples of people who have worked in this arena for many years building up a great deal of experience, expertise and respect, seemingly without the negative effects of burnout. At the same time, many do experience the work to be highly stressful and experience burnout, and/or stop working with this group of offenders. The differences between these two groups and the potential causes of such differences have yet to be investigated, despite the fact that the findings of such research could be important in the recruitment and selection of treatment staff, and in the implementation of strategies to reduce stressors and burnout.

In the past, the impact of sex offender work on staff has been overlooked, yet this is an important aspect in terms of maintaining treatment integrity (see Chapter 2). If staff find the work overwhelming, distance themselves from offenders or slip into an overly confrontational style, programme drift can occur. Furthermore, the delivery of the programme may be affected by high levels of staff illness or staff turnover. The increased focus on treatment integrity through accreditation and licensing systems has placed more emphasis on issues related to treatment staff, yet there is a lack of knowledge about how to manage these issues. Research has suggested a number of strategies that can be employed to reduce the impact of the negative aspects of the work, with the most important seeming to be the creation of a supportive network and work environment. However, these findings are based solely on the self-reports of staff, and there are no studies comparing staff doing similar work in environments with different protective factors, or studies evaluating the protective strategies that staff have identified. If treatment integrity is to be maintained, and the well-being of staff given greater consideration, more research is needed into these issues.

Sex offender treatment staff frequently report that it is helpful to differentiate the offender from the offence and fortunately, this is the recommended therapeutic approach. As will be seen in later chapters, the impact of staff on programme effectiveness has largely been overlooked, despite the fact that therapeutic alliance is considered a key issue in other areas of therapy and clinical intervention. Research now suggests that a non-confrontational approach is the most effective therapeutic style, but more investigation into the impact of staff and their therapeutic style on programme effectiveness is required.

Although, 'treatment' is the word most frequently used to describe cognitive-behavioural sex offender programmes, it does not describe the process accurately, as offenders have to take responsibility for their behaviour and subsequent behaviour change. In this context, treatment is not something that is done to offenders, it is something that offenders actively take part in. Thus, whether 'treatment' is officially enforced or not, it is effectively voluntary, as offenders who choose not to participate fully in the programme and the act of change will demonstrate no treatment effect. Perhaps because of the perception of 'treatment' as a passive process that absolves an offender from guilt, the media and public often suggest that sex offender treatment is a 'soft option', yet offenders who fully engage in the treatment process find it difficult, emotional and stressful. This is because they are required to be open and honest about all their behaviours including their offending, their thoughts, sexual fantasies, life history including their own abuse, fears, shortcomings and progress in their attempt to change. The experiences of offenders and the impact this has on the effectiveness of treatment is another area that has been neglected by researchers, although a greater understanding of what is expected of offenders can be obtained from the next chapter, which describes the range of treatment activities and treatment targets that are included in most cognitive-behavioural programmes.

Chapter 6

Cognitive-behavioural sex offender treatment goals

The cognitive-behavioural approach to sex offender treatment developed out of the realization that sex offending results from an interaction of socioeconomic, cognitive, behavioural, and emotional variables. Consequently, programs have become multidimensional and have looked at a number of components.

(Valliant and Antonowicz 1992: 222)

This approach assumes that offenders are shaped by their environment, and have learned certain cognitive skills, or have developed inappropriate ways of behaving (Vennard *et al.* 1997). McGuire (1996, cited in Vennard *et al.* 1997) stresses, however, that this approach does not attribute the causes of offending solely to individual or psychological factors. It also takes account of sociological explanations of criminal activity, such as the way social conditions affect individual development. As Hudson *et al.* (1995: 69) pointed out:

From a cognitive-behavioural perspective, the problems sex offenders present can be addressed by changing the offender's attitudes and thinking, and by teaching him skills that will reduce his offence proclivities and enable him to satisfy his needs in more pro-social ways.

Marshall (1992) stated that the emphasis of this approach lies in targeting five problem areas. These are: (1) cognitive factors, i.e. dealing with the offender's denial and minimization, while also focusing on the development of empathy, remorse and non-deviant attitudes; (2) sexual issues, i.e. decreasing deviant arousal while increasing appropriate arousal; (3)

social functioning, which involves developing skills to initiate and maintain appropriate relationships and increasing self-confidence, self-esteem, communication skills and assertiveness; (4) life management, which involves developing leisure activities and work skills; and (5) relapse prevention, which helps to integrate what offenders have learnt and apply it to real life, including also the development of strategies for dealing with difficult situations and deviant thoughts or fantasies. Marques, Nelson *et al.* (1994: 578), however, provided the following five treatment objectives for their sex offender programme:

> (a) an increased sense of personal responsibility and decreased use of justifications for sexual deviance; (b) a less deviant pattern of sexual arousal; (c) an understanding of and ability to apply the basic concepts and techniques of the RP [Relapse Prevention] model; (d) an ability to identify high-risk situations; and (e) improve skills in coping with these high-risk situations.

From a US survey of 755 adult and 745 juvenile treatment programmes provided in 1992, McPherson *et al.* (1994) discovered that 80 per cent of the programmes addressed the following areas: victim empathy; anger management; sex education; communication; cognitive distortions; assertiveness training; personal victimization/trauma; the relapse cycle; and relapse prevention. In addition, over two-thirds also incorporated victim apologies, impulse control, values clarification, positive pro-social sexuality, sex-role stereotyping, journal keeping, relaxation techniques and stress management. Most included elements that train offenders to accept responsibility for their illegal behaviour and to reduce exposure to situations where they are at risk of reoffending. Schwartz (1992) found that most specialized programmes in Washington state focused on a number of specific goals: helping the offender overcome denial and take responsibility for his/her behaviour; developing empathy for others; identifying and treating deviant sexual arousal; identifying social deficits and inadequate coping skills; challenging cognitive distortions that may perpetuate acting out; and developing a comprehensive relapse-prevention plan.

Beckett (1994) found that most UK programmes focused on four main areas: altering patterns of deviant arousal; correcting distorted thinking; increasing social competence; and educating offenders about the effects of sexual abuse and theories of offending cycles. Similarly, most programmes provided by the Probation Service of England and Wales contained the common elements of controlling sexual arousal; reducing denial; enhancing victim empathy; and improving family relationships (Proctor 1996). HM Inspectorate of Probation (1998) found the programmes they examined commonly comprised the following topics:

identifying the offence cycle; challenging distorted thinking; increasing willingness to accept responsibility for behaviour; developing victim awareness and empathy; and training in social skills and relapse prevention.

Most programmes use a variety of methods to achieve their treatment goals. A pool of techniques is common to this approach, although each programme may differ in the combination of techniques used and the emphasis that is placed on each of these. Beckett *et al.* (1994) stated that common techniques that are employed (in UK group programmes) include: group discussion and brainstorming; small group or pair work that is eventually fed back to the whole group; role-play exercises; groupwork that focuses on a particular individual, referred to as 'being in the hot seat'; work based on videos or written material; and homework assignments. In addition, behavioural techniques and drama therapy may be used. Calder (1999) and Carich and Calder (2003) provide detailed examples of cognitive-behavioural sex offender treatment techniques and exercises.

As can be seen from these examples, and the treatment programmes outlined in Chapter 3, programmes display diversity in their treatment goals; however, they also show a great deal of overlap and similarity. Most programmes tend to have the same core elements, although there may be great variety in the way in which this content is delivered to the offenders. These core programme elements will be described later and the empirical support for them considered. Treatment targets can be grouped into three broad categories: those that are offence-specific (i.e. more directly linked to sexual offending); those that are not offence-specific (i.e. related to feelings, thoughts and skills that may have an impact on offending or the ability to resist offending) and relapse prevention. It is not possible here to describe all treatment components in detail, particularly the range of non-offence-specific treatment targets, and so most attention has been focused on the elements that are included in the majority of programmes, and which are often given the most attention in these programmes. Offence-specific targets of denial and minimization, cognitive distortions/restructuring, victim empathy and sexual arousal/fantasy are considered first, followed by non-offence-specific targets and finally, relapse prevention.

Offence-specific treatment goals

Denial and minimization

Sex offenders show numerous and subtle forms of denial (Langevin *et al.* 1988). In addition, offenders also frequently minimize their crimes, often even after denial has been overcome (Marshall 1994). Minimization reduces perceived culpability for behaviour(s). Barbaree (1991) distinguished three forms of minimization: minimization of harm to the victim; minimization of the extent of previous offences; and minimization of responsibility for the offence.

In a paradoxical sense, denial (and minimization) is positive as it shows that the offender has an internal view that he or she did wrong, or at least that he/she is aware of the cultural disapproval for his/her actions (Sheath 1990). Certainly, denial is understandable given the consequences of admittance and the fact that all stages of the criminal justice system encourage it (Gocke 1991; Perkins 1991).

> From an adaptational model, the sex offender is attempting to cope
> with a highly adversarial setting with far reaching consequences for
> him/her. Non-admission of anomalous behaviour is understandable
> in light of these consequences.
>
> (Rogers and Dickey 1991: 58)

Hanson *et al.* (1991) argued that sex offenders employ two strategies to avoid negative sanctions: first, they deny they committed the offence(s) (or only admit to part of their crimes); and second, they provide rationales to excuse their behaviour. Usually, Hanson and colleagues claimed, they use both strategies.

Denial is a complex, multidimensional phenomenon (Grubin and Gunn 1990; Haywood *et al.* 1994). Salter (1988) suggested that denial changes over time along a continuum; however, Grubin and Gunn (1990) and Gocke (1991) argued that denial is more complex than this. Grubin and Gunn pointed out that offenders might deny some aspects of their behaviour, while freely admitting to others. Gocke highlighted the fact that denial does not change in a 'uni-directory trajectory', as it fulfils a functional role, and consequently can change dramatically in form and content across time, location and context.

Hudson *et al.* (1995) believed that denial and minimization functioned at least in some part to protect offenders from self-blame and the resulting low self-esteem, but Nugent and Kroner (1996) challenged the view that denial is a self-protective strategy. Instead, they described an ingrained and pervasive response that is not related to whether or not offenders admit their offence. This implied that child molesters might be largely unaware of the presence of denial, which suggested that denial would be resistant to treatment. Barbaree (1991), Marshall (1994) and O'Donohue and Letourneau (1993), however, have all shown significant reductions in denial and minimization following treatment programmes targeted solely at reducing these behaviours. Furthermore, O'Donohue and Letourneau (1993) showed that offenders reported that the fear of the consequences of disclosure, especially from loved ones, was the major reason they were in denial, which suggests a conscious rather than unconscious process.

Rogers and Dickey (1991: 58) suggested that 'our hopes for relatively complete self disclosure of sexual deviations may well be unrealistic'. This view is supported by the findings of Snell *et al.* (1989) who studied university students' willingness to disclose sexual behaviours, fantasies and attitudes to therapists and their intimate partners. These students exhibited considerable variability in the material they were willing to disclose and few, if any, shared all their experiences. Furthermore, Anderson and Boffitt (1988) studied healthy sexually active women and found considerable variation in their self-reports over a four-month period, despite the use of a standardized measure. 'If the adult population in general is not forthcoming or consistent in reporting their sexual fantasies and experiences, how can we expect honest and complete disclosure from sex offenders?' (Rogers and Dickey 1991: 58). Reduction of both denial and minimization, however, is a primary target for treatment (Beckett *et al.* 1994). Early programmes tended to refer to working on denial and minimization as a separate component of treatment that was distinct from elements of the programme addressing cognitions distortions, but later developments (and consequently many later treatment descriptions) subsumed denial within a broader goal/ component of cognitive restructuring. It has been claimed that reducing denial is an important prerequisite for change, as offenders have to admit their behaviour and take full responsibility for their crimes. 'Until denial and minimization are overcome, it is difficult, if not impossible, to proceed with other aspects of treatment' (Marshall and Eccles 1996: 298).

In support of this view, some have shown that continued denial (and extensive minimization) is prognostic of poor treatment outcome (Marshall and Barbaree 1988; Simkins *et al.* 1989; Barbaree 1991). However, in contradiction to these early findings, Maletzky (1993) did not find any differences in the long-term outcome of treated deniers versus treated admitters and Beckett *et al.* (1994) found that reducing denial and minimization did not necessarily equate with changes in other treatment targets. Moreover, Hanson and Bussiere (1998) found, in a meta-analysis of sex offender recidivism studies, that, in both treated and untreated offenders, denial or admission did not predict reoffending. Hanson (2003) points out that there is some evidence to show that attitudes that are tolerant of sexual offending are related to recidivism (Hanson and Harris 2000; Hudson *et al.* 2002). Hence, he reasons that, as there is a limited link between denial and recidivism, 'excusing one's own behaviour is less problematic than believing that it is okay for others to do the same thing' (Hanson 2003: 19).

Thus, there seems to be some debate regarding the link between denial and minimization with recidivism. Beech and Fisher (2002) argue that equating denial with risk is a logical fallacy. They cite evidence that many high-risk offenders, such as fixated paedophiles, are quite open about their offending (i.e. have low denial and minimization), in contrast to incest offenders, who are low-risk offenders but have higher levels of denial (Fisher, Beech *et al.* 1998). Furthermore, they refer to the work of Lund (2000) who questioned the findings of Hanson and Bussière (1998). Lund pointed out that in the studies reviewed by Hanson and Bussiere, the definition of denial was unclear, deniers were often excluded from treatment and it was unclear if deniers stayed in treatment for long. Thus, Lund suggested that as failure to complete treatment is related to risk, and denial is linked to failure to complete treatment, then denial must be associated with risk. This view seems to be supported by the findings of Hanson and Harris (2000) who showed that denial was a dynamic risk factor. Given these latest findings, Beech and Fisher argued that denial should be addressed at the start of treatment, as it is difficult to work on other aspects of offending if denial is maintained. Furthermore, they claimed that admitting details of the offence(s) allows offenders to take responsibility for their behaviour and encourages change.

The presence and degree of denial and minimization has long been considered a significant factor in offenders' 'treatability' (Marshall and Barbaree 1988; Barbaree 1991). Consequently, offenders who have high levels of denial and minimization are routinely excluded from treatment (see Chapter 3), as it is believed that these offenders will inhibit the progress of the rest of the treatment group. However, Hudson *et al.* (1995) argued that this was irresponsible, since deniers are a higher risk group of offenders compared to admitters who fail to receive treatment (Marshall and Eccles 1991). Furthermore, they stated that deniers attending their programme had profited from being in a group with offenders who admitted their offences. Offenders who persisted in their denial following the cognitive restructuring component of the programme (Kia Mamara, New Zealand), however, would be asked to leave. The success of programmes focusing on denial and minimization suggest that exclusion on the basis of denial is misguided, although it might be sensible for some offenders to attend an introductory component dealing with this issue, prior to attendance at the full programme. Such programmes are described by Brake and Shannon (1997) and Schlank and Shaw (1996).

One of the key ways denial and minimization are addressed in treatment is described by Marshall and Eccles (1996). In brief, offenders are asked to describe their offence(s) in detail. While they are doing this, other offenders in the treatment group challenge the offenders' account, for example by asking for clarity when an offender has been vague in his or her description, or pointing out minimizations.

Offenders are encouraged to do this in a firm but supportive manner rather than in an aggressive confrontational way. Furthermore, offenders use their own experiences as the basis for these challenges. Marshall and Eccles explained that in order for staff to facilitate challenge and avoid confrontation, they obtained accounts of the offence that were independent of the offender, e.g. a victim statement, so that they could evaluate the accuracy of the offenders' account and frame challenges to the offender in an appropriate way. Offenders repeat their accounts with further challenges until their account is acceptable to the group.

Despite attempts to change levels of denial and minimization, some offenders refuse to admit their offences. Marshal and Serran (2000) explain why these offenders present a problem: in Canadian penitentiaries they cannot be moved to lower security establishments and they cannot be granted parole. So they 'clog up the system, only to be eventually released untreated when they have served their full sentences and are under no jurisdictional control' (p. 212). Marshall and Serran describe how Thornton pointed out that some research had shown no link between denial and poor treatment outcome (discussed previously) and so, he suggested that deniers be offered treatment addressing their presumed sexual offending, but without the need for them to admit their offence(s) (for a description of this programme, see Marshall, Thornton et al. 2001). Consequently, Marshall (1998, cited in Marshall and Serran 2000) implemented a programme that provided all the usual treatment components, but omitted those focusing on denial. The findings of this initiative are yet to be published, although the programme was being evaluated; however, Beech and Fisher (2002) report that a programme for deniers run by HM Prison Service was discontinued due to its lack of success (Mann, personal communication, cited in Beech and Fisher 2002).

This issue highlights the importance of evaluating all the individual targets and components of treatment: an endeavour that has been neglected to date. Clearly more work is needed on denial: much recent work has focused on the cognitions of sex offenders (see the next section), but not specifically on the issue of denial. Consequently, offenders with high levels of denial have tended to be overlooked and excluded from treatment; yet, if these offenders do have a high risk of reoffending, more work is needed to reduce this risk, particularly if these offenders are eventually to be released back into the community.

Cognitive distortions/cognitive restructuring

Both feminist and cognitive-behavioural theorists have argued that attitudes and beliefs contribute to sexual offending (Hanson et al. 1991), although they disagree on the exact role of these attitudes. Feminists suggest that sexual violence perpetrated against women and children is the result of offenders' strong beliefs in the cultural values of society that condone male sexually coercive behaviour (see Herman 1988; Scully 1990). Many cognitive-behavioural researchers, however, believe that child molesters develop attitudes that enable them to cope with, and neutralize, the conflict between their offending behaviour and societal norms and values (see Abel *et al.* 1984, 1989). Thus, Abel and his colleagues argued that these attitudes are a result of, rather than the cause of, sexual offending. According to this view, offenders adjust their internal standards to allow them to continue a personally pleasurable activity. These views are rather simplistic in nature and subsequent theoretical developments, which are discussed later, present a more complex picture that incorporates elements of both these arguments. Yet, despite the simplicity of these early views, they were important in highlighting the importance of cognitions in the development and maintenance of sexual offending.

The attitudes and beliefs that support offenders' behaviour are often referred to as cognitive distortions:

> Learned assumptions, sets of beliefs, and self-statements about deviant sexual behaviours such as child molestation and rape which serve to deny, justify, minimize, and rationalize an offender's actions.
>
> (Calder 1999: 122)

Common cognitive distortions in sexual offenders who offend against children include ideas: that children want sexual contact with adults, that children consent to such contact, that children are under no pressure to have sex with an adult, that sexual contact between children and adults is not harmful, that children behave in a sexually seductive manner towards adults, and that adult men are entitled to satisfy their sexual needs no matter what the cost to others (Calder 1999). A similar range of cognitive distortions can be found in offenders who offend against adults and include ideas: of sexual entitlement; of the uncontrollability of sexual arousal/behaviour; that women mean yes when they say no; that women want to be raped or enjoy being raped; that rape does not cause harm; and that victims 'ask', or deserve, to be raped (see Burt 1980, 1998; Burt and Albin 1981)

Cognitive distortions (and denial and minimization) are not exclusive to sex offenders. Most of us display cognitive distortions, or thinking errors, to defend ourselves or push our point of view; however, when these distortions continue or become extreme they may inhibit our ability to function in a healthy manner (Calder 1999). These thinking errors are closely related to work on denial and minimization, and in a similar manner, treatment programmes aim to highlight offenders' cognitive distortions and correct these thought processes.

> This study demonstrates that child molesters do report beliefs and attitudes that are dramatically different from those of non-child molesters, suggesting that the normalization of these faulty cognitions may be an integral part of the successful treatment of child molesters. . . . Successful treatment should expose these cognitions and help the molester understand their illogical nature. Without such beliefs, child molesters would find it more difficult to justify their child molestation behaviour, with a resultant decrease in their child molestation.
>
> (Abel *et al.* 1989: 147)

Earlier studies typically focused on two aspects of cognition: beliefs and attitudes, with researchers identifying only the content of cognitive distortions. For example, in a vignette study describing sexual contact between an adult and a child, Stermac and Segal (1989) found that child molesters' perceptions about the vignettes differed from those of other (non-abuser) respondents. Child abusers perceived more benefits to the child resulting from the sexual contact, and ascribed greater complicity to the child and less responsibility to the adult. Stermac and Segal concluded that sex offenders interpret sexual information in maladaptive ways, which contributes to their offending. Murphy (1990) suggested that cognitive distortions were used to deny, minimize and/or rationalize behaviour and Abel *et al.* (1984) proposed that child abusers developed cognitions and beliefs that supported their sexual activities with children. However, Ward *et al.* (1997) criticized these conclusions as they assumed that cognitive distortions occurred in the same way in every offender. They argued further that previous work had focused on developing psychometrically robust methods that centred on the measurement and content of relevant cognitions.

The use of psychometric scales is a contentious issue, as many see them as being transparent (i.e. it is easy for an offender to identify 'desirable' responses from those that more accurately reflect what the offender believes) and hence, the findings from these scales are open to misrepresentation (Blumenthal *et al.* 1999). Tierney and McCabe (2001), who investigated the psychometric properties of a number of psychometric tests measuring cognitive distortions and empathy, found that many of these scales had poor psychometric properties. Furthermore, in a review of scales measuring cognitive distortions, Vanhouche and Vertommen (1999) revealed that only one, the Child Molest Scale, was able to discriminate between a group not promised anonymity and a group that was. Thus, the majority of the scales were subject to social desirability bias.

It has also been pointed out that psychometric measures of cognitive distortions have focused on the content of these cognitions rather than the *processes* that underlie the initiation, maintenance and justification of sexual offending (Ward *et al.* 1998). Ward and colleagues proposed that self-report scales are relatively crude measures of deviant beliefs and attitudes, as they rely on investigating static thoughts, rather than discursive strategies. They argued further that emotions, cognitions and behaviours change throughout the process of offending and can be activated or inhibited in the course of different stages of the offence cycle. Importantly, Ward *et al.* stated that there has been a 'failure in most research to distinguish between attitudes that emerge as a consequence of sexual offending and those that predispose men to offend' (p. 409). Explaining the complexity of sex offenders' cognitions, Ward *et al.* (1997) identified different types of cognitive variables such as cognitive structures (beliefs, schemata), cognitive operations (biased information processing) and cognitive products (self-statements, attributions) and considered maladaptive beliefs and distorted thinking as fundamental to cognitive distortions.

The complex nature of cognitions and cognitive distortions has been revealed by the use of qualitative methods, such as Grounded Theory (Ward *et al.* 1998) and Discourse Analysis (Auburn and Lea 2003). The results of such analyses have provided an important contribution to theory development in this area. While traditional explanations have focused on *why* sex offenders employ distorted thinking patterns to justify and deny their behaviours, qualitative research has concentrated on *how* language is represented and constructed in relation to offenders' feelings, thoughts and place in society. It is believed that examining *what* is said might tell us more about what these individuals are doing with their words in terms of justifying and denying, rather than just explaining the cognitive structures that these words represent. Thus, cognitive distortions are conceptualized as something offenders *do*, rather than being something offenders *have* (Auburn and Lea 2003). Ward *et al.* (1997) claimed that much attention in the past has focused on post-offence cognitions and called for increased awareness of the temporal component of sexual offending, where understanding the cognitive processes at all stages of the offence cycle is necessary. Consequently, Ward (2000) argued that sexual offenders' cognitive distortions are unlikely to stem from unrelated independent beliefs but emerge from 'underlying causal theories about the nature of their victims' (p. 492).

Ward (2000) suggests that the content of causal theories, which he terms 'implicit theories' from the use of this idea in developmental, cognitive and personality psychology, are likely to be maladaptive and constructed during the child abusers' early development, possibly as a result of sexual abuse or exposure to inappropriate behaviour. Ward explained that these implicit theories are similar to scientific theories, in that they are used to explain, predict and interpret interpersonal situations. Ward proposes that from an early age knowledge is organized into theories that are applied to explain empirical regularities (e.g. other people's actions) and to make predictions about the world. These predictions usually take the form of expectations and guide the processing of information. Ward explains that sexual offenders' implicit theories regarding their victims are structured around two core sets of mental constructs: beliefs and desires, which form the framework from which behaviour is interpreted. For example, the claim that 'children often initiate sex and know what they want' suggests that an offender's implicit theory conceptualizes children as having specific desires, wants and preferences. Within this view, a child's everyday behaviour, such as sitting on an offender's knee, could be interpreted as revealing sexual preferences and may generate distorted statements such as 'the child sought sex out; the child wanted sex'. Thus, this implicit theory can lead to the interpretation of everyday behaviour as revealing sexual preference and intent (Ward and Keenan 1999).

Ward and Keenan (1999) argued that offenders develop maladaptive implicit theories about children's sexuality that guide the processing of information or 'evidence'. Consequently, the friendly behaviour of a child (evidence) is possibly interpreted by the offender in sexual terms. Perhaps more importantly, Ward and Keenan pointed out that it takes consistent contradictory evidence for a theory to be replaced. Instead, anomalous observations such as 'she may not want sex on this occasion, but usually when she is behaving in this way, she does' are accounted for by a minor adjustment within the offender's implicit theory. A replacement theory will only be applied if the counterevidence outweighs the offender's existing hypothesis. The idea within these implicit theories is that cognitive distortions in child sex offenders may constitute pre-existing assumptions and beliefs rather than simply post-offence rationalizations.

The main advantage of this model is that cognitive distortions are construed as cognitive processes that are used by offenders to apply theories to situations and evaluate their fit with the evidence (the child's behaviour). Evidence that does not 'fit' the theory's basic assumptions is either rejected or interpreted in accordance with the offender's core assumptions. In addition, the implicit theory framework could be used to explain the various typologies of child sexual abusers by differentiating between the diverse contents of their beliefs. For example, one abuser's implicit theory might emphasize the child's need in sexual terms, while another might see a child as a source of intimacy. Similarly, a child abuser might theoretically conceive a child as seductive and desiring sexual contact, whereas another might assume he is entitled to have sex with whoever he wants. Thus, a child abuser will use his or her knowledge in relation to particular situations and victims and this specific theory will facilitate his/her understanding of not only his/her victims' behaviour but will guide his/her planning in relation to future actions.

As it is believed that implicit theories emerge from sexual offenders' early experiences, it is logical to assume that they could derive from differential learning experiences. For example, offenders who have been sexually abused as a child might, despite the fact that the abuse was unpleasant, develop an assumption that it is normal for adults and children to engage in sexual activity. Drake *et al.* (2001: 29) suggested that 'this implicit theory might remain active because the abuse is often kept secret, hence the belief that sexual behaviour is normal for young children is neither tested nor discarded'. Furthermore, child abusers may lack a satisfactory alternative theory perhaps because they are socially isolated or have social skills deficits, which might persuade them to stick with the familiar. Consequently, these maladaptive implicit theories cause the offender to evaluate the world in an offence supportive manner. Thus, the implicit theory perspective of cognitive distortions suggests that sexual offending is a dynamic phenomenon in which an offender's maladaptive thoughts can be elicited at different points in time and within different contexts.

Ward and Keenan (1999) identified five implicit theories underpinning child molesters' cognitive distortions: children as sexual objects; entitlement; dangerous world; uncontrollable; and nature of harm. Offenders holding the 'children as sexual objects' theory believe that children are primarily motivated by pleasure or are sexual beings. Thus, children are seen as possessing sexual needs, desires and preferences and are able to develop plans to achieve these goals. Ward and Keenan speculate that this theory is developed from early sexual experiences or abuse. The 'entitlement' theory encompasses the idea that some people are superior to others and hence, they have the right to impose their desires on others, i.e. those who are less important. This theory may develop from early rejection and the subsequent threat to self-esteem, such that entitlement is a way of compensating for this distress, or results in an elevated sense of self-importance. Those holding the 'dangerous world' theory believe that the world is a dangerous place and that others are inherently abusive and rejecting. Accordingly, they may feel unable to retaliate against adults and that children are more likely to understand them. It is postulated that this theory results from early and continued physical or emotional abuse, where the individual learns to take measures to avoid harm or to satisfy needs and desires. The 'uncontrollable' theory has the core belief that sexual preferences and personality are unchangeable and that some, namely the offender themselves, have no control over their expression, which is analogous to having an external locus of control. Ward and Keenan argue that this theory develops from experience of feeling out of control in relation to sexual or emotional drives. Those holding the final theory, 'nature of harm', believe that there are degrees of harm that can be inflicted on other people and that sexual activity alone is unlikely to hurt another person. Thus, they believe that if more harm could have been inflicted, i.e. through the use of physical violence, they see themselves as having regard for the victim's well-being. This is linked with a belief that sexual activity is beneficial. Ward and Keenan argue that this theory is likely to be used in conjunction with other theories.

Drake *et al.* (2001) argue that treatment programmes have tended to regard cognitive distortions as isolated, independent variables that should be detected and challenged (Murphy 1990; Langton and Marshall 2000). Thus, treatment programmes challenge cognitive distortions in much the same way as they do denial and minimization, although they may use a framework of the offenders' cycle (or chain) of offending (which the offender is encouraged and helped to identify) to guide this process (for description of more traditional treatment approaches see Calder 1999; Marshall and Eccles 1996; Carich and Calder 2003). Drake and colleagues (2001), however, argue that within this approach, cognitive distortions are not understood as being linked to more general theories of behaviour, are seen as only being used to support offending behaviour (rather than also being used to explain both offending and non-offending behaviour), and are explained as post-offence rationalizations. Drake and colleagues propose that if these assumptions are used in treatment and distortions are addressed individually with no explanation of how similar beliefs are related to one another, offenders will not grasp the purpose and structure of cognitive restructuring. Drake *et al.* believe that if cognitive distortions are presented as arising from a limited set of underlying beliefs (i.e. the five implicit theories outlined previously), then offenders can understand the wider implication of their thinking errors. Consequently, these authors have developed a component on cognitive restructuring to reflect their views and describe this approach.

Drake *et al.* describe that the first treatment step is to identify the offence chain (see the relapse-prevention section and Ward, Louden *et al.* 1995; Ward and Hudson 1998b; Hudson *et al.* 1999). Then similarities between the wide range of cognitive distortions reported during the offence process are identified; hence, they are reframed as implicit theories (examples of how each of the five implicit theories can be reframed and elaborated are provided by Drake *et al.* (2001)). The third step involves offenders identifying specific experiences that gave rise to their interpretations and the irrational and erroneous aspects of these interpretations. The group discusses how these cognitions predispose individuals to offend and how they are maintained to facilitate offending. Offenders are then assisted in developing interpretations that are more realistic and in adapting these to everyday situations. A second feature of this stage, which at the time of writing Drake and colleagues state was only applicable to some cognitive distortions, is to induce an emotional response in offenders that is incompatible with their cognitive distortions. This, the authors argue, functions to motivate offenders to rapidly develop cognitions that are more realistic. The final stage is to review this module, by providing offenders with an opportunity to say how they have changed, which allows the treatment staff to assess the usefulness of the strategies outlined.

Although (as was shown earlier), there has been extensive work in recent years enhancing our understanding of cognitive distortions, these theories have yet to be extensively empirically validated. In addition, there has been little work evaluating the cognitive distortion/restructuring component of treatment. Consequently, it is not possible to ascertain how effective cognitive restructuring is at changing offenders' cognitions, or how such changes are linked to recidivism. Nor is it currently possible to assess whether the treatment described by Drake et al. (2001) is more effective than more traditional methods. Such work is clearly needed to ensure that this key aspect of treatment is effective, as it is generally believed. Finally, it should also be noted that much of the work discussed here is related to sex offenders who offend against children, and the cognitions or implicit theories of offenders who offend against adults have so far been neglected. Some of the implicit theories identified by Ward and Keenan could possibly be applied to non-child abusers (e.g. entitlement); however, the majority contain theories about children, which clearly cannot be generalized to all offenders.

As will be noted in Chapter 9, treatment with offenders who offend against adults has dubious efficacy in comparison with offenders who offend against children and this looks set to continue if research into offenders' cognitions ignores the former group of offenders. The likely difference between the implicit theories for different groups of offenders (assuming this the most helpful way of explaining and treating offenders' cognitions) also raises doubt about the efficacy of treating all types of offenders in a single group programme, as is the current treatment practice. Perhaps separately developed programmes for different groups of offenders would prove to be a more effective method of treatment. The bias that has tended to exist in treatment theory and research towards sex offenders who offend against children could explain why treatment has tended to be less successful with other groups of offenders.

Victim empathy

Abel and his colleagues were the first to report using empathy enhancement as a treatment component (Murphy *et al.* 1980), yet within a few years, most descriptions of treatment programmes had empathy training components (see Marshall 1996a). Sex offenders frequently fail to appreciate the damage they have inflicted on their victims and thus they often demonstrate little remorse for their crimes (Beckett *et al.* 1994). Perpetrators often blame victims for the offence and interpret the victim's behaviour as provocative (Beckett *et al.* 1994). Consequently, most practitioners believe that it is important to instil in offenders an understanding of the harm they have caused their victim(s) (Marshall and Eccles 1996), based on the premise that low levels of empathy contribute to offending by disinhibiting sexual arousal. This is despite the fact that there is only limited and confusing evidence to suggest that sex offenders are pervasively unempathic (Marshall *et al.* 1994). 'No one has yet offered any evidence in support of these ideas, perhaps because they appear to be self-evident truths' (Marshall and Eccles, 1996: 302). Research on empathy has been complicated by a lack of agreement regarding the definition of this construct.

> Despite the wide spread recognition of empathy as an important human characteristic, there has been little consensus among theorists on its formal definition. Most of the disagreement appears to be on whether or not empathy involves actual vicarious experience of another's emotions or simply the willingness and ability to put oneself in another's place (role taking).
>
> (Chlopan *et al.* 1985: 635)

Mehrabian and Epstein (1972) argued that there is a critical difference between these two perspectives (the cognitive role-taking process and empathic emotional responsiveness): the former is the recognition of another's feelings whereas the latter includes the sharing of these feelings. However:

> Recent years have seen increased movement toward an integration of these two hitherto separate research traditions. In fact, it is a growing belief among empathy theorists and researchers that our understanding of empathy can improve only with the explicit recognition that there are both affective and cognitive components to the empathic response.
>
> (Davis 1983: 113)

Marshall *et al.* (1994) have suggested a four component model of empathy: (1) recognition of another person's emotional state; (2) an ability to perceive the world from that person's point of view; (3) an ability to replicate the emotional state of the other person; and (4) a change in behaviour towards the other person. However, Pithers (1999) has criticized this model. He argued that the model is not able to explain a bystander's response to an endangered person who is unconscious, as there the unconscious person would have no emotional response to recognize or replicate. Thus, Pithers argued that the bystander would be left to feel nothing and would thus do nothing for the person in danger. Furthermore, he argued that recognizing empathy is an inadequate treatment goal if the offender recognizes empathy only once he or she has committed an offence. Hence, offenders must be taught to predict an empathic response before the response has happened, if empathy training is to be able to inhibit future offending. Accordingly, Pithers's (1994: 565) preferred definition of empathy is: 'the capacity to cognitively perceive another's perspective, to recognize affective arousal within oneself, and to base compassionate behavioral responses on the motivations induced by these percepts.' Hudson et al. (1993) discovered that sex offenders were deficient in recognizing emotions in others, especially anger, disgust, surprise and fear. Thus, they argued that treatment should include elements that enabled offenders to recognize these emotions as well as to understand the affective feelings being experienced.

In conjunction with this shift to a more complex understanding of empathy, the measurement of this construct has shifted from general measures to context-specific measures. For example, the Child Molester Empathy Measure (CHEM) developed by Fernandez et al. (1999) assesses empathy in three contexts: towards a child who was in a motor vehicle accident and was disfigured; towards a child who had been sexually molested by an unknown assailant over a period of time; and towards the offender's own victim(s). However, the same concerns about the use of psychometric tests to measure cognitive distortions also apply to the measurement of empathy. Webster (2000, cited in Webster et al. 2004) found that sex offenders could identify the socially desirable responses from forced choice questions; however, they were unable to provide appropriate empathic justifications for their choice of responses.

Despite the fact that there has been some agreement on the complexity of the components that comprise empathy, there is still debate surrounding whether sex offenders suffer from generalized empathy deficits (see Marshall and Eccles 1996; Calder 1999). Initially, many treatment programmes focused on assessing and improving perpetrators' generalized empathy skills; that is, it was accepted that empathy is a trait that is unaffected by the situation (Marshall and Eccles 1996). However, Marshall and his colleagues have found little evidence to suggest that sex offenders have generalized empathy deficits (Marshall et al. 1993;

Marshall *et al.* 1994), but Marshall *et al.* (1994) and Fernandez *et al.* (1999) found that child molesters displayed empathy deficits towards children who have been sexually abused, and even greater deficits towards their own victim(s). Hence, Marshall and his colleagues have argued that treatment should be targeted towards enhancing empathy towards victims and the potential future victims of sexual abuse (for example, see Marshall and Eccles 1996). However, Teuma *et al.* (2003) found, using Australian samples (and using Fernandez and colleagues's CHEM), that child molesters did not differ significantly from a non-offender community sample in empathy levels for the accident victim or for the sexual abuse victim of an unknown perpetrator. Furthermore, Smallbone *et al.* (2003) found that empathy did not correlate with sexual offence convictions in a sample of Australian sex offenders; however, it did correlate with non-sexual offence convictions, particularly violent convictions (which were also correlated with higher levels of fantasy). Thus, they argued that the needs of criminally versatile and non-criminally versatile offenders should be distinguished and examined more carefully, to further develop empathy training for these two groups.

To complicate the issue further, Burke (2001), in the USA, found that 23 male sex offenders between the ages of 13 and 18 showed significantly lower empathy levels (as measured by Davis's Interpersonal Reactivity Index, a generalized measure of empathy) than 23 non-offenders of the same age. These results were supported by Farr *et al.* (2004) who investigated an English sample of 44 adolescent offenders (mean age 17.3) and 57 non-offending adolescents (between 16 and 18 years old, with a mean age of 17.4). Using the Empathy Test for Girls (adapted from Hanson's and Scott's empathy test for women), which contains eight vignettes that describe a variety of interactions between females and males, Farr *et al.* (2004) found that the adolescent sex offenders had significantly lower empathy levels that the non-offending adolescents.

The relationship between empathy and sexual offending, then, remains unclear. Moreover, Pithers (1999) has argued that several logical problems render much of the research on empathy meaningless. He pointed out that operational definitions of empathy are not consistent across studies and that measurement techniques vary. In addition, he stated that although there have been some noteworthy attempts to develop empathy measures for sex offenders, they all rely on the self-report of sex offenders, which is problematic as test items are often transparent. Finally, he argued that researchers have ignored the context and conditions under which offenders complete these self-report measures.

If it is true that sex offenders do not suffer from generalized empathy deficits, then the lack of empathy they show towards their own victim(s) is better construed under the banner of cognitive distortion. Essentially offenders deny the need to feel sympathy for their victim(s), perhaps because the offenders believe that the victim(s) initiated the sexual encounter, deserved it and/or wanted it. This view is supported by the findings of Webster and Beech (2000) who found that total scores derived from participants' 'victim letters', which were generated during treatment, correlated with psychometric measures of cognitive distortions about offenders' victims, but did not correlate with general measures of empathy. Further support was provided by Marshall *et al.* (2001) who found that the level of empathy child molesters exhibited towards their victims was significantly correlated with their level of cognitive distortions.

Hanson and Scott (1995) made an important point about empathy deficits by arguing that some offenders may be able to accurately identify suffering in others, but are indifferent to, or even attracted to this suffering, e.g. for sadistic reasons. Thus, aiming to improve these offenders' levels of empathy (using the assumption most commonly applied that increased an awareness of suffering will inhibit offending) is likely to have little impact on recidivism; in fact, it could even be argued that it might make offenders worse. For example, Rice *et al.* (1994) found that increasing the salience of suffering increased the arousal of rapists. In support of these arguments, Hanson and Scott (1995) found that offenders who used overt force in their offences (and hence, who may be indifferent or attracted to the suffering of their victims) did not show perceptive-taking deficits, compared to offenders who did not use overt force, who did show such deficits. Hanson and Scott argued that a failure to differentiate between these two types of offenders, and to differentiate and assess perspective-taking from sympathetic feelings, might account for the hitherto complex and contradictory empirical findings.

In 2003, Hanson suggested a model of empathy where uncompassionate responses are explained by an adversarial or indifferent relationship, perspective-taking deficits and inappropriate methods for coping with the perceived distress of others. Hanson (2003) argues that the most serious threat to sympathetic responding is an indifferent or adversarial relationship. He points out that although we tend to think that only deviant individuals take pleasure in the suffering of others, most of us react positively to another's suffering when the other is an enemy or adversary; for example theatre crowds cheer when the bad guys are killed and political partisans delight when their opponents are humiliated. Thus, Hanson argues that it is easy to imagine case histories in which adversarial relationships contribute to sexual offending. According to Hanson, perspective-taking deficits are likely to be important in less aggressive sexual assaults. Here, offenders may believe that friendly advances are sexual in nature and misinterpret victims' resistance.

Finally, even when the relationship is non-hostile and the suffering has been accurately perceived, Hanson argues that people do not always react with sympathy and compassion. Using this model, and the findings discussed previously, Hanson suggests that different empathy treatment is needed for different types of offenders, as increasing the salience of victim suffering is unlikely to reduce recidivism in sadistic rapists, or in offenders who are unable to cope with their own guilt.

Pithers (1999) pointed out that if offenders do have empathy deficits, these are most likely to be manifested when emotional precursors to abuse are active, e.g. because of anger, acute anxiety or profound loneliness. Yet, Pithers was unable to identify any research that examined empathy in offenders who were actively experiencing affective precursors to past instances of offending. Interestingly, a similar argument was developed by Hanson (1999) who suggested that for sex offender treatment to be effective, offenders should practise their newly learnt attitudes, beliefs, skills and techniques in conditions that more closely mirrored those under which they had committed their offence(s). These context-dependent arguments are interesting and perhaps important, although it is hard to imagine that a treatment programme would safely be able to routinely induce anger, intoxication and anxiety in its clients, let alone be allowed to do this on ethical grounds, to achieve improved treatment efficacy.

The arguments of Pithers and Hanson can be linked to the concept of cognitive deconstruction, which has been applied to sex offenders by Ward, Hudson and Marshall (1995). The concept was originally described by Baumeister (1989, 1990, 1991, cited in Ward, Hudson and Marshall 1995) and explains a state where people avoid the negative implications of self-awareness to escape from the effects of traumatic or stressful events, which may develop into an entrenched behaviour pattern. It is argued that during deconstructive states, attention narrows in focus from abstract or higher levels of awareness, for example where attention is focused on the social consequences of actions (which may well include feelings of empathy), to concrete or lower levels of awareness, for example a focus on feelings of pleasure such as sexual arousal. 'Sex is a very effective means of escaping the self; almost by definition, it is a deconstructed state in which self-awareness is low and standards for behaviour are virtually nonexistent' (Laws 1999: 296).

Ward, Hudson and Marshall (1995) used this concept and the idea that sex can be used to escape the self to link many of the treatment components discussed in this chapter (i.e. denial and minimization, cognitive distortions, affective states, intimacy and social skills deficits, empathy, and relapse-prevention concepts such as the problem of immediate gratification) to explain sexual offending; however, they also stressed that it is unlikely that all offenders will enter deconstructive states. Laws (1999: 296) argued that this theory 'is probably the most important explanatory construct to emerge in this field [sex offender treatment] in the past decade'. Yet, this theory could suggest that treatment is less likely to be effective in sex offenders who enter deconstructive states, as treatment changes learnt in 'normal' states could be eliminated when an offender enters a deconstructive state; unless through treatment an offender learns to avoid entering such a state. The theory also suggests that different types of treatment are needed for different types of offenders.

Despite the arguments of Hanson and Pithers (and Ward *et al.*), empathy treatment has tended to be delivered to all offenders who are engaged in treatment in the same way. Marshall and Eccles (1996) described how they ask offenders to describe an emotionally distressing experience they have had, other than being arrested. Offenders are encouraged to 'relive' the experience and consequently, these disclosures are emotional for both the offender describing the events and for those listening. After such descriptions, the listening offenders are asked to describe how they felt during the account and it is explained to them that this is empathy. In another component, Marshall and Eccles ask offenders to explain what they think the effects of sexual abuse are and to distinguish the immediate, post-abuse and long-term effects. When all offenders have contributed to the list of effects, this list is used as the basis of a general discussion. Then offenders are asked to describe the offence from their victim's perspective and are challenged by the group if this description is self-serving and/or contains cognitive distortions. Finally, offenders are asked to write two letters (which are not sent): one from the victim and the other a reply to this letter. Offenders read these letters to the group and are challenged by other group members until the group is satisfied with the letters' content. In a third component, treatment staff read descriptions written by survivors of abuse, or show a video of a survivor describing their abuse and its consequences. Although Marshall and Eccles stated that they do not commonly have a survivor visit the group, this technique is used by some programmes. After the account, offenders are asked to describe how they felt listening to the account and these feelings are defined as empathy by the treatment staff. Offenders are also asked what they now feel for their own victims and they are asked to explain how they would feel if a family member was sexually assaulted. Similar techniques are described by Hudson *et al.* (1995) and similar and additional techniques are described by Carich and Calder (2003).

Roys (1997) suggested that a lack of understanding of the mechanisms of empathy has resulted in a situation where 'it appears unclear exactly what it is we are asking the offender to do when we tell him that it is necessary that he develop empathy' (p. 54). Consequently, Roys argued that more research and training for practitioners and treatment providers is needed in order to provide a greater understanding of the complexities of empathy, and in particular, to develop methods that are successful at enhancing empathy in others. However, Pithers (1994) developed a programme that was effective in increasing sex offenders' empathetic skills, which encouraged:

> the current inclusion of empathy training in comprehensive treatment programs for sex offenders, although it remains to be seen whether or not these short-term changes will be associated with long-term maintenance of behavioural change and avoidance of subsequent offences (p. 570).

In the England and Wales prison programme, sex offenders reported that the empathy component of treatment, which includes role-play, has the most profound effect in getting them to understand the harm that they caused their victims (Beech *et al.* 1998). However, Beech and Fisher (2002) argue that this component has to be delivered carefully, as it would seem that it can be counterproductive if it is delivered too early in the treatment process. Beckett *et al.* (1994) found that 25 per cent of offenders in short programmes (around 50 hours) had less victim empathy. Consequently, it was hypothesized that offenders experience negative feelings about themselves early in the treatment process and do not have the capacity to cope with further negative messages. Thus, it was felt that offenders could only deal with victim empathy work when they have developed the personal resources to cope with the knowledge of the harm they have caused.

Baim *et al.* (1999) found that a psychodrama component delivered in England to nine offenders (12 started the component but three dropped out) significantly improved offenders' levels of victim empathy and reduced distortions about child sexuality; however, the small sample involved in this study raise doubt about the reliability of these findings. In terms of empathy towards their own victim(s), offenders showed improved empathy levels but there was no significant statistical difference and there was great variability among the offenders. However, offenders with the worst scores at pre-treatment showed an improvement at post-treatment, while those with good scores at pre-treatment were the ones who showed no improvement or a slight worsening in their empathy levels. There was a significant improvement between the pre- and post-treatment empathy levels for a general victim of sexual abuse. Despite these group differences, Baim and colleagues found that there was very little change in offenders who offended against adult women. Nevertheless, they reported these results as encouraging and championed the use of psychodrama in this context.

As with other treatment goals, the role that empathy plays in sex offending is not clear, and consequently the effect of empathy training on recidivism is undetermined. The reasons for this situation could be the hitherto simplistic understanding of many of these concepts and the failure to consider the links between treatment goals. For example, as discussed earlier, the link between cognitions and empathy is important, as empathy will not be felt if the offender does not see the need to feel empathic towards the victim. An offender may not think of his or her victim as a victim in need of empathy. Empathy and cognition are also linked to affective factors, such as emotion regulation and social skills, and factors that combine these issues, such as intimacy and relationships (for reviews of these issues and the links between these components see Geer *et al.* 2000; Covell and Scalora 2002). Cognitive deconstruction may also be an important factor that has an impact on the cognitions and empathy levels experienced by offenders. Thus, research and theoretical developments are producing an ever more complex picture of sexual offending that can be difficult to fully incorporate into treatment programmes. This is particularly the case when the demands of the criminal justice and health systems require a range of offenders to be treated together, often in short periods of time. Yet, many of the developments outlined earlier suggest that different empathy components (including no component at all) may be required for different offenders. Clearly more work is needed on this component of treatment to determine if work on empathy (in its current form) is effective in reducing recidivism; and further to identify whether different empathy training/work is needed for different types of offenders. The timing of such treatment to produce the maximum positive impact also needs investigation.

Sexual arousal/sexual fantasy

As discussed in Chapter 2, early theorizing regarded sexual offending as an outcome of deviant sexual arousal and thus, attempts to eliminate sexual offending focused on modifying this deviant arousal. 'Since, *prima facie*, this is rather too simplistic, it is historically interesting to note that this basic approach, in one form or another, held sway for many years . . .' (Laws 1995: 42). However, there has been much theorizing (e.g. from a feminist perspective) and the emergence of empirical evidence suggesting that there is more to sexual behaviour than sexual arousal. For example, Marshall and Eccles (1991) argued that fantasies that supported sexually deviant behaviour included expressions of power, control, aggression and a desire to humiliate. Furthermore, Marshall and Eccles (1996) argued that the role deviant sexual preferences have in initiating and maintaining deviant sexual behaviour is often exaggerated. Empirical evidence shows that many sexual offenders do not have primary arousal to deviant sexual stimuli. For example, Marshall and Eccles (1991) reported that less than 50 per cent of perpetrators who offended against children outside their families and less than 30 per cent of perpetrators who offended against children within their families showed deviant sexual arousal.

There is an assumption in such studies that arousal to certain images (e.g. to pictures of children or to depictions of aggressive and/or non-consenting sex) is 'deviant'. However, this issue is complex and there are many studies that show how 'normal', non-offending men are aroused by children and non-consenting and/or violent sexual contact. For example, Marshall and Barbaree (1993, cited in Marshall and Eccles 1996) found that only 30 per cent of a sample of rapists met the criteria for deviant arousal; yet, 26 per cent of a group of non-offenders also met this criteria. Furthermore, there is a wide range of stimuli that produce sexual arousal in both 'normal' and 'abnormal' groups. Thus, a difficulty with this issue is the lack of a clear understanding of what 'normal' sexual arousal is (for a more detailed discussion of a range of issues regarding sexual arousal and sexuality, see McConaghy 1999b); and therefore, what sort of arousal treatment therapists should try to develop in offenders.

Many have claimed that sex offenders engage in fantasies about deviant acts that form the basis of offending behaviours and are used to plan offences (see Pithers 1990; Eldridge and Wyre 1998). Some suggest that such fantasies can lead to an escalation in offence frequency and severity (Wyre 1990, cited in Howitt 1995). However, as Marshall and Serran (2000) point out, there is scare evidence to support these ideas, citing the following examples. O'Donohue et al. (1997) found that sexual offenders rarely reported deviant fantasy, although child molesters did reported significantly more fantasies involving children than comparison groups. Marshall et al. (1991) observed that 32 per cent of child molesters with female victims and 41 per cent with male victims reported fantasies of sex with children. Pithers, Beal et al. (1989) revealed that only 17 per cent of rapists had fantasized about rape during the six months before the offence. These figures in themselves tell us little, for they do not give an indication of the frequency of the fantasizing or the content. As Howitt and Cumberbatch (in press, cited by Howitt 1995) pointed out, an offender's fantasy may be different to the actual offence: a mismatch between fantasy and behaviours that is also apparent in non-offending groups (Howitt 1995).

In a related issue, the link between the use of pornography and offending is far from clear (Howitt 1995; Seto et al. 2001). Howitt (1995) argued that research has shown little strong and consistent evidence that sex offenders use pornography more than comparison groups. Howitt's research with 11 paedophiliac sex offenders who were completing assessment and treatment at a private clinic (in England) revealed a complex picture of pornography use. Howitt found no evidence that early exposure to pornography was a cause of later offending; in fact, many offenders' first exposure to pornography occurred after they had begun offending. Furthermore, the use of child pornography was rare; however, some offenders would cognitively manipulate other forms of pornography to meet their needs, or adapt non-pornographic material. There is a general assumption that use of pornography and fantasy leads to offending, but Howitt reported examples of a link in the opposite direction, where offending was used to generate sexual fantasy. Seto *et al.* (2001) concluded that there was little evidence to show that there is a direct causal link between pornography and offending, although exposure to pornography may be linked to other measures of sexual aggression, such as belief in rape myths and physical aggression. However, Seto and colleagues argued that many studies did not consider the range of interactions involved, and argued that men who showed a greater propensity to sexually aggress were more likely to show an effect from exposure to pornography, which was not found in men with no such propensity to sexually aggress. Further, Gee *et al.* (2003) argue that although pornography has an important function for many offenders it does not directly 'cause' offending. Instead, pornography may serve to disinhibit an offender and increase the likelihood of an offence. In addition, Gee *et al.* point out that pornography is just one of the many sources of information that may be used to generate fantasy.

In an interesting development to these debates, Gee *et al.* (2003) used Grounded Theory to investigate the function that sexual fantasy may serve for sex offenders. They interviewed 24 offenders convicted of a range of offences in Victoria, Australia. From these interviews, Gee and colleagues developed the Sexual Fantasy Function Model (SFFM) that revealed four key functions of fantasy. The first is *affect regulation*, where fantasy is used to regulate offenders' mood. This could be done to alleviate negative mood/affect, elevate ambivalent mood/effect, or enhance positive mood/affect. The second function, *sexual arousal*, is used by a large proportion of offenders to either induce or enhance sexual activity. *Coping* was the third function, whereby offenders used fantasy to exert actual or perceived control over internal or external threats by using distortion and/or manipulation, or used fantasy to escape the realization of their situation. The final function of fantasy is *modelling*. Here fantasy is used to relive experiences or to create new ones. Gee *et al.* contend that the SFFM is consistent with the Self-Regulation Model of Relapse (Ward and Hudson 2000) as sexual offending could result from active engagement (approach) in fantasy behaviour, or from a failure to inhibit (avoidance/passive) fantasy when it has been triggered.

Despite the fact that sex offender treatment started with attempts to modify deviant sexual arousal only (as discussed in Chapter 2), the lack of a clear link between sexual arousal and sexual offending has led some to argue that work on sexual arousal is not a necessary requirement for all offenders completing sex offender treatment (see for example Beech and Fisher 2002). This sort of work cannot be done in groups and so offering extensive work in an attempt to modify arousal has resource implications. There are also ethical implications in completing such work, as some have argued that it is unethical to show offenders sexually explicit pictures of children, or of non-consenting aggressive sexual contact, even if these pictures are then paired with negative stimuli. Consequently, as can be seen in the programme descriptions in Chapter 3, such work is not included in many programmes, or is only offered to offenders who are believed to be in need of such modification, e.g. offenders with arousal to children.

However, some programmes continue to provide such work as a key element to their programme and as such, this work is completed by all offenders, for example the Kia Marama programme in New Zealand (Hudson et al. 1995). Hudson and colleagues argued that there was sufficient evidence to warrant directly treating deviant arousal, despite the fact that they also pointed out that there was limited evidence to support the efficacy of such work and that many offenders did not have deviant sexual arousal. Furthermore, despite claiming that the link with deviant fantasy and behaviour had been exaggerated, Marshall and Eccles (1996) argued that thoughts and feelings about deviant acts are frequently entertained by offenders, particularly prior to sexual offending. Thus, they stated that all offenders will have had at least some thoughts about deviant acts that have come to be associated with satisfaction, and that treatment should attempt to reduce the probability that such thoughts produce satisfaction. Marshall and Eccles therefore described a range of techniques used in their programmes. These techniques included covert sensitization, masturbatory reconditioning and other similar techniques. Hudson et al. (1995) explained the masturbatory reconditioning techniques used in the Kia Marama programme in New Zealand.

Despite the use of these techniques in some programmes, as was discussed in Chapter 2, research showing that behavioural techniques can change deviant arousal is equivocal. There is some evidence to show that such techniques produce short-term changes in arousal, but little support that long-term changes in behaviour can be induced from these short-term changes (hence, the need to revise treatment and include cognitive elements, as discussed in Chapter 2). Furthermore, Marshall (1997) showed that deviant arousal was modified without any specific treatment component aimed at modifying deviant arousal. He argued that providing the skills and attitudes required to meet pro-social needs eliminated the need to modify deviant arousal.

This, then, is another treatment component that is surrounded by controversy and supported by very limited empirical evidence. In contrast to some of the treatment goals discussed previously, this component also has a poor theoretical basis, with much relevant theory pointing towards the omission of such a component, perhaps for all but a minority of offenders who show primary arousal to deviant stimuli. And for these offenders, the ability to modify deviant arousal seems limited. Sexual arousal is an area that is so poorly understood in 'normal' populations that it is not surprising that there is a poor understanding of this aspect in 'deviant' populations. As sexual arousal and sexual fantasy is a taboo topic that is so rarely discussed (see research discussed earlier in this chapter about the poor reliability of reports of sexual behaviour in normal populations), it is difficult to see how our understanding of this issue will improve. However, the work of Gee and her colleagues (2003) in developing the SFFM is an interesting recent development in this area, which may help to improve treatment on sexual fantasy. It would seem from this model that, rather than trying to change sexual arousal, efforts would be better placed in using the model in conjunction with relapse-prevention training, guiding offenders away from using fantasy in a way that is likely to enhance the likelihood of future offending behaviour and encouraging the inhibition of such fantasy once it has been triggered.

Non-offence-specific treatment goals

As well as the offence-specific goals outlined earlier, many treatment programmes also target a range of non-offence-specific goals. Although there is general agreement about the offence-specific targets of treatment (i.e. virtually all programmes target all the goals discussed previously), there is less agreement about the non-offence-specific targets. For example, Beech and Fisher (2002) described the targeting of self-esteem problems, intimacy deficits, attachment problems, assertiveness difficulties, management of negative emotional states and problem solving deficits. Hudson et al. (1995) outlined components that address social problem solving, stress management, substance abuse, life skills, interpersonal skills, relationship issues, anger management and sex education.

There is often a clear logic behind the provision of these components and many have empirical support in the form that sex offenders have been shown to be deficient in these areas compared to control groups. For example, Seidman et al. (1994) showed that sex offenders had intimacy deficits and were more lonely compared to control groups. Marshall and Hambley (1996) showed that intimacy was correlated with loneliness, and that these measures were also correlated with hostility towards women. A number of these issues have also been reviewed and theories developed accordingly by a number of authors. For example, Marshall (1989) reviewed intimacy and loneliness in offenders; Marshall (1993b) examined the role of attachments, intimacy and loneliness in offending; Ward, Hudson, Marshall and Seigert (1995) developed a theoretical framework for attachment style and intimacy deficits; Ward *et al.* (2000) linked cognitive, affective and intimacy deficits in offenders; and Ward and Hudson (2000) reviewed intimacy, empathy and cognitive distortion under the heading of interpersonal competency. Some non-offence-specific treatment targets also develop from other treatment components; for example, the use of relapse-prevention techniques requires problem-solving and coping skills (see the next section of this chapter).

Some research has shown that sex offenders have lower levels of self-esteem than the 'normal' population (Marshall and Mazzucco 1995; Marshall *et al.* 1995; Marshall, Champagne, Brown and Miller 1997). In 1990, Marshall and Barbaree (1990a) claimed that low self-esteem was one of the main factors that led to the commission of a first sexual offence, and in 1997, Marshall, Anderson and Champagne argued that sex offenders share an extensive array of features with low self-esteem individuals. Thus, self-esteem appears to be linked in complex relationships with many other factors, such as empathy deficits and poor intimacy skills, which are believed to play a factor in either the causation or maintenance of sexually abusive behaviours (Marshall, Champagne, Sturgeon and Bryce 1997; Marshall, Champagne, Brown and Miller *et al.* 1997). In addition, Marshall, Champagne, Sturgeon and Bryce (1997) suggested that low self-esteem impedes the treatment process as low self-esteem individuals may be reluctant to try new behaviours, adopt new attitudes and commit to change. Furthermore, Marshall (1996a) linked self-esteem to Bandura's *et al.*'s (1977) notion of self-efficacy (see discussion on relapse prevention) which suggested that offenders are more likely to engage in a behaviour if they are confident that they will engender the desired results. Thus, Marshall and his colleagues argued that increasing self-esteem is an important treatment goal (Marshall 1996a, 1996b; Marshall, Champagne, Sturgeon and Bryce 1997; Marshall, Champagne, Brown *et al.* 1997).

As can be seen from this summary, there is a great deal of overlap in the authors reviewing these areas and developing theory. Some of these authors have also been responsible for developing treatment programmes, so it is not surprising that components addressing these issues have been included in treatment provision. However, there is insufficient research into the levels of these deficits during treatment and the impact of treatment on them, so that it is not possible to identify if reducing these deficits in sex offenders improves treatment outcome. In some offenders, increased self-esteem may well be linked to a poor treatment outcome; for example, it would not seem to be a good idea to increase levels of self-esteem in offenders with strong beliefs in sexual entitlement. It is also possible that increasing some offenders' self-esteem and improving their intimacy, social and relationship skills will enable them to more effectively ingratiate themselves in social settings and gain access to future victims. After reviewing the evidence for the deficits in affect and emotion outlined earlier, Howells *et al.* (2004) argued that, as sex offenders are a heterogeneous group, different treatment programmes will be needed for different offenders, and it may not be needed at all for some. Thus, more research is needed to empirically validate the theories of Marshall and Ward and their colleagues and to evaluate the treatment components linked to these non-offence-specific deficits.

Relapse prevention

Marlatt (1982; see also Marlatt and Gordon 1985) originally developed the relapse-prevention model in the area of addictions (i.e. the study of addiction to alcohol, drugs and so on) and its main concern was the maintenance of treatment-induced abstinence. As Laws (1995) explained, Marlatt argued that the probability of treatment success was greatest at the end of treatment; however, within a year, relapse rates of 80 per cent could be observed. Marlatt reasoned that if a programme addressing the issue of relapse could be added to the end of the original treatment, then the effects of the treatment could be maintained; and thus, the number of relapses reduced.

> Relapse-prevention programs teach people to recognize 'warning signs,' patterns of behaviour (including thoughts, feelings and actions) that increase the risk of relapse. By learning alternative ways of coping with urges in high-risk situations for relapse, clients are better equipped to prevent backsliding or to recover from lapses if they occur.
>
> (Marlatt 1992: 159, cited in Laws 1995: 43)

This approach was extended to sex offenders by Pithers and his colleagues (Pithers *et al.* 1983, 1988; Pithers 1990, 1991). Marshall and Eccles (1996) argued that this approach provided a model for cognitive-behavioural treatment that was compatible with, and incorporated, much of the work that was already being conducted. In addition, it provided a cohesive framework within which the various elements of treatment could be understood. As described previously, Marlatt originally intended relapse prevention to be a strategy for treatment maintenance (Laws 1995); however, it has become common to incorporate relapse-prevention components into treatment programmes (see Hudson *et al.* 1995; Marshall and Eccles 1996; Beech and Fisher 2002), or even to use relapse prevention for the framework for an entire programmes (see for example, Marques *et al.* 1989; Pithers, Martin *et al.* 1989), although Polaschek (2003) queries whether these two approaches differ significantly. However, as can be seen from the programme descriptions in Chapter 3, more recently in some jurisdictions there has been a return to Marlatt's original conception, with the development of 'relapse-prevention' or 'maintenance' programmes, delivered in a package of treatment programmes.

Bandura *et al.*'s (1977) model of self-efficacy is particularly influential in this approach. This model suggests that target behaviour is more likely to be performed if the individual believes that he/she has the skills necessary to perform the behaviour (efficacy expectations), and that the performance of this behaviour will lead to a positive outcome (outcome expectations). Bandura and colleagues suggested that the strength of self-efficacy determines whether or not a client will attempt to change his/her behaviour, how much effort he/she will put into it and how easily they will give up in the face of obstacles. Thus, a relapse-prevention approach encourages the practice of coping strategies to increase the strength of self-efficacy. In addition, as outlined earlier, Marshall (1996a) argued that creating a therapeutic context that enhances a sense of self-worth is essential, as this will manifest in increased self-esteem, the ready acquisition of coping skills and increased self-efficacy expectations.

According to Pithers' original model (1990, 1991), an offender leaves (or should leave) a treatment programme in a state of abstinence, i.e. with confidence and high self-efficacy that they can avoid future reoffending. However, at some point the offender will make a seemingly irrelevant decision (often referred to as a SID), which is essentially a slip or lapse that makes reoffending more likely. For example, an offender may have a 'deviant' thought or fantasy, or 'find' themselves in an environment with children. Despite seeming an unimportant decision, the SID increases the offender's risk of reoffence and each SID takes the offender a step closer to relapse. When used in sexual offender programmes, 'lapse' is used to describe a 'slip' in behaviour (or thoughts or feelings) that makes an offence more likely and 'relapse' is used to refer to such a reoffence. This is different from the use of these terms in many other programmes, where, for example, having a single drink or cigarette could be considered a 'lapse' in abstinence, rather than a full-blown 'relapse' into addictive behaviour. As well as making SIDs, it is also likely that an offender will be using maladaptive coping strategies that also make relapse more likely. If an offender can make an adaptive coping strategy in a high-risk situation, then abstinence is maintained (and self-efficacy maintained), and further lapses or relapse prevented (for a while at least). At some point offenders are likely to experience the Abstinence Violation Effect (AVE), which is recognition that they are struggling to maintain abstinence (and avoid reoffending). Pithers and his colleagues included four forms of AVE that are likely to increase the probability of relapse: self-depreciation; expectation of failure; the problem of immediate gratification (PIG); or erroneous self-attribution. All of these reduce feelings of self-efficacy and make relapse more likely. However, if the lapse is attributed to something outside the control of the offender (e.g. an external unstable attribution), if an adaptive coping strategy can be employed, or the AVE can be reversed or ignored, then self-efficacy can be increased and hence, relapse is less likely.

Many publications outline treatment approaches for this element of treatment (see Carich and Calder 2003; Pithers *et al.* 1983, 1988; Laws 1989, 1995; Marques and Nelson 1989; Pithers 1990, 1991; Hildebran and Pithers 1992; Hudson *et al.* 1995; Marshall and Eccles 1996). Using the principles of the model described earlier, offenders are taught in treatment to recognize risky or problematic situations and/or precursors (e.g. stress) that could lead to further offending. This is usually done by having offenders identify and outline their offending cycles (see Chapter 4) and/or the chain of events and thoughts that led to their offending (for an example of an offending chain, see Laws 1995, 1999, 2000a). Offenders are then encouraged to identify warning signs that they are likely to reoffend and to recognize SIDs. Eventually offenders are asked to formulate and practise strategies (including thoughts and behaviours) relevant to their offence cycle/chain that will enable them to cope with (or avoid) these situations in future and hence, avoid offending. Finally, offenders develop this information into a relapse-prevention plan. Many programmes also ask offenders to identify a network of support (see Marshall and Eccles 1996).

> Like the treatment components discussed previously, empirical support for relapse prevention is poor.
> The dominance of RP [relapse prevention] in treatment should arguably make the evaluation of whether it reduces reoffending a top-priority task. It comes as a surprise then to find how little empirical analysis has been undertaken of its effects.
>
> (Polaschek 2003: 364)

Marlatt (2000) reported that the relapse-prevention outcome studies in the alcohol, smoking and drug intervention literature created a mixed picture, with most studies showing that relapse-prevention programmes are not associated with higher rates of abstinence. However, Dowden *et al.*'s (2003) research provides a more positive conclusion. They completed a meta-analysis of 40 relapse-prevention programmes (including sex offender and non-sex offender programmes) and found a small treatment effect, with a mean effect size of 0.15, although the effect sizes ranged from −0.15 to 0.45. Yet, 90 per cent of the studies yielded positive outcome data. Dowden *et al.* observed that the more relapse-prevention components used, the greater the treatment effect. However, the mix of sex offender and non-sex offender programmes in this meta-analysis means that it does not give a good indication of how well relapse-prevention techniques work with sex offenders. The two well-documented sex offender treatment programmes based entirely on the relapse-prevention framework have shown mixed results. One programme reported positive outcome data but no comparison group was used in the study (see Chapter 7 for a discussion of why this is problematic) (Pithers, Martin *et al.* 1989; Pithers 1991) and the other initially reported encouraging results but later found no treatment effects (see Chapter 8 and Marques, Day *et al.* 1994; Marques 1999; Marques *et al.* 2000). However, Marques, Nelson *et al.* (1994: 586) argued that:

> One of the strongest predictors for a new sex offence in our treatment sample was the ability of offenders to utilize some of the RP [relapse prevention] techniques that are emphasized in the treatment program. We suspect that one reason this relationship is strong is that the RP measures require the S [subject] to both understand and *apply* what he has learned. That is, these written RP exercises require the S to actually apply the skills to his own thoughts and behaviours, rather than just endorse appropriate attitudes.

The lack of evaluation studies investigating the impact of the relapse-prevention component of treatment means that it is not possible to say if this aspect of treatment is effective or not. Indeed, Marshall and Anderson (2000) argue that there is little evidence that treated offenders can describe the relapse-prevention components that they have been 'taught' or that they can explain 'acquired' coping strategies. However, this issue was investigated by Fisher *et al.* (2000), who found significant pre-treatment to post-treatment improvements in awareness of risk situations and coping strategies (measured using a relapse-prevention questionnaire). After a nine-month follow-up period, however, only offenders who showed other significant treatment effects (e.g. in levels of cognitive distortion) maintained these improvements, which was particularly noticeable in offenders who completed short (less than 80 hours) treatment programmes. Thus, Fisher *et al.* argued that relapse-prevention training is only useful when offenders have made significant treatment gains, which would actually fit with Marlatt's original conception of the relapse-prevention model. Further, they suggested that relapse prevention should only be undertaken as part of an extensive treatment programme.

Despite the lack of empirical support for relapse-prevention techniques, they have remained unchanged and unchallenged for many years. 'Perhaps the most remarkable thing about RP [relapse prevention] is the way it has been uncritically accepted' (Laws 1999: 290). However, beginning in the mid 1990s the literature on relapse prevention increased dramatically with both theoretical and empirical work. This led to the identification of many weaknesses in the original model and the development of revised models and techniques.

It has been argued that the main criticism of the relapse-prevention approach is that it suggests that offenders offend when they experience negative emotions/moods and lack the skills to deal with these in an appropriate manner (Ward and Hudson 1998b; Beech and Fisher 2002). However, as Beech and Fisher point out (see also Marshall and Serran 2000) many would now argue that there are many pathways or routes to offending (see Chapter 4 and Ward and Siegert 2002). Moreover, many offenders do not follow the route outlined by the relapse-prevention model; for example, they may have good skills and have different motivations to offend. Launay (2001), however, argues that the fact that the relapse-prevention model does not fit with all offenders is an irrelevant criticism, as it was never meant to be applied to all offenders. The original model was designed for offenders who left treatment with a commitment to abstinence (to avoid reoffending). Thus, Launay suggests that relapse-prevention programmes should be delivered after treatment (according to Marlatt's original idea) and following a thorough assessment to ensure that they are only offered to offenders who are appropriate for this form of intervention.

Marshall and Anderson (2000) argue that it can be counterproductive to outline in excessive detail offence chains and relapse-prevention plans (see also Marshall and Serran 2000). They explain that in doing this, treatment staff may create an impression that the task of avoiding relapse is monumental; and hence, they reduce offenders' beliefs that they can achieve such a goal (i.e. it reduces self-efficacy). Marshall and Anderson also suggest that excessive post-treatment supervision is ill advised, as it encourages offenders to believe that they can only avoid relapse with such supervision and support. This may be a successful strategy while the supervision and support is available, but leaves offenders feeling vulnerable and less able to avoid relapse when this is removed. Marshall and Anderson use recent data provided by Marques (personal communication, cited in Marshall and Anderson 2000; Marshall and Serran 2000) to support this argument, as the data revealed that the level of reoffending dramatically increased once community supervision was removed. Hence, Marshall and Anderson propose reducing the relapse-prevention component and claim that this will: make it easier for offenders to remember other factors about the programme; make it more likely that offenders will develop a general, rather than a situation-specific approach to avoiding relapse; and increase offenders' beliefs that they are in control of their lives.

Some have found that sex offenders have difficulty completing the offence chain (Laws 1999). For example, Marques *et al.* (2000) discuss the complexity and difficultly in identifying offence chains and in planning and practising ways to intervene to avoid reoffending, particularly for rapists. Marques and colleagues argue that issues of power and control exist in a wide variety of settings, and movement through the offence chain can happen very rapidly; thus, it is difficult to cover this in a way that will have a real impact in everyday life. Laws (1999) reported that it was a difficult task if offenders denied fantasizing and overt planning and claimed that the offence 'just happened'. Ward, Louden *et al.* (1995) investigated the cognitive-behavioural chain and found a number of weaknesses in the original conception that led them to produce a revised chain. This has nine stages of which six have two or three subcategories that describe different aspects of the stage and can account for the differences between offenders. Laws (1999) argued that the revised model was noteworthy because it integrates affective, environmental, cognitive and behavioural variables into a clear description of the offence chain. Furthermore, that it could account for a range of offenders and offender characteristics, supports features of the traditional relapse-prevention model and, most importantly, places greater emphasis on cognitive-distortions and affect states over the entire course of the chain.

Pithers (personal communication, cited in Laws 1999) noted that offenders who are comfortable with their lifestyle (and/or whom presumably wish to continue offending) might not experience the AVE. In fact, these offenders may find comfort in their lapses, rather than distress. Ward, Hudson and Siegert (1995) critiqued the sex offender relapse-prevention model, arguing that many problems stemmed from the recategorization of 'lapse' and 'relapse' (explained previously). In the original model the AVE is experienced after a lapse, but before a relapse; however, Hudson *et al.* reported that few of the offenders they investigated (Ward *et al.* 1994) reported negative emotions (i.e. AVE) after a 'lapse', although they did after a 'relapse'. Furthermore, they suggested that the problem of immediate gratification (PIG) was more important at the stage of 'lapse' than as part of the AVE. Ward, Hudson and Siegert (1995) suggested that post-relapse AVE could return an offender to their original level of offending, or could even lead to more extreme/severe forms of offending. Thus, Laws (1999) argued that this aspect of the relapse-prevention model was more important than had been believed before, which warranted more research. Launay (2001), however, diminished the importance of these theoretical criticisms, saying that they had little clinical relevance and further, that the new model added little to the old.

In the UK, the core programme (see Chapter 3) originally stressed the importance to offenders of not putting themselves in risky situations, so that they would avoid reoffending; however, the latest version of the programme (Core 2000) places more emphasis on the idea that there are positives to not reoffending (Beech and Fisher 2002). This is likely to be a result of observations made by Mann (1998, cited in Marshall and Serran 2000) that relapse-prevention plans focus on avoidance goals; yet, research indicates that avoidance goals are difficult to attain, compared to approach goals which are easier to achieve. Thus, in the latest version of the programme, offenders are encouraged to adopt new 'appealing life goals' and the idea that a 'new me' can replace the 'old me' is stressed. This approach is more in accordance with the 'Good Lives' model of rehabilitation (Ward 2002a; Ward and Stewart 2003).

Ward and Hudson (1998b) used the findings from self-efficacy research and their own work describing the sex offence process to develop a new model of relapse prevention: the Self-Regulation Model. They argued that this model avoided the weaknesses of the original model; most notably that it only included one pathway for offending. The Self-Regulation Model contains nine different phases in the relapse process: life event; desire for deviant sex or activity; offence-related goals established; strategy selected; high-risk situation entered; lapse; sexual offence; post-offence evaluation; attitude towards future offending. The offender can leave the process (i.e. avoid relapse) during any of these nine phases. Ward and Hudson pointed out that offenders can move backwards and forwards through the phases and remain in some phases for long periods of time, such that the whole relapse process may occur over a long period. As discussed in Chapter 4, Ward and Hudson also categorized offenders into a typology that described the strategies they use to avoid or to instigate new offences.

> This represents a considerable theoretical and practical break-through in sex offender treatment because the new model can accommodate persons who wish to change their behavior, those who are uncertain, and those who are clearly content with being sex offenders. It is my prediction that this model will be warmly supported and rapidly adopted in the field.
>
> (Laws 1999: 291)

Thornton (1997, cited in Laws 2000a) questioned whether we needed relapse prevention at all. In a similar argument to that of Marshall and Serran (2000), he stated that it made offending too salient, particularly when the recidivism rates for sex offenders are actually quite low. He also pointed out that sex offenders are not highly motivated and although they may learn relapse-prevention techniques during treatment, there is no guarantee that they will actually use them. Thus, he suggested that it was possible to omit relapse prevention and focus instead on offenders' criminogenic factors/needs. Perhaps the most damning criticism of the relapse-prevention approach was made by Hanson (2000), who pointed out that the model assumes that lapses are to be expected (rather than being seen as a failure) and that all offenders are considered high risk: offenders who claim they are not a risk are considered to be in denial and uncooperative. 'For men who are genuinely low risk to reoffend, it is hard to understand how constantly telling them that they are dangerous should help with anything' (Hanson 2000a: 29). Hanson argues further that the model of offence cycles/chains may not be the most appropriate to describe sex offences, as some offenders may quite simply offend on impulse. He states that the assumption of high levels of motivation to abstain from offending is 'a serious weakness in the application of the RP [relapse prevention] model to the sexual offender'. (p. 35) However, such negative views are not shared by all. For example, Launay (2001) argues that, provided the techniques are used with appropriate offenders in an appropriate manner (i.e. as a post-treatment component following assessment), relapse prevention has important clinical relevance and hence, its use should continue.

Clearly, there is still a great deal of debate about the use of relapse-prevention techniques in sex offender treatment. Like many of the other treatment components, recent theoretical developments have led to revisions in the conceptualization of the component itself and the way it is delivered in treatment. Also, like other treatment components, evidence for the efficacy of the component is scarce. Poor outcome results may be a reflection of the way in which the relapse-prevention model has been used in treatment (and outcome studies will not yet reflect the more recent developments in this component). Although it was designed as an add-on to treatment, many programmes now incorporate it into the main treatment programme. Furthermore, all offenders are given the same relapse-prevention training, which might not be appropriate for offenders who follow different offending pathways. Moreover, Marlatt (2000) states that, although the core elements of relapse prevention can be taught in groups, it is important that an individualized approach is used to ensure that the core elements are tailored to meet the needs of each individual. Although offenders are encouraged to develop their own offending cycles/chains and relapse-prevention plans, there is little time in group programmes for extensive individual work. Thus, it may be necessary to develop a range of relapse-prevention programmes to meet the needs of different groups of offenders and/or extend individual work on this issue. However, if the views of Marshall and his colleagues, Thornton and Hanson are correct – i.e. in some instances (or even all instances) relapse prevention increases the salience of reoffending and reduces self-efficacy possibly making offenders more likely to reoffend – then it is important that this component is effectively evaluated and omitted (for some or all offenders) if it is not shown to be effective, or if it is shown to have a detrimental effect.

From the above discussion, it is clear that although many of the treatment goals were logical and intuitive, there was actually little empirical support for them. Rather than providing this support, increased empirical research has highlighted weaknesses in many of the treatment components and led to revisions and in some cases the elimination of the component from some programmes. Initially the aims of treatment seemed quite straightforward and were contained in discrete treatment goals that applied fairly equally to all offenders: reducing denial and minimization; eliminating cognitive distortions; improving victim empathy; developing a range of non-offence-specific skills; and constructing and practising a relapse-prevention plan. However, research and theoretical development has shown how these components overlap and interlink in complex relationships that may vary from offender to offender and at different stages in the offence chain or cycle. Thus, the goals of treatment must also become more fluid and interlinked, for example offenders need not only to be able to demonstrate empathy but cognitively they also need to understand that their future/potential victim is deserving of such empathy. In addition, many of the latest theories and empirical findings suggest that having a single treatment model/programme for all offenders, where a range of offender types are treated together, is misguided. Although treatment is delivered in modular components to allow the flexibility to provide different amounts of treatment to offenders with differing levels of risk and treatment needs, these components do not always provide the flexibility that is suggested by the theories/studies described here. For example, it is not always possible to vary the amount or type of empathy training received.

The greatest weakness with the treatment goals discussed is the lack of empirical support for their efficacy. In some cases there is evidence that offenders significantly improve in the treatment goals from pre-treatment to post-treatment, but this is often measured with transparent psychometric tests and the limited research reveals a far from conclusive picture. More importantly, there is scarce evidence showing links between treatment changes and recidivism; thus, it is far from clear if changes in the treatment goals outlined earlier would produce actual changes in offending behaviour. This lack of evidence is a great concern and research on this issue is clearly needed. The lack of empirical support for these treatment goals, and the revisions in some that have become necessary from the little empirical evidence that has been produced, may account for the poor evaluation results of many treatment programmes and the equivocal nature of the evaluation literature as a whole. Clearly, treatment programmes containing unnecessary and/or ineffective treatment components are likely to have a limited impact on recidivism. While the revisions outlined here may improve programme efficacy, it will be some time before these changes are revealed in the outcome literature. The findings of the outcome literature published to date will be reviewed in Chapters 8 and 9; however, an examination of the methodological issues surrounding programme evaluation is given first, in the next chapter.

Chapter 7

Are programmes effective?
Part 1: Difficulties in evaluating
programmes

As discussed in the previous chapters, the use of sex offender treatment programmes has expanded in the last two decades. Yet, there is still considerable debate concerning the effectiveness of these programmes. A general shift towards evidence-based practice has meant that most now recognize and accept the need to use interventions that have been proved effective; however, it is vitally important that *all* treatment programmes are evaluated for a number of reasons.

First, the use of these programmes within criminal justice and mental health systems across the world implies that they are effective in reducing recidivism. Hence, it is possible that sex offenders who have been or are being treated are being released into the community or treated in other ways on the assumption that they have a lower risk of reoffending, when perhaps they may otherwise (without the use of treatment) have been detained in secure accommodation or treated in other ways, on the assumption that they constitute a higher risk. There will clearly be devastating consequences to potential future victims if these assumptions are incorrect.

Second, it is often assumed that North American research findings, which the majority of published evaluations are, can be generalized to other countries; however, 'while North American studies are informative, they may not be relevant to the British experience' (Proctor 1994: 31) or to the experiences of other countries. As Grubin and Thornton (1994) pointed out, we are unable to ascertain if North American sex offenders are in some way different to offenders from other nations, or whether sex offending occurs in the same contexts and in similar ways throughout the world. In addition, as discussed in Chapter 3, although based on a similar approach, programmes from different countries and the structures in which they are provided do differ.

Third, despite the fact that most treatment programmes are based on the same principles, each one is different, not least because they have different programme staff and different offenders attending the programmes. Moreover, programmes will change slightly over time and across deliveries. Thus, it cannot be assumed that *all* programmes are effective because *some* programmes have demonstrated positive effects, or that each delivery of a programme will be effective because *one* or *some* deliveries of the programme have been shown to be effective. As will be discussed in more detail later, these programme differences have generally been overlooked in the evaluation research in this field; however, developments over the last few years have shown that some differences between programmes, such as the style of therapists, can have an effect on treatment outcome.

Fourth, research has demonstrated that offenders who drop out of treatment programmes have higher rates of recidivism than offenders who do not undertake any treatment (Cook *et al.* 1991; Marques, Day *et al.* 1994; Miner and Dwyer 1995; Harris *et al.* 1998; Marques 1999). Hanson and Bussiere (1998) and Bench *et al.* (1997, cited in Grossman *et al.* 1999) found that failing to complete treatment was a significant predictor of sexual recidivism. Furthermore, it was the strongest predictor in a broader definition of recidivism (including non-sexual offences and parole and probation violations) (Bench *et al.* 1997, cited in Grossman *et al.* 1999). While it is likely that this elevated recidivism is due to pre-treatment characteristics of the offenders who drop out of treatment, rather than due to the treatment itself, it may also be that poor or ineffective programmes actually increase the risk of recidivism in their clients. Consequently, it is important that ineffective programmes are identified and modified or terminated.

Finally, Knopp *et al.* (1992) noted that if all sex offender programmes were evaluated a 'gold mine' of data would be generated. This knowledge could be used to protect future generations of potential sex abuse victims. Moreover, best practice and the principles of evidence-based practice promote a model whereby all interventions are delivered, evaluated and modified with the aim to make improvements which are based on the findings from the evaluation and other relevant empirical evidence; delivered, reevaluated, remodified and so on continually, to ensure that interventions are not only effective, but that they are as effective as can be given the knowledge available.

Although it is clear that sex offender treatment programmes need ongoing evaluation, conducting such assessment is not a straightforward process. There are many methodological issues, problems and dilemmas that make executing evaluation research and drawing firm conclusions from this work difficult and complex. In this chapter, these issues will be examined in more detail. Problems surrounding the design of evaluation research will be explored and the various outcome measures and their associated strengths and weaknesses described. This discussion will be completed by examining the issues and problems that are present in all evaluation research studies, regardless of the methodology employed. Please note that while this chapter is written with sex offender programmes in mind, the difficulties and issues discussed below also apply to the evaluation of other psychological treatment or intervention programmes within both criminal justice and mental health settings.

Design

In order to produce reliable and valid findings, researchers strive to isolate and examine the specific effects one group of variables (or a single variable) has on another. Hence, in an evaluative study, researchers aim to demonstrate that the identified outcomes (for example, the reduction in recidivism) were directly attributable to the intervention under examination (for example, the treatment programme). The methodological design that is best able to achieve this ideal is the experimental design, more commonly referred to as the randomized control trial (RCT) in evaluation research. This design has long been regarded by researchers in many fields of experimental enquiry as the most effective and most desirable (see Farrington (1983) for a discussion of the strengths of this design in criminal justice research).

Experimental design/randomized control trials

This design requires the researcher to randomly assign a group of similar participants to one of two (or more) conditions. In one condition, the participants should receive the particular intervention under examination, while in the other condition (the control group), participants should be given a placebo intervention. This should be as similar as possible to the real intervention, so that participants are not able to identify which condition they have been assigned to (other conditions may include participants who receive no intervention, or participants who drop out of the treatment). Throughout the study, all groups of participants should be treated identically (or as identically as possible). In addition, those conducting the study, the deliverers of treatment (where this is possible) and the participants should be blind to the conditions to which participants have been allocated. After a period of time when it can reasonably be assumed that the intervention would have produced the desired effects (follow-up period), the participants should be tested/measured in such a way that these effects can best be identified. If the experiment has been conducted competently, the differences identified from the outcome measures of each group can be attributed to the intervention being evaluated. Although ideal in nature, and frequently utilized within many fields (perhaps most notably in medical research), for a number of reasons it is virtually impossible to use this design fully when evaluating sex offender treatment programmes (and other similar forms of psychological intervention).

Placebo interventions

McConaghy (1999a) reported that the most consistent finding of meta-analyses of psychological treatment outcomes is that placebo treatment groups have better outcomes than waiting-list or no-treatment groups. Furthermore, at times they show greater effect sizes than specific treatment interventions. Hence, McConaghy argued that it is possible that a placebo effect, rather than the treatment itself, could be the only cause of a positive treatment outcome. While it is often relatively easy to give participants a placebo intervention that appears to be identical to the real intervention in some research, such as the use of dummy pills in medicine, it is difficult to see how participants could attend a programme that appeared to be focusing on sex offender treatment work without generating any changes in the clients. Thus, in psychological treatments, it is impossible to control for the placebo effect (see also McConaghy 1995); that is, that clients change merely because they are receiving a form of intervention, no matter what or how effective that intervention is. If participants are randomly allocated to a treatment or a no-treatment (control group) condition, it is impossible to evaluate the effects on the control group of the awareness that they were not receiving any treatment (McConaghy 1995), or the effects on the treatment group of the knowledge that they were receiving treatment. Thus, we cannot be sure that any differences identified between the treatment and control groups were actually directly attributable to the psychological intervention.

In addition, practitioners may be wary of conducting RCTs, from fear of the potential negative effects on the control group, who will be aware, and possibly not at all happy, that they have not been chosen to receive the treatment. Such a concern was raised by the staff at HMP Grendon Prison (England) who feared that offenders assessed as suitable for the therapeutic community regime but allocated to the non-treatment group may decompensate and become involved in more negative behaviour than if they had never been involved in the RCT, i.e. never offered the treatment (Campbell 2003). If allocation to the control group does have adverse effects on the individuals in this group, this increases further the differences between the two groups, such that identified post-follow-up differences cannot be attributed to the treatment alone. As suggested in the Home Office feasibility studies (Farrington and Jolliffe 2002; Campbell 2003), it may be possible to randomly allocate participants prior to them being offered, or assessed for, treatment; however, this requires a greater number of participants for the RCT, as many individuals may be assessed as not being suitable for treatment, or they may decide that they do not wish to complete the treatment. This will have the greatest impact when numbers are already low, and is likely to impact on the statistical power of the study, which will be discussed in more detail later in this chapter. A further difficultly with the control group may be participants' reluctance to continue with the study when they perceive that they are gaining nothing from their participation. Thus, it might be difficult to obtain follow-up data from the control group, although this is likely to have a limited impact when the follow-up assessment is officially recorded recidivism rates.

Random allocation

Regardless of the problem of the placebo effect, random allocation to experimental conditions is generally upheld as an ideal within the experimental design, as this method ensures that there are no differences, other than those generated by chance, between the participants allocated to each condition. It is possible that randomization could result in non-equivalence between the treatment and comparison groups, an issue raised by Hanson (1997) and Miner (1997) as one that justified the use of other methodological approaches. Lack of equivalence of groups formed in this way, though, is inevitable and is taken into account by statistical tests of significance (see also McConaghy 1999a). Furthermore, differences occurring through randomization are likely to be less systematic (which might have less impact on treatment outcome) than those generated by other allocation methods.

Although methodologically desirable, random allocation raises a number of ethical issues. It can be argued that it is never acceptable to withhold a potentially beneficial intervention from someone who may benefit from its use, although this problem is often overshadowed (for example in medical research) by the need to ensure that the intervention is safe. In the evaluation of sex offender treatment programmes, researchers have fiercely debated the ethics of deliberately withholding this form of intervention, when the negative consequences of such an approach potentially affects not only the client from whom the intervention is being withheld (and who can give informed consent for his/her participation in the study), but also innocent members of society who the client may harm as a result of this withholding (and who do not and cannot consent to their 'involvement' in the study).

Quinsey *et al.* (1993: 513) stated:

If the treatment has not yet been shown to be effective or if the comparison/control treatment was the intervention most sex offenders would receive anyway, psychologists have an ethical obligation (cf. Canadian Psychological Association 1988) to reduce the present ambiguity about the effects of sex offender treatment.

Thus, they argue that random allocation is necessary, and hence ethical, as it is a requirement of the methodological design that is essential to show *conclusively* whether treatment is effective or not. For as McConaghy (1999a: 184) stated:

Failure to provide methodologically adequate evidence of the efficacy of particular psychological treatments could therefore have serious consequences for the continued use of those treatments and for the esteem in which the treatments and their practitioners are held by other psychologists and psychiatrists.

Some researchers, however, most notably Marshall and his colleagues, believe that random allocation is an unethical method that should be avoided. Marshall and Pithers (1994) pointed out that withholding treatment can be expected to result in the psychological and physical injury (or even death) of innocent women, men or children who had no say at all in the implementation of the random-allocation design. Furthermore, Marshall (1993c: 527) argued:

Most members of society are quite understandably reserved, if not hostile, to the release into their community of sex offenders. If they were to find out we were deliberately denying these men access to treatment, I am quite certain their anger would find public expression, which would result in either the termination of the evaluation project or the closing of the programme altogether.

Thus, Marshall and Pithers (1994: 24) concluded:

We cannot see how any ethically concerned researcher would suggest a random design treatment outcome study for sex offenders. The pursuit of ideal scientific standards is not, in our view, of greater concern than the protection from victimization of innocent women, men and children.

The latter arguments, though, clearly assume that sex offender treatment is effective, or at least potentially effective and therefore, that those allocated to the control group are missing out on this valued intervention. The key difference, then, between the arguments of Marshall and his colleagues and Quinsey *et al.* and McConaghy, is their belief in the current effectiveness and thus, potential value of sex offender treatment, rather than in differences of ethical understanding and ideologies. Marshall and his colleagues (Marshall 1993c; Marshall, Jones *et al.* 1991) have repeatedly shown a more positive outlook for sex offender treatment than Quinsey and his colleagues (Quinsey *et al.* 1993). It is understandable that a strong belief in the positive value of treatment would lead to concern about the withholding of this intervention. Similarly, it is understandable that a firm belief that an intervention has yet to demonstrate effectiveness (and may possibly not be effective), would lead to a greater concern regarding the demonstration of effectiveness, to avoid the potential problems that may follow if the intervention is being used as if it were effective. Innocent victims can be generated in either scenario. If treatment is effective and withheld from some people, then they may go on to offend against others. On the other hand, if treatment is not effective, but treated as if it was, treated offenders may be released as 'safe', which allows them to offend against others.

Interestingly, it is Quinsey *et al.*'s viewpoint that is supported by the American Psychological Association's (APA) Task Force on Promotion and Dissemination of Psychological Procedures (1993, cited in McConaghy 1999a). They considered that research contrasting treatment groups with waiting list comparison groups, rather than using randomized control groups, was not sufficient. In addition, they recommended requiring empirical validation of treatments. In the UK, after consultation with representatives from ethics committees and researchers who had sought ethical approval for proposed RCTs, Farrington and Jolliffe (2002) concluded that an RCT investigating a new programme for Dangerous and Severe Personality Disordered individuals would be granted ethical approval, as the benefits of the study, i.e. conclusions about the programme's effectiveness, would outweigh the costs, the withholding of treatment to the randomized control group.

Marshall (1993c) did concede that random allocation might be acceptable in some situations when certain conditions are imposed on researchers, for example if circumstances beyond the control of the researcher limit the number of treatment places (this was also a consideration in the feasibility study of Farrington and Jollife, which was discussed above). Such a situation was encountered by Marques, Day *et al.* (1994: 32) who argued:

When resources are made available specifically for the empirical investigation of the treatment of sex offenders and when that support would not be available otherwise, the ethical dilemmas involved with randomized designs are minimal.

The programme evaluated by Marques and her colleagues was provided under legislation in California that required the evaluation to be based on a valid experimental design. This, and the fact that the treatment programme was limited to 50 beds when there were 15,000 sex offenders in California, made it possible to match and randomly assign volunteers to treatment and non-treatment conditions.

When such conditions do not exist, a compromise position suggested by McConaghy (1995) is possible: to randomly assign participants to one of two or more treatment programmes: 'There would appear to be no ethical objection to random allocation of offenders to different treatments when there is no acceptable evidence that one is superior to another' (p. 397). Strictly speaking, however, while this approach may be ethically more acceptable, it is only able to say which programme(s) produced better outcome(s). It is unable to tell us *conclusively* whether treatment is effective or not. If all treatments in the study are equally effective or ineffective, no differences will be identified.

Given that it is impossible for researchers to provide a placebo sex offender treatment programme and the issues surrounding randomization, the most strict experimental design/RCT is unattainable for the majority of workers in this field (and similarly for those working with many other psychological interventions). In certain conditions, however, it may be possible for a small number of studies to adopt an experimental approach that employs random allocation. For the majority of evaluators, though, these conditions will not be present and they will be forced to adopt a quasi-experimental design.

Quasi-experimental designs

There are many different methodological designs in this category. Generally, quasi-experimental designs attempt to maximize control over the variables being studied, while taking into account the limitations enforced by the natural environment or ethical considerations, as discussed previously. In order to isolate treatment effects, researchers attempt to compare the treatment group(s) with groups (or existing data representing these groups) of participants (comparison group(s)) who are as similar as possible to the treatment group. Without a comparison group of similar untreated offenders, it is impossible to say whether the outcomes identified in the treatment group were due to the intervention being evaluated, or to some other effect (see also Marques, Day *et al.* 1994) such as maturation, identification as an offender, imprisonment, differences in the treatment group and so on.

Larzelere *et al.* (2004) stated that the regression discontinuity design is the most robust quasi-experimental design, as it specifies the selection processes involved in identifying treatment and non-treatment groups explicitly. Next best, they argued, is the interrupted time series design, which controls for pre-existing, pre-treatment differences and trends. The comparison of non-equivalent groups is, according to Larzelere *et al.* the third best design. Few sex offender treatment evaluation studies (and studies of other psychological interventions employed in criminal justice systems) use the more robust designs and most commonly compare the average/aggregated outcome of a treatment group with that of a control/comparison group. Some studies use a slightly better design and match the participants in the treatment and comparison group on variables thought to impact on the problematic behaviour (i.e. sexual offending), although exact matching on more than two variables is difficult and often fails (Hanson and Nicholaichuk 2000). When this is done, most studies use the less effective method of matching variables retrospectively, i.e. after the intervention, rather than the prospectively. As Friendship *et al.* (2002) discuss, retrospective matching is poorer as it is often only possible to match participants on a small number of variables, because of the lack of information from the comparison group(s). Prospective matching, they argue, is preferred as it attempts to control for extraneous variables in advance of the treatment/ intervention, and there is more opportunity to select a range of variables likely to impact on the problematic behaviour, and to collect relevant data from both the treatment/intervention groups and the comparison group.

Many different comparison groups have been used in studies evaluating sex offender treatment programmes (and other psychological interventions): offenders who received a different form of intervention (for example incarceration); offenders released prior to the implementation of a treatment provision; offenders who were unable (or unwilling) to attend a treatment programme; offenders on a treatment waiting list; and offender characteristics inferred from the literature. Marques, Day *et al.* (1994: 32) argued:

> In a comparison study, it is important that a subject's group assignment not be made on the basis of factors related to the risk of reoffence and that care is taken to examine and control for possible differences between treatment and comparison groups on recidivism-related characteristics.

Ultimately, however, regardless of the type of comparison group employed, it is always possible that the differences identified between the treatment and comparison groups are attributable to some extraneous variable(s), rather than to the treatment programme under examination (hence, the preference, methodologically, for RCTs). Specific problems identified in sex offender treatment evaluations (which may also apply to other psychological interventions) are the use of selection criteria, problems in identifying and gaining access to suitable comparison groups, and the difficulty in accurately identifying untreated offender characteristics from the literature. In addition, some authors have questioned the suitability of this approach for evaluation research, as will be discussed below.

Selection criteria

The majority of treatment programmes employ some form of screening strategies to identify and exclude offenders deemed unsuitable for the intervention. For example, as described in Chapter 3, offenders who have high rates of denial are routinely refused treatment. Such selection criteria introduce differences between the treatment and comparison groups. Decisions made by the offenders themselves can also be included in this category. Offenders who are unwilling to attend treatment may be used as a comparison group, but the willingness (or lack of it) to attend treatment may be a crucial characteristic that influences the outcome variable. Thus, it is always possible that these differences, rather than the intervention programme, account for identified differences in outcome.

Larzelere et al. (2004) argue that selection bias is often the most important threat to making valid conclusions from intervention evaluation research. Sex offender treatment outcome is one of a range of interventions they assess in their paper, which, they argue, is confounded by selection bias. One reason for this is the use in many studies (which include meta-analyses that aggregate the findings of these problematic original studies) of comparison groups consisting of treatment refusers or drop-outs, who are known to have high rates of recidivism (Cook et al. 1991; Marques, Day et al. 1994; Miner and Dwyer 1995; Harris et al. 1998; Marques 1999). Thus, Larzelere and colleagues question claims of positive treatment outcome and of treatment effectiveness. They refer to an interesting conclusion drawn by Harris et al. (1998: 103) on this issue:

> Agreeing to and persisting with treatment over the long term serves as a filter for detecting those offenders who are relatively less likely to reoffend, but the nature of the treatment has little or no detectable specific effect on outcome.

Larelere *et al.* suggest ways to control for selection bias and point out that the failure to consider this bias masks the difference between more effective and less effective treatments, which may ultimately hinder the development of the intervention.

Identification of, and access to, a comparison group

Marques, Day *et al.* (1994) argued that one of the most difficult obstacles in evaluating sex offender treatment programmes is finding adequate comparison groups (see also Marshall and Eccles 1991; Marshall, Jones *et al.* 1991). Difficulties may arise in identifying a group of untreated offenders who are as similar as possible to the treated offenders. Furthermore, while it may be possible to identify such offenders, it may not be possible to include them in the research. With the provision and use of sex offender treatment becoming more common, untreated offenders are less likely to be found, particularly in organizations or groups, where access for study can be gained relatively easily. In addition, untreated offenders who remain in organizations are likely to be those for whom treatment was deemed unsuitable, or who are more serious and/or at high risk. As discussed previously, with such characteristics, these offenders are unsuitable as comparison participants. Finally, offenders who would be suitable comparison participants, but who are not engaged in treatment, may be less willing to participate in this type of research. Thus, researchers in this field find it difficult to employ comparison groups that provide reliable and valid research findings. These difficulties also result in many different types of comparison groups being used, which makes comparison of results across studies extremely difficult.

Identifying characteristics from the literature

Given the problems associated with identifying and employing appropriate comparison groups, some researchers have compared the characteristics of the offenders in their treatment groups, usually recidivism, with data obtained from the literature for untreated offenders. Marshall and Eccles (1991) believe it is possible to infer from the literature untreated recidivism rates that can be used to compare recidivism rates of the treated group; however, Furby *et al.* (1989) considered this impossible. The major difficulty with this approach is identifying recidivism rates for offenders who, apart from being untreated, are as similar as possible to the offenders being treated. Although this method may provide some form of comparison for studies where it is impossible to locate a more suitable comparison group, it should not be advocated as a good quasi-experimental design.

Critique of quasi-experimental approach

In a scathing attack on the quasi-experimental approach, Pawson and Tilley (1994: 291) stated: 'One has to ask, should we press on with the evaluation of such programmes given the tendency to end in a state of collective puzzlement at the inconsistency of it all?' They argue that this methodological approach is limited because programmes cannot be considered as an external force that impacts on the subjects. Treatment only works if subjects choose to make it work and are placed in the right conditions for this to take place. The quasi-experimental approach, they suggest, is designed to iron out differences that could be crucial in understanding why programmes are successful, or in identifying the most effective programmes (or particularly effective elements of programmes). Pawson and Tilley believe that it is important to understand how and why treatment is effective, as well as whether or not it is effective, and suggest that evaluations should address the following questions:

(1) Has the problem been cracked?

(2) Did the initiative alter the size of the problem?

(3) What did the initiative do that impacted on the problem?

(4) How was the problem affected by the initiative?

(5) What else resulted from the initiative as well as effects on the problem?

(6) How, where and for whom could the effects be replicated?

(7) What more do we know at the end of the evaluation about the patterns of outcome effectiveness of the initiative, and what else do we need to know?

Thus, evaluation research should take the format of a progressive series of studies. The authors conclude that the quasi-experimental design only answers questions (1) and (2), which 'leaves us with a one-off series of studies and leaves us clueless about how the very next trial will turn out' (p. 304).

As will be discussed in more detail in the next chapter, many of Pawson and Tilley's criticisms can be applied to sex offender treatment evaluation, which despite many years of research, is still unable to draw firm conclusions regarding the efficacy of these programmes. Perhaps, then, the reliance on the quasi-experimental approach has been misguided and other designs, such as the within-treatment method, that are able to address the remaining questions posed by Pawson and Tilley should be given more consideration. For as McPherson *et al.* (1994: 38) argued: 'ideally, an evaluation should be able to specify why a program was effective or ineffective'.

Within-treatment studies

Despite being the weakest design methodologically (in terms of addressing the question of whether or not treatment is effective), the within-treatment design is frequently adopted in evaluation research because of the problems identified above and because it is more efficient in terms of time and resources. In 1997, Barbaree argued that problems with outcome studies give greater validity and importance to alternative evaluation methods, such as within-treatment studies.

Essentially, this method tests clients on a number of variables prior to the start of the programme and on completion of the programme, more commonly referred to as pre- and post-treatment testing or comparison. Any differences between these results are argued to be a result of the treatment intervention. In most sex offender treatment (and other psychological interventions) evaluations, offenders are tested on a battery of psychological scales that measure attitudes believed to be related to the commission of the problematic behaviour (based on treatment theory and/or research findings).

This design has a number of problems. It has very little internal validity (Shaughnessy and Zechmeister 1997) and it is always possible that identified differences were due to something other than the intervention; for example, that offenders benefited from the initial testing or merely changed over time. These problems can be reduced if a comparison group (who does not receive the intervention) is also tested at the same time as the treatment group, using the same tests, and the results of the two groups compared; however, the use of comparison groups in within-treatment designs is very rare.

McConaghy (1999a) argued that the major danger of within-treatment studies is that they can support false beliefs or ineffective treatments. He used an example initially provided by Barbaree (1997), who argued that offenders in relapse-prevention programmes have been shown to acquire coping skills designed to prevent relapse, which have been shown to be related to the risk of recidivism. The implication being that programmes which produced such coping skills have been shown effective in reducing reoffending. McConaghy (1999a), however, postulated another explanation: offenders who acquire coping skills have characteristics that would make them less likely to reoffend without the acquisition of these coping skills. Marques, Day *et al.* (1994, cited in McConaghy 1999a) found that 26 offenders who had initially volunteered for treatment, but later decided against it, displayed the best outcome. None of the offenders reoffended. McConaghy suggested that these 26 men made considered, intelligent decisions in rejecting treatment: characteristics that may be related to better outcome. Chaffin (1994, cited in McConaghy 1999a) discovered that offenders who completed treatment had more social/sexual skills and were typically more socially competent. Thus, evidence of within-treatment change does not in itself provide evidence that the treatment or intervention was effective in reducing the problematic behaviour (e.g. sexual offending).

McConaghy's viewpoint is supported by Hanson *et al.* (1991) and Hanson (1997) who, although recommending within-treatment studies, also highlighted the need to relate treatment changes to recidivism. Hanson *et al.* (1993) identified a number of treatment effects: offenders felt more in control of their lives, more extroverted, less subjective distress, less hostile, less depression and improved self-esteem. These changes, however, bore little relation to recidivism. More research investigating the relationship between treatment change and recidivism is needed.

Another problem with within-treatment studies is the sole focus on significant treatment change (that is, whether there has been a statistically significant improvement in scores on the outcome measures used), without an analysis of the pre- or post-treatment positions of the clients. Some changes related to recidivism may be very subtle and not actually show as a statistically significant change, although even a small, non-statistically significant change may be related to recidivism. Given the small sample sizes likely to be involved in these analyses (see the discussion of power later in this chapter), significant changes will only be revealed in many statistical analyses when the treatment effect is large. Moreover, it may be easier to produce a statistically significant change in clients who start from a very poor position, and less easy to make these changes in clients who start from better positions. A programme that treats high-risk offenders with very poor pre-treatment scores on a battery of psychometric tests may show a significant treatment effect, i.e. a significant change between the pre- and post-treatment scores. However, another programme may have a group of low-risk offenders who begin the treatment with moderate or good scores on the same battery of psychometric tests. Although offenders' scores may improve at post-treatment, the programme may not show a significant treatment effect. Yet, a comparison of the two programmes may reveal that the post-treatment scores of the high-risk offenders are actually worse than the pre-treatment scores of the low-risk offenders. If significant treatment change is the only measure examined and is used to determine release into the community, the programme working with low-risk offenders will be considered a failure and the offenders with the highest risk may be released as treatment success, when their level of risk is higher than those designated as treatment 'failures'.

Although within-treatment designs have a number of weaknesses, the most prominent of which is that they cannot show *conclusively* whether or not a treatment intervention has been successful, they have an important role to play (alongside experimental and quasi-experimental research) in the overall development of sex offender treatment programmes. As Marques, Nelson *et al.* (1994: 577) argued:

> If we are to evaluate and improve our treatment interventions, we must be able to identify behaviours, skills and attitudes to target for change, determine that they can be altered by particular treatment approaches and demonstrate that they are relevant to the risk of re-offending.

Thus, within such a strategy, researchers should attempt to use the design that best suits their research aims, within the constraints of the resources and situations with which they are faced.

Cost-benefit analysis

The designs discussed so far have focused on whether treatment or interventions are effective or not. Yet, even if we believe that an intervention is successful, a key policy question is whether the costs of the treatment can be justified relative to the cost of the treatment. In order to answer this question, cost-benefit analysis, which is a comprehensive economic evaluation technique, is required (see Dhiri and Brand (1999) and Cohen (2000) for a more detailed discussion of this method). The methodological principles of this analysis derive from economic theory, and it is widely used in many fields of study. To date, however, this type of evaluation has not featured much in the analysis of offender treatment programmes (see Brown (2000) for a brief review). In terms of sex offender treatment, a review by Plotnick and Deppman (1999) found no cost-benefit analyses published between 1990 and 1995 for child abuse intervention programmes, although Prentky and Burgess reported such an analysis for the rehabilitation of child molesters in the US in 1990, and Shanahan and Donato published an analysis of paedophile treatment programmes in Australia in 2001. In addition, Marshall (1992) and Williams (1996b) have made more crude assessments of the value of sex offender treatment. Trends in policy and politics towards more evidence-based and accountable practice, however, has increased the awareness of and requests for such analyses. For example, the UK Home Office requires evaluators of crime reduction interventions to complete cost-benefit analyses for all programmes (Colledge *et al.* 1999) and has produced guidance for this research (Dhiri and Brand 1999).

Cost-benefit analysis requires an estimate of all the costs of a treatment programme per offender, which should include both fixed and incremental costs. This estimate is then offset against an estimate for all the benefits of the programme per offender. This aspect of the analysis is more complex. Some costs may be more easy to calculate, e.g. the saving in incarceration costs, if the programme diverts offenders away from incarceration; however, the full estimate of benefits will depend on the effectiveness of the programme. Clearly, the benefits of the programme will depend on how many offenders the treatment successfully diverts from reoffending. As will be seen in the next chapter, drawing conclusions about this for sex offender treatment programmes is difficult. When assumptions are made about the effectiveness of the programme, estimating a value for all the benefits is difficult. Some benefits may have a clear tangible cost, e.g. the cost of reconvicting a reoffender, yet, some assumption must be made about whether to assume just one reoffence or more for each recidivist. In addition, calculating a monetary cost for intangible benefits, such as the cost of harm to the victims and/or society, is difficult. However, there are precedents for some of these calculations, e.g. payments for damage in criminal and civil law that can be used. Thus, it is possible to make estimates of the value, in monetary terms, of any programme. The findings of the limited research in this area will be discussed in Chapter 9.

Outcome measures

Hollin (1994) distinguished between two types of outcome variables: measures of 'criminogenic' variables, which are specific to the commission of crime, and measures of personal or clinical characteristics, which are related to personal functioning. Evaluations of sex offender treatment programmes employ both of these groups of variables to measure outcome. The 'criminogenic' variable, recidivism, is widely used in experimental and quasi-experimental studies, while measures of personal or clinical characteristics are normally associated with within-treatment studies and involve the measurement of personality traits, attitudes and behaviours which are believed to be related to recidivism. There are many issues and difficulties associated with the use of both groups of outcome measure and these will be explored in more detail below.

Recidivism

Intrinsically recidivism, or the rate of reconviction, appears to be the best and most obvious method of measuring outcome for interventions that aim to eliminate the commission of criminal behaviour: 'ideally, a program's adequacy should be measured by how effective it is in reducing recidivism' (McPherson et al. 1994: 86). However, despite being the most valid, and thus most desirable measure of programme effectiveness, there are many problems associated with the use of this measure: determining successful outcome; measuring recidivism effectively; choosing an appropriate follow-up period; and combating the problem of low base-rates. In addition, some researchers have queried the potential of this method of measuring outcome.

Determining successful outcome

In order to evaluate effectively sex offender treatment programmes, providers and researchers must decide on the criteria that they consider best represent the successful outcome of the intervention. Intuitively, it may be argued that the elimination of the offending behaviour is the goal, for example Zonana (1997) argued that the consequences of recidivism were such that a zero rate of recidivism is the only acceptable level. However, unless we detain all convicted sex offenders for the rest of their lives, this is unrealistic as 'no rehabilitation program can expect to be 100 per cent effective' (McGrath 1991: 329). But, as Grubin and Thornton (1994: 69) pointed out, determining more realistic criteria is problematic:

> Measuring the success of treatment programs ... are [sic] not straightforward. Any decrease in the expected recidivism rate may be counted as an achievement, but it is the program failures who will attract the most publicity. One also has to decide whether to count as treatment success the individual who reoffends but in a less violent manner or the offender whose reoffending is delayed over time. ... If it is accepted that the goal of programs ... is not to cure but to help offenders control their behaviour, then expectations should not be raised falsely, and targets will be achieved more easily.

If any decrease in the recidivism rate is counted as a successful outcome, researchers and practitioners risk being accused of setting standards that are too low, and of conducting outcome studies where it is almost inevitable that positive results will be obtained. However, Marshall (1992) pointed out that preventing only 1 or 2 per cent of sexual offenders from reoffending will have a real impact on the lives of possible victims and save society a significant amount of money. On the other hand, programmes aiming for a total elimination in recidivism are doomed to failure. Setting a position between these two extremes is an arbitrary process: just how much of a reduction in recidivism should be considered to represent a successful outcome? Furthermore, effectively measuring whether an offender has reoffended in a less violent manner, or has taken longer to reoffend than he might have done having not completed treatment, is problematic.

Laws (2000b: 37) argues that current models adopt a 'zero tolerance position':

> Although total elimination of problem behaviour might be a highly desirable goal, it is very likely also an unachievable one. Despite adherence to this approach, most professionals would acknowledge that sex offending is probably a chronic condition that cannot be cured but can be managed, if somewhat imperfectly. This is what harm reduction is all about. A harm reduction perspective acknowledges that lapses and relapse are probably inevitable and that the job of treatment is, at minimum, to reduce the frequency and intensity of those instances.

In taking these views, Laws has been criticized and, in his own words: 'accused of giving up, throwing in the towel, saying that a little sex offending is all right' (Pare 1997; Maletzky 1998, both cited in Laws 2000b). Clearly, this issue is an emotive one and one that is complicated by the fact that researchers rarely state in their evaluation reports the criteria they are using to assess successful outcome. In practice, however, most sex offender treatment outcome studies consider programmes effective if they demonstrate a statistically significant difference (usually at the 5 per cent significance level) between the recidivism rates of the treatment group(s) and the control/comparison group(s).

In recent years, there has been a trend in psychological research to report the treatment effect size which, strictly speaking, is a measure of the degree that two or more variables are related, or that an independent variable affects an independent variable. This has partly been in response to some of the methodological issues already discussed, and to enable easier comparison between studies (and also to allow research to be more easily collated into meta-analyses). This trend has been reflected in sex offender treatment outcome studies, although there is still debate about what constitutes an acceptable effect size, or what effect size a successful programme would produce. Cohen (1988, cited in Clark-Carter 1998) defined that an effect size (d) in the region of 0.2 represents a small effect size, a d of around 0.5 a medium effect size, and a d of approximately 0.8 a large effect size. Yet, the question remains as to whether a small, medium or large effect size represents a successful intervention. Marshall and McGuire (2003) point out that some interventions with physical health problems that have been deemed effective actually have very small effect sizes, some of which are below Cohen's small d of 0.2. They adopt the approach of comparing effect sizes across a number of different interventions and conclude that the effect sizes of sex offender treatment programmes are comparable, if not superior, and hence they draw positive conclusions. However, given that four of the six reported effect sizes fall in the range of, or below, Cohen's small effect size, there is still room for others to draw more equivocal or negative conclusions.

Recidivism or reconviction rates are usually based on a dichotomous variable, i.e. whether the offender was reconvicted of a new offence or not. The number of new offences and the severity of the offences (particularly compared to pre-treatment offences) are hardly ever taken into account. Consequently, current analyses compare the recidivism rates (i.e. percentage of offenders in both groups who reoffended at least once) of treatment and control/comparison groups. Yet, more detailed recordings of recidivism data and analyses that are more complex might show more reliably the differences between treatment and non-treatment groups, or identify the effects of treatment more fully. Perhaps treatment has a greater impact on the severity of the new offences committed rather than the overall recidivism rate. Whether this could be argued a success would be hotly debated; however, the data would provide a greater understanding of the impact of treatment, and perhaps help to identify differences between treatment programmes more effectively. However, collecting data that are more detailed may prove difficult and time consuming because of the practices, such as plea-bargaining, and procedures of criminal justice systems. For example, in England and Wales, the official rates of reconviction published by the Home Office refer only to the first offence committed by the offender (Friendship and Thornton 2001).

Another difficulty in determining successful outcome is the question of whether this should be measured in terms of sexual reoffending, violent reoffending or any reoffending. There is no consensus on this matter (Marques, Day et al. 1994), although most researchers use sexual recidivism. The reason for this approach is outlined by Marshall et al. (1991: 468).

> We will only report reoffences for sex crimes since the primary goal of therapy is not, as yet, to eliminate all criminal tendencies but only sexual offending. We might hope that treatment would reduce antisocial behaviour in general, but unless that is a specific target of treatment we cannot reasonably expect nonsexual crimes to constitute one of the dependent variables in evaluating outcome.

Quinsey et al. (1993), however, argued that studies should also include non-sexual recidivism because of the practice of plea-bargaining, and the possibility that these offences may be positively or negatively affected by treatment. In practice, many researchers (although not all; for example see Cook *et al.* (1991); Hanson *et al.* (1993)) report more than one measure of recidivism. Some focus on sexual and violent reoffending (see Marques, Day *et al.* 1994; Marques, Nelson *et al.* 1994), some on sexual and non-sexual recidivism (Zgoba *et al.* 2003), whereas others report all three measures of recidivism (see Nicholaichuk 1996; Hanson *et al.* 2004).

As pointed out earlier, some officially recorded data may produce results that mask sexual reconvictions. In data such as that recorded by the Home Office, where only the first reoffence is recorded (Friendship and Thornton 2001), a person who first commits an offence against property and then later a sexual offence, will not be recorded officially as a sexual recidivist. In addition, Quinsey and his colleagues (1993) pointed out that the best method of determining recidivism is by examining offence descriptions; however, these are not usually available to researchers and this method is very time consuming.

Measuring recidivism

Marques, Day *et al.* (1994: 32) argued that criminal justice systems have many sources of error and that 'officially reported numbers of sex offenders are widely recognized to be gross underestimates of the true number of crimes that have been committed'. For example Lloyd *et al.* (1994) wrote that only 50 per cent of offences are reported to the police, and only 3 per cent result in a caution or conviction. For sexual offences, Mayhew *et al.* (1989) estimated that the rate of reporting is much lower, with only one in five sexual offences being reported to the police. In addition, official rates of recidivism are 'noisy' in that they reflect police efficiency, offenders' luck and other uncontrolled factors (Marshall and Barbaree 1988). Thus, the use of recidivism rates can be problematic. Yet, Lloyd *et al.* (1994) argued that these rates are a key indicator of performance, and are thus, an essential criminological tool.

In an attempt to combat the problems associated with official data sources, some researchers have used unofficial sources to measure recidivism. For example, Marshall and Barbaree (1988) considered that an offender had reoffended when there was sufficient evidence that implicated the offender on reasonable grounds, but where arrest and prosecution had not been possible because of a lack of legally acceptable corroboration of the victim's story. These authors reported that they tried to err on the side that suggested the offenders had reoffended. Using this method, unofficial records revealed 2.4 failures and 2.7 victims for every one revealed by official records. In 1993, Marques, Day *et al.* found reviewing parole office records in addition to computerized law enforcement data produced a 33 per cent increase in estimates of recidivism.

Other researchers have used sex offender self-report measures (for example see Abel *et al* 1988). Clearly, this approach relies on the honesty of offenders to report their criminal behaviour. Marques, Day *et al.* (1994), however, reported that studies which were able to guarantee confidentiality revealed large numbers of offences that had not resulted in arrest (see for example Abel *et al.* 1987).

In addition to using a variety of methods to measure recidivism, many different definitions of recidivism are employed, such as rearrest, reconviction, or reincarceration (McPherson *et al.* 1994). Thus, sex offender treatment evaluations employ different criteria to measure and define recidivism. For example, Gordon and Nicholaichuk (1996) measured offences that resulted in custody, whereas Nicholaichuck (1996) used police information databases to include arrests, convictions, parole and probation violations for sexual, violent and all offences. Marques, Day *et al.* (1994) obtained information from Department of Justice rapsheets and parole reports, and offenders were judged to have reoffended if either source indicated that they had been arrested for a new sexual crime or a new non-sexual violent crime. Marshall *et al.* (1991) used official police records of offences and recorded only sexual offences. These differences in definitions and measures make it extremely difficult to compare recidivism rates and effectiveness across evaluation studies, or to use the literature to provide untreated recidivism rates when comparison groups are unavailable. These problems are exacerbated by the fact that many studies fail to report the definitions and criteria they used to measure recidivism.

Follow-up period

Once a sexual offence has been committed, it can take a long period of time to appear in official records or statistics (if, that is, it is reported or recorded at all). This period varies depending on the measure being employed: arrest records reflect reoffences sooner than do records recording convictions. It is not inconceivable that more than a year will pass between arrest and conviction. Consequently, recidivism studies must employ follow-up periods that provide adequate time for treatment failures (that is, those who reoffend) to be represented in the records or statistics being employed. Studies that use follow-up periods of a year should be considered unreliable for this reason.

Regardless of the type of recidivism, the measures used and the type of offence, the cumulative reconviction rate for a group of offenders is greater if reconvictions are measured over longer periods of time. Thus, long follow-up periods are required to produce the most valid and reliable evaluations. The results of this, however, are that evaluations measuring recidivism are costly and take many years to complete. For example, Marques, Day *et al.* (1991, cited in Marques, Day *et al.* 1994) estimated a follow up of five years would be needed for 75 per cent of offenders who would reoffend to appear in the official records. In England and Wales, the convention has been to use a two-year follow-up period. Friendship *et al.* (2002) state that this is based on two key arguments. The first is the need to provide adequate time for reoffenders to show up in the statistics, i.e. allow for the time between arrest and reconviction. The second is because most offenders who are reconvicted are convicted within the first two years following release. They report the findings of Kershaw *et al.* (1999) who found that 55 per cent of prisoners released from prison in England and Wales in 1988 were reconvicted within the first two years of release, with only a further 9 per cent being reconvicted in the third and fourth years after release. However, these statistics are based on the general prison population. Many studies have shown that sex offenders remain a risk for much longer periods than other offenders, so perhaps Marques *et al.*'s suggestion of five years is more reliable with sex offender populations. However, the resources required to complete such a study are unlikely to be available to most evaluators, although studies with longer follow-up periods can be found in the literature: McGrath *et al.* (2003) followed up offenders for an average of six years; Zgoba *et al.* (2003) used a 10-year period; and Hanson (2004) used an average follow-up period of 12 years. These studies are far from the norm, however, and although they may tell us whether the programme evaluated was successful or not, by the time the study is published, the programme has probably changed and developed a great deal, or may even have ceased to exist. Moreover, this model is not helpful for staff who wish to monitor the ongoing effectiveness of their programmes, due to the delay between the programme delivery and the evaluation outcome results.

Low base rates

Contrary to the impression created by the media, sex offenders have relatively low rates of recidivism, regardless of society's response to them upon their identification as sex offenders. Hanson and Bussière (1996, 1998) studied the recidivism data from 98 reports of 61 unique data sets ($n = 23,393$), with an average follow-up period of five years. They found that the overall sexual recidivism rate was 13 per cent and the overall general recidivism rate was 36 per cent. In comparison, recidivism rates in England and Wales seem to be much lower: Friendship and Thornton (2001) found that sexual reconviction rates within a four-year follow-up period had fallen dramatically from 12 per cent in offenders released in 1980, to just 4 per cent in offenders released in 1993. Thus, the majority of sex offenders will not be convicted of a new sex offence, or any other type of offence, even if they receive no treatment. This means that unless the treatment is dramatically successful, it will be difficult to identify the impact of treatment, and that large sample sizes are needed to demonstrate a significant difference in recidivism between treated and untreated groups. Thus, although low reconviction rates are clearly desirable, low base rates create a serious methodological problem (Friendship and Thornton 2001).

Obtaining samples that are large enough to produce studies that are reliably able to demonstrate such statistically significant reductions is not an easy task. Not only does this method require researchers to locate large groups of suitable offenders but it also requires a great deal of investment in terms of time and money (Marshall 1993c; Marques, Day et al. 1994), which are rarely available. For example, in England and Wales, even if HM Prison Service had the resources to treat all sex offenders in custody, the sample size would still be limited by the relatively small number of sexual offenders discharged from prison each year (Marshall 1994, cited in Friendship and Thornton 2001). Furthermore, a long follow-up period (e.g. 10 years), would be politically difficult. The selection of a sample size and the implications of low base rates are more problematic when we consider statistical power, which is discussed in more detail later in this chapter. Moreover, the techniques that can be employed to increase sample sizes, e.g. combining the results from a number of similar programmes, or the deliveries across a range of locations of the 'same' programme (such as the evaluation of the SOTP in England and Wales, which is treated as one programme, although it is delivered in a number of prisons by different staff), or combining the results from several deliveries of the same programme over a number of years, causes problems that affect the reliability and validity of the evaluation. The programmes may have changed over time, or they may be delivered slightly differently in different locations, or by different staff. Thus, it is difficult to determine the programme that is actually being evaluated, and the treatment effects or differences across locations and time will be hidden and may even have an impact on the results of the evaluation. These issues of programme differences will be discussed in more detail later in the chapter.

Friendship and Thornton (2001: 290) conclude:

The methodological problems presented by the low base rate of sexual reconviction, in addition to the wide gap between reconviction rates and levels of actual sexual crime, put into jeopardy the use of sexual reconviction rates *per se* in the evaluation of prison-based treatment for sex offenders. The development of other outcome measures to supplement reconviction rates is essential.

They point out that this issue will also affect probation and community-based programmes.

Objections to the use of recidivism

Doob and Brodeur (1989: 181) made the following interesting point:

> The advocates of 'rehabilitation' appear sometimes to do their argument and society a disservice. ... They ... are defining 'rehabilitation' or 'treatment' programs in 'corrections' in such a way that the concepts become defined as anything that reduces recidivism. ... Presumably then, by using such a nice and neat operational definition ('the reduction of recidivism'), any incapacitative strategy would, effectively, qualify as being 'rehabilitative' if its effects were permanent.

Thus, they suggest that many treatment programmes should be evaluated in terms of goals quite different from recidivism. It is indeed true that the term 'rehabilitation' tends to imply that some improvement in the clients' moral or living standards have been achieved, which enable them to live more pro-social, fulfilling lives. However, the extent to which these orientations apply to sex offenders can be questioned. Many practitioners and researchers argue that treatment is necessary given the reality that most sex offenders eventually return to the community, and because of the damage that can be inflicted on innocent members of society. Thus, their main goal is to protect potential victims, rather than improve the lives of perpetrators. In this context, emphasis on recidivism seems to be an appropriate response. More recently, however, Ward (2002a) and Ward and Stewart (2003) have argued for the adoption of a 'Good Lives' model, which is very much in keeping with Doob and Brodeur's understanding of 'rehabilitation'. If this approach is embraced more fully with sex offenders, then the comments of Doob and Brodeur will need to be taken more seriously and research reflecting these points conducted.

Although rigorous methodological studies involving the measurement of recidivism are seen to be crucial in effectively answering the question of whether or not sex offender treatment is effective, there is also a growing feeling that this method alone is inadequate for the continued development and improvement of this form of intervention (see Furby *et al.* 1989; Marques, Nelson *et al.* 1994; Marshall and Pithers 1994; Barbaree 1997). Some authors argued that the problems discussed above give greater validity to other methodological designs (Barbaree 1997), some that more sensitive measures of maintenance and therapeutic change are needed (Marshall and Pithers 1994), whereas others argued that we need to understand how and why these programmes are effective (Pawson and Tilley 1994). For as Furby *et al.* (1989: 7) stated: 'Without the capacity to relate treatment activities or in-program changes to long-term adjustment, one runs the risk of learning very little of practical use from an outcome study.' In order to address these issues researchers have examined within-treatment changes in offenders' personal traits, behaviours and attitudes.

Personal and clinical characteristics

The measurement of these constructs is primarily associated with the within-treatment research design. Essentially researchers measure offenders on a number of characteristics at the start and end of the programme, with the assumption being that identified changes in these variables were produced by the treatment programme. However, a number of problems have been identified with this approach: questions regarding the extent to which these variables are related to recidivism; which constructs should be measured; which measurement tools best measure the appropriate constructs; and the extent to which this approach is valid.

Relationship with recidivism

Hollin (1994: 195) pointed out that 'it is possible for intervention programmes to produce significant outcomes in terms of positive personal change, but for that personal change to have no impact on criminogenic variables'. Furthermore, Hanson *et al.* (1993) argued that research linking treatment effects to recidivism is inconclusive and that there is little relationship between personality measures and recidivism. 'None of the psychological measures that have been used in previous research have been useful in predicting recidivism' (p. 646). This conclusion was supported by Proulx *et al.* (1997) who found that psychometric data did not predict recidivism in rapists and child molesters. Given that the majority of characteristics measured by researchers are chosen on the basis of treatment theory or research findings from comparisons of sex offending populations with 'normal' populations, it is not clear why this should be the case. 'There is little research, however, documenting how changes in treatment are associated with reduced recidivism' (Hanson *et al.* 1991: 179). Clearly, more research is needed to address this issue.

Which construct?

Researchers attempting to evaluate treatment programmes by examining within-treatment change must initially decide on the psychological and personality constructs they wish to examine. In order to maximize the reliability and validity of the research, these constructs should be chosen because of their relationship to sexual offending and treatment theory, or because they have been identified as differentiating sex offenders from the 'normal' population. An examination of the literature, however, reveals an enormous variety of constructs that meet these requirements and, in addition, that have been used in previous evaluation studies. Popular constructs include: denial, cognitive distortion, empathy, self-esteem, locus of control, expectancy of success, aggression/hostility, loneliness, intimacy, social competence and attitudes towards women and children.

Realistically, it would be impossible for researchers to measure all these constructs because of the time that this would involve. It is necessary, therefore, to try to determine which of these characteristics are the most suitable, that is, which best differentiate offenders from non-offenders, or which are theoretically the most important concepts. However, reviewing the literature reveals that this is far from obvious and the vast array of constructs that have been used in evaluation studies confirm this point. Consequently, few, if any, studies have used the same set of constructs to evaluate their treatment programme, with the result that comparison between evaluations is extremely difficult, if not impossible.

Which measure?

Having decided on a number of constructs to include in the evaluation, researchers must then choose the best method of measuring this construct. Unfortunately, this too is far from straightforward. For most of the constructs listed above, a number of psychometric scales have been developed, some of which have conflicting theories or arguments over the way in which the construct should be interpreted and measured (for example see research on empathy, which is briefly mentioned in Chapter 6). Given the time taken to complete each scale, researchers are limited in the number of scales they can employ in their evaluation. In addition, many of these scales have limited norm data for both the 'normal' and sex offender populations. From the literature, the best choice of scales is far from obvious and this confusion means that not only do evaluators employ different constructs, but that even studies using the same constructs employ different psychometric scales to measure these constructs. Thus, comparability is virtually impossible. Furthermore, the lack of norm data and the limited use of each scale for evaluations of this kind means that researchers have no indication of the scores that could be considered to be acceptable or unacceptable post-treatment outcome scores.

Validity

A criticism of treatment programmes, and hence of this method of evaluating them, is that programmes merely teach offenders how to respond appropriately to the psychometric scales being used for assessment, rather than engendering any real change in the men in terms of their offending behaviour (as discussed earlier there appears to be a poor relationship between treatment change and recidivism). The fact that psychometric scales are relatively transparent, in that it is possible to identify the purpose of the scale and tailor responses accordingly, is a large factor in this criticism. As Hanson *et al.* (1991: 182) pointed out:

> Clinical assessments are not anonymous and offenders who appear at risk for reoffending can face serious consequences related to sentencing, conditional release, and child custody. A useful way of conceptualizing the offenders' test taking behaviours is as a communication between the offender and the examiner (Rogers 1991). Sexual offenders rarely volunteer for assessments. Such assessments are typically completed at the request of some authority. Offenders likely perceive assessments as an occasion to present an image of themselves and their actions that the examining authority would find least objectionable.

Evidence for the transparency and the inadequacy of psychometric scales can be found in Webster and Marshall's (2004) discussion of the use of qualitative data in sex offender research. For example, Webster and Beech (2000) found that offenders could identify the correct and most socially desirable responses when given forced response choices in an empathy assessment; however, when asked to justify their responses, offenders revealed a different, less socially desirable, empathic response.

In 1991, Hanson and his colleagues questioned the reliability and validity of a number of psychometric tests designed to measure attitudes and cognitions. They concluded that although there was strong theoretical support indicating that these factors are related to sexual offending:

> The available research . . . does not support the validity of any of the existing measures for the prediction of sexual recidivism in correctional populations. . . . there may also be fundamental problems with using abstract attitude questionnaires with a population so prone to denial, minimization, and distortions.
>
> (p. 196)

Furthermore, they argue that researchers are better off constructing new measures rather than relying on existing scales and that more work is necessary to improve existing outcome measures for sex offenders.

Hanson *et al.* (1991: 200) suggested that it is important to find ways of eliminating the transparency associated with the majority of existing measures and they believe:

One potentially useful strategy for circumventing self-presentation biases is to use skill or competency measures. These measures can address knowledge gained in treatment (e.g. relapse-prevention techniques) as well as skill deficits that are thought to contribute to sexual offending (e.g. difficulty decoding the reactions of women).

These measures are perhaps more valid because they require offenders to generate their own responses rather than choose the best response from those that are already provided. Another solution, although one that is likely to overlap with Hanson and colleagues' suggestion, is, as Webster and Marshall suggest, to use and develop qualitative methods for assessing offender characteristics, as these seem better able to assess the complexities of offender characteristics and also appear to produce more reliable and valid data. In the course of treatment programmes, information is produced that could be analysed using qualitative methods, so additional time is not required to collect data (Mann 1999, cited in Webster and Marshall 2004); however, these methods require more time for analysis and also involve techniques that many practitioners are less or unfamiliar with. Some might also suggest that the use of qualitative data is less reliable and that interpretations of these data are less consistent across researchers and time. Furthermore, if each programme generates its own treatment-specific measure, there is a danger that these programmes reinforce the major criticism of this approach, which is that programmes merely teach offenders how to respond better to assessment measures, rather than changing offending behaviour. Thus, such measures must also be related to recidivism. Furthermore, the adoption of individual treatment measures would make it extremely difficult to compare the effectiveness of different treatment programmes, and with the small numbers of offenders generally involved with each treatment programme, effectively assessing the reliability and validity of each of these measures would be problematic.

Finally, Kroner and Weekes (1996) highlighted the importance of checking that the reliability and validity of measures is maintained when they are used on inmates. They argued that issues such as loss of freedom, adapting to structure, or guilt and anxiety may influence the relevance of test items, so that non-prison measures may not be transferable to prison settings. Few studies, however, have examined this factor. In fact, only a small number of psychometric tests that measure constructs that have been theoretically or empirically related to sexual offending have been tested or 'normed' on sex offender populations.

This review has shown that there are many problems associated with the outcome measures that have been employed to assess programme effectiveness. Essentially researchers must assess the strengths and weaknesses of each group of measures, and choose those that they can fund and which best address the question(s) they are researching. Recidivism is the most valid measure but it has a number of problems in terms of reliability, especially when comparing results across studies. In addition, the effective use of this method is expensive in terms of time and resources and it does little to address the question of how and why programmes are effective. The measurement of personality and clinical characteristics can help to address this question and is less costly and more reliable; however, the major weakness of this approach is that it has poor validity. Ultimately, the most meaningful evaluation would use a combination of these outcome measures (for example, see the work being conducted by Marques and her colleagues in 1993 and all in 1994) but the resource implications of this approach make it unlikely for all but a few studies.

Generic evaluation problems

When evaluating sex offender treatment programmes a number of issues and difficulties arise, no matter what methodological design or outcome measures are employed. These can be categorized into treatment characteristics, offender characteristics, problems associated with drop-outs and problems with statistical power.

Treatment characteristics

Describing cognitive-behavioural programmes or other psychological interventions is far from straightforward. It is reasonably easy to provide a basic description of a treatment programme, despite the fact that most evaluation studies fail to do this (Marshall and Pithers 1994; McPherson *et al*. 1994). However, it is much more difficult to provide a description of a programme that would enable others to replicate the programme, or to describe all the details that may have an impact on programme efficacy. In fact, word restrictions in journal publications and book chapters serve to actively discourage the inclusion of such descriptions. Marshall *et al*.'s (1998) publication is unique in that it describes a wide range of sex offender programmes operating in a variety of settings; however, it would still be difficult to replicate programmes using these descriptions. Without programme descriptions, it is impossible for the reader to know what was or was not effective. Practitioners are therefore unable to compare their own programmes with those that have been evaluated and so it is extremely difficult to amend and develop programmes from the evaluation literature.

It is commonplace now for treatment programmes to have strict manuals and protocols explaining how the programme should be delivered; however, if checks are not made to programme implementation, the programme that is actually delivered can vary greatly from that outlined in official documentation. Rutter and Giller (1983, cited in Perkins 1991) suggested that in many instances planned interventions are not actually delivered. More recently, Gendreau *et al.* (1999) stated that the issue of programme implementation has been relatively ignored in the evaluation of correctional treatment programmes. They argued that the effectiveness of any treatment programme is diminished if careful attention is not paid to implementation processes. In addition, they revealed that there is tentative evidence to suggest that recidivism is correlated with the quality of implementation. Marshall and Pithers (1994) argued that one of the issues affecting treatment effectiveness is the extent to which therapists adhere to treatment protocol; however, this issue is rarely covered in the evaluation literature (see Pithers (1997) for a discussion of the problems that can arise if some treatment staff veer from treatment protocols). Although this aspect has largely been ignored in the past, some guidance for evaluators of crime reduction interventions suggest that this aspect must be taken into consideration (Colledge *et al.* 1999). However, this issue has rarely been addressed to date in the sex offender treatment outcome literature.

Sex offender treatment is referred to in the evaluation literature almost as if it were a simple, single entity, that can easily be transferred from one location, context, time, group of offenders and so on to another. Yet, Shaughnessy and Zechmeister (1997) pointed out that treatment programmes are actually a 'package' of smaller components (as can be seen in Chapter 6) but most evaluations measure the effectiveness of the overall package, not the individual components. Consequently, it is not possible to know if one component is more critical than the other components to the overall effectiveness of the programme. There are important resource implications if only a small part of a programme is responsible for the effectiveness of the programme. Programmes could be delivered over shorter periods, using fewer resources. Thus, more sex offenders could be treated with the same resources, or valuable resources could be used for other purposes, yet this aspect is largely ignored in the evaluation literature.

This form of intervention, like other psychological interventions, operates via a series of complex social interactions. Furthermore, these complex interactions result in different treatment experiences for each client. Perkins (1991) argued that the context in which treatment is provided can be very important. In addition, as has been discussed previously, each treatment programme is different. Perhaps these differences are small but important aspects, such as the therapeutic style of treatment staff and the response of treatment clients, inevitably change from one programme to the next. This makes evaluating effects across programmes and isolating treatment effects difficult (McPherson *et al.* 1994). Marshall and Pithers (1994) believed that the best treatment programmes are likely to be those that respond to the clients' changing needs over time, which will be different for all clients. Thus, they argued that evaluations employing time-limited, inflexible sequences of interventions are likely to underestimate the potential effectiveness of treatment programmes.

The main model adopted in sex offender treatment, and many other forms of cognitive-behavioural therapy, is group treatment (see Chapter 5). Group processes and group cohesiveness, particularly when groups are discussing sensitive issues such as sexual and/or offending behaviours, are likely to play an important part in the outcome of the treatment. It would seem logical that a programme is less likely to be effective if group cohesiveness is low and offenders do not feel comfortable discussing issues in their treatment group, compared to a group where cohesiveness is high and offenders feel supported by the group and comfortable during discussions. These issues have rarely been evaluated in treatment programmes (see Beech *et al.* (1998) for an evaluation that unusually includes the assessment of group processes). Beech and Fordham (1997), using data from the aforementioned evaluation, revealed that treatment groups showing greater group cohesion demonstrated the best treatment outcome, though this issue has been discussed little since (although see Jennings and Sawyer (2003) for a rare discussion of techniques to improve the effectiveness of group processes).

From this brief discussion, it can be seen that the methodology traditionally adopted in sex offender treatment evaluations encourages researchers to overlook the complexities of these programmes and, more importantly, the subtle differences between programmes. The emphasis in behavioural techniques, early in the development of the cognitive-behavioural approach, where emphasis was placed on procedures rather than therapists, may account for the lack of consideration of these factors (Marshall, Fernandez *et al.* 2003). Yet, in other areas of therapy, these issues, particularly the importance of the therapist style, the perceptions the clients have of the therapist, and the therapist/client relationship, have been shown to be of great importance in treatment effectiveness. For example, a quarter of the variance in treatment effectiveness was shown to be related to the quality of the therapist/client relationship (Morgan *et al.* 1982). It is surprising, therefore, that these issues have not been explored more fully in sex offender treatment, where the nature of the issues being discussed is sensitive and difficult, and thus it could be expected that the way in which the treatment staff and clients approach this issue would have an impact on outcome. Yet, these problems have largely been overlooked, although in the last two to three years they have been investigated mostly by Marshall and his colleagues (see Marshall *et al.* 2002; Marshall, Fernandez *et al.* 2003; Marshall, Serran *et al.* 2003; Serran *et al.* 2003). These issues also lend further support to the suggestions of Pawson and Tilley (1994) and McPherson *et al.* (1994) that evaluations must address how and why interventions are effective.

Offender characteristics

As was briefly discussed in Chapter 1, a number of factors have been shown to be related to the risk of recidivism; for example, the number of previous convictions. It is probable that many of these factors may also influence treatment outcome. However, current methodological designs mask these effects (Gordon and Nicholaichuk 1996). For example, the same treatment is provided for all types of offenders and in evaluation studies results are pooled across offender types, or are compared with groups of untreated offenders who vary in terms of level of risk. Thus, it is possible that evaluation studies are not identifying effective programmes, or subgroups of offenders for whom treatment has been successful. In 1996, Nicholaichuk explored this issue by examining treatment outcome for samples of low- and high-risk offenders. For low-risk offenders, he found that the treatment group displayed a higher rate of recidivism than the control group; however, for high-risk offenders, the treatment group had a recidivism rate that was 59 per cent lower than the control group. But when these two groups were combined, no treatment effects were shown. Thus, when evaluating these programmes, it is important to consider (and specify in research reports) risk factors, including offender types, offence characteristics and offence histories (Marshall and Pithers 1994; McPherson *et al.* 1994; Nicholaichuk 1996; Williams 1996b).

Clients' perceptions of the therapeutic relationship and positive outcome in non-sex offender treatment appear to be positively correlated to treatment outcome (Walborn 1996). Frost (2004) revealed, from a grounded theory analysis, four distinct therapeutic engagement styles of child sexual offenders in a group treatment programme; styles that may be related to treatment outcome, although this aspect has yet to be evaluated. As mentioned earlier, Marshall and Pithers (1994) believe that the best treatment programmes are likely to be those that respond to the client's changing needs over time. Given that the risk and responsivity principles (see Chapter 2 and Andrews 1995) are two important principles of effective crime reduction interventions, it is surprising, and concerning, that these issues have largely been ignored in sex offender outcome research to date. Clearly, research is needed to address the range of questions posed by Pawson and Tilley (1994: 338; Andrews and Bonta 1994), which may help identify the characteristics, treatment response and treatment styles of offenders for whom treatment appears to be more effective. This could prove to be a key aspect in determining progress in treatment and risk following the completion of treatment – issues that could improve the risk management of, and thus, public protection from, sexual offenders.

Drop-outs

Throughout the duration of treatment, some clients will choose to leave the programme, while others will be asked to leave by treatment providers. These clients are commonly referred to as drop-outs. Marques, Day et al. (1994) pointed out that rates of treatment withdrawal and termination vary widely depending on a number of factors, such as offender motivation, programme requirements and the consequences of leaving.

As McPherson et al. (1994) revealed, this problem is not restricted to a small number of offenders. McPherson and her colleagues asked treatment providers to complete forms on the completion records of all sex offenders who were treated in Minnesota in 1992. Forms were completed for 1,551 offenders (59 per cent of the total number of offenders treated). Forty-eight per cent of these offenders were still engaged in treatment. Of the offenders who had left treatment, 53 per cent had satisfactorily completed treatment; however, the remaining 383 offenders (47 per cent) left before they had successfully completed the programme. Many of these drop-outs (40 per cent) were asked to leave by staff because they did not comply with the requirements of the programme (that is, they failed to make progress, violated rules, threatened others or exhibited violent behaviour), or they were not considered to be amenable to treatment (for example because they continued to deny their offences). One third (33 per cent) chose to leave the programme or absconded, while 13 per cent were transferred to another programme. Six per cent of these drop-outs reoffended, and sentences or probation orders expired before treatment was completed in 8 per cent of the cases. A community-based programme operating in Victoria, Australia reported similar drop-out rates (Lee et al. 1996). Of the 58 offenders accepted onto the programme over a three-year period, 21 (36 per cent) failed to complete the programme. Sixty-seven per cent of these drop-outs failed to continue to attend weekly sessions, 28 per cent were excluded for being disruptive in group sessions and 5 per cent were unable to attend as a result of jail sentences. Hall (1995) reported a drop-out rate of one-third for the cognitive-behavioural studies included in his meta-analysis. However, Shaw et al. (1995) found that 86 per cent of sex offenders admitted failed to complete a correctional treatment programme.

There is considerable debate regarding the inclusion of drop-out data in evaluation studies. Marshall (1993c) argued that the effectiveness of a programme can only be assessed by studying the offenders who actually completed the programme; however, Quinsey *et al.* (1993) suggested that such an approach overestimates the effectiveness of treatment. Furthermore, Foa and Emmelkamp (1983) noted that the value of a programme is measured not only by the success of those who complete it, but also by the number who refuse it or drop out after beginning treatment. In addition, excluding the outcome of drop-outs, when it is not possible to exclude offenders with similar characteristics from the control group, biases the outcome of evaluations in favour of treatment (McConaghy 1999a). This practice also violates the randomization procedure (Cook and Cambell 1979, cited in McConaghy 1999a). However, including drop-out data is often problematic as it may be more difficult to track the progress of these offenders (in recidivism studies), or to persuade these men to complete assessment once they have left the programme (personal/clinical change studies).

In 1989, Furby and his colleagues stated that schemes must be developed to account for drop-outs; however, Marques, Day *et al.* (1994) pointed out that there is still no consensus on how these offenders should be dealt with in evaluation research. In some studies, drop-outs are counted as failures (see Maletzky 1991), whereas in other studies outcome data from treatment groups which include and exclude drop-outs are examined (for example see Marques, Day *et al.* 1994). However, more often than not, drop-outs are not described or included in analyses.

Even if researchers believe that it is important to include drop-outs in their analyses, this is not a straightforward process. In a large treatment programme, where random allocation was being employed to evaluate programme effectiveness, 132 offenders were initially randomly assigned to treatment (Marques, Day *et al.* 1994). Of these offenders, 26 withdrew their consent prior to the start of programme. Of the 106 who began treatment, 20 did not complete it (13 voluntarily withdrew, while seven were returned to prison). Thus, the authors questioned which of these offenders should be considered the treatment group: all those who were assigned to the treatment group; only those who started the programme; or only those who successfully completed the intervention.

It is also difficult to draw comparisons and conclusions regarding the effectiveness of programmes with differing drop-out rates. For example, a programme may have a 100 per cent completion rate but be able to be effective with only 50 per cent of those who complete it; another programme, however, may have a 50 per cent drop-out rate but demonstrate effective outcomes with all the clients who complete the programme. If 100 offenders begin both these programmes, successful outcome would be demonstrated in 50 offenders from each treatment group. Should these programmes be considered equally effective? In theory, perhaps, they should be, but research has shown that drop-outs have much higher rates of recidivism than those who do not begin treatment (Cook *et al.* 1991; Marques, Day *et al.* 1994; Miner and Dwyer 1995; Harris *et al.* 1998; Marques 1999). However, factors that result in offenders dropping out of treatment may be related more to the characteristics of the offenders rather than the characteristics of the programmes (although more research is needed in this area). For example, Marques, Day *et al.* (1994: 50) stated that 'those who are the most impulsive and exercise the least amount of self-control are likely to be the ones to withdraw or be terminated from treatment'. In addition, Chaffin (1994) showed that drop-outs had fewer social/sexual skills and Cook *et al.* (1991) found that they had a higher number of previous offences and were the 'most troublesome recidivists' (p. 241). Despite these findings, Lee *et al.* (1996) managed to reduce the drop-out rate from 42 to 29 per cent by enhancing offenders' motivation for treatment. One way Lee *et al.* did this was by providing individual treatment for offenders, before allowing them to participate in the group programme, until they acknowledged their problems and were prepared to work on them.

This review suggests that drop-outs should not be ignored in evaluation research, but that treatment strategies need to be developed for this group of offenders who are: 'the offenders for whom intervention appears to be the most desperately needed and who present the greatest challenge for the development of new and innovative approaches.' (Marques, Day *et al.* 1994: 50).

Statistical power

In 1997 Barbaree pointed out that most discussion and concern regarding the evaluation of sex offender treatment programmes (and indeed of many other psychological intervention evaluation) focuses on the possibility of making a Type I error; that is, of concluding that treatment is effective, when in fact it is not (or rejecting the null hypothesis when it is in fact true). To date, he argued, serious consideration had not been given to the issue of making a Type II error; that is, of concluding that treatment is ineffective, when in fact it is effective.

The concept of 'power', specifically the probability that the null hypothesis will be rejected when it is in fact false (or the probability of avoiding a Type II error, which is $1-\beta$, where β is the probability of making a Type II error) was first described by Cohen (1962). This concept was slow to become accepted in psychological research but in the last decade has gained prominence, so much so that it is now commonplace for funding bodies to require power calculations in research bids. Cohen (1988, cited in Clark-Carter 1998) suggested that, as a rule of thumb, a reasonable level of power to aim for under normal circumstances is 0.8. The power of a statistical hypothesis, the level of α (i.e. the level of significance, or of making a Type I error), the sample size(s), and the size or strength of the treatment effect (more commonly referred to as effect size) are all interrelated; for example, when sample size and treatment effect are constant, the lower the α level (preferred and usually set at 0.05), the lower the power (when higher power values are preferred). However, by increasing the sample size it is possible to have both the level of α and the level of power at what have come to be accepted as desirable levels (0.05 and 0.8 respectively).

There are many ways of using these factors in statistical calculations and considerations. Traditionally, however, psychological research has tended to give prominence to setting the α level (usually at 0.05) and focusing less on the other factors, such that samples sizes have largely been determined by the number of participants available to researchers, and effect sizes and power levels have largely been ignored. However, when the level of power has been calculated on studies using this approach, power has been shown to be low, and not improved even after Cohen's publication in 1962 (Barbaree 1997). In recent years, though, there has been an increased focus on both effect sizes (see Marshall and McGuire (2003) for a discussion of effect sizes in sex offender treatment) and level of power (see Barbaree 1997), with emphasis being put on selecting a sample size that will provide an acceptable level of power, given the predicted expected effect size(s) and level of α. What these calculations have revealed is that much larger sample sizes are needed than had previously been thought or utilized. This is particularly problematic in sex offender research because of the low base rates and the problems in accessing large sample sizes, as discussed previously.

Barbaree (1997) manipulated the four factors described above (sample and effect size, α and power levels) in a number of ways, taking into account a range of base rates, to discuss the power of sex offender evaluation research. He found that when $n = 100$, and treatment effects were moderate (0.50) and large (0.66) acceptable levels of power (> 0.80) were obtained when base rates were above 0.60 and 0.40 respectively. However, these base rates do not reflect the average base rates described above, of 0.13 or below, and the treatment effects are larger than those described by Marshall and McGuire (2003), which ranged from 0.10 to 0.28. Yet, when Barbaree used a small treatment effect size (0.33, still higher than the highest effect size described by Marshall and McGuire), an acceptable level of power was not achieved at any of the tested base rates (0.10 to 0.70). When n was increased to 150, an acceptable level of power was only achieved when the base rate was 0.70.

When Barbaree used the values obtained by Hall (1995), a base rate of 0.27 and an effect size of 0.29 (which incidentally is different to the 0.24

effect size reported by Marshall and McGuire for the same study), he found that the sample size would have to be 495 to achieve a power level of 0.50 (described as the power level of the 'average' study in the literature), and a sample size of 916 would be needed for a power level of 0.80. Finally, Barbaree calculated that the treatment effects sizes required for three prominent studies (Hanson *et al.* 1991; Rice *et al.* 1991; Marques, Day *et al.* 1994) were 0.42, 0.37 and 0.49 respectively to achieve a power level of 0.50, and 0.56, 0.50 and 0.63 respectively for a power level of 0.80. Given that these effect sizes exceed those of published research, and are high for any kind of psychological and many medical interventions (see Marshall and McGuire 2003), this is unrealistic. Thus, it could be concluded that these studies will fail to find a treatment effect, even if there is one, as the power level of their study, given the likely treatment effect, stated sample size and base rate, is not sufficient. Given that these studies are relatively well resourced and have relatively large sample sizes that many evaluators would find difficult to obtain, this finding is particularly concerning.

Clearly, what these calculations reveal is that Barbaree's concern about the likelihood of Type II, rather than Type I errors, is justified. Studies of recidivism require large sample sizes that are likely to be unachievable in many locations. Where these can be achieved, it is through combining many deliveries of the 'same' programme, over several locations, or many years, or both. The problems of this approach have been discussed above. Furthermore, relatively large samples are needed to assess pre- and post-treatment change, or to compare the psychometric test scores from more than one programme, or programme delivery. Given that treatment groups are small, with 10 or fewer clients, analyses using a single group are likely to have insufficient levels of power. Hanson *et al.* (2002), however, argue that sample size is less important than careful consideration of the comparison group, to ensure a comparison group that can be considered to be equivalent in all important respects to the treatment group. Although the individual study may not have sufficient power, a number of methodologically sound studies, albeit with small samples, can be combined in a meta-analysis. Yet, although this approach may help to answer the overall question of whether treatment is effective or not, it does not help in the reliable assessment of each individual programme.

Given the methodological debate in the outcome literature, and the focus on employing robust, appropriate designs, there is a great deal of pressure on researchers/evaluators, particularly in programmes with small numbers of clients, and it is not surprising that some researchers have stated that new methods of evaluation and/or new outcome measures are required (Barbaree 1997; Friendship and Thornton 2001). One method employed to overcome some of these problems is the meta-analysis. These studies combine the effect sizes from published studies to assess if, across all the studies included in the analysis, there is an overall treatment effect. However, the reliability of these studies depends on the quality of the evaluations incorporated in the analysis. As will be seen in the next chapter, there has been debate about the findings of published meta-analyses, with some suggesting they reveal positive outcome, while others, using the same studies, argue that they reveal negative outcome, or suffer from so many methodological problems that the results cannot be relied upon.

A methodology that has previously been overlooked in the evaluation literature is the use of qualitative methods, although these methods, too, have issues with regard to reliability and validity. It is rather surprising to note in the evaluation literature that the offenders or clients themselves are not asked what they thought of the programme, what they felt they achieved, learnt and so on. Offenders' progress is turned into an array of numbers ranging from recidivism rates to scores on psychometric tests. Yet, an offender who shows a significant treatment change, who says he has benefited nothing from the programme, who says he does not believe that he can avoid reoffending, or who insists that he does not understand what the programme staff were telling him, is likely to remain a risk and become a treatment failure. As Webster and Marshall (2004) show, qualitative methods can provide useful information that reveals complexities often hidden in quantitative research. Furthermore, qualitative research does not require the large sample sizes of quantitative research.

Garret *et al.* (2003) distributed questionnaires to treated offenders to elicit their views on the treatment they had received. Although this type of research is unable to assess conclusively if the programme was effective or not, it was able to highlight a number of areas that could be improved, and it raised awareness of aspects of the programme that offenders preferred and believed they benefited from most, some of which went against what might have been expected. Similarly, Drapeau *et al.* (2004) interviewed 24 offenders completing a treatment programme investigating the offenders' impression of the voluntary basis of treatment, the nature of motivation for treatment, and the ways that treatment was or was not helpful. In addition, Murphy (1998) also reported qualitative information about offenders' views, which they obtained from interviews with offenders in their cells. Recommendations for change were also obtained from this study. Clearly, this type of information is useful and can be used to develop and improve programmes. In addition, it may be able to begin to answer Pawson and Tilley's (1994) third, fourth and fifth questions: what it is about the programmes that engender changes, how the programmes work, and what the range of outcomes are (other than an effect on recidivism) –

questions that are currently being neglected in sex offender treatment outcome research.

This review has shown that designing evaluations of sex offender treatment programmes is not a simple process. There are a variety of issues to be considered and a number of difficulties to overcome. Essentially, each evaluator must chose the methodology that best addresses the aims of their evaluation, within the constraints placed on the research by the availability of resources and the research environment within which they are based. The result of this, however, is that virtually every evaluation employs a slightly different methodology, which makes comparisons across studies particularly difficult. In addition, each evaluation is inevitably compromized in that a number of methodological weaknesses will make drawing firm conclusions regarding the effectiveness of the programme problematic. However, some attempts have been made to standardize the approach, by setting guidance for evaluators or minimum standards.

In 1999, Colledge *et al.* produced guidance for evaluators of crime-reduction interventions funded by the Home Office (England and Wales), based on the principle that all offender programmes must be evaluated for their impact on crime. In their general principles for evaluations, Colledge and colleagues suggest the following points: evaluation methods need to be built in from the start; the depth of evaluation needs to be considered, with different designs adopted according to whether the programme is new, being developed and/or expanded, or being monitored on a regular basis; the standard of operation, or implementation of the programme needs to be monitored/evaluated; the use of short-term (e.g. within-treatment psychometric test changes) as well as long-term (e.g. recidivism) outcome measures should be considered; the choice of outcome measures should suit the intended purposes of the programme; the numbers being evaluated must be sufficient to produce robust statistical results; a control or comparison group (using randomization if possible) should be used, if possible; selection effects should be accounted for, which includes ensuring that drop-outs are taken into account; and finally, independent verification of results should be ensured. This guidance also requires the completion of a cost-benefit analysis.

More focused on sex offender treatment outcome, the committee appointed by the Association for the Treatment of Sexual Abusers (ATSA) to review sex offender treatment outcome, set the minimum standards for a study to enter an evaluative review as having a satisfactory comparison group of untreated sexual offenders, that is that there is an untreated comparison group from the same setting as the treatment group, which approximately match the treated offenders on relevant offence history and demographic characteristics (Hanson *et al.* 2002).

Practical and resource constraints will mean that some evaluators and practitioners, particularly those who treat small numbers of clients/ offenders, will be unable to meet these guidelines, although the guidelines do enable a more consistent sifting of reliable from unreliable or less reliable studies in an attempt to address the question of whether treatment is effective or not, which is the issue addressed in the next chapter.

Chapter 8

Are programmes effective?
Part 2: Research evidence

Despite many attempts to evaluate the effectiveness of sex offender treatment programmes, the interpretation of the findings of such studies remains controversial. The conclusions of some authors seem to have changed little over the last two decades. For example, the Howard League (1985) argued that reported examples of change are not hard to come by but conclusive, scientific proof is more difficult to obtain. Later, Furby *et al.* (1989) claimed that only tentative conclusions could be made as every evaluation study has methodological flaws. Thus, they concluded that 'there is no evidence that treatment effectively reduces sex offence recidivism' (p. 25). Similarly, in 1993, Quinsey *et al.* argued that 'the effectiveness of treatment in reducing sex offender recidivism has not yet been demonstrated' (p. 521) and almost 10 years after the Howard League report was published, McPherson *et al.* (1994: 38) stated: 'there have been few studies that have achieved the level of scientific rigor needed to arrive at definitive conclusions about treatment effectiveness'.

It is interesting to note, given the previous review of the methodological problems associated with evaluating sex offender treatment programmes, that all these negative conclusions are based on methodology. Essentially, these authors have argued that researchers have been unable to *prove conclusively* that treatment is effective because of methodological weaknesses. These conclusions say very little about the actual treatment programmes being evaluated. Interestingly, none of these authors suggest that research has been unable to demonstrate conclusively that treatment is *not* effective. But as Marshall, Jones *et al.* (1991: 466) argued:

There are far too many people who are ready to seize on the conclusion of the methodological idealists, that treatment for sex offenders has not been demonstrated to be effective. Unfortunately, this gets readily converted into the declaration that these men cannot (usually this means ever) be treated.

These methodologically based conclusions imply that it is, or one day will be, possible to address the problem of poor methodology and demonstrate conclusive proof of effectiveness; however, this is unrealistic. Firstly, it can be argued that social science research can never prove anything *conclusively*, rather that a particular body of research suggests that a particular hypothesis is supported until a study (or, more realistically, a group of studies) reveals that this is not the case. Secondly, as the discussion in the previous chapter has shown, sex offender evaluations can never hope to be methodologically perfect, a point also made by West (1996: 65): 'given the nature of the prison and probation approaches to the treatment and rehabilitation of sex offenders, the prospect of rigorous scientific validation of outcome is remote'. Thus, in the real world, research can never prove *conclusively* whether or not sex offender treatment programmes are effective.

This conclusion does not mean that we should abandon all efforts to monitor the effectiveness of treatment programmes. As was pointed out at the beginning of the previous chapter, it is important that all treatment programmes are continually assessed, given the possible consequences of poor, ineffective treatment. In addition, although research may not be able to prove effectiveness beyond doubt, over time, with enough studies, and the use of meta-analysis, it can reveal patterns and trends about treatment efficacy. As Marshall (1993c) pointed out, little evaluation research would be conducted if too much emphasis was placed on doing the perfect study, and Shaughnessy and Zechmeister (1997: 353) stated that 'some knowledge about the effectiveness of a treatment is more desirable than none'. Thus, Marshall (1993c) argued that a climate has to be created that will encourage the reporting of programme effectiveness with a goal to answering the question: 'can we discern grounds for optimism in the treatment outcome literature?' (p. 525). This does not mean, however, that we pay no attention to methodological issues: 'to ignore certain criteria in reviewing the literature . . . will not encourage any reader to have confidence in the conclusions drawn from the review' (Marshall, Jones *et al.* 1991: 466). Consequently, a balance between the two extremes must be found where researchers adopt the most rigorous methodology possible and draw conclusions that take account of the methodological weaknesses of each study.

North America

Evidence demonstrating the effectiveness of North American cognitive-behavioural treatment programmes was provided by many studies in the

1980s. Davidson (1984, cited in Marshall, Jones *et al.* 1991) found that child molesters and rapists treated at an Ontario penitentiary had a sexual recidivism rate (derived from official police records) of 11 per cent compared to a rate of 35 per cent for untreated matched controls released in the eight years prior to the start of the programme. Gordon (1989, cited in Grossman *et al.* 1999; Marshall, Jones *et al.* 1991) revealed a sexual recidivism rate (reconviction recorded in police records, follow-up average of two years and a maximum of seven years) of 10 per cent for treated child molesters and rapists (Saskatchewan Federal Penitentiary) who were similar to those studied by Davidson. No comparison group was included, but using the untreated recidivism rates from Davison's study, Marshall and colleagues concluded that the programme was effective.

Marshall and Barbaree (1988) demonstrated lower rates of sexual recidivism (official criminal record and unofficial police and child welfare reports of reoffending, follow-up of one to four years) in 68 treated (13.2 per cent), compared to 58 untreated (34.5 per cent) paedophiles who had abused girls, paedophiles who had abused boys and incest offenders. They also reported a significant within-treatment reduction in deviant arousal. Treated offenders were treated via an outpatient service in the Kingston Sexual Behavioural Clinic. In 1989, a 3 per cent sexual recidivism rate (rearrest, seven-year follow-up) was exhibited by 147 treated child molesters (Vermont State corrections facility) and 15 per cent for treated rapists (Pithers and Cumming 1989, cited in Marshall, Jones *et al.* 1991). Across both groups a sexual recidivism rate of 6 per cent in treated offenders was compared to a rate of 33 per cent in untreated offenders (Pithers and Cumming 1989, cited in Grossman *et al.* 1999).

Although these results are promising, many of these studies suffered from less robust methodology, for example the comparison group in Marshall and Barbaree's study were deemed suitable for treatment, but subsequently declined to attend the programme. Following criticism of the choice of control group (Quinsey *et al.* 1993), Marshall (1993c) argued strongly that this was an acceptable group and that reasons for not attending treatment were not necessarily to do with factors related to risk, e.g. that offenders lived too far away from the treatment centre, rather than they were not motivated to attend. More importantly in terms of assessing current treatment programmes, the programmes evaluated in these early studies bear very little resemblance to the comprehensive programmes delivered today. For example, the programme evaluated by Marshall and Barbaree in 1988 contained aversion therapy, masturbatory reconditioning (rarely being the main focus of current programmes, see Chapter 3) and social skills training. Programmes evaluated by Abel *et al.* (1988), Gordon (1989), and Pithers and

Cumming (1989) contained elements that were more similar to today's programmes (see Grossman *et al.* 1999), but were likely to be much less sophisticated.

In the 1990s, many more reports of positive outcomes were published. Freeman-Longo and Knopp (1992) reported a reduction in recidivism of approximately 50 per cent for treated men. A sexual recidivism rate (rearrest, six-year follow-up) of 3 per cent for treated child molesters and rapists compared with a sexual recidivism rate of 20 per cent for untreated controls was obtained in an evaluation in a Vermont state corrections facility (Hildebran *et al.*, cited in Grossman *et al.* 1999). Bingham *et al.* (1995) stated that from a sample of 202 offenders mandated to a community-based programme in Florida, USA, who had been followed up for an average of five years, only four offenders had been rearrested for a sexual offence. However, there was no comparison group in this study.

Further support for sex offender treatment was provided by the analysis of data from the Clearwater programme, delivered in a Regional Psychiatric Centre (Saskatoon) in Canada (Prairies region) (Nicholaichuk *et al.* 2000). A total of 296 high-risk sex offenders treated between 1981 and 1996 (168 rapists, 49 paedophiles, 47 offenders who offended against adults and children, 32 incest offenders) and 283 untreated sex offenders (although they were untreated at Clearwater, some may have been treated at other institutions) drawn from a sample of over 2,600 offenders were matched on age at index offence, date of index offence, and prior criminal history, and followed up for an average of six years. Missing data meant that there were some difficulties in matching offenders, and difficulties in matching offenders on all variables meant that treated offenders often had more previous convictions than the 'matched' untreated offenders.

The officially recorded conviction rate for new sexual offences for the treated offenders was 14.5 per cent, compared to 33.2 per cent for untreated offenders. This difference was not statistically significant, but it was considered, by Nicholaichuk *et al.* to be clinically significant as recidivism was reduced by 50 per cent. Furthermore, only 8.8 per cent of the treated offenders who had no prior offences sexually reoffended, compared to 27.3 per cent of their untreated counterparts; whereas 23.5 per cent of treated recidivist offenders committed new sexual crimes, compared to 43.0 per cent of the untreated comparison group. Forty-eight per cent of treated offenders remained out of prison compared to 28.3 per cent untreated offenders, and treated offenders committed fewer new sexual crimes than untreated comparisons. Finally, survival analysis revealed that untreated offenders committed new offences sooner than treated offenders, and committed new offences at a higher rate through-out the follow-up period. This is a comparatively robust methodology (for sex offender treatment evaluations) and reports some promising results that were consistent across analyses. However, as Nicholaichuk and colleagues discuss, there were problems matching offenders and it is possible that the untreated comparisons were treatment refusers or drop-outs, or that some had treatment at other institutions, and the 'matching' of criminal histories meant that treated offenders had more previous offences than untreated offenders.

McGrath et al. (1998) reported a significant treatment benefit from an outpatient cognitive-behavioural programme in a rural Vermont county, compared to a non-specific treatment programme and a non-treatment control group. Recidivism rates (new offences identified from criminal record checks and probation violations) were examined for 122 sex offenders (23 rapists, 92 child molesters and eight hands-off offenders) placed under correctional supervision in Addison County, Vermont from 1984 to 1995. Seventy-one offenders completed a specialized cognitive-behavioural treatment programme, while 32 offenders received less specialized mental health treatment, and 19 offenders received no treatment as they refused it. Retrospective pre-treatment comparisons revealed that the non-treatment group had more extensive criminal histories, but no other differences were identified between the three groups. Most offenders were considered low to medium risk. After an average period at risk of 62.9 months, the specialized treatment group had a significantly lower rate of general recidivism than the non-specialized treatment and non-treatment groups. Furthermore, the specialized treatment group had a significantly lower sexual recidivism (one recidivist, 1.4 per cent) rate than the non-specialized treatment group (five recidivists, 15.6 per cent).

In a later study in Vermont, McGrath et al. (2003) compared the recidivism rates (all new charges of offences based on criminal record checks), over a mean follow-up period of six years, of 56 sex offenders (rapists, non-contact sex offenders, incest offenders and child molesters) who completed a prison-based cognitive behavioural programme in the Vermont Department of Corrections, with 49 programme drop-outs, and 90 men who refused treatment services. Although the groups are clearly not fully equivalent, McGrath et al. found that there were no group differences in the offenders' pre-treatment risk as assessed by the RRASOR and Static-99 actuarial measures. The sexual reoffence rate of 5.4 per cent for the treated offenders was significantly lower than the rate of 30.6 per cent for the treatment drop-outs and 30.0 per cent for the group who refused treatment. Furthermore, the treatment group had a significantly lower violent recidivism rate (12.5 per cent) than those who refused treatment (31.1 per cent). The drop-outs had a violent recidivism rate of 16.3 per cent, which was not significantly different from the rates of the other groups. No significant differences were found in the rates of other (i.e. non-sexual or non-violent recidivism) or any (all offences combined) recidivism.

Interestingly, McGrath et al. (2003) found that only four of the 45 (9 per cent) sexual recidivists reoffended while completing follow-up treatment in the community, and only seven (16 per cent) while under community correctional supervision. Furthermore, sexual recidivists were significantly much less likely to have received community supervision. Sixteen offenders (14 per cent) who received community supervision reoffended compared to 29 offenders (35 per cent) who received no such supervision. Similarly, sexual recidivists were significantly less likely to be in community treatment: five (8 per cent) who were in community treatment reoffended compared to 40 (31 per cent) who were not. McGrath and colleagues also observed that the longer offenders remained in community treatment, or under community supervision, the less likely they were to reoffend, either sexually or violently. Clearly, this is a strong endorsement for long-term treatment and supervision in the community.

Not every published evaluation of North American programmes, however, has shown positive treatment effects. In 1991, Rice et al. reported that there were no significant differences in the recidivism rates (arrest or conviction, average 6.3-year follow-up) of two groups of offenders who had each been given one of two different behavioural therapies to control their sexual arousal to inappropriate stimuli. In a later study, Rice et al. (1994, cited in Marshall and Pithers 1994) found that the reoffence rate for treated offenders was higher than that of untreated offenders. There are, however, many criticisms of this report and of the treatment programme being evaluated (Marshall, Jones et al. 1991; Marshall and Pithers 1994; Peebles 1999). This treatment was limited in that it used a single behavioural technique (for example, aversion therapy) (Marshall, Jones et al. 1991), provided only a brief intervention with no aftercare or clinical follow-up (Grossman et al. 1999) and as such is not comparable to the majority of cognitive-behavioural treatment programmes. Marshall and Pithers (1994) argued that such limited treatment could not be expected to be effective. Furthermore, in one report, treatment was said to have been terminated a decade before the report was published (Quinsey et al. 1993). In addition, only 18 of the 29 treated men 'successfully' completed the treatment (Marshall, Jones et al. 1991), the patients were in a maximum-security facility and the sample was most likely dominated by high-risk offenders, many of whom had psychiatric disorders (see Grossman et al. 1999). Thus, it is not surprising that the results were negative (Marshall, Jones et al. 1991).

The Sex Offender Treatment and Evaluation Project (SOTEP) is unique and produced what is generally perceived as one of the methodologically strongest set of studies (Miner et al. 1990; Marques et al. 1993, 2000; Marques, Day et al. 1994; Marques, Nelson et al. 1994). SOTEP was designed to evaluate the effectiveness of an innovative relapse-prevention-based programme at the Atascadero State Hospital in California, which operated from 1985 until 1995. Rapists and child molesters recruited from Californian prisons who qualified for the programme were matched on age, criminal history and type of offence. One offender of each pair was randomly assigned to treatment and the other to no treatment (volunteer control group). A third group (non-volunteer controls), which consisted of matched offenders who did not want to attend treatment, was also monitored. Offenders who dropped out of treatment formed another group in follow-up analyses. Within-treatment changes that were linked to the treatment model and measured using a battery of psychometric and skills-based tests were monitored along with rearrests over a five-year period. The project also reviewed the programme in discussions with treatment staff and a small number of recidivists ($n=9$), and uniquely published these findings and their recommendations for change (see Marques et al. 2000).

In 1993, Miner et al. reported that 50 SOTEP treated offenders (rapists and child molesters) demonstrated a significant reduction in their expression of cognitive distortions and justifications, and that these treated offenders did this significantly less than the 48 untreated volunteer controls. Similarly, treated offenders showed an increased acceptance of responsibility for their behaviour and the consequences of that behaviour, and a deceased sexual arousal to deviant sexual themes. Finally, treated offenders developed more effective coping and relapse-prevention skills. These findings were mirrored in an analysis of 79 treated child molesters (Marques, Nelson et al. 1994), although there is some overlap in the offenders included in these two analyses. In 2000, Marques et al. reported that their evaluation data indicated that treatment subjects made significant progress towards each of the five treatment goals in that they demonstrated an increased sense of personal responsibility and decreased justification of sexual deviance, a decrease in deviant sexual interests, an understanding of and ability to apply relapse-prevention concepts and techniques, an improved ability to identify high-risk situations, and improved skills in avoiding and coping with high-risk situations.

The most recent published recidivism data (see Marques et al. 2000) showed that after about five years at risk, the 167 treated offenders had a lower sexual rearrest rate (10.8 per cent) than the 225 volunteer controls (13.8 per cent) and the 220 non-volunteer controls (13.2 per cent). This continued earlier trends (Marques, Day et al. 1994), but as with earlier analyses, there was no statistically significant difference. The drop-out group consistently demonstrated the highest levels of recidivism: after an average of five years follow-up, the recidivism rate of the 37 drop-outs was 18.9 per cent.

Cognitive distortions and justifications were found to be related to sexual and violent recidivism in 34 rapists (20 treated, 10 volunteer controls and four drop-outs), with fewer distortions and justifications indicating a reduced likelihood of recidivism (Marques *et al.* 1993). Twenty-seven rapists (13 treatment, 13 volunteer control and one drop-out) completed a test to measure awareness and recognition of relapse-prevention factors. Although no significant relationship was identified for sexual recidivism, four subscales were linked to violent recidivism. In child molesters (76 in the treatment group and 79 in the volunteer controls) at risk on average for 38.4 months, no significant relationship was identified between cognitive distortions, justifications and risk for sexual offences, although there was a relationship for violent offences (higher cognitive distortions and justifications at release in-dicated a increased risk of violent reoffending) (Marques, Nelson *et al.* 1994). Higher levels of deviant sexual arousal in both pre- and post-treatment measures were related to higher risk of sexual offences, but a lower risk of violent offences. One of the strongest predictors of risk of sexual offence was the ability to use relapse-prevention techniques: offenders able to identify high-risk situations, formulate adequate coping responses and present a complete picture of the consequences of reoffence were less likely to commit a new sex offence. Subsequent analyses, however, did not find this effect for the whole treatment group, although this finding applied to a sub-group of offenders with a more extensive history of sexual offending. Among these high-risk offenders, those who mastered relapse-prevention techniques had a lower risk of reoffence. In the remainder of the offenders, recidivism rates were not influenced by performance in relapse-prevention tasks.

As mentioned previously, the SOTEP evaluation used a robust methodology and is revered by many. So, the fact that significant differences in recidivism between the treatment and control groups have consistently not been identified is quite damning. Yet, concern has been raised about the SOTEP treatment programme, which relied almost exclusively on relapse-prevention techniques and theory. Maletzy (1998, cited in Maletzky and Steinhauser 2002) and McConaghy (1998) have both suggested that this approach may not be the most effective treatment method. However, a quick comparison of the sample sizes that Barbaree (1997) calculated were needed for power levels around 0.8 would suggest ($n = 916$) that even though the eventual sample sizes in the SOTEP were relatively large (167 treated, 220 and 225 controls), it is still probable that the study had insufficient power to identify any treatment effect. Yet, if this study, which was set up and resourced specifically to include adequate evaluation, is unable to produce a study with sufficient power, there is little hope that any study will be able to achieve this. Furthermore, this project revealed that the relationship between within-treatment changes and recidivism was complex. While significant treatment effects were consistently demonstrated, some changes were related to sexual recidivism in some subgroups, and some to violent recidivism in some subgroups. No treatment change seemed to reliably predict recidivism across the whole group, and the analyses do not reveal a simple pattern of relationships.

In 2004, Hanson et al. conducted a study with a relatively long average follow-up period of 12.5 years (range seven to 14 years) and an unusually large sample of offenders (734 offenders). In the 1980s, the Correctional Service Canada introduced weekly community treatment sessions for all sex offenders released in the Pacific Region. This allowed Hanson and his colleagues to compare sex offenders released prior to the introduction of this policy (321 offenders) with those who were released following its instigation (403 offenders), which they argued reduced selection bias. No significant differences were found in sexual recidivism (21.8 per cent compared to 21.1 per cent), violent recidivism (44.5 per cent versus 42.9 per cent) or general recidivism (60.4 per cent compared to 56.6 per cent) of the two groups. The outcome remained unchanged when a variety of variables, such as age, length of follow-up, static risk factors and year of release were controlled for. Methodologically speaking, this is a very robust study and so the findings of this study are quite negative; however, there are questions over the standard of the programme. Hanson et al. (2004) point out that the programme was well regarded at the time, although they admit that it would not meet the current Canadian Service of Correction's accreditation standards. The authors emphasize that the study shows that the programme evaluated did not have a significant impact on recidivism, with the implication being that this finding does not necessarily apply to all other programmes.

Other evaluation results are more equivocal. Abel et al. (1988) used self-report data to calculate recidivism rates after a one-year follow-up period. A rate of 12 per cent was reported for treated offenders, which, according to Marshall et al. (1991) suggests the results were poor; however, with no reliable self-report comparisons for untreated men (and given the widely accepted belief that official data underreports offences), it is difficult to draw any conclusions about the effectiveness of this programme. Abel et al. (1988, cited in Grossman et al. 1999) reported a recidivism rate of 34.9 per cent for offenders who dropped out of the programme; however, the problem of using drop-outs as a comparison group was discussed in the previous chapter, and this information does little to improve our understanding of the effect of this programme.

In 1993, Hanson and his colleagues reported on the long-term (93 per cent of the men were followed up for more than 15 years and 63 per cent for more than 20 years) recidivism rates (police records of reconviction)

of a relatively large group of child molesters who had attended a behavioural treatment programme between 1965 and 1973. These researchers found no significant differences between the recidivism rates of the treatment group ($n = 106$) and the two comparison groups (group 1 were from the same institution but before the start of programme ($n = 31$), so they were not treated; group 2 were from same institution at the same time but they did not complete treatment ($n = 60$)). However, post-treatment results did suggest that the treated men felt more in control of their lives, were more extroverted, experienced less subjective distress and less depression, and had improved self-esteem. But these factors were not related to recidivism. Hanson *et al.* concluded: 'Our findings of substantial long-term recidivism suggest that any short-term treatment, no matter how well conceived and well delivered, is unlikely to effectively control many child molesters' (p. 651). But although this study had a lengthy follow-up period and large sample sizes, it highlights one of the issues of using recidivism data discussed in the previous chapter, as the treatment was quite outdated by time of publication.

Zgoba *et al.* (2003) investigated the 10-year sexual and non-sexual recidivism (officially recorded reconviction) rates for 236 sex offenders released from New Jersey's general prison system and for 163 offenders from New Jersey's correctional facility and treatment centre for repetitive-compulsive sexual offenders (ADTC). They found that the offenders released from the ADTC had lower rates of committing sexual offences than the comparison prison population group (9 per cent compared to 13 per cent), but this difference was not significant; however, the ADTC group had a significantly lower non-sexual recidivism rate (23 per cent) than the comparison group (44 per cent). Zgoba and colleagues argued that low base rates may account for the lack of a significant difference, and suggested that the ADTC offenders were therapeutically more challenging as their offending was identified as being part of a repetitive and compulsive sexual behaviour pattern, whereas the offending of the sex offenders in the general prison population were not identified as such. They also noted that the ADTC offenders had on average more previous sexual convictions than the comparison prison sex offenders, a factor related to higher levels of risk.

Two recent studies show how methodological issues dominate evaluation research and limit and confuse the conclusions that can be drawn about sex offender treatment programmes. Looman *et al.* (2000) examined recidivism data from the Regional Treatment Centre in the Ontario region of the Correctional Service of Canada, which had been evaluated previously, and mentioned briefly above, by Davidson (1984, cited in Marshall, Jones *et al.* 1991). Quinsey *et al.* (1998) also evaluated data from the same institution, using the same pool of treated offenders; however, the conclusions of the two studies were in opposition.

Quinsey and colleagues followed up 213 offenders released prior to 1992 who completed the treatment programme between 1976 and 1989, and 183 offenders assessed as not needing treatment – 52 who refused to be assessed, 27 who were assessed but judged unsuitable, and 9 who were considered to require treatment but did not receive it. The sexual and violent recidivism rate for the treated sample was 35 per cent, and the sexual reconviction rate 25 per cent. The corresponding sample for offenders assessed as not requiring treatment was 6 per cent. The untreated and treated samples had different risk levels and so could not be compared directly. So, the recidivism rates were adjusted by Quinsey *et al.* using regression analysis. They developed an equation for risk that accounted for 15 per cent of the risk of recidivism. When the groups were compared using this equation, the sexual recidivism rate for the treated group was significantly higher than that for the untreated group. Looman and colleagues, however, criticized the statistical method used by Quinsey *et al.* pointing out that the method is not the same as a matched control study, as the regression only accounts for variables used in the equation. Hence, Looman *et al.* argued that Quinsey *et al.*'s conclusion that treatment had a negative impact, was 'rather strong'. Although Looman *et al.*'s point about regression analysis is correct, it should also be remembered that matched studies only account for variables that are included in the 'matching' process, which usually consist of only two or three variables. It should also be noted that offenders assessed as not needing treatment in Quinsey *et al.*'s comparison group could have been assessed in this way for positive reasons, i.e. they were not deemed to be in need of treatment, which would mean that some of these offenders might constitute a lower risk compared to the treated offenders.

Looman and colleagues used a sub-set of the treated sample examined by Quinsey and colleagues (there were some disagreements between the two studies in terms of who had received treatment) and matched these offenders using a sample of more than 3,000 offenders incarcerated in the Prairie region of the Correctional Service of Canada from 1983 to 1996. Offenders were matched on age at index offence (within one year), date of index offence (within the same calendar year) and prior criminal history (number of criminal convictions plus or minus two). The follow-up period ended in 1996, and so offenders were followed up on average for four years more than in Quinsey *et al.*'s study. Due to the serious nature of the treated group's criminal history, it was not possible to find a match for 63 treated offenders. So comparisons were completed on 89 treated and 89 matched untreated offenders.

After an average time at risk of 9.9 years, the untreated group had significantly more sexual reoffences (51.7 per cent) than the treatment group (23.6 per cent), which constituted a moderate effect size of 0.48. In offenders who had no previous sexual offences prior to the index offence 20.9 per cent sexually reoffended, which was significantly lower than the rate of 42.9 per cent in the untreated comparisons (effect size 0.51). For men with previous sexual offences prior to the index offence, 26.1 per cent of the treated offenders sexually reoffended compared to 73.1 per cent of the untreated comparisons (effect size 0.59), which is a statistically significant difference. Looman *et al.* argue that this indicates that the programme was effective at reducing sexual recidivism, particularly in high-risk offenders. However, it should be remembered that the highest risk offenders were not included in the study, as they could not be matched with untreated men.

The debate between these two studies is interesting and clearly illustrates the methodological issues that blight the evaluation of these programmes. Both studies evaluated the same programme, and some of the same offenders, yet the conclusions they reached were very different, and serve to give support to retorts such as 'anything can be proved with statistics'. Quinsey *et al.*'s sample included more high-risk offenders than Looman *et al.*'s sample, but Quinsey *et al.*'s comparison group is questionable. Although Looman *et al.* argued that Quinsey *et al.*'s regression method did not include the full range of variables controlled for in matched studies, they only matched three variables and these matches were far from exact. Thus, these studies provide ammunition for both the 'treatment works', and 'treatment is ineffective' camps. Most clearly, these studies demonstrate the difficulty, if not impossibility, of reaching firm conclusions about sex offender treatment effectiveness.

UK and Ireland

In the UK, fewer evaluations have been published and initially those that were published were generally less methodologically rigorous than the studies discussed earlier. However, as treatment provision has developed and become incorporated more firmly in the criminal justice system, evaluation has become more prominent and methodologically more robust.

In an early evaluation of the prison-based SOTP, Thornton and Hogue (1993) demonstrated a significant treatment effect, which was measured on a goal-attainment scale and the Sexual Offence Information Questionnaire (both scales were developed by Hogue but no further details were supplied). This effect was maintained a year after the completion of treatment. More recently, Beech *et al.* (1998) reported significant treatment effects: a reduction in denial and increase in admittance of deviant sexual interests and level of offending behaviour; a decrease in pro-offending attitudes; a positive change on scales measuring personality factors which predispose offenders to sexual offending; and an improvement in relapse-prevention skills. Of a subset of offenders (56) who agreed to be interviewed after a follow-up period of nine months, most had maintained these treatment effects. Interestingly, offenders who had shown a significant reduction in pro-offending attitudes maintained their relapse-prevention skills, whereas offenders who had not demonstrated such a reduction in attitudes had lost these skills.

Friendship *et al.* (2003a, 2003b) examined the two-year officially recorded reconviction rates of 647 sex offenders who completed the SOTP between 1992 to 1994, and 1,910 sex offenders who had not participated in the programme and who were matched to the treatment group by year of discharge. There was no significant difference in the sexual recidivism rates of the two groups (2.6 per cent treatment, 2.8 per cent comparison); however, there was a significant difference between the sexual and/or violent recidivism rates (4.6 per cent treatment, 8.1 per cent comparison). No significant difference was found in recidivism for any type of offence (13.3 per cent treatment, 16.5 per cent comparison). At this stage, although this programme seems to demonstrate effective treatment changes, it does not seem to have an impact on recidivism, or at least on sexual recidivism. However, these findings can be questioned as, although the sample sizes are relatively large, the base rate of sexual recidivism for UK incarcerated sex offenders is extremely low, so a study with a longer follow-up period is needed before confidence in the results can be achieved.

Murphy (1998), in a preliminary study evaluating the impact of the programme in Arbour Hill Prison, Ireland, on 30 offenders, reported that the programme had significantly reduced offenders' cognitive distortions and sexual fantasies and significantly increased their sense of personal control over their lives. However, significant differences were not found in other treatment measures, such as hostility, social desirability, social avoidance and distress. Murphy also reported findings obtained from interviews with offenders who had completed the programme. Offenders reported that the programme had had an impact and suggested that the sessions be longer with greater emphasis on relapse prevention.

In 1991, the HM Inspectorate of Probation noted that the small amount of research that had been undertaken to evaluate treatment programmes provided by the Probation Service had shown promising results. Eldridge and Gibbs (1987), reporting on programmes provided by Nottinghamshire Probation Service, revealed that none of the 18 offenders who had been followed up for three or four years after the completion of their programme had reoffended. Staffordshire Probation Service, which ran the longest and most intensive non-residential programme, claimed a 97 per cent success rate (Garrison 1992).

In 1994, Proctor reported on an evaluation of a treatment programme run by the 'Cherwell Group' in the Oxfordshire Probation Service. He found the programme had been effective in changing attitudes. Although little impact had been made on the offenders' beliefs that they were a danger to women and children, a major shift in the acceptance of responsibility was demonstrated and levels of empathy were increased. Two years later, Proctor (1996) compared 54 sex offenders (rapists, exhibitionists and child molesters) who started the Cherwell programme between 1989 and 1992 with a matched group from the same jurisdiction released prior to the introduction of the programme between 1986 and 1989. The offenders were matched on seven variables: age, number of previous convictions for sexual offences, type of offence, age of victim, gender of victim, whether force was evident, whether genital to genital contact was evident and the length of time that the offender was followed up. After a five-year follow-up period, the officially recorded sexual reconviction rate was 5.6 per cent for the treatment group compared to 13.0 per cent for the comparison group. Although three times as many offenders in the comparison group reoffended as in the treatment group, this difference was not statistically significant. Hanson *et al.* (2004) state that this is among the better studies of treatment outcome, but the sample size is quite small which, combined with the low base rate, is likely to mean that the study has a low level of statistical power, which may account for the lack of statistical significance.

An evaluation of six Probation Service programmes and one residential sex offender programme (using the within-treatment design and psychometric tests as outcome measures) was conducted for the Home Office by Beckett *et al.* (1994). This research determined that at the end of 54 hours of treatment (although this did not represent all the treatment offenders would have received, particularly in the more extensive programmes), 54 per cent of child abusers demonstrated a treatment effect, in terms of displaying profiles that fell mostly in the non-offending range. That is, they could not be distinguished from non-offending men on their levels of assertiveness; cognitive distortions; emotional congruence; ability to empathize with victims; and their sexual obsessiveness. Scores on some factors, such as self-esteem and emotional loneliness, did not reach 'normal' levels, but they did reveal marked, positive changes after treatment. In addition, this research demonstrated that highly deviant offenders needed a considerably longer time in treatment before they produced a non-deviant profile. In 2001, Beech *et al.* investigated the officially recorded recidivism rates, after a six-year follow-up period, for 53 of the offenders investigated in the original study. The sexual recidivism rate was 15 per cent, but it is difficult to assess the efficacy of these programmes using this recidivism data, as the data from a comparison group were not presented.

Allam (1999, reported by the Home Office 2003) conducted an evaluation of the West Midlands probation sex offender programme that became one of the three community accredited programmes in England and Wales (see Chapter 3). The sexual reconviction rate of those completing the programme was reduced by 7.4 per cent (3.2 per cent, compared to 10.6 per cent for matched controls). Furthermore, the reconvition rate for violent offences was reduced by 11 per cent and the rate for other types of crime reduced by 22 per cent. In 2004, Bates *et al.* reported on a follow-up study of 183 sex offenders treated in the Thames Valley Sex Offender Groupwork Programme, an accredited community-based programme. The average follow-up period was 3.9 years, ranging from two to six years. In measuring recidivism, Bates *et al.* used officially recorded reconviction data combined with unofficial data of incidences of reoffences and rearrests. Ten men (5.4 per cent) were reconvicted of at least one sexual offence, and two men (1.1 per cent) reoffended unofficially. A comparison group was not included in the study, but Bates and colleagues investigated in more detail the types of reoffences, comparing these to previous convictions. There was some evidence to show that some offenders were reconvicted for less serious offences, although this discussion is largely anecdotal with little formal analysis.

Australia

Although programmes in Australia have developed on a similar time scale to the UK and New Zealand, Australia has very few published evaluation studies. In 1996, Lee *et al.* showed that offenders (25 paedophiles, eight exhibitionists and two paraphiliacs) had gained and maintained, over a one-year follow-up period, significant treatment effects (in a community-based treatment provided by the Community Forensic Psychiatry Service in Victoria, Australia). These effects included an increase in the acceptance and control of their sexual problems, an enhancement of their social and assertiveness skills, an improvement in their sexual knowledge and a reduction in their cognitive distortions. Reconviction rates, using official criminal records, after a one-year follow-up period were also obtained. Three out of 37 offenders were reconvicted (8.1 per cent), although none of the paedophiles were reconvicted in the one-year period. These data were compared to the reconviction rates of 21 offenders who dropped out of the programme. Four of these offenders were reconvicted (19 per cent), but there was not a significant difference between the rates of the two groups. Clearly, this is not a strong study because of the drop-out comparison group and the one-year follow-up period. The study could be used to begin to unravel how significant treatment effects are related to recidivism, although the numbers involved in the study at this point (particularly with the small number of recidivists) make analyses of these data problematic.

New Zealand

Like the UK, New Zealand was slow to introduce sex offender treatment programmes. Despite this, there is now a coordinated approach to treatment, which is well managed and documented, with a clear committed to evaluation. Kia Marama, the first programme for offenders imprisoned for sexual offences against children in Christchurch, New Zealand, was evaluated by Bakker *et al.* (1998) when the programme had been running for seven years (established in 1989) and its first three years of graduates (283 men) had been in the community for six years. A comparison group was selected from sex offenders convicted between 1983 and 1987 who offended against children. The treated group had a sexual recidivism (any subsequent officially recorded reconviction) rate of 8 per cent and the comparison group a rate of 21 per cent. This was a statistically significant difference, but the comparison group had been at risk for almost twice as long as the treated group. However, survival analysis also revealed a statistically significant difference, with the treated group having half the failure rate (10 per cent) than the comparison group (22 per cent), even when factors such as age, ethnicity and number of previous convictions had been controlled for. Although these results were considered to demonstrate an effective programme, the quality of the comparison group could be questioned, as there may be a cohort effect due to the different years of release. The longer time at risk for the comparison group is also of concern. Nevertheless, a recidivism rate of eight per cent for untreated offenders after a six-year follow-up period would suggest a recidivism rate comparative to other treatment programmes with more positive outcomes.

The Te Piriti Special Treatment Programme is interesting because it has been designed in a context that seeks to combine Māori culture and beliefs with those of western psychology, to deliver a programme at Aukland Prison for offenders imprisoned for sexual offences against children. In 2003, the programme had been in operation for over eight years, employing the core components of its sister programme, Kia Marama, in a manner that is culturally appropriate for Māori. A group of 201 treated men (68 Māori and 133 non-Māori), who had been released into the community for at least a year and had an average time at risk of 2.4 years, were compared to the comparison sample used in the Kia Marama study described above (Nathan *et al.* 2003). The Te Piriti programme was found to be effective in reducing sexual recidivism in both Māori and non-Māori sex offenders. Treated offenders displayed an officially recorded sexual reconviction rate of 5.5 per cent, compared to 21 per cent in comparison offenders, but comparison offenders had a longer period at risk than the treated offenders. However, the mean time to sexual reoffence between the two groups was not statistically significantly different. Māori men who completed the Te Piriti pro-grammes had significantly lower sexual recidivism (4.4 per cent) than Māori men who completed the Kia Marama programme (13.6 per cent). Nathan *et al.* (2003) concluded that the programme was effective, although the short follow-up period and the choice of comparison group raises concerns about the validity of this conclusion. A follow-up study when the treated men have been at risk for longer with a matched comparison group would provide results that are more convincing. Nevertheless, this evaluation has shown that the Te Piriti programme is more effective for Māori sex offenders than the Kia Marama programme, without loss of effectiveness for non-Māori offenders. This can be related to the 'what works?' focus on treatment responsivity that has largely been ignored in sex offender outcome studies, but will be discussed in more detail in the next chapter.

Lambie and Stewart (2003) evaluated community-based treatment programmes provided by SAFE Network Inc., Aukland, STOP Welling-ton Inc. and STOP Trust Christchurch, all independent organizations providing treatment for both court-mandated and non-mandated clients in New Zealand. They compared the recidivism rates of 175 treated offenders with 28 offenders who had been assessed but untreated for a number of reasons, and historical data provided by the New Zealand Department of Corrections of a probation comparison group of 186 offenders convicted during 1995 who did not receive treatment. The groups were comparable on many variables, but the treated group had more victims, but fewer offences prior to treatment, than the assessed only group. The probation group had fewer prior offences than the treatment group. Lambie and Stewart argued that the groups were 'relatively comparable' except that the treated group had a more extensive offending history than the probation group, and a less extensive history than the assessment only group. This is quite an important 'except', as these factors are likely to be related to levels of risk. The median follow-up period was four years.

The overall sexual recidivism rate across the three programmes for treated offenders was 8.1 per cent, and the sexual recidivism rate for offenders who successfully completed the programmes was 5.2 per cent. In comparison the rate for the assessment-only group was 21 per cent and for the probation group 16 per cent. Survival analysis revealed a significant difference between the treatment and assessed-only groups, but only a 'borderline significant' difference ($p = 0.06$) between the treatment and probation groups. Lambie and Stewart argued that recidivism 'occurred less and later' in the treatment group in comparison with the other two groups. No significant differences were found between the non-sexual recidivism rates of 10 per cent for the treated group, 25 per cent for the assessment only group and 12 per cent for the probation group. Higher recidivism related to non-completion of the programme, which is not surprising, but of concern as the programmes had an average drop-out rate of 45 per cent, with one programme having a drop-out rate of 70 per cent. Unusually, recidivism was found not to be related to offender age, ethnicity, number of previous convictions, victim gender, number of previous sex offences, or total number of previous offences. These results seem promising but the numbers in the assessment-only group are small, and the comparability of the tested groups can be questioned, particularly of the treatment and assessment-only groups. The drop-out rate is a concern and Lambie and Stewart put forward suggestions to address this, such as more research, sentencing changes to require attendance to the end of the programme, and programmes for deniers.

Overall, these studies paint a confused picture. Most of the studies in the UK, Australia and New Zealand are limited in terms of their validity, as are many of the studies in North America, particularly those published in the 1980s or those that evaluated treatment delivered at, or prior to, this time. Nevertheless, there are many studies that are at least reasonably well-designed that reveal a positive outcome; however, a small number of well-designed studies producing results in the opposite direction question whether it can be assumed that treatment is effective. It is possible, of course, that the robust studies showing no, or negative, effects reflect an ineffective programme; however, with so few robust studies it is very difficult to assess this reliably. In addition, it is possible that the studies with negative outcomes were located in secure institutions or treated high-risk offenders, which may account for the poor outcome; however, there is not a great enough range of evaluations comparing offenders with comparable risk levels to allow reliable comparisons to be made in terms of risk or treatment settings. Because of these difficulties, researchers have combined these (and other) studies in meta-analyses to identify trends across the range of published literature.

Meta-analyses

Meta-analysis pools together treatment effects from a number of studies and so provides a method of assessing the consistency of results across studies. In addition, combining the samples of a number of studies increases the power of the statistical analysis, so that even small effects might be identified. This method is considered by some to be state of the art in reviewing quantitative evaluation research, and thus, the best method for integrating sex offender treatment data. Since 1995, a number of meta-analyses have attempted to draw conclusions about the effectiveness of sex offender treatment programmes.

In 1989, Furby and his colleagues attempted to complete a meta-analysis on sex offender treatment, but they were unable to do so because of the poor quality of the published research. So they published a review of the studies, concluding that there was no evidence of effectiveness. Many of the programmes included in the review, however, had been discontinued because their approach was deemed obsolete.

> Thus, although the conclusions of Furby *et al.* no doubt reflect the ineffectiveness of early, unspecialized approaches to sex offender treatment, such conclusions may not be justified when we consider the outcome of more modern, highly specialized intervention and management strategies.
>
> (Marshall and Pithers 1994: 14)

In addition, Marshall and Pithers (1994) showed that at least one-third of the samples reviewed by Furby *et al.* overlapped, creating a bias against positive results. Nevertheless, this study is frequently cited as evidence that treatment is ineffective. Yet Furby and colleagues (1989) claimed to have made only tentative conclusions regarding treatment effectiveness and Furby (quoted in Freeman-Longo and Knopp 1992) later expressed concerns that his report had been misinterpreted and used to discredit contemporary approaches to treating sex offenders.

In 1995, Hall conducted a meta-analysis on 12 studies published since Furby *et al.*'s (1989) review that he argued had employed relatively rigorous and robust methodology (i.e. they compared, using samples of 10 or more, treated offenders with comparison groups, using arrest records for sexual recidivism as outcome data). Hall initially reviewed 92 studies, but discarded 80 of these, as they did not meet his specified methodological requirements. Only three of the remaining 12 studies employed randomization to control and treatment groups, and only four studies evaluated cognitive-behavioural programmes (although Hall categorized five studies as cognitive-behavioural, one was a multi-systemic programme for adolescents, which had a particularly large treatment effect). The mean follow-up period of the 12 studies was 6.9 years. Hall found that treated sex offenders had fewer rearrests (9 per cent) compared to untreated controls (12 per cent), with an average effect size of 0.12. This study showed that cognitive-behavioural treatment was significantly more effective than behavioural treatment alone (but the multi-systemic programme with the large treatment effect may have biased this analysis). The effects sizes for the cognitive-behavioural programmes were 0.45 (Hildebran and Pithers 1992), 0.14 (Marques, Day *et al.* 1994), 0.47 (Marshall and Barbaree 1988) and 0.56 (Marshall and Eccles 1991). The treatment effect sizes were significantly greater in outpatient/community-based treatment than treatment in institutional settings. Furthermore, the effect sizes were greater in studies with follow-up periods of five years or more, and with offenders with greater base rates of recidivism. This either suggests that it is easier to treat high-risk offenders, or that it is easier to show a decrease in recidivism when starting with higher base rates.

Grossman *et al.* (1999: 359) argued that Hall's conclusions that treatment had an impact on recidivism constituted a 'robust finding'. However, others have criticized Hall's study. Becker and Murphy (1998) criticized the small number of studies included, which is indeed low for a meta-analysis. They also reported problems with the categorization of some treatments as cognitive-behavioural. Finally, they noted that some comparison groups received some treatment, when other comparison groups received no treatment, although this difference was not taken into account in the analysis. Hanson *et al.* (2004) also point out that a major limitation of the study was that many of the comparison groups were made up of non-completers (drop-outs), which Hall did acknowledge in his report. When Rice and Harris (1997) reanalysed the data from Hall's study, they concluded that the treatment effects were confined to studies using non-completers and an analysis excluding drop-out studies failed to find a treatment effect. As noted in Chapter 7, meta-analyses are only as good as the studies they include and Hall's analysis has suffered from the poor quality of the studies available for analysis. Remember that Hall excluded 80 studies that did not meet 'appropriate' methodological standards.

In 1999, Alexander reported the findings of an analysis of the results of 79 evaluation studies ($n = 10,988$) published from 1943 to 1996. Alexander recognized that the majority of studies included in her analysis did not have the methodological rigor of those assessed by Hall (1995), although she too excluded studies with fewer than 10 participants. She hoped, however, that the larger data set employed in her study would reveal patterns that were not so readily discernible in Hall's data set, which had relatively low base rates (Alexander 1999). Alexander omitted studies with overlapping datasets, unclear or no outcome data, biomedical treatment and physical castration. In addition, data for drop-outs, because of a lack of consistency in data and analyses, were omitted, which Alexander acknowledges could have skewed the results.

Alexander found that less than 11 per cent of the treated sex offenders reoffended, and when offenders were subdivided by type of offence, the efficacy for some groups of offenders became more apparent. Treated offenders had lower recidivism rates than untreated offenders in all categories (rapists, child molesters, exhibitionists, type not specified), except for type 'not specified'. Rates for treated child molesters averaged 13.9 per cent, while those for untreated child molesters averaged 25.8 per cent. Similarly, treated incest offenders had lower recidivism rates (4.0 per cent) compared to untreated incest offenders (12.5 per cent). There was little difference, however, in comparisons for treated and untreated rapists (20.1 per cent and 23.7 per cent respectively). Relapse-prevention-based programmes consistently yielded recidivism rates below 7 per cent. Offenders treated in prison had a 9.4 per cent recidivism rate compared to 17.6 per cent in untreated comparison offenders, but offenders treated in hospital settings had higher recidivism rates (16.6 per cent) than their untreated counterparts (11.5 per cent). Alexander noted in her discussion that more standardization of definitions, types of offenders, types of treatment and reporting of data would increase the viability of future meta-analyses. While Alexander's study seems to suggest that treatment is effective, Hanson *et al.* (2002) pointed out that there were some anomalies in Alexander's results and suggested that there was too much variance in the methods employed across the range of studies analysed to enable firm conclusions to be drawn.

Polizzi *et al.* (1999) adopted a different approach to assessing and comparing the evaluation studies of 21 prison and non-prison based programmes evaluated in the 10 years prior to their study. They examined the quality of the research, as well as the results of these studies, using techniques developed by University of Maryland researchers for a Crime Prevention Report completed for the US Congress (Sherman *et al.* 1997, cited in Polizzi *et al.* 1999). In order to provide a clear presentation of the quality of empirical research Sherman and colleagues developed a rigour scale, where each study was scored on a scale of one to five on its ability to control extraneous variables, minimize error and use appropriate statistical tests. From this assessment, eight studies, which scored a one on the scale, were deemed too low in scientific merit to be included in the analysis. Eight studies evaluating prison-based programmes (six with rigour scale scores of two, and two with rigour scale scores of four), and five studies evaluating community-based programmes (two with rigour scale scores of four, two with scores of three and one with a score of two) were included in the analysis. Approximately half of these studies showed a statistically significant treatment effect in favour of the benefit of treatment programmes. Non-prison based programmes were deemed to have been effective in curtailing future offending. At least two studies, judged to be of scientific merit, demonstrated a significant reduction in recidivism. Overall, for prison-based programmes only one study, which scored above three on the rigour scale, showed a significant effect for treatment (effect size 0.45), although the studies with scores of two were consistent with these findings. Hence, prison-based programmes were judged by Polizzi *et al.* to be promising, but the evidence was not strong enough to support the conclusion that they had demonstrated effectiveness. There were too few studies involved to analyse programme outcome for different classifications of offenders.

Gallagher et al. (1999) included 22 studies with 25 treatment comparisons in their meta-analysis. They argued that Hall's study was compromized because it included only published studies, which may represent a positively biased sample of evidence. This is because authors and/or journals editors may be more inclined to publish studies that have a positive outcome. Thus, Gallagher et al. attempted to broaden and update Hall's study by including published and unpublished literature that had a measure of sexual reoffence as outcome, a non-treatment comparison group, and was reported in English after 1975 and delivered treatment after 1970. Gallagher criticized Hall for choosing to include studies published after 1989 as they said this was an arbitrary date in terms of treatment development, although it was chosen by Hall to include all studies published after Furby et al.'s (1989) review. However, Gallagher and colleagues can also be criticized for choosing to have such an early cut-off date, as treatment delivered in the 1970s differed enormously from that delivered more recently (note Marshall's comments on Furby's study above). In addition, the type of programmes included in Gallagher et al.'s study varied enormously, including two they categorized as behavioural, two as augmented behavioural, 10 as cognitive behavioural/relapse prevention, three as cognitive behavioural, one as surgical castration, four as chemical castration and three other psychosocial treatments. Becker and Murphy's (1998) criticism of Hall's classification of the multi-systemic programme can also be applied to Gallagher et al.'s study, which used the same categorization as Hall. All but one of the studies reviewed by Gallagher and his colleagues was North American in origin, and three studies investigated programmes for juvenile offenders.

Twenty studies demonstrated a better outcome for treated offenders, four a better outcome in untreated comparisons, and one study revealed no difference between treated and untreated groups. The average effect size was 0.43, which the authors argued could be considered statistically significant and a 'medium' effect size. The behavioural, cognitive-behavioural (both relapse prevention and other) and augmented chemical-medical programmes showed substantial reductions in risk of post-treatment sexual recidivism. Gallagher et al. concluded that cognitive-behavioural programmes were effective, with programmes that included relapse prevention being as effective as programme that did not. However, Hanson et al. (2004) point out that many of the studies reviewed contained threats to validity. Many used drop-out comparison groups and some contained preliminary reports which were contradicted by later studies. In addition, some offenders would be double or triple counted, as they formed the treatment sample in more than one study.

Hanson *et al.* (2002) attempted to bring some order to these method-ological concerns. They included all 'credible' studies of psychological treatment of sex offenders identified by May 2000 in which treated sex offenders were compared to sex offenders who received no treatment or a form of treatment judged to be inadequate or inappropriate. Forty-three studies with combined sample sizes of 5,078 treated sex offenders and 4,376 untreated sex offenders were reviewed. When more than one study evaluated the same sample of treated offenders, the study with the largest sample size or longest follow-up period was included in the analysis. If a different method was used in more than one study using the same sample, the study that was determined to have the best methodology was included. Two studies were omitted due to unresolved anomalies in the data. Twenty-three published studies and 20 unpub-lished studies were included in the analysis. Most studies were North American (21 from the USA, 16 from Canada) in origin, with five from the UK and one from New Zealand. The median publication year was 1996 with 10 (23 per cent) evaluations published in 1999 or later. The authors argued that the studies were mostly recent, although the earliest publication year was 1977, and treatment was delivered between 1965 and 1999 (80 per cent of the offenders received treatment after 1980). Most studies examined adult male sex offenders, but four investigated adolescent sex offenders, and one studied female offenders. More than half the programmes evaluated (23 out of 43) were based exclusively in institutions, with 17 based in the community and three in both settings.

Averaged across all the studies, with an average follow-up period of 46 months, the sexual recidivism rate of 12.3 per cent for treated offenders was lower than the sexual recidivism of 16.8 per cent for untreated offenders. This pattern was similar for general recidivism, with a rate of 27.9 per cent for treated offenders and 39.2 per cent for untreated comparisons. The better outcome displayed by treated offenders was statistically significant, but there was a great deal of variability across studies. The treatment effect was stronger in unpublished studies, which perhaps counters arguments of a publication bias towards positive outcomes. Offenders who dropped out of treatment had higher rates of sexual recidivism; an effect that was consistent across the 18 studies that included drop-out data. However, surprisingly, offenders who refused treatment did not have higher rates than those who had attended at least some treatment. Offenders referred to treatment based on need had higher recidivism rates than offenders not considered to need treatment. These results suggest that the findings of studies which include comparison groups of drop-outs or offenders assessed as not needing treatment are more related to the method used, rather than the quality of the treatment provision. On average, the 20 studies with the best methodological designs revealed an overall treatment effect, although there was a great deal of variability between studies. The average recidivism rates across the best 15 methodological studies evaluating current treatments were 9.9 per cent for treated groups and 17.4 per cent for untreated comparison groups. Institution and community-based programmes seemed to be equally effective, as were programmes targeting adults or juvenile offenders. Hanson and colleagues concluded that the study indisputedly showed that recidivism rates were lower in treated sex offenders. However, what can be disputed, they argued, is the reason for this: either treatment is effective, or other differences between the treated and untreated offenders account for the differences in recidivism. Hanson *et al.* believe that current treatments are effective at reducing recidivism, but argued that 'firm conclusions await more and better research' (p. 186).

Conclusions

Although there have been many criticisms of some of these meta-analyses, they appear to paint a more promising picture than the range of published evaluations discussed previously. However, the issue is still not fully resolved. For as Hanson *et al.* (2002: 170) state:

> Despite more than 35 review papers since 1990, and a review of reviews (United States General Accounting Office 1996), researchers and policy makers have yet to agree on whether treatment effectively reduces sexual recidivism.

This is because methodological issues allow professionals to legitimately disagree on the value of evaluation studies which contain a range of threats to validity (Hanson 1997). Thus, this debate is set to continue.

Nevertheless, the results of the meta-analyses appear to support the claim made by Peebles (1999) that there is a growing body of scientific literature which suggests that untreated sex offenders have higher rates of recidivism and reoffend more quickly than treated sex offenders. This would suggest that:

> While there are difficulties in reaching scientific certainty, there are enough promising results on record to justify investment in more treatment schemes and more treatment research and evaluation.
> (Howard League 1985: 164)

Yet, Grossman *et al.* (1999: 359) end their review with a note of caution:

An optimistic perspective must be entertained cautiously and accompanied by a commitment to the advancement of scientific knowledge in the field. . . . Treatments for sex offenders does exist, and the outcome data are not uniformly discouraging. They are, however, complex, difficult to interpret, and cause for cautious optimism at best.

More confident in the merits of sex offender treatment programmes and at a stage when the data did not fully support this view, Marshall and Eccles (1991: 87) argued that 'treatment for sex offenders is effective'; however, more importantly they went on to point out that:

Not all forms are effective and not all applications of all forms are effective. We are not uniformly effective with all offender types, and find rapists the least responsive to our efforts to date. We need to modify our programs to deal with our current failures. But sex offenders can be treated.

This is an important point, as most of the research discussed in this chapter seems to have been concerned with whether treatment is effective or not, rather than with which programmes are effective, with which offenders programmes are effective, or even how we can answer these questions reliably in a time span that enables programme providers (or others) to intervene if the treatment is not working.

In 1978, Kempe and Kempe estimated that approximately 10 per cent of child sexual abusers were untreatable and remained dangerous for a variety of reasons to do with their psychiatric condition or their refusal to acknowledge their behaviour. Tilley (1992), however, argued that it was difficult to define 'untreatable' as new methods were being devised all the time. However, it is probably true that a proportion of sex offenders will not benefit from treatment programmes (although at present we seem to be unable to easily and reliably identify these offenders). They remain a challenge to the criminal justice system, which often has no choice but to release these potentially dangerous men back into the community. However, Marshall et al. (1991: 468) argued that:

A neglected factor . . . concerns the benefits to society of even marginal success in treating sex offenders. Since most sex offenders who do reoffend after release from prison or discharge by the courts, do so against more than one victim, then just effectively treating one offender who would otherwise have reoffended, is beneficial in that it saves two or more innocent victims from suffering.

Furthermore, Marshall and Pithers (1994) believe that if we are able to treat some offenders, but are unable to identify who they are, then we must be morally obliged to treat as many offenders as possible given the potentially disastrous consequences if they reoffend. Although not extensive, there is a growing body of literature addressing the question of what works and with whom, which will be discussed in the next chapter.

Chapter 9

Are programmes effective?
Part 3: What works?

Much of the evaluation literature investigating cognitive-behavioural sex offender treatment programmes has addressed the question of whether or not treatment works. As was discussed in the previous chapter, although not conclusive, this research suggests that treatment can be effective; however, what is not clear is what treatment programmes are effective, what characteristics distinguish effective treatments from non-effective treatments and for whom effective treatment programmes work. Furthermore, there has been very little exploration of why treatment might be effective and what aspects of programmes have an impact on offenders. These issues will be discussed in this chapter; however, the chapter will begin by examining whether or not these programmes are cost effective.

Cost benefit

As well as wishing to know if sex offender treatment is effective in reducing recidivism, social policy makers and managers also want to know if the treatment is cost effective. A recent meta-analytic review of correctional treatment programmes (Aos *et al.* 1999, cited in Brown 2000), showed that, based on tangible costs alone, every dollar spent on human-service-oriented correctional interventions ($n = 88$) saves the taxpayer approximately $5.00, and the victim, $7.00. Punishment-oriented interventions, on the other hand, produced substantially smaller savings ranging from 50¢ to 75¢. Cognitive-behavioural programmes aimed at adult populations generated estimated per-dollar savings ranging from $2.54 to $11.48.

In terms of cognitive-behavioural sex offender treatment programmes, Marshall, Eccles and Barbaree (1993) argued that a three-tiered programme in Canada treating offenders in both prison and the community was cost effective. They calculated the cost to society of a reoffence as being 200,000 Canadian dollars. Assuming a 25 per cent reduction in recidivism, the saving following the treatment of 100 offenders was calculated to be five million Canadian dollars. The cost of the treatment provision was estimated at 600,000 Canadian dollars. Thus, the saving to society was in excess of four million Canadian dollars. This analysis was based on tangible costs only, and so does not include intangible costs to victims and society. Marshall *et al.* explained that on average, each offender who sexually reoffends does so against at least two victims, and so a 25 per cent reduction in recidivism would eliminate the potential suffering of 50 women or children. Marshall *et al.*'s 25 per cent reduction rate is perhaps a little excessive, but calculations based on their cost estimates reveal that only three reoffences need to be eliminated to recoup the costs of the treatment provision – any additional reductions in recidivism would produce cost-benefits.

Similar estimates have been made for treatment provision in the USA. McGrath (1995) conducted a cost-benefit analysis based only on tangible costs of outpatient sex offender treatment in Vermont. He calculated costs for 100 treated and 100 untreated offenders based on the 6 per cent recidivism rate for treated offenders in Vermont's treatment programme, calculated in 1992. When this recidivism rate was used for both treated and untreated offenders, not surprisingly, the programme was neither effective nor cost-effective. However, when McGrath used a 7 per cent recidivism rate for untreated offenders and 6 per cent rate for treated offenders, the programme was found to be cost effective. The total cost for untreated offenders was calculated at $936,768, for treated offenders at $971,796, producing a treatment saving of $35,028. Thus, McGrath argued that a 1 per cent decrease in sexual reoffence rates would more than offset the cost of providing treatment services. Furthermore, if the untreated reoffence rate was increased to 8 per cent, savings in excess of $1,000,000 would be produced.

Bakker *et al.* (1998) suggested that, as the Kia Marama programme costs were two million dollars, and the savings from reduced recidivism $5.6 million, the New Zealand Department of Corrections had made a net saving of more than $3 million. In a more detailed cost-benefit analysis, Shanahan and Donato (2001) also calculated the cost benefit of sex offender treatment. They calculated the costs of a 'generic' prison-based programme, based on data from Kia Marama in New Zealand, and Australian programmes in Moreton, Queensland, Casuarina and Bunbury in Western Australia and Ararat in Victoria. They estimated annual running costs per offender at Australian $8,175. In order to make a conservative cost-benefit calculation, they used a figure of Australian $10,000. The total tangible costs per new victim were calculated at $19,890, which was considered a conservative estimate. Different ways of calculating intangible per-victim costs resulted in a lower figure of $19,650 and an upper figure of $198,900. Finally, offender-related costs were calculated at $137,400. Using these figures, total costs ranged from $157,290 to $356,190. Cost benefits were calculated if the reduced recidivism rate varied between 2 and 14 per cent. With a 2 per cent reduction in recidivism, the programme costs exceeded the programme benefits in all calculations. However, an 8 per cent reduction in recidivism revealed cost benefits in all calculations. If only tangible costs were considered, the benefit costs matched the costs of the programme, and adding intangible costs meant that the programme was cost effective with this level of recidivism. With a 4 per cent reduction in recidivism, the programme was only cost effective if the higher calculations of intangible costs were included in the calculation. Shanahan and Donato (2001) argued that with plausible calculations, recidivism reductions of 6 to 8 per cent and lower calculations of intangible costs, the net economic benefits ranged from Australian $62,000 to $1.05 million.

Although the number of cost-benefit analyses of cognitive-behavioural sex offender treatment programmes is small, the findings seem to be consistent, although the levels of analysis in all but the last study are rather basic. Shanahan and Donato's study reveals the complexity of thorough cost-benefit analyses and the difficulties of estimating intangible costs (omitted from the other studies). This study suggests that programmes have to be more effective in reducing recidivism to produce cost benefits than some of the earlier studies suggest. A review of the outcome studies discussed in the previous chapter does not make it clear whether a reduction in recidivism of 6 per cent is feasible. Some studies show reductions well in excess of this, but many show much smaller reductions if they show any at all. More cost-benefit research employing the detailed, comprehensive calculations completed by Shanahan and Donato is needed before we can firmly conclude that treatment is cost effective in financial terms. Clearly, in human suffering terms, any reduction in recidivism, no matter how small, is a positive outcome.

What works, with whom?

The majority of evaluative work has focused on the question of efficacy, which has meant that other important issues have been neglected. It would seem reasonable to conclude from this literature that some treatment programmes work with some offenders, hence some pro-grammes do not work and furthermore, some programmes do not work with some offenders, or possibly all programmes do not work with particular groups of offenders. For reasons of both resources and risk-management it is important that we are able to identify which programmes are effective and with which offenders, yet these issues have so far received very little attention. Information that sheds light on these issues has often been a by-product of the research discussed previously, with studies directly investigating some of these issues only being published in the last few years.

Treatment drop-outs

The most consistent finding in the evaluation literature is that treatment drop-outs have higher rates of recidivism, compared to treated offenders, and often compared to untreated offenders. At a simplistic level of explanation, there could be two reasons for this: firstly, that something about the process of not completing a full treatment programme produces a higher recidivism rate; or secondly, something about the offenders before they begin treatment makes them more likely to drop out of treatment and means they also have higher risks of reoffending. There has been very little research investigating the process of treatment that would enable a sound assessment of the former hypothesis; however, most research tends to support the latter argument by demonstrating a range of factors that distinguish drop-outs from treatment completers.

Federoff and Wright (1993, cited in Miner and Dwyer 1995) found that process measures were the most reliable factors that distinguished between treatment completers and drop-outs. Offenders who fitted into treatment social interactions were more likely to complete it. Miner and Dwyer (1995) found that drop-outs had fewer extrinsic motivations for treatment, appeared to be rigid with very conventional attitudes, and lacked awareness or concern about the consequences of their behaviour; however, these factors accounted for only a small proportion of the variability between the two groups. Miner and Dwyer argued for an interactive model of treatment and stressed the need for more research into the social, interactive processes involved in treatment.

Abel et al. (1988) found three factors that differentiated treatment completers from treatment drop-outs: the extent of pressure the offender was under to complete treatment; a diagnosis of personality disorder; and a lack of discrimination in the choice of victim or sexually deviant act. Shaw et al. (1995) discovered that offenders with a stable marital relationship and better reading skills were more likely to have a better treatment outcome. But, contrary to other studies, offence type and antisocial personality disorder did not predict treatment outcome. Marques, Day et al. (1994) suggested that offenders who were the most impulsive and exercised the least amount of self-control were the ones most likely to withdraw or be terminated from treatment. Geer *et al.* (2001) revealed that treatment completers had more years of education and fewer previous incarcerations than treatment non-completers. In addition, offenders who reported sexual abuse as children, and those who demonstrated higher levels of denial and minimization, were more likely to drop out of treatment. In plethysmograph analyses, drop-outs showed lower levels of arousal to consensual peer sexual interactions.

Browne *et al.* (1998) identified nine variables that were significant in differentiating treatment drop-outs from treatment completers. Offenders with a violence-related index offence, a previous conviction for a violence-related offence or a history of contact offences were more likely to drop out of treatment than non-violent offence counterparts. Furthermore, offenders with previous police contact or previous time spent in prison were more likely to drop out of treatment, as were offenders who were unemployed or who had casual employment with children at the time of the offence. In addition, a history of alcohol and drug abuse and the presence of delinquent behaviour were associated with non-completers. When these variables were used to predict whether offenders would remain in treatment for the duration of the programme, 78 per cent of the offenders were classified correctly, identifying 83 per cent of those who remained in treatment and 70 per cent of those who dropped out of treatment.

Although these studies identify a range of variables, the variables are inconsistent across studies, and so it is currently not possible to reliably test offenders at pre-treatment for 'drop-out potential'. Lee *et al.* (1996) reported reduced drop-out rates (from 42.3 per cent to 28.5 per cent) when they introduced an individual treatment that worked on denial and motivation to attend treatment, which was delivered to some offenders prior to the start of the treatment programme. These results may suggest a means of reducing drop-out rates, but the numbers of offenders studied by Lee and colleagues was small and no detailed analysis was reported. Nevertheless, this seems an area worthy of further investigation.

Treatment compliance

It is intuitive that behaviour in treatment will be related to outcome, i.e. that those appearing to be more motivated and compliant will have a better outcome than those who seem to be more difficult, less motivated, and reluctant to participate. Indeed, there is some evidence to suggest that this is the case with non-sex offending populations (Muran *et al.* 1995; Startup and Edmonds 1994). However, this issue has been the subject of a great deal of debate as regards sex offenders, as many professionals believe sex offenders to be particularly manipulative. Thus, they are able to create the impression that they are committed and working hard, when perhaps they are just behaving in this way to complete the treatment, even though they may have no interest in actually changing their sex-offending behaviour when they have completed the programme (and/or their sentence requirements). Consequently, some argue that treatment merely teaches sex offenders the 'correct answers' and actually serves to make 'better' offenders who can more easily avoid future detection. Despite this debate, the research evidence on this issue is sparse.

Harris *et al.* (1991) found that forensic patients (including sex offenders) who committed a new violent offence were more likely to have behaved poorly in treatment, which was indicated by clinical record entries of non-compliance or aggressive behaviour, number of times disciplined, and time that passed before receiving a staff recommendation for discharge from the programme. Similarly, Beech *et al.* (2001) discovered that 10 per cent of offenders who were classified as 'benefiting from treatment' were reconvicted compared with 23 per cent of men classified as 'not having responded to treatment', and furthermore, that none of the low-risk offenders who were 'responsive' to treatment reoffended. However, in 1999, Seto and Barbaree found that good treatment behaviour (positive and appropriate behaviour in group sessions, good homework assignments, positive ratings of motivation and overall change) was not related to parole failure or rates of general recidivism. More worryingly, they found that it was related to 'serious' recidivism, i.e. a new violent or sexual offence. Furthermore, they found that men who scored higher in psychopathy (as measured by Hare's PCL-R) and behaved better in treatment were almost three times as likely to commit any kind of reoffence and five times as likely to commit a serious reoffence as other groups of offenders (i.e. men who performed poorly in treatment regardless of their psychopathy rating, and men who performed well in treatment who had low psychopathy scores). Perhaps, then, this research shows there is some merit in the belief that some sex offenders, at least, are manipulative individuals, whose behaviour in treatment may not be a good indication of level of future risk. Obviously, this issue needs to be taken into account in risk assessment and risk management, although more research is needed to clarify this relationship.

Offender characteristics

Men who offend against children seem to be fairly responsive to treatment, although the efficacy of treatment for men who rape is still equivocal (McGrath 1995). Generally, as can be seen in the literature discussed in the previous chapter, a range of sex offenders are evaluated together, so there is limited research investigating the differential impact of treatment on different types of offenders. However, Davidson (1984, cited in Marshall, Jones *et al.* 1991), Marshall and Eccles (1991), Hildebran and Pithers (1992), and Marshall (1996a) have all noted that programmes were not successful with rapists, and in her meta-analysis, Alexander (1999) found no significant differences between treated and untreated rapists (20.1 per cent recidivism compared to 23.7 per cent). Marshall (1993a) discussed why this might be the case and how treatment can be adapted to make it more effective with this group of offenders. It is not clear if these suggestions have been implemented and even if they have, there is no published empirical research evaluating these adaptations. It would seem that the issue has not been resolved, as more recently, Marx *et al.* (1999) asked whether we could do better with cognitive-behavioural treatment for rapists. They pointed to research that showed that rapists were more like the normal prison population than other categories of sex offenders and highlighted the heterogeneity of rapists. They made a number of suggestions for adjustments to current sex offender treatment programmes, in the hope that these would improve programme efficacy with rapists; however, they pointed out the need for these suggestions to be empirically tested.

Other offenders who seem to be resistant to treatment include those who have multiple sexual offence convictions, fixated deviant arousal patterns and severe psychopathic personality traits (McGrath 1991). Marques *et al.* (2000) found that sex offenders who offended against male children were more responsive to treatment than those who offended against female children (although the trend was not statistically significant). Offenders in the treatment group who had substance abuse problems or prior treatment experience did significantly better than their counterparts in both control groups, but offenders with evidence of thought disorder (this was not defined more clearly) did not respond as well to treatment as the control groups. In Seto and Barbaree's study (1999), PCL-R scores predicted serious recidivism (new sexual or violent offence).

Offenders who believe that they have little influence or control over what happens in their lives, i.e. they have an external locus of control, are likely to have more limited success in a treatment that relies on them taking responsibility for changing their lives/behaviour, than offenders who have an internal locus of control (Beech and Fisher 2002). There is limited support for this assumption, as external locus of control has been found to be related to risk of reoffending and having an internal locus of control at pre-treatment has been linked to treatment success (measured using psychometric tests) (Fisher, Beech *et al.* 1998). This research would suggest that it is important for offenders to develop an internal locus of control during treatment and Beech and Fisher suggest that this can be done by showing offenders that offences did not 'just happen', that they were planned in some way. Whether such an approach would be effective for offenders with a strong external locus of control, though, is yet to be determined.

When treated recidivists (19) were compared with treated non-recidivists (219), by Bakker *et al.* (1998), the recidivists were found to have attitudes supportive of offending, cognitive distortions, conservative attitudes towards women, less empathy and a tendency to internalize anger. Furthermore, compared to non-recidivists, recidivists tended to have lower IQs, and were nearly three times more likely to report the death of a parent or caregiver in childhood, and five times more likely to have severe literacy problems. In terms of offence characteristics, recidivists were less likely to report female victims, more likely to report male victims or victims of both genders, and almost twice as likely to report an onset of offending before adulthood.

Maletzky (1993) found that characteristics of victims were the factors that most significantly differentiated treatment failures from treatment successes. An offender was classified as a treatment failure if he did not complete all treatment sessions, reported any incidence of overt or covert deviant sexual behaviour at the end of treatment or during follow-up sessions, had deviant arousal greater than 20 per cent on the plethysmograph at the end of treatment or at any follow-up session, or was charged with any new sexual crime throughout the duration of the study period. Maletzky observed that offenders who abused a child not living within his home were seven and a half times more likely to be considered treatment failures than offenders who abused children with whom they lived. Furthermore, offenders who abused multiple victims were six times more likely to fail treatment than those who abused against a single child. Some non-victim characteristics differentiated treatment failures from successes. Offenders who denied their crimes were two and a half times more likely to fail than offenders who admitted their crime, and offenders with IQs below 90 were 2.75 times more likely to fail than those with higher IQs. Offenders with erratic employment and unstable personal relationships were three times more likely to fail than offenders with more stable histories. Finally, offenders with high pre-treatment deviant sexual arousal were two and a half times more likely to fail, and offenders with low pre-treatment arousal to adult heterosexual consenting stimuli were one and a half times more likely to fail, compared to offenders with more 'normal' arousal levels. These comparisons were all made between different categories of treated offender. No comparison untreated group was included in the study.

Evaluating the same treatment programme but with a 25-year follow-up period, Maletzsky and Steinhauser (2002) reported the following treatment failure rates: 6.3 per cent for offenders who molested girls; 9.4

per cent for men who molested boys; 9.7 per cent for heterosexual paedophiles; 16.3 per cent for homosexual paedophiles; and 21.2 per cent for rapists. Further analyses (mainly from reoffences) also revealed that the latter two groups failed more quickly than offenders in other groups. They confirmed data from many other studies, that leaving treatment early predicted recidivism. Of 1,669 drop-outs, 136 (8.1 per cent) were reconvicted of a sexual crime, compared to 69 (1.4 per cent) of the 5,607 treatment completers.

These findings would suggest that offenders who had higher levels of risk were more likely to be treatment failures, although the research on risk and treatment outcome is equivocal. As suggested in Chapter 7, the main difficulty with level of risk is that different researchers use the terms 'high', 'medium' and 'low' risk without always clearly defining how offenders were given these assessments. Furthermore, within a treatment setting, offenders may be rated as high and low risk; however, this is a reflection of their risk in comparison to other offenders on the programme rather than all other offenders in the population. For example, 'high'-risk offenders in a community setting may actually be a lower risk than 'low'-risk offenders in a secure psychiatric setting. Consequently, comparison between studies is difficult.

Gordon and Nicholaichuk (1996) reported that a sample of high-risk (based on previous convictions for sexual offences) sex offenders (rapists, paedophiles, incest offenders and offenders with mixed sexual crimes) treated in the Clearwater Programme at the Corrections Service of Canada Regional Psychiatric Centre (Saskatoon) had a significantly lower sexual recidivism rate, of 6 per cent, compared to an untreated sample (national sample of offenders released from prison) of high-risk offenders (14.6 per cent). Yet, there was no significant difference in the rates of treated and untreated offenders when all offenders (low and high risk) were included in the analysis (4.7 per cent for Clearwater compared to 6.2 per cent for national sample).

Nicholaichuk (1996) used the same information and compared this with outcome data from a programme for provincially incarcerated sex offenders (26 offenders), whom he argued were lower-risk offenders (only 15 per cent had a previous conviction for a sex offence) than those at the Regional Psychiatric Centre. A matched comparison group (35 men) was created from a sample of offenders incarcerated for similar numbers and types of sex offences. Average time at risk in the community (follow-up period) was 31.2 months for the treated group and 28.8 months for the comparison group. The groups did not differ significantly in the rates of reconviction, although the comparison group actually had a lower reconviction rate (3 per cent compared to 11 per cent). Despite this, the treatment group did show improvements in anxiety rates and social functioning. Thus, Nicholaichuk argued that treatment was effective for high-risk offenders but not for low-risk offenders (no difference was found when the data for the two groups was pooled), who should accordingly be directed to low-intensity, low-cost provision, with more intensive programmes being reserved for high-risk offenders.

Other studies, however, seem to show that high-risk offenders, such as those in secure psychiatric hospitals, or other high-security prisons, are resistant to treatment (see Quinsey *et al.* 1998). In England and Wales, the prison SOTP did not seem to have an impact on high-risk offenders (Friendship *et al.* 2003b); while in community-based programmes, Beckett *et al.* (1994) were able to demonstrate that programmes were not equally effective with all offenders: 65 per cent of the men with low deviancy profiles were 'successfully' treated (as measured by pre- and post-treatment changes in psychometric test scores) compared to 42 per cent of the offenders with high-deviancy profiles. Short-term therapy was successful with 62 per cent of the low-deviancy offenders but with only 20 per cent of the high-deviancy offenders. Long-term treatment, however, was more successful in treating high-deviancy men (60 per cent). Clearly more research is needed to clarify this issue. Such research should include a careful and thorough assessment of risk, using standardized risk-assessment tools, so that reliable comparisons can be made between studies, and offenders with differing levels of risk.

In a qualitative study of the experiences of minority ethnic sex offenders attending the SOTP, Patel and Lord (2001) discovered that a significant minority of black offenders felt that race and culture had been an issue during the programme. Over half felt that they had been treated differently than white offenders, and two-thirds reported a clash of interest between the two groups that resulted in them being stereotyped and victimized. Following this report, the Prison Service instigated a number of changes to staff training and developed a specialized training course. In addition, they conducted an evaluation of the impact of the SOTP on minority ethnic clients (Webster *et al.* 2004).

Fifty-two black sexual offenders who completed the SOTP were identified from the SOTP national database and compared to a matched sample of white sex offenders who were identified from the same database. Apart from the obvious differences in ethnicity, the two groups did not differ on victim and offence variables. Analysis revealed that the programme had similar within-treatment effects on both groups of offenders. However, some differences were identified between the two groups, most notably the higher levels of pre-treatment denial in black sex offenders, and a greater post-treatment reticence to acknowledge future risk of reoffence. The authors discussed possible reasons for these findings and point out that the small sample sizes and a lack of norm psychometric test data for minority ethnic groups raise concerns about the validity of these findings. This study is preliminary in nature and forms only part of the effort to ensure that treatment is equally effective for all groups of offenders. Work in New Zealand shows that programmes can be adapted to take account of the cultural differences. Here, the Te Piriti programme, which was adapted from the original Kia Marama programme to take account of Māori culture and values, was shown to be more effective with Māori sex offenders than the Kia Marama programme (Nathan *et al.* 2003). Clearly, these considerations are an important part of the responsivity principle that until recently has largely been ignored in the sex offender literature.

Treatment characteristics

In sex offender treatment, cognitive-behavioural programmes and relapse-prevention programmes have repeatedly been shown to produce the greatest average treatment effects (Alexander 1999; Gallagher *et al.* 1999; Grossman *et al.* 1999; Hall 1995). In addition, poor outcome seems to be demonstrated in programmes based in hospital settings (Quinsey *et al.* 1998; Alexander 1999) or institutional settings compared to community-based settings (Polizzi *et al.* 1999). Yet, these findings were not replicated by Hanson *et al.* (2002: 1048) who found that institutional and community-based programmes were equally effective.

As was discussed in Chapter 2, effective intervention programmes target criminogenic needs that are skills based and deliver treatment in a manner that is consistent with offenders' learning styles; however, there has been insufficient research to know whether these features are also important for treating sex offenders (Hanson *et al.* 2004). Gendreau (1994) stressed the holy trinity of risk, need and responsivity. Treatments should be matched with offender risk level, be cognitive-behavioural in nature and target criminogenic needs and be delivered in a manner that promotes pro-social skills. Similarly, Mailloux *et al.* (2003) discussed the issue of 'dosage', pointing out that best use of resources, as well as risk and responsivity principles, demand that the extent of treatment is tailored to the risk needs of the clients.

In addition, Beckett *et al.* (1994) argued that programmes should be flexible to fit clients rather than clients being placed into the existing provision, or that clients should be selected on the basis of whether they are best suited to the provision available. While these arguments are laudable, in practice such individualization of programmes would be difficult to manage by services with limited resources and small numbers of clients to allocate to each type of provision. Extended provision of individual offence-base work carried out by supervising officers in conjunction with a treatment programme may perhaps provide the best solution to this predicament.

As Marshall and Serran (2000) point out, there is little empirical evidence to support how much treatment sex offenders need; yet, there seems to be a strongly held belief that as offence behaviours are so well entrenched, 18 months to two years of treatment is needed, if not longer. Marshall and Serran argue, however, that this is not necessarily the case and point to some positive outcome studies where treatment takes place over a relatively short period of time (see for example, Hudson *et al.* (1998), where treatment is completed in 31 weeks). There are obvious resource issues, not to mention ease of providing treatment for offenders with short sentences, if treatment can be delivered in short periods and/or in a less intensive manner. Thus, more research is needed to investigate this issue.

Treatment is actually a 'package' of smaller components (Shaughnessy and Zechmeister 1997), yet as Marshall and Serran (2000) highlight (and as discussed in more detail in Chapter 6), these smaller components are poorly evaluated. Marshall and Serran argue that treatment components should satisfy three requirements: they should meet their goals; they should be an essential requirement in the achievement of these goals (e.g. that the empathy component, rather than the other components, produces changes in empathy); and they are necessary to produce a long-term reduction in recidivism. Although there are a few studies that address the first of these issues (see Chapter 6), research investigating the second and third of these issues is scarce. Given the importance of these components in treatment – essentially they are the core element of treatment – this is surprising, and rather worrying. In addition, as was discussed in more detail in Chapter 6, Marshall and Serran point out that there has been debate about whether some treatment targets, most notably empathy and relapse prevention, should be included in treatment programmes.

McGrath *et al.* (2003) found lower sexual recidivism for participants who received aftercare treatment and correctional supervision services in the community. Marshall *et al.* (1998) pointed out that despite adopting a relapse-prevention approach, most programmes do not provide the post-treatment provision that was recommended in the relapse-prevention models developed by Marques and Nelson (1989), Pithers (1990) and Pithers *et al.* (1989) – an issue discussed briefly in Chapter 5. Whether the extended maintenance programmes described by these authors would produce better results than either treatment without post-treatment support or treatment with minimum post-treatment support, remains to be determined, although Marshall and Anderson (1996) failed to obtain encouraging results. Moreover, as discussed in Chapter 6, Marshall and Serran (2000) questioned the use of extensive supervision and support, as this created a reliance on this support (which perhaps encouraged a belief on the offenders' part that they could not avoid reoffending) that produced an increase in reoffending when the support was removed.

Marques *et al.*'s (2000) chapter is unique in that the authors discuss at length the strengths and weaknesses of the treatment programme they reviewed and make associated recommendations for change for programme improvement. Such discussions can help all practitioners develop their programmes, and it is surprising that these issues are not discussed more frequently in the literature. Marques and colleagues believed that they could have strengthened offenders' commitment to abstinence (teaching the model is of no benefit if offenders have no intention in using it), stressed and challenged participants more, focused more on affective factors (particularly in developing empathy and having offenders link this to their own victims), practised coping skills more (saying what you might do is not the same as being able to do it well in situations that may arise and develop quite quickly), and provided a strong conditional release component (to ease the sudden change from hospital to community life) and longer-term aftercare. Interviews with nine offenders who had reoffended reinforced these ideas. Although these offenders had learnt the concepts taught in the programme, many had little motivation to use them, and some believed that they would not be able to cease offending and so the things they learnt had little impact. Most of these offenders also lacked empathy for their own victims. 'These individuals clearly did not "get" the program that we provided' (Marques *et al.* 2000: 329).

Marques *et al.* (1993) remarked that intervention must be based on theory and that this should be tested via evaluation, so that, as the intervention is tested, the theory is also tested. Interestingly, such practice has now become a feature/requirement of accreditation in jurisdictions (UK and Canada) that have introduced such systems. Marques and colleagues also suggest that the programme must address not only the common causes of sexual offending, but also risk factors that may be unique to each offender. However, this issue is less likely to be fully incorporated, as accreditation procedures have demanded strict programme protocols and manuals, which effectively reduce the scope to tailor programmes to individual needs (unless of course this is somehow built into the programme manual). However, developments in theory (see Drake and Ward 2003) and research into therapeutic styles (see Marshall, Fernandez *et al.* 2003; Marshall, Serran *et al.* 2003; Serran *et al.* 2003) have led these authors to question the use of manuals. It would seem that the principle of programme integrity, for which manuals are seen to be a great benefit, is at odds with the principle of responsivity. More research is needed on this issue to inform the debate that is just beginning on the suitability of manuals. It is perhaps possible that a compromise position would be to provide manuals and protocols that have in-built flexibility, providing programme staff with a range of options that allow them to respond to the sex offenders in their groups, without the risk of programme drift. Programmes could also have more extensive individual treatment components, but this has resource implications.

Group cohesion

As discussed in Chapter 5, it is believed that group rather than individual work with sex offenders is more effective for a variety of reasons, yet there has been little work to explore if this reasoning is correct. The lack of provision delivered to individuals makes it difficult to compare individual and group treatment, but more could be done to explore whether groups do provide the advantages discussed in Chapter 5 and whether there are any negative factors in such a method of delivery. When the dangers of the potential negatives of group work (e.g. the formation of offending groups) are considered, it is surprising that this issue has not been given greater consideration in evaluation research.

The two STEP studies (Beckett *et al.* 1994; Beech *et al.* 1998) revealed that group cohesiveness was correlated with treatment success (as measured by pre- and post-treatment changes in psychometric tests). That is, groups that displayed the highest level of agreement between clients and leaders in terms of the group's goals and expectations (Beckett *et al.* 1994), and those that were better able to deal with the open expression of negative feelings and disagreements (Beech *et al.* 1998) were more effective. Beech *et al.* reported that one group they studied had a very disruptive member who intimidated the other members of the group and, consequently, was likely to have affected the group's progress overall. Thus, Beech and his colleagues suggested that the group environment should be monitored throughout treatment. In addition, it is important that steps are taken to effectively control or exclude disruptive group members. Furthermore, research is needed to identify the characteristics of offenders who are likely to be disruptive (Beech *et al.* 1998).

Therapist characteristics

West (1996: 65) argued that 'perhaps the most important element in treatment, although the hardest to assess, is the therapist's ability to form an empathic relationship with these unattractive characters'. This element of treatment provision is difficult to assess and is rarely included in evaluation research; yet, Beckett *et al.* (1994) argued that it was clear that the effectiveness of programmes had been dependent on the skill, experience and the therapeutic style of programme staff. Thus, 'we need to focus research on treatment processes and on the optimal therapist characteristics that facilitate the effectiveness of our procedures' (Marshall 1996b: 332). Beckett *et al.* (1994) commented that treatment was delivered competently and sensitively by programme staff. However, Beckett and his colleagues also found that some staff used too much jargon and assumed too much about their clients' level of comprehension. Using the Group Environement Scale (GES), Beech and Fordham (1997) found that a helpful and supportive leadership style was important in creating an atmosphere conducive to producing positive treatment outcome, while overcontrolling leaders were felt to have a negative effect on the group.

To investigate this issue further, Marshall and his colleagues (2002) embarked on a series of studies to investigate the impact of therapists' styles on treatment outcome. First, they established that researchers could reliably identify 18 therapist features that occurred with reasonable frequency in videos of HM Prison (England and Wales) treatment sessions. These features included warmth, being directive, being confident, using appropriate humour and being confrontational. In the second phase (reported in the same article), a different selection of videotapes from the same programme was examined, so that therapeutic style could be compared with treatment change (as measured using psychometric test data) in offenders. Although 17 therapist features were initially recorded, only 13 occurred with sufficient frequency to be included in the analysis.

The results revealed clear relationships between treatment benefits and therapist features. Being empathic and warm was related to seven measures of treatment change, each of which was linked to a key treatment target. Furthermore, being directive and rewarding was related to significant changes in at least five measures of treatment progress. Firm but supportive challenging was related to a reduction in offenders' victim blaming. Thus, Marshall et al. argued that being directive and rewarding with empathy and warmth were the four 'cardinal virtues' of therapists when treating sex offenders (Marshall et al. 2002). In a preliminarily study, a confrontational style was negatively correlated with offenders' increased competence in coping (Marshall, Serran et al. 2003); however, this finding was not replicated in the later study (Marshall et al. 2002). Marshall and colleagues argued that this was due to changes made to the therapists' training and to the SOTP monitoring system, which discouraged the use of a confrontational style. They argued that this was evident as there were very few instances of confrontation in the tapes reviewed. These studies clearly show that the style the therapist uses in treatment has an effect on treatment change measured using psychometric data; however, it would be interesting to see if these effects are also related to recidivism. These findings are unique to one treatment programme and one country and they clearly need to be replicated elsewhere. Nevertheless, they provide evidence that subtle differences in treatment delivery can have an impact on treatment change that may account for overall differences in programme effectiveness (and may account for the contradictory evaluation findings reported in the previous chapter).

Why does it work?

Research investigating the question of why sex offender treatment programmes work, assuming of course that they do, is virtually non-existent. There is an assumption that as programmes have been developed on sound theoretical concepts, treatment targets based on empirical findings, and treatment goals linked to recidivism, they will work. However, as can be seen from the discussion in Chapter 4, theoretical debate in this arena has been limited, and as was explained in Chapter 2, many programme developments occurred rapidly, based on clinical practice, general ideas in psychology, and the 'good ideas' of treatment staff, rather than on sound empirical research. Furthermore, as discussed in Chapter 6, the empirical support for many of the treatment goals and for links between treatment goals and recidivism is at best equivocal and in many instances non-existent. Even if theory and treatment had been devised entirely on sound empirical research, it does not necessarily follow that treatment would work in the manner suggested by the theory or inferred from the empirical data. Hence, it is important that research addresses the issue of why treatment works, and even where appropriate, why it does not work. Some research, using qualitative designs, is beginning to emerge which asks, from the offenders' perspective, why treatment works, or what it was about the treatment that had an impact on them.

Drapeau *et al.* (2004) interviewed 24 sex offenders attending the La Macaza Clinic at the La Macaza penitentiary in Québec. After completing only the first phase of the programme, offenders reported that it had been helpful as it provided an opportunity for them to express themselves openly and freely. Furthermore, they argued that they had become better able to avoid confrontation and make use of a larger range of responses in difficult situations. Many expressed a sense of confidence and pride in their learning. The programme provided the men with a better understanding of sexual abuse in general and paedophilia in particular, but most were disappointed that the aim of the programme was not to provide them with an individual explanation for their behaviour. The offenders reported that the programme had given them simple and useful techniques to use to avoid relapse and helped them to better understand their victims, and by extension to better understand themselves. Although the offenders found the sessions where they had to explain their crimes in detail to the rest of the group among the most difficult, they also reported that they were beneficial.

Interestingly, when asked why they were attending treatment (offenders attended the clinic on a 'voluntary' basis), offenders cited a range of reasons, yet these reasons rarely included consideration of their past or potential future victims. Some said they attended to learn new tools, but when they were asked to explain this, it became clear that they had 'borrowed' this term from treatment staff. Some offenders referred to lacking control of their impulses and others about lacking self-understanding and wanting to gain a mastery of these impulses or to understand themselves more. Some offenders also wanted to learn about paedophilia. Another reason given was to have a safe and supportive environment to discuss these issues, and a wish to be part of a group of peers. Some offenders wanted to avoid another sentence and others wanted to prove to loved ones that they could be successful at something, or that they were committed to change. Other reasons given by single offenders were to get out of the penitentiary, to be kept busy, deal with feelings of guilt, or merely as a response of pressure to attend.

Scheela and Stern (1994) conducted 20 interviews and 65 direct observations of 43 male sex offenders completing the Sex Abuse Treatment (SAT) programme at a Health Centre in Northern Minnesota (see also Scheela 1995). These offenders described a process that involved remodelling themselves, relationships and environments. In the offenders' words, this process involved 'falling apart'; 'taking on' responsibility for the abuse; 'tearing out' the damaged parts; 'rebuilding' to make necessary changes; 'doing the upkeep' to maintain these changes; and 'moving on' to new remodelling projects. Scheela explained how this model could be used to help offenders understand the processes that they will go through as part of treatment and help clinicians understand these processes too. Although it is a useful model in this respect and it tells us that the process of treatment can be extensive and have far-reaching effects, it does not fully answer the question of why treatment works. For example, it is not clear what treatment therapists do that helps offenders remodel their lives, rather than give up at the 'falling apart' stage. Answering the question of why treatment works is going to be difficult, but more studies like the two described here should help to build up a picture of effective treatment processes.

This chapter has shown that there are huge gaps in our knowledge about the efficacy of sex offender treatment programmes. Although it may now be possible to say with a little more confidence that some treatment works for some offenders, there can be little confidence in assertions about the type of treatment and type of offenders. Throughout this chapter, calls have been made for more research into these issues and it seems that the criticisms of evaluation research made by Pawson and Tilley in 1994 continue to be a problem in this area of intervention. It is surprising that so very few evaluations actually ask the people who complete the treatment or intervention what helped or hindered them, what had the most impact, or even if they believed that the programme was likely to have an impact on their future behaviour; yet, evaluators find all sort of elaborate ways to assess outcome using quantitative, numerical data. Reluctance in psychology to use qualitative data has probably contributed to this problem, despite the fact that the few sex offender treatment studies that have been conducted using qualitative designs have revealed interesting, detailed data that can be used to inform and improve treatment practice. Although this chapter has revealed a dearth in knowledge about many of the issues discussed, it has also shown that these issues are beginning to attract attention, empirical research and professional debate. Such work should enable the development of treatment, but perhaps more importantly, a greater understanding of the processes involved and the factors that make treatment successful. Other issues that should be considered to improve treatment and the reduction of sex offences will be discussed in the next, and final chapter.

Chapter 10

Conclusion / the future of sex offender treatment

In the last 35 years, the criminal justice response to sex offenders has changed considerably in many countries. As they are increasingly demonized by the media, the public and politicians, an image of sex offenders has developed that focuses on 'stranger danger', rather than an awareness that sex offenders are more like 'normal' people and live within 'normal' communities, and further that most victims are abused by those they know and trust.

> Clearly the public has a pervasive fear of sex offenders. At the same time they also believe that they are somewhere 'out there': Sex crime is a problem happening to someone else, in another neighbourhood, in another city. Sex offenders do not live on their street, belong to their social groups and churches, work with them, teach their children, or interact with the public in ordinary ways.
>
> (Laws 2000b: 34)

Consequently, this group of offenders is seen as needing more punitative and more specialized responses than most other groups of criminals. This is despite the fact that evidence showing that sex offenders are a distinct group of offenders with different criminogenic needs and deficiencies, and requiring different criminal justice interventions, is scarce. However, legislative changes have made custodial sentences more likely, increased the length of these sentences and introduced greater monitoring and supervision procedures. At the same time, however, a rehabilitative approach – the use of cognitive-behavioural treatment for sex offenders – has developed to such an extent that it now forms a key role in the criminal justice provision of many countries (e.g. the USA, Canada, the UK, Australia and New Zealand).

Despite the widespread use of this provision in both custodial and community settings, the public seems largely ignorant of this form of intervention (Brown 1999), perhaps because of its neglect by the media.

> People don't really understand what we do. They know that we lock paedophiles up, but by and large we don't get good publicity. When you see how the TV portrays therapy being done in prison it's not particularly good, and some of these prison dramas are awful. . . . It really isn't helpful the kind of publicity that we get.
> (Female principle officer in charge of the SOTP at HMP Wayland, cited in Silverman and Wilson 2002: 65)

HM Inspectorate of Probation (1998: 154) noted that only a minority of services sought opportunities to explain and promote sex offender work to the public.

> This was not surprising at a time when any intervention with sex offenders may be portrayed as naive and ineffective in the media but it did mean that much of the excellent work taking place was unknown to the general public.

Thus, educating the public about treatment programmes and their impact on offenders may help to engender a more aware culture, although given the current climate this seems unlikely. For as Worrell (1997: 125) lamented:

> . . . official government discourse now rejects the language of rehabilitation in favour of the language of surveillance and control through information. . . . The sex offender has been constructed as irredeemable. It is no longer his crimes that are unacceptable; he himself is unacceptable as a member of the community. He is forever non-reintegratable.

Although largely unnoticed by the public, sex offender treatment has developed significantly since treatment with this group of offenders was first introduced. Initially based on a uni-dimensional theory that sex offending was caused solely by deviant sexual arousal/fantasy, both theoretical debate and empirical research has led to a much more complex and comprehensive understanding of the multiple pathways that lead to sex offending behaviours. Alongside this more complex understanding of sex offenders' behaviour (and thoughts, affective states, and deficiencies), treatment programmes have expanded to account for the range of factors now believed to play a role in the development and/or maintenance of sexually abusive behaviours. Perhaps rather surprisingly, given the range of countries, treatment settings, groups of offenders, and treatment providers, cognitive-behavioural programmes are remarkably similar. Most use the same range of treatment techniques, provide treatment in group settings and address the same core treatment goals.

Despite this similarity and the length of time that these programmes have been provided, empirical support and validation for these treatment goals is limited. Much of the evaluation research to date has focused on addressing the question of whether programmes are effective or not. Although examining whether each treatment component contributes towards overall programme effectiveness would provide an important contribution in determining overall effectiveness, this aspect of programme evaluation has tended to be ignored. Thus, empirical data neither provide consistent support for the effectiveness, and thus inclusion of these components in treatment programmes, nor do they reliably suggest that they are ineffective and therefore should be excluded. However, the empirical basis for the inclusion of empathy training seems problematic, particularly in terms of whether sex offenders lack empathy, or cognitively deny the need for empathy in their own victims, or perhaps actually enjoy the pain and suffering of their victims. Furthermore, although used extensively and often regarded highly by practitioners, evidence for the efficacy of relapse prevention is poor, particularly when used as a central treatment component for all sex offenders. Similarly, empirical support for the use of sexual arousal/ fantasy modification techniques is lacking, although many programmes now omit work on this issue, and some include it only for offenders who have particular problems in this area. Although work on non-offence-specific factors seems logical, such a range of factors are addressed in a wide range of treatment components that it is impossible to identify at present if these elements have the expected effect on recidivism. Finally, more work is needed to develop treatment for offenders who show high levels of denial, as they are often excluded from programmes despite the fact that they may present a high risk of reoffence. Thus, it is possible that treatment programmes' aims to address denial and minimization, cognitive distortion, victim empathy, sexual arousal/fantasy, relapse prevention and non-offence-specific goals are misguided.

> Treatments are ... limited by the uncertain state of scientific knowledge of the causes of deviant sexuality and the complex linkages that can occur between violent and sexual impulses.
>
> (West 1996: 66)

Hence, 'there is a desperate need for more fundamental research and for experimental treatment centres' (p. 66).

One reason for the gap in knowledge about separate treatment components could be the difficulty of measuring progress on treatment goals, such as denial, empathy and relapse-prevention skills. Existing measures tend to be very transparent, as it is easy for offenders, and particularly offenders who have completed some treatment sessions, to identify socially desirable responses. Furthermore, there is a huge range of measures used throughout the evaluation literature that does not provide for comparison across offenders, programmes or studies. What is urgently needed is a range of tools that measure the key treatment goals targeted by the majority of programmes in a manner that is less transparent than current measures, perhaps by the inclusion of open-ended responses as well as, or instead of, fixed-choice responses. Context-dependent rather than general, trait type measures may also be more reliable and valid. Such measures would need to be empirically validated across a range of sex offender populations and, importantly, linked to risk assessments and recidivism. If these measures were used consistently by all treatment providers, treatment components could be evaluated more reliably, and different programmes and different deliveries of programmes could be compared.

Furthermore, empirically validated links to risk and recidivism would allow practitioners to use these tools to assess post-treatment risk and treatment progress, such that more reliable decisions could be made about whether more treatment is needed (and of what type/addressing which treatment goals) and whether offenders should be released, supervised and so on. For although the risk assessment of all offenders, including sex offenders, has developed and improved enormously in recent years, the factors that have been shown to be the most reliable in the assessment of sex offenders are static risk factors (i.e. factors that change little over time). Currently there is very little empirical evidence that shows how the completion of treatment impacts on risk, or how this factor can be combined with existing risk assessment measures to improve post-treatment assessment. Similarly, there is a lack of knowledge of the characteristics of offenders at the end of treatment that differentiate treatment successes from treatment failures, and/or those who could be considered to be a reduced risk on the basis of treatment success. The development of reliable measures of treatment-targeted variables could also be used in the long-term monitoring of offenders, with treatment booster sessions provided if responses fall below a certain level.

Although at first glance this sounds logical and relatively straightforward, the development of such measures would not be an easy task. In addition, validation linked to long-term risk and recidivism would take many years to complete. In the meantime, the identification of the best psychometric tools that have at least some 'norm' data for sex offenders (which is often lacking in the psychometric tests used by treatment practitioners and evaluators) from those currently available, coupled with an agreement by practitioners, evaluators and researchers to use the same core set of these psychometric tests examining key treatment targets, would at least enable comparison across programmes and studies (which is currently lacking). Such an approach would also produce more reliable 'norm' data that could be pooled to identify scores that may be predictive of future offending or abstinence from offending. Yet, as programmes are delivered in many countries and there is no organization akin to a governing body, it is not clear who would be in a position to identify the most reliable and valid psychometric measures and/or request a policy employing a standardized set of psychometric tests. Moreover, it is far from clear if researchers, practitioners and evaluators would support and adopt such a policy.

This is not to say that those working in this arena do not support evidence-based practice. One of the greatest changes in treatment provision in the last 30 years has been the widespread shift towards evidence-based practice, and furthermore, the embedding of such practice within criminal justice systems with the introduction of accreditation and/or licensing procedures. However, evaluation could be embedded more fully in the provision in some countries, although this impression is generated from the lack of published evaluation research in countries such as the USA and Australia, which does not necessarily mean that the programmes are not being evaluated. Nevertheless, it is important that evaluation procedures are incorporated into treatment provision to allow for the continued monitoring and development of treatment programmes. As well as requiring the use of interventions and techniques that have demonstrated effectiveness, the adoption of evidence-based practice principles has also led to the more widespread production of clearly described treatment targets, and theoretical models of treatment change. In addition, these practices have required the production and use of treatment manuals.

Initially manuals were introduced as a positive measure to increase programme integrity and avoid programme drift. However, in recent years, many developments in treatment theory and the findings of empirical research suggest that the manual and 'one treatment fits all' approach may be misguided. Theory of sexual offending (especially of child sexual abuse) now suggests that there are multiple pathways to the development of sexual offending behaviours and typologies of offenders exist with different treatment needs. Similarly, work on denial, minimization, cognitive distortions, empathy, sexual arousal/fantasy, non-offence-specific deficits and relapse prevention all suggest that offenders have a varied range of treatment needs that cannot be addressed or incorporated in a single programme. Thus, it seems that the most effective treatment will be that which is targeted towards these varied needs.

Indeed, such an approach is supported by the 'what works?' literature, which identifies effective treatment as that which is targeted towards offenders' criminogenic needs, taking into account their level of risk, in a manner that uses the methods and techniques best suited for each offender. Given the importance of these principles in evidence-based practice, it is surprising that more work has not been done on these issues in sex offender treatment provision and in the evaluation of this intervention. Although some programmes have been adapted for some specific groups of offenders, such as special needs offenders and for offenders with a variety of cultural backgrounds, and some jurisdictions have a variety of programmes that can incorporate treatment for offenders with different levels of risk in both community and custodial settings, the general approach has been to develop a single programme that is delivered to all offenders. The dependence on groupwork with sex offenders and limited resources may account for the reliance on this approach; nevertheless, the theory and research suggest that such an approach is likely to be ineffective.

This may account for the mixed evaluation findings, as evaluation studies have generally concentrated on a range of offenders completing a single programme used for all offender types. Furthermore, the poor outcome with rapists may reflect a focus/bias towards sex offenders who offend against children (which dominate the theoretical and empirical literature) and the lack of a fit between the treatment targets of current programmes and the criminogenic needs of rapists. Clearly more work is needed to address this issue, although it is difficult to see how group treatments can be provided when the numbers in some offender groups, particularly when offenders are widely geographically spread, is small. A modular approach providing a range of treatments for each treatment component/goal may be a possible solution, with each offender assigned to different modules based on risk, needs and responsivity principles. This approach would allow for the provision of treatment manuals. Another approach would be to write treatment manuals that suggest a variety of treatment approaches depending on the offenders being treated; thus, treatment staff could incorporate flexibility while also avoiding programme drift. However, it is difficult to see how such an approach could encompass the wide range of needs without the manual becoming overly complex and difficult to use in practice.

As indicated earlier, the outcome literature for cognitive-behavioural programmes provides a far-from-clear picture as to the effectiveness of this form of intervention. While many maintain that this form of intervention is effective (for example Marshall), many are equally adamant that effectiveness has not been demonstrated (for example,

Quinsey). A range of methodological problems contributes to this confusion. This is exacerbated by the fact that treatment has actually changed over time (due to changes in treatment theory, treatment targets and treatment methods), so that a range of programmes is being evaluated (particularly in meta-analyses). This is despite the fact that the term cognitive-behavioural treatment (and the treatment evaluation studies themselves) creates the impression that treatment is a single entity that remains constant across time and location. These problems are compounded further by the inclusion of, and pooling of results for, a range of offenders, with a range of risk levels and criminogenic needs. This is aggravated yet further by the omission of factors such as therapeutic alliance, characteristics and style of treatment staff, group processes and dynamics, and the responses of offenders completing treatment. Hence, it is hardly surprising that clear patterns have not emerged from evaluation studies.

Pawson and Tilley (1994) critiqued quasi-experimental designs such as those employed by sex offender treatment evaluators, arguing that the result of such work is a confused picture. With this form of intervention, these arguments are certainly supported. Pawson and Tilley argued that evaluation research should address a broader range of questions, rather than just focus on whether the intervention works or not. Hence, questions such as why and how the intervention worked (if it did work), and where and for whom it was effective (if it was) should be addressed. In recent years some researchers have begun to address these issues in sex offender treatment, although the body of literature remains limited, as is our understanding of these issues. More research is needed on these questions, rather than on the general 'does it work' question, as by building up a knowledge of whether each treatment component has an impact, what it has an impact on, what other factors have an impact on offenders, how treatment components/factors have an impact, how they are linked to offending and so on, it may be possible to more effectively answer the question of whether treatment works or not. Crucially, rather than a yes or no response, this answer would be more detailed, describing exactly what treatment worked, with whom, in what settings, with what characteristics, etc. The greater use of qualitative methods and actually asking the offenders (treatment clients) themselves what they thought of the treatment, what had an impact and so on, is likely to help in this endeavour.

An interesting point regarding the evaluation and perception of this form of intervention with sex offenders was made by Laws (1999: 293):

> ... It is my belief that we made a serious mistake in the field a number of years ago when we characterized our efforts as sex offender treatment rather than sex offender management. The word

treatment conjures a disease model that was long ago abandoned in this field. Because it suggests remission or cure, it establishes false expectations for treatment efficacy. This has had unfortunate consequences as the judicial system, the media, and the public have gradually become aware of the reoffence rates among so-called treated offenders.

Moreover, it should also be noted that no matter how effective treatment becomes, this provision alone cannot eliminate the problem of sexual offending. As Konopasky (1996) pointed out, practitioners do not get to treat sex offenders until the behaviour is already well entrenched and has been reported. Furthermore, the current social climate does not encourage offenders to come forward and seek help (Groth and Oliveri 1989; Konopasky 1996). In addition, current treatment provision is focused in criminal justice/corrections systems and so is only (or mostly) available to those who have been convicted of a sexual offence. Thus, treatment will do nothing to prevent undetected sex offenders (the majority of offenders) from sexually abusing.

> The best way to stop sexual abuse is to prevent it before it begins.
> ... most public health officials will confirm that primary prevention
> is much less costly and more effective than tertiary prevention.
> (Freeman-Longo 1996: 97)

Furthermore, those arguing from a feminist standpoint would suggest that the problem of sexual offending is not going to diminish so long as social and cultural attitudes and behaviours support the dominance of men, rape myths and other attitudes supportive of sexually abusive behaviours. Thus, policy makers and social policy agencies should focus more attention on primary (and secondary) prevention, within a public health approach.

Laws (1996, 2000b) has been one of the main proponents of a public health approach to sexual offending, arguing that the criminal justice system in not effective in reducing all but a minority of sexual offences, and furthermore that such approaches inflate public fears and exacerbate the rejection of sex offenders by the public (which does little to prevent offences). Hanson (2000), too, pointed out that treatment, in the form of relapse prevention, did little to protect the public by preventing sexual offences, and moreover, did not help generate strategies that may be successful in the more widespread prevention of such abuse. A public health approach focuses on preventing the targeted behaviours/incidents, in this case sexual offending, before it happens/takes place, by focusing on three levels of prevention (for more detailed discussions of the application of the public health approach to child sexual abuse see

Becker and Reilly 1999; McMahon and Puett 1999; Mercy 1999; McMahon 2000). Primary prevention aims to stop behaviour before it starts and:

> ... may be achieved through universal preventive measures which are directed at everyone in an eligible population of selective preventive measures which are directed at those with higher than average risk for unhealthy behaviour. A third type of effort, indicated preventative measures, centres on individuals who have already engaged in unhealthy behaviour or have a disease.
>
> (Mercy and Hammond 1999, cited in McMahon and Puett 1999: 258)

Secondary prevention focuses on those who are at risk of engaging in the unwanted behaviour, or developing the unwanted disease/problem, i.e. it would target those most at risk of becoming sex offenders and/or those most at risk of victimization. Tertiary prevention focuses on those who have demonstrated the target behaviour at least once, i.e. identified sexual offenders and working with those who have been victimized. Currently, the majority of provision aimed at preventing sexual offences by focusing on potential or actual offenders takes place at the tertiary level, with the primary and secondary levels of intervention virtually ignored by social policy. However, there are a number of programmes operating at the primary (and to a lesser extent secondary) level of prevention that focus on the prevention of victimization (see Becker and Reilly 1999; McMahon and Puett 1999), although there is doubt about the effectiveness of these programmes, with mixed evaluation results (Becker and Reilly 1999). Furthermore, some (for example, Chasan-Taber and Tabachnick 1999; Tabachnick and Dawson 2000) have argued that prevention should be aimed at potential offenders who have responsibility for abuse, rather than at potential victims who are not responsible for the abusive behaviour.

The 'Stop It Now' Programme, which was developed in the state of Vermont (USA), is an innovative approach that addresses sexual abuse at the primary and secondary levels of prevention (Chasan-Taber and Tabachnick 1999; Tabachnick and Dawson 2000).

> The programme relies on two key premises: that adults – not children – must prevent child sexual abuse and that child sexual abuse can be prevented using the tools of public health awareness and education.
>
> (Tabachnick and Dawson 2000: 1)

Hence, the programme involves two key areas of intervention: public health campaigning (promoted through a public awareness campaign and outreach work), designed to raise the awareness of child sexual abuse and provide accurate information about sex offenders, their ability to change and the dangers of an overly punitive response; and a confidential telephone helpline for people worried about their own behaviour, and for those worried about the behaviour of others (e.g. of relatives or friends). This approach increased the percentage of Vermonters who could explain child sexual abuse from 44.5 per cent in 1995 to 84.8 per cent in 1999. Furthermore, 90 per cent could correctly identify abuse scenarios and the proportion of respondents who recognized that abusers were likely to live in their communities rose from 67.0 per cent to 73.7 per cent. In addition, the proportion of Vermonters who could identify at least one sign that an adult or juvenile was experiencing sexual behaviour problems and the number who said they would take direct action if they knew of a case of abuse increased. In four years of operation, the confidential telephone service received 657 calls, of which 99 (15 per cent) were from self-identified abusers (Tabachnick and Dawson 2000). A similar programme was introduced in the UK (see Kemshall *et al.* 2004) and a helpline developed in Merseyside (see Hossack *et al.* 2004). As the introduction of this programme is more recent, extensive evaluation data is limited (see Kemshall *et al.* 2004), although 40 per cent of callers to the helpline were concerned about their own behaviour. This approach is a good example of a public health approach to sexual offending. Yet, in order for it to achieve its maximum potential, it needs to be adopted at a governmental level and to form the principle of intervention and prevention, rather than run alongside a punitive, often misinformed approach, which largely contradicts the principles of the public health model.

As Hanson *et al.* (1993) pointed out, recidivism is most likely to be prevented when interventions attempt to address the lifelong potential for reoffences, and do not expect sex offenders to be permanently 'cured' following a single set of treatment sessions. To this end, many including Wyre (1989, 1992, cited in McAlinden 1999) have argued that telephone helplines could be successfully used as a support for treated offenders. In addition, Wyre suggests that this approach could be used as an avenue for diversionary treatment; that is, where the offender is encouraged to attend treatment programmes without the consequence of criminal prosecution. While the latter use of this scheme is likely to be controversial (a factor indeed recognized by Wyre), the former application could provide crucial post-treatment support. Evidence that sex offenders and those completing treatment would use such a helpline is provided by Hossack *et al.* (2004). In total, 37 calls were received to a helpline in Merseyside (England) between July 2000 and December 2001. Of these calls, 31 per cent were from high-risk callers who described serious intentions to abuse, had abused or were currently abusing and

29 per cent were from offenders in treatment programmes who were experiencing problems that they felt unable to discuss in their treatment group or from partners of offenders in treatment. This suggests that the more widespread use of helplines would be of benefit. Furthermore, for treatment to target the maximum number of offenders, some provision for offenders outwith the criminal justice (and mental health) system is required.

In addition, attention should be focused to increase public awareness of treatment and to attempt to engender an environment where treated sex offenders are successfully reintegrated into the community; as 'the public wish for more punitive responses toward perpetrators has the unintended effect of creating a climate in which fewer offenders are held accountable for their crimes' (Groth and Oliveri 1989: 326). Furthermore, offenders who are thwarted in their attempts at a fulfilling non-offending lifestyle, i.e. those who cannot get a job, are hounded out of their communities, cannot develop meaningful relationships (because of the response to them, as much as their skills in developing such relationships), are perhaps more likely to return to their offending behaviours. Eldridge and Wyre (1998: 91) argued for a need to involve the community in offender monitoring. They pointed out that:

> In order for relapse prevention to be effective, sexual offenders need to be able to engage in a social life that is safe in the context of their individual pattern of offending. This requires an aware culture in which the offender is not an outcast but neither is he the subject of naïve trust.

An innovative approach that could be used to support offenders undergoing treatment and assist their reintegration back into the community is the Community Reintegration or Circles of Support and Accountability Project (John Howard Society 1997, cited in Nash 1999) developed in British Columbia in 1994 (see also Wilson and Prinzo 2001; Petrunik 2002; Silverman and Wilson 2002; Drewery 2003). This project takes on offenders from federal institutions who would be released back into the community with high needs and little, if any, community support. Circles of six volunteers are created for each offender who must agree to live by the consensus of the circle, participate in counselling sessions and identify and address any substance abuse problems. Furthermore, circle members assist with offenders' daily living needs, maintain open and honest communication and mediate between the offender and the community (for a description of how this works in practice see Silverman and Wilson 2002). Between 1994 and 2000, 30 circles were set up in the Toronto-Hamilton area and 12 in other parts of Canada (Petrunik 2002). In the first two years, the project claimed not a single relapse (John Howard Society 1997, cited in Nash 1999). In a later and more detailed analysis, Wilson and Prinzo (2001) reported that three from 30 high-risk offenders (at risk in the community for an average of 36 months, ranging from 16 months to just over six and a half years) reoffended, each in a less serious manner than the offence for which they had been imprisoned (see also Silverman and Wilson 2002). Using risk assessment scales to determine how many of the group would be likely to reoffend, Wilson concluded that the circle members reoffended at a rate that was less than 40 per cent of that predicted by the risk scales (which would predict seven reoffences in the group of 30 offenders). This model is currently being piloted in the UK, although it is too early, and the number of offenders supported in this way too small, to say if it has been effective in this country. Generally, the circle volunteers have tended to be members of faith communities, but if this approach is to have more widespread support and utility, particularly in communities with a variety of faiths and/or limited religious beliefs, a pool of volunteers from a range of community settings is required.

The treatment of sex offenders has clearly developed enormously in the past 35 years; however, many issues still need to be addressed. Most notably, these involve questions regarding the effectiveness of specific treatment goals, what treatment works, which offenders it works with, in what contexts it works, what characteristics make it work and how it works. Although treatment has become a key aspect of the criminal justice approach to dealing with sexual offences, this approach neglects primary and secondary levels of prevention that could arguably have a greater impact on the reduction of sex offences. Thus, if government policy is truly aimed towards public protection (a more frequent claim in recent years), more emphasis is needed to reduce the likelihood that people develop sexually abusive patterns of behaviour; to ensure that such behaviours are not overlooked, ignored, condoned, supported or unreported; and that intervention is targeted at those who are more likely to engage in such behaviours but who have yet to do so; and provides for offenders/potential offenders outwith the criminal justice system. Ultimately, the treatment of known/convicted sex offenders will have a limited impact on the rate of sexual offending, as the majority of sex offences go unreported and hence, the majority of offenders are unidentified.

References

Abel, G.G. (1994) 'Commentary', *Behavior, Research and Therapy*, **32(5)**, 529–31.

Abel, G.G., Becker, J.V. and Cunningham-Rathner, J. (1984) 'Complications, consent and cognitions in sex between children and adults', *International Journal of Law and Psychiatry*, **7**, 89–103.

Abel, G.G., Becker, J.V., Cunningham-Rathner, J., Rouleau, J. and Murphy, W. (1987) 'Self-reported sex crimes of nonincarcerated paraphiliacs', *Journal of Interpersonal Violence*, **2(1)**, 3–25.

Abel, G.G., Blanchard, E.B. and Becker, J.V. (1978) 'An Integrated Treatment Program for Rapists' in R. Rada (ed.) *Clinical Aspects of the Rapist* (pp. 161–214). New York: Grune & Stratton.

Abel, G.G., Gore, D.K., Holland, C.L., Camp, N., Becker, J.V. and Rathner, J. (1989) 'The measurement of cognitive distortions of child molesters', *Annals of Sex Research*, **2**, 135–53.

Abel, G.G., Mittelman, M.S., Becker, J.V., Rathner, J. and Rouleau, J.L. (1988) 'Predicting Child Molesters' Response to Treatment' in R.A. Prentky and V.L. Quinsey (eds) *Human Sexual Aggression: Current Perspectives*. New York: Annals of the New York Academy of Sciences.

Alexander, M.A. (1999) 'Sexual offender treatment efficacy revisited', *Sexual Abuse: A Journal of Research and Treatment*, **11(2)**, 101–16.

American Psychiatric Association. (1994) *Diagnostic Manual of Mental Disorders* (4th ed.). Washington, DC: APA.

Anderson, B.L. and Boffitt, B. (1988) 'Is there a reliable and valid self-report measure of sexual behaviour?', *Archives of Sexual Behaviour*, **17(6)**, 509–25.

Andrews, D.A. (1989) 'Recidivism is predictable and can be influenced: using risk assessments to reduce recidivism', *Forum of Correction Research [On-Line]*, **1(2)**, 11–18. http://www.csc-scc.gc.ca/text/pblct/forum/e012/12j_e.pdf.

Andrews, D.A. (1995) 'The Psychology of Criminal Conduct and Effective Treatment' in J. McGuire (ed.) *What Works: Reducing Reoffending: Guidelines from Research and Practice*. Wiley series in Offender Rehabilitation (pp. 35–62). Oxford: John Wiley & Sons.

Andrews, D.A. and Bonta, J. (1994) *The Psychology of Criminal Conduct*. Cincinnati, OH: Anderson.

Andrews, D.A., Bonta, J. and Hoge, R.D. (1990) 'Classification for effective rehabilitation', *Criminal Justice and Behavior*, **17(1)**, 19–52.

Andrews, D.A., Zinger, I., Hoge, R.D., Bonta, J., Gendreau, P. and Cullen, F.T. (1990) 'Does correctional treatment work? A clinically relevant and psychologically informed meta-analysis', *Criminology*, **28**, 369–404.

Atkinson, J.L. (1996) 'Female sex offenders: a literature review', *Forum of Correction Research [On-Line]*, **8(2)**. http://www.csc-scc.gc.ca/text/pblct/forum/e082/082m_e.pdf.

Auburn, T. and Lea, S. (2003) 'Doing cognitive distortions: a discursive psychology analysis of sex offender treatment talk', *British Journal of Social Psychology*, **42(2)**, 281–98.

Aubut, J., Proulx, J., Lamoureux, B. and McKibben, A. (1998) 'Sexual Offenders' Treatment Program of the Phillippe Pinel Institute of Montreal' in W.L. Marshall, Y.M. Fernandez, S.M. Hudson and T. Ward (eds) *Sourcebook of Treatment Programs for Sexual Offenders* (pp. 221–34). New York: Plenum Press.

Bailey, W.C. (1966) 'Correctional outcome: an evaluation of 100 reports', *Journal of Criminal Law, Criminology and Police Science*, **57**, 153–60.

Baim, C., Allam, J., Eames, T., Dunford, S. and Hunt, S. (1999) 'The use of psychodrama to enhance victim empathy in sex offenders: An evaluation', *The Journal of Sexual Aggression*, **4(1)**, 4–14.

Bakker, L., Hudson, S., Wales, D. and Riley, D. (1998) *And There Was Light: Evaluating the Kia Marama Treatment Programme for New Zealand Sex Offenders against Children*. New Zealand Department of Corrections. http://www.corrections.govt.nz/public/pdf/research/kiamarama/kiamarama.pdf.

Bandura, A., Adams, N.E. and Beyer, J. (1977) 'Cognitive processes mediating behavioral change', *Journal of Personality and Social Psychology*, **35(3)**, 125–39.

Barbaree, H.E. (1991) 'Denial and minimisation among sex offenders: assessment and treatment outcomes', *Forum of Correction Research [On-line]*, **3(4)**. http://www.csc-scc.gc.ca/text/pblct/forum/e034/034h_e.pdf.

Barbaree, H.E. (1997) 'Evaluating treatment efficacy with sexual offenders: the insensitivity of recidivism studies to treatment effect', *Sexual Abuse: A Journal of Research and Treatment*, **9(2)**, 111–28.

Barbaree, H.E., Peacock, E.J., Cortoni, F., Marshall, W.L. and Seto, M. (1998) 'Ontario Penitentiaries' Program' in W.L. Marshall (ed.) *Sourcebook of Treatment Programs for Sexual Offenders* (pp. 59–77). New York, NY: Plenum Press.

Barker, M. and Morgan, R. (1991) 'Probation practice with sex offenders surveyed', *Probation Journal*, **38(4)**, 171–6.

Barker, M. and Morgan, R. (1993) *Sex Offenders: A Framework for the Evaluation of Community-Based Treatment*. London: HMSO.

Barron, P., Hassiotis, A. and Banes, J. (2002) 'Offenders with intellectual disability: the size of the problem and the therapeutic outcomes', *Journal of Intellectual Disability Research*, **46(6)**, 454–63.

Bates, A., Falshaw, L., Corbett, C., Patel, V. and Friendship, C. (2004) 'A follow-up study of sex offenders treated by Thames Valley Sex Offender Groupwork Programme, 1995–1999', *Journal of Sexual Aggression*, **10(1)**, 29–38.

BBC News (2002) 'Top paedophile clinic shuts', *BBC News On-Line*, 31 July. http://news.bbc.co.uk/1/hi/england/2161518.stm.

BBC News (2004) 'New sex offender hostels planned', *BBC News On-Line*, 9 September. http://newsvote.bbc.co.uk/mpapps/pagetools/print/news.bbc.co.uk/1/hi/uk/3639484.stm.

Becker, J.V. and Murphy, W.D. (1998) 'What we know and do not know about assessing and treating sex offenders', *Psychology, Public Policy and Law*, **4(1/2)**, 116–37.

Becker, J.V. and Reilly, D.W. (1999) 'Preventing sexual abuse and assault', *Sexual Abuse: A Journal of Research and Treatment*, **11(4)**, 267–78.

Beckett, R.C. (1994) 'Assessment of Sex Offenders' in T. Morrison, M. Erooga and R.C. Beckett (eds) *Sexual Offending Against Children: Assessment and Treatment of Male Abusers*. London: Routledge.

Beckett, R.C. (1998) 'Community Treatment in the United Kingdom' in W.L. Marshall, Y.M. Fernandez, S.M. Hudson and T. Ward (eds) *Sourcebook of Treatment Programs for Sexual Offenders*. New York: Plenum Press.

Beckett, R.C., Beech, A.R., Fisher, D. and Fordham, A.S. (1994) *Community-based Treatment for Sex Offenders: An Evaluation of Seven Treatment Programmes*. London: HMSO.

Beech, A.R. and Fisher, D.D. (2002) 'The rehabilitation of child sex offenders', *Australian Psychologist*, **37(3)**, 206–14.

Beech, A.R. and Fordham, A.S. (1997) 'Therapeutic climate of sexual offender treatment programs', *Sexual Abuse: Journal of Research and Treatment*, **9(3)**, 219–37.

Beech, A.R. and Ward, T. (2004) 'The integration of etiology and risk in sexual offenders: a theoretical framework', *Aggression and Violent Behavior*, **10(1)**, 31–63.

Beech, A.R., Fisher, D. and Beckett, R.C. (1998) *STEP 3: An Evaluation of the Prison Sex Offender Treatment Programme*. London: HMSO.

Beech, A.R., Erikson, M., Friendship, C. and Ditchfield, J. (2001) *A Six-year Follow-up of Men Going Through Probation-based Sex Offender Treatment Programmes*. Research, Development and Statistics Directorate: Research Findings No. 144. London: HMSO.

Behroozi, C.S. (1992) 'Groupwork with involuntary clients: remotivating strategies', *Groupwork*, **5(2)**, 31–41.

Bélanger, N. and Earls, C. (1996) 'Sex offender recidivism prediction', *Forum of Correction Research [On-line]*, **8(2)**. http://www.csc-scc.gc.ca/crd/forum/e082/e082g.htm.

Bickley, J. and Beech, A.R. (2002) 'An investigation of the Ward and Hudson Pathways Model of the sexual offense process with child abusers', *Journal of Interpersonal Violence*, **17(4)**, 371–93.

Bingham, J.E., Turner, B.W. and Piotrowski, C. (1995) 'Treatment of sexual offenders in an outpatient community based program', *Psychology Reports*, **76**, 1195–200.

Birkett, D. (1997) 'Monsters with human faces', *The Guardian*, 27 September, pp. WEE 22.

Blumenthal, S., Gudjonsson, G. and Burns, J. (1999) 'Cognitive distortions and blame attribution in sex offenders against adults and children', *Child Abuse and Neglect*, **23(2)**, 129–43.

Blyth, E. and Milner, J. (1990) *The Process of Inter-agency Work in the Violence against Children Study Group. Taking Child Care Seriously: Contemporary Issues in Child Protection Theory and Practice.* London: Unwin Hyman.

Bond, I. and Evans, D. (1967) 'Avoidance therapy: its use in two cases of underwear fetishism', *Canadian Medical Association Journal,* **96**, 1160–2.

Borduin, C.M., Whiteman, M. and Gordon, A.S. (1990) 'Multisystemic treatment of adolescent sexual offenders', *International Journal of Offender Therapy and Comparative Criminology,* **34**, 105–14.

Borzecki, M. and Wormith, J.S. (1987) 'A survey of treatment programmes for sex offenders in North America', *Canadian Psychology,* **28(1)**, 30–44.

Bourke, M.L. and Donohue, B. (1996) 'Assessment and treatment of juvenile sex offenders: an empirical review', *Journal of Child Sexual Abuse,* **5(1)**, 47–70.

Brake, S.C. and Shannon, D. (1997) 'Using Pretreatment to Increase Admission in Sex Offenders' in B.K. Schwartz and H.R. Cellini (eds) *The Sex Offender: New Insight, Treatment Innovations and Legal Developments.* Kingston, NJ: Civic Research Institute.

Briere, J. and Runtz, M. (1989) 'University males' sexual interest in children: predicting potential indices of "pedophilia" in a non forensic sample', *Child Abuse and Neglect,* **13**, 65–75.

Brody, S. (1976) *The Effectiveness of Sentencing.* Home Office Research Study No. 35. London: HMSO.

Brown, S.J. (1999) 'Public attitudes towards the treatment of sex offenders', *Legal and Criminological Psychology,* **4(2)**, 239–52.

Brown, S.L. (2000) 'Cost-effective correctional treatment', *Forum of Correction Research [On-Line],* **12(2)**. http://198.103.98.138/text/pblct/forum/e122/122n_e.pdf.

Brown, J. and Blount, C. (1999) 'Occupational stress among sex offender treatment managers', *Journal of Managerial Psychology,* **14(1–2)**, 108–20.

Browne, K.D., Foreman, L. and Meddleton, D. (1998) 'Predicting treatment dropout in sex offenders', *Child Abuse Review,* **7**, 402–19.

Burdon, W.M. and Gallagher, C.A. (2002) 'Coercion and sex offenders: controlling sex offending behavior through incapacitation and treatment', *Criminal Justice and Behavior,* **29(1)**, 87–109.

Burke, D.M. (2001) 'Empathy in sexually offending and nonoffending adolescent males', *Journal of Interpersonal Violence,* **16(3)**, 222–33.

Burt, M.R. (1980) 'Cultural myths and supports for rape', *Journal of Personality and Social Psychology,* **38(2)**, 217–30.

Burt, M.R. (1998) 'Rape Myths' in J. Clay Warner and M.E. Odem (eds) *Confronting Rape and Sexual Assault* (pp. 129–44). Wilmington, DE: SR Books/Scholarly Resources Inc.

Burt, M.R. and Albin, R.S. (1981) 'Rape myths, rape definitions, and probability of conviction', *Journal of Applied Social Psychology,* **11(3)**, 212–30.

Calder, M.C. (1999) *Assessing Risk in Adult Males who Sexually Abuse Children: A Practitioners' Guide.* Lyme Regis: Russell House Publishing.

Campbell, S. (2003) *The Feasibility of Conducting an RCT at HMP Grendon.* London: Home Office Online Report. http://www.homeoffice.gov.uk/rds/pdfs2/rdsolr0303.pdf.

Cann, J., Falshaw, L. and Friendship, C. (2004) 'Sexual offenders discharged from prison in England and Wales: A 21-year reconviction study', *Legal and Criminological Psychology*, **9(1)**, 1–10.

Carich, M.S. and Calder, M.C. (2003) *Contemporary Treatment of Adult Male Sex Offenders*. Lyme Regis: Russell House Publishing.

Carnes, P.J. (1983) *Out of the Shadows: Understanding Sexual Addiction*. Minneapolis: Compare.

Carnes, P.J. (1990) 'Sexual Addiction' in A.L. Horton (ed.) *The Incest Perpetrator*. Beverly Hills, CA: SAGE.

Census 2001 (2003) *United Kingdom*. http://www.statistics.gov.uk/census2001/profiles/uk.asp.

Chaffin, M. (1994) 'Research in action: assessment and treatment of child abusers', *Journal of Interpersonal Violence*, **9(2)**, 224–37.

Chasan-Taber, L. and Tabachnick, J. (1999) 'Evaluation of a child sexual abuse prevention program', *Sexual Abuse: A Journal of Research and Treatment*, **11(4)**, 279–92.

Chlopan, B.E., McCain, M.L., Carbonell, J.L. and Hagen, R.L. (1985) 'Empathy: review of available measures', *Journal of Personality and Social Psychology*, **48**, 635–53.

Clark, N.K. (1993) 'Sexual Offenders: An Overview' in N.K. Clark and G.M. Stephenson (eds) *Sexual Offenders: Context, Assessment and Treatment. D.C.L.P. Issues in Criminological Psychology, Occasional Paper No. 19*. Leicester: British Psychological Society.

Clark-Carter, D. (1998) *Doing Quantitative Psychological Research: From Design to Report*. Hove: Psychology Press.

Cohen, J. (1962) 'The statistical power of abnormal social psychological research: a review', *Journal of Abnormal and Social Psychology*, **65**, 145–53.

Cohen, M.A. (2000) 'To Treat or Not To Treat? A Financial Perspective' in C.R. Hollin (ed.) *Handbook of Offender Assessment and Treatment* (pp. 35–49). Chichester: John Wiley & Sons.

Coleman, E. and Haaven, J. (1998) 'Adult Intellectually Disabled Sexual Offenders' in W.L. Marshall, Y.M. Fernandez, S.M. Hudson and T. Ward (eds) *Sourcebook of Treatment Programs for Sexual Offenders* (pp. 273–86). New York: Plenum Press.

Coleman, E., Dwyer, S.M., Abel, G., Berner, W., Breiling, J., Eher, R., *et al.* (2000) 'Standards of care for the treatment of adult sex offenders', *Journal of Psychology and Human Sexuality*, **11(3)**, 11–17.

Colledge, M., Collier, P. and Brands, S. (1999) *Crime Reduction Programme and Constructive Regimes in Prison. Programmes for Offenders: Guidance for Evaluators. Crime Reduction Programme – Guidance Note 2*. London: HMSO.

Cook, B., David, F. and Grant, A. (2001) *Sexual Violence in Australia*. Research and Public Policy Series No. 36. Canberra: Australian Institute of Criminology.

Cook, D.A.G., Fox, C.A., Weaver, C.M. and Rooth, F.G. (1991) 'The Berkeley Group: ten years' experience of a group for non-violent sex offenders', *British Journal of Psychiatry*, **158(2)**, 238–43.

Cooke, D.J. and Philip, L. (2000) 'To Treat or Not To Treat? An Empirical Perspective' in C.R. Hollin (ed.) *Handbook of Offender Assessment and Treatment* (pp. 17–34). Chichester: John Wiley & Sons.

Correctional Service of Canada (2003) *Standards for Correctional Programs 726–1.* http://www.csc-scc.gc.ca/text/prgrm/correctional/standards_e.shtml.

Covell, C.N. and Scalora, M.J. (2002) 'Empathic deficits in sexual offenders', *Aggression and Violent Behavior,* **7(3)**, 251–70.

Cowburn, M. and Dominelli, L. (2001) 'Masking hegemonic masculinity: reconstructing the paedophile as the dangerous stranger', *British Journal of Social Work,* **31**, 399–415.

Cowling, M. (1998) *Date Rape and Consent.* Aldershot: Ashgate.

Craven, S., Brown, S. and Gilchrist, E. (under review) 'Sexual grooming: review of literature and theoretical considerations', *Psychology, Crime and Law.*

Crighton, D. (1995) 'Sex offender groupwork', *Issues in Criminology and Legal Psychology,* **23**, 15–21.

Cull, D.M. and Wehner, D.M. (1998) 'Australian Aborigines: Cultural Factors Pertaining to the Assessment and Treatment of Australian Aboriginal Offenders' in W. L. Marshall, Y.M. Fernandez, S.M. Hudson and T. Ward (eds) *Sourcebook of Treatment Programs for Sexual Offenders* (pp. 431–44). New York: Plenum Press.

Davies, J. (1999) 'Aboriginal sex offender treatment program Greenough regional prison'. Paper presented at the *Best Practice Interventions in Corrections for Indigenous People Conference* convened by the Australian Institute of Criminology in conjunction with Department for Correctional Services SA, Adelaide, 13–15 October.

Davies, N. (1998) 'The epidemic in our midst that went unnoticed', *The Guardian,* 2 June, pp. 4–5.

Davis, G.E. and Leitenberg, H. (1987) 'Adolescent sex offenders', *Psychological Bulletin,* **101(3)**, 417–27.

Davis, M.H. (1983) 'The effects of dispositional empathy on emotional reactions and helping: a multidimensional approach', *Journal of Personality,* **51(2)**, 167–84.

DesLauriers, A. and Gardner, J. (1999) 'The Sexual Predator Treatment Program of Kansas' in A. Schlank and F. Cohen (eds) *The Sexual Predator: Law, Policy, Evaluation and Treatment.* Kinston, NJ: Civic Research Institute.

Dhiri, S. and Brand, S. (1999) *Crime Reduction Programme. Analysis of Costs and Benefits: Guidance for Evaluators.* London: HMSO.

Di Fazio, R., Abracen, J. and Looman, J. (2001) *Group Versus Individual Treatment of Sex Offenders: A Comparison.* Ottawa: Correctional Service of Canada.

Doob, A.N. and Brodeur, J.P. (1989) 'Rehabilitating the debate on rehabilitation', *Canadian Journal of Criminology,* **31(2)**, 179–92.

Dowden, C., Antonowicz, D.H. and Andrews, D.A. (2003) 'The effectiveness of relapse prevention with offenders: A meta-analysis', *International Journal of Offender Therapy and Comparative Criminology,* **47(5)**, 516–28.

Drake, C.R. and Ward, T. (2003) 'Practical and theoretical roles for the formulation based treatment of sexual offenders', *International Journal of Forensic Psychology [On-line],* **1(1)**, 71–84. http://ijfp.psyc.uow.edu.au/index2.html.

Drake, C.R., Ward, T., Nathan, P. and Lee, J.K.P. (2001) 'Challenging the cognitive distortions of child molesters: an implicit theory approach', *Journal of Sexual Aggression,* **7(2)**, 25–40.

Drapeau, M., Körner, A., Brunet, L. and Granger, L. (2004) 'Treatment at La Macaza Clinic: a qualitative study of the sexual offenders' perspective', *Canadian Journal of Criminology and Criminal Justice*, **46(1)**, 27–44.

Drewery, H. (2003) 'The people behind circles of support', *Criminal Justice Matters*, **2003(52)**, 18–19.

Duncan, L.E. and Williams, L.M. (1998) 'Gender role socialization and male-on-male vs. female-on-male child sexual abuse', *Sex Roles: A Journal of Research [On-line]*, **39(9–10)**, 765–85. http://www.findarticles.com/cf_0/m2294/9-10_39/53857390/print/jhtml.

Eccles, A. and Walker, W. (1998) 'Community-based Treatment with Sexual Offenders' in W.L. Marshall, Y.M. Fernandez, S.M. Hudson and T. Ward (eds) *Sourcebook of Treatment Programs for Sexual Offenders* (pp. 93–103). New York: Plenum Press.

Eldridge, H. and Gibbs, P. (1987) 'Strategies for preventing reoffending: a course for sex offenders', *Probation Journal*, **34(1)**, 7–9.

Eldridge, H. and Wyre, R. (1998) 'The Lucy Faithfull Foundation Residential Programme for Sexual Offenders' in W.L. Marshall, Y.M. Fernandez, S.M. Hudson and T. Ward (eds) *Sourcebook of Treatment Programs for Sexual Offenders*. New York: Plenum Press.

Ellerby, L. and Stonechild, J. (1998) 'Blending the traditional with the contemporary in the treatment of Aboriginal sexual offenders: A Canadian experience' in W.L. Marshall, Y.M. Fernandez, S.M. Hudson and T. Ward (eds) *Sourcebook of Treatment Programs for Sexual Offenders* (pp. 399–417). New York: Plenum Press.

Elliott, M. (1993) *Female Sexual Abuse of Children*. New York: Guildford Press.

Elliott, M. (1998) 'Female Sexual Abuse; "The ultimate taboo" ' in S. Hayman (ed.) *Child Sexual Abuse: Providing for Victims, Coping with Offenders. Proceedings of Two Conferences Held on 2 February and 12 March 1998*. London: The Institute for the Study and Treatment of Delinquency, King's College London.

Elliott, M., Browne, K. and Kilcoyne, J. (1995) 'Child sexual abuse prevention: what offenders tell us', *Child Abuse and Neglect*, **19(5)**, 579–94.

Ennis, L. and Horne, S. (2003) 'Predicting psychological distress in sex offender therapists', *Sexual Abuse: A Journal of Research and Treatment*, **15(2)**, 149–57.

Epps, K. (1996) 'Sex Offenders' in C.R. Hollin (ed.) *Working with Offenders: Psychological Practice in Offender Rehabilitation* (pp. 150–87). Chichester: John Wiley & Sons.

Farr, C., Brown, J. and Beckett, R. (2004) 'Ability to empathise and masculinity levels: comparing male adolescent sex offenders with a normative sample of non-offending adolescents', *Psychology, Crime and Law*, **10(2)**, 155–68.

Farrenkopf, T. (1992) 'What Happens to Therapists Who Work with Sex Offenders?' in E. Coleman, S. M. Dwyer and N.J. Pallone (eds) *Sex Offender Treatment: Psychological and Medical Approaches* (pp. 217–23). London: The Haworth Press.

Farrington, D.P. (1983) 'Randomized Experiments on Crime and Justice' in M. Tonry and N. Morris (eds) *Crime and Justice: A Review of Research* (pp. 257–307). Chicago: University of Chicago Press.

Farrington, D.P. and Jolliffe, D. (2002) *A Feasibility Study Into Using A Randomised Controlled Trial To Evaluate Treatment Pilots At HMP Whitemoor*. London: Home

Office Online Report. http://www.homeoffice.gov.uk/rds/pdfs2/rdsolr1402. pdf.

Federoff, J.P. and Moran, B. (1997) 'Myths and misconceptions about sex offenders', *The Canadian Journal of Human Sexuality*, **6(4)**, 263–76.

Feldman, M.P. (1977) *Criminal Behaviour: A Psychological Analysis*. Chichester: John Wiley & Sons.

Fernandez, Y.M., Marshall, W.L., Lightbody, S. and O'Sullivan, C. (1999) 'The child molester empathy measure: description and examination of its reliability and validity', *Sexual Abuse: A Journal of Research and Treatment*, **11(1)**, 17–37.

Fieldman, J.P. and Crespi, T.D. (2002) 'Child sexual abuse: offenders, disclosure and school-based initiatives', *Adolescence*, **37(145)**, 151–60.

Finkelhor, D. (1984) *Child Abuse: New Theory and Research*. New York: Free Press.

Finkelhor, D. (1986) *A Sourcebook on Child Sexual Abuse*. Beverly Hills, CA: SAGE.

Finkelhor, D. (1994) 'Current information on the scope and nature of child sexual abuse', *Future of Children*, **4(2)**, 31–53.

Finkelhor, D. and Lewis, I.A. (1988) 'An epidemiologic approach to the study of child molestation', *Annals of the New York Academy of Sciences*, **528**, 64–78.

Fisher, D. and Beech, A.R. (1999) 'Current practice in Britain with sexual offenders', *Journal of Interpersonal Violence*, **14(3)**, 240–56.

Fisher, D., Beech, A.R. and Browne, K. (1998) 'Locus of control and its relationship to treatment change and abuse history in child sexual abusers', *Legal and Criminological Psychology*, **3(1)**, 1–12.

Fisher, D., Beech, A.R. and Browne, K. (2000) 'The effectiveness of relapse prevention training in a group of incarcerated child molesters', *Psychology, Crime and Law*, **6(3)**, 181–95.

Fisher, D., Grubin, D. and Perkins, D. (1998) 'Working with Sexual Offenders in Psychiatric Settings in England and Wales' in W.L. Marshall, Y.M. Fernandez, S.M. Hudson and T. Ward (eds) *Sourcebook of Treatment Programs for Sexual Offenders*. New York: Plenum Press.

Fisher, D., Beckett, R., Beech, A.R. and Fordham, A.S. (1995) 'The therapeutic impact of sex offender treatment programmes', *Probation Journal*, **42(1)**, 2–7.

Foa, E.B. and Emmelkamp, P.M.G. (1983) *Failures in Behavior Therapy*. New York: John Wiley & Sons.

Freeman-Longo, R.E. (1996) 'Feel good legislation: prevention or calamity', *Child Abuse and Neglect*, **20(2)**, 95–101.

Freeman-Longo, R.E. and Knopp, F.H. (1992) 'State of the art sex offender treatment: outcome and issues', *Annals of Sex Research*, **5(3)**, 141–60.

Freeman-Longo, R.E., Bird, S.L., Stevenson, W.F. and Fiske, J.A. (1995) *1994 Nationwide Survey of Treatment Programs and Models Serving Abuse-Reactive Children and Adolescent and Adult Sex Offenders*. Brandon, VT: Safer Society Press.

Frenken, J. (1999) 'Sexual offender treatment in Europe: an impression of cross-cultural differences', *Sexual Abuse: A Journal of Research and Treatment*, **11(1)**, 87–93.

Friendship, C. and Thornton, D. (2001) 'Sexual reconviction for sexual offenders discharged from prison in England and Wales: implications for evaluating treatment', *British Journal of Criminology*, **41**, 285–92.

Friendship, C., Beech, A.R. and Browne, K.D. (2002) 'Reconviction as an outcome measure in research: a methodological note', *British Journal of Criminology*, **42**, 442–4.

Friendship, C., Mann, R.E. and Beech, A.R. (2003a) 'Evaluation of a national prison-based treatment program for sexual offenders in England and Wales', *Journal of Interpersonal Violence*, **18(7)**, 744–59.

Friendship, C., Mann, R.E. and Beech, A.R. (2003b) *The Prison-Based Sex Offender Treatment Programme – An Evaluation*. Research, Development and Statistics Directorate: Research Findings No. 205. London: HMSO.

Fromuth, M.E., Burkhart, B.R. and Jones, C.W. (1991) 'Hidden child molestation: An investigation of adolescent perpetrators in a nonclinical sample', *Journal of Interpersonal Violence*, **6(3)**, 376–84.

Frost, A. (2004) 'Therapeutic engagement styles of child sexual offenders in a group treatment program: a grounded theory study', *Sexual Abuse: A Journal of Research and Treatment*, **16(3)**, 191–208.

Furby, L., Weinrott, M.R. and Blackshaw, L. (1989) 'Sex offender recidivism: a review', *Psychological Bulletin*, **105(1)**, 3–30.

Gallagher, C.A., Wilson, D.B., Hirschfield, P., Coggeshall, M.B. and MacKenzie, D.L. (1999) 'A quantitative review of the effects of sex offender treatment on sexual reoffending', *Corrections Managements Quarterly*, **3(4)**, 19–29.

Garrett, T., Oliver, C., Wilcox, D.T. and Middleton, D. (2003) 'Who cares? The views of sexual offenders about the group treatment they receive', *Sexual Abuse: A Journal of Research and Treatment*, **15(4)**, 323–38.

Garrison (1992) *Working with Sex Offenders: A Practical Guide*. Social Work Monographs 112. Norwich: University of East Anglia.

Gee, D., Ward, T. and Eccleston, L. (2003) 'The function of sexual fantasies for sexual offenders: a preliminary model', *Behaviour Change*, **20(1)**, 44–60.

Geer, J.H., Estupinan, L.A. and Manguno Mire, G.M. (2000) 'Empathy, social skills, and other relevant cognitve processes in rapists and child molesters', *Aggression and Violent Behavior*, **5(1)**, 99–126.

Geer, T.M., Becker, J.V., Gray, S.R. and Krauss, D. (2001) 'Predictors of treatment completion in a correctional sex offender treatment program', *International Journal of Offender Therapy and Comparative Criminology*, **45(3)**, 302–13.

Gendreau, P. (1981) 'Treatment in corrections: Martinson was wrong', *Canadian Psychology*, **22(4)**, 332–38.

Gendreau, P. (1996) 'The Principles of Effective Intervention with Offenders' in A.T. Harland (ed.) *Choosing Correctional Interventions That Work: Defining the Demand and Evaluating the Supply* (pp. 117–30). Newbury Park, CA: SAGE.

Gendreau, P. and Ross, R.R. (1979) 'Effective correctional treatment: bibliotherapy for cynics', *Crime and Delinquency*, **25**, 463–89.

Gendreau, P., Goggin, C. and Smith, P. (1999) 'The forgotten issue in effective correctional treatment: program implementation', *International Journal of Offender Therapy and Comparative Criminology*, **43(2)**, 180–7.

Gendreau, P., Goggin, C., Cullen, F.T. and Andrews, D.A. (2000) 'The effects of community sanctions and incarceration on recidivism', *Forum of Correction Research [On-Line]*, **12(2)**. http://www.csc-scc.gc.ca/text/pblct/forum/e122/122c_e.pdf.

Gibbens, T.C.N., Soothill, K.M. and Way, C.K. (1981) 'Sex offences against young girls: a long-term record study', *Psychological Medicine*, **11**, 351–7.

Glaser, D. and Frosh, S. (1993) *Child Sexual Abuse* (2nd ed.). Basingstoke: Macmillan.

Glasser, M., Kolvin, I., Campbell, D., Glasser, A., Leitch, I. and Farrelly, S. (2001) 'Cycle of child sexual abuse: links between being a victim and becoming a perpetrator', *British Journal of Psychiatry*, **179**, 482–94.

Gocke, B. (1991) *Tackling Denial in Sex Offenders: A Therapeutic Dilemma Exacerbated by the Criminal Justice System*. Probation Monograph 98. Norwich: Social Work Monographs, University of East Anglia.

Goldman, J.D.G. and Padayachi, U.K. (2000) 'Some methodological problems in estimating incidence and prevalence in child sexual abuse research', *Journal of Sex Research [On-line]*, **37(4)**, 305–14. http://www.findarticles.com/cf_0/m2372/72272302/print.jhtml.

Gordon, A. and Nicholaichuk, T.P. (1996) 'Applying the risk principle to sex offender treatment', *Forum of Correction Research [On-Line]*, **8(2)**. http://198.103.98.138/text/pblct/forum/e082/082Le.pdf.

Gordon, A. and Porporino, F.J. (1990) *Managing the Treatment of Sex Offenders: A Canadian Perspective*. Abbotsford Correctional Service of Canada.

Grayston, A.D. and De Luca, R.V. (1999) 'Female perpetrators of child sexual abuse: a review of the clinical and empirical literature', *Aggression and Violent Behavior*, **4(1)**, 93–106.

Griffiths, D., Hinsburger, D. and Christian, R. (1985) 'Treating developmentally handicapped sexual offenders: the Nork Behavior Management Services Treatment Program', *Psychiatric Aspects of Mental Retardation Reviews*, **4**, 49–54.

Griffiths, D., Quinsey, V.L., Hinsburger, D. and Christian, R. (1989) *Changing Inappropriate Sexual Behavior: A Community-based Approach for Persons with Developmental Disabilities*. Baltimore, MD: Brooks.

Grossman, L.S., Martis, B. and Fichtner, C. (1999) 'Are sex offenders treatable? A research overview', *Psychiatric Services*, **50(3)**, 349–61.

Groth, A.N. (1977) 'The adolescent sexual offender and his prey', *International Journal of Offender Therapy and Comparative Criminology*, **21**, 249–54.

Groth, A.N. (1983) 'Treatment of the Sexual Offender in a Correctional Institution' in G.J. Greer and I.R. Stuart (eds) *The Sexual Aggressor: Current Perspective on Treatment* (pp. 160–76). New York: Van Nostrand Reinhold.

Groth, A.N. and Lorendo, C. (1981) 'Juvenile sex offenders: guidelines for assessment', *International Journal of Offender Therapy and Comparative Criminology*, **25**, 31–9.

Groth, A.N. and Oliveri, F.J. (1989) 'Understanding Sexual Offence Behaviour and Differentiating Among Sexual Abusers: Basic Conceptual Issues' in S.M. Sgroi (ed.) *Vulnerable Populations: Sexual Abuse Treatment for Children, Adult Survivors, Offenders, and Persons with Mental Retardation* (Vol. 2). New York: Lexington Books.

Grubin, D. and Gunn, J. (1990) *The Imprisoned Rapist and Rape*. London: Institute of Psychiatry.

Grubin, D. and Thornton, D. (1994) 'A national program for the assessment and treatment of sex offenders in the English prison system', *Criminal Justice and Behavior*, **21(1)**, 55–71.

Grubin, D. and Wingate, S. (1996) 'Sexual offence recidivism: prediction versus understanding', *Criminal Behaviour and Mental Health*, **6**, 349–59.

Hall, G.C.N. (1995) 'Sexual offender recidivism revisited: a meta-analysis of recent treatment studies', *Journal of Consulting and Clinical Psychology*, **63(5)**, 802–9.

Hall, G.C.N. (1996) *Theory-based Assessment, Treatment, and Prevention of Sexual Aggression*. Oxford: Oxford University Press.

Hall, G.C.N. and Hirschman, R. (1991) 'Toward a theory of sexual aggression: a quadripartite model', *Journal of Consulting and Clinical Psychology*, **59**, 662–9.

Hall, G.C.N. and Hirschman, R. (1992) 'Sexual aggression against children: a conceptual perspective of etiology', *Criminal Justice and Behavior*, **19(1)**, 8–23.

Hanson, R.K. (1997) 'How to know what works with sexual offenders', *Sexual Abuse: A Journal of Research and Treatment*, **9(2)**, 129–45.

Hanson, R.K. (1998) 'What do we know about sex offender risk assessment?', *Psychology, Public Policy, and Law*, **4(1–2)**, 50–72.

Hanson, R.K. (1999) 'Working with sex offenders: a personal view', *Journal of Sexual Aggression*, **4(2)**, 81–93.

Hanson, R.K. (2000) 'What Is So Special About Relapse Prevention?' in D.R. Laws, S.M. Hudson and T. Ward (eds) *Remaking Relapse Prevention with Sex Offenders* (pp. 27–38). New York: Guildford Press.

Hanson, R.K. (2003) 'Empathy deficits of sexual offenders: a conceptual model', *Journal of Sexual Aggression*, **9(1)**, 13–23.

Hanson, R.K. and Bussière, M.T. (1996) 'Sex offender risk predictors: a summary of research results', *Forum of Correction Research [On-line]*, **8(2)**. http://198.103. 98.138/text/pblct/forum/e082/082c_e.pdf.

Hanson, R.K. and Bussière, M.T. (1998) 'Predicting relapse: a meta-analysis of sexual offender recidivism studies', *Journal of Consulting and Clinical Psychology*, **66(2)**, 348–62.

Hanson, R.K. and Harris, A.J.R. (2000) 'Where should we intervene? Dynamic predictors of sexual assault recidivism', *Criminal Justice and Behavior*, **27(1)**, 6–35.

Hanson, R.K. and Nicholaichuk, T. (2000) 'A cautionary note regarding Nicholaichuk et al. (2000)', *Sexual Abuse: A Journal of Research and Treatment*, **12(4)**, 289–93.

Hanson, R.K. and Scott, H. (1995) 'Assessing perspective-taking among sexual offenders, nonsexual criminals, and nonoffenders', *Sexual Abuse: A Journal of Research and Treatment*, **7(4)**, 259–77.

Hanson, R.K. and Thornton, D. (2000) 'Improving risk assessments for sex offenders: a comparison of three actuarial scales', *Law and Human Behavior*, **24(1)**, 119–36.

Hanson, R.K., Broom, I. and Stephenson, M. (2004) 'Evaluating community sex offender treatment programs: a 12-year follow up of 724 offenders', *Canadian Journal of Behavioural Science*, **36(2)**, 87–96.

Hanson, R.K., Cox, B.J. and Woszczyn, C. (1991) 'Assessing treatment outcome for sexual offenders', *Annals of Sex Research*, **4(3–4)**, 177–208.

Hanson, R.K., Scott, H. and Steffy, R.A. (1995) 'A comparison of child molesters and nonsexual criminals: risk predictors and long-term recidivism', *Journal of Research in Crime and Delinquency*, **32(3)**, 325–37.

Hanson, R.K., Steffy, R.A. and Gauthier, R. (1993) 'Long-term recidivism of child molesters', *Journal of Consulting and Clinical Psychology*, **61(4)**, 646–52.

Hanson, R.K., Gordon, A., Harris, A.J.R., Marques, J.K., Murphy, W., Quinsey, V.L., *et al.* (2002) 'First report of the collaborative outcome data project on the effectiveness of psychological treatment for sex offenders', *Sexual Abuse: A Journal of Research and Treatment*, **14(2)**, 169–94.

Harris, G.T., Rice, M.E. and Cormier, C.A. (1991) 'Psychopathy and violent recidivism', *Law and Human Behavior*, **15(6)**, 625–37.

Harris, G.T., Rice, M.E. and Quinsey, V.L. (1998) 'Appraisal and management of risk in sexual aggressors: implications for criminal justice policy', *Psychology, Public Policy, and Law*, **4(1–2)**, 73–115.

Haywood, T.W., Grossman, L.S., Kravitz, H.M. and Wasyliw, O.E. (1994) 'Profiling psychological distortion in alleged child molesters', *Psychological Reports*, **75(2)**, 915–27.

Henham, R. (1998) 'Sentencing sex offenders: some implications of recent criminal justice policy', *The Howard Journal*, **37(1)**, 70–81.

Herman, J.L. (1988) 'Considering sex offenders: a model of addiction', *Signs: Journal of Women in Culture and Society*, **13(4)**, 695–724.

Hildebran, D.D. and Pithers, W.D. (1992) 'Relapse prevention: Application and Outcome' in W. O'Donohue and J.H. Geer (eds) *The Sexual Abuse of Children: Clinical Issues* (pp. 365–93). Hillsdale, NJ: Lawrence Erlbaum.

HM Inspectorate of Probation (1991) *The Work of the Probation Service with Sex Offenders*. London: HMSO.

HM Inspectorate of Probation (1998) *Exercising Constant Vigilance: The Role of the Probation Service in Protecting the Public from Sex Offenders*. London: HMSO.

HM Prison Service (2004) *Annual Report 2004*. London: HMSO.

HMP Barlinie (unpublished) *Creating Control: Statement of Results*. HMP Barlinie: Scottish Prison Service.

Hollin, C.R. (1994) 'Designing effective rehabilitation programmes for young offenders', *Psychology, Crime and Law*, **1**, 193–9.

Hollin, C.R. (1995) 'The Meaning and Implications of "Programme Integrity" ' in J. McGuire (ed.) *What Works: Reducing Reoffending: Guidelines from Research and Practice* (pp. 195–208). Chichester: John Wiley & Sons.

Home Office (1991) *Criminal Statistics for England and Wales 1990*. London: HMSO.

Home Office (1995) *Home Office Statistical Bulletin. Notifiable Offences in England and Wales, 1994. Issues 5/95*. London: Home Office Research and Statistics Department.

Home Office (2001a) *Home Office Statistical Bulletin. Recorded Crime, England and Wales, 12 months to March 2001. Issue 12/01*. London: Home Office Research and Statistics Department.

Home Office (2001b) *Prison Statistics England and Wales, 2001*. London: HMSO.

Home Office (2002) *The Treatment and Risk Management of Sexual Offenders in Custody and in the Community*. London: National Probation Directorate.

Home Office (2003) *Working with Offenders: What Works in Reducing Re-Offending*. http://www.crimereduction.gov.uk/workingoffenders1.htm.

Home Office (2004) *Home Office Statistical Bulletin. Crime in England and Wales 2003/04*. London: Home Office Research and Statistics Department.

Home Office Communication Directorate (2002) *SOTP: Why bother? SOTP, The Sex Offender Treatment Programme: A Brief Guide for Prisoners*. London: HMSO.

Home Office National Probation Directorate (2001) *Working with Offenders*. http://www.crimereduction.gov.uk/workingoffenders13.htm.

Hood, R. (1967) 'Research on the Effectiveness of Punishments and Treatments' in European Committee on Crime Prevention (ed.) *Collected Studies in Criminological Research* (pp. 73–113). Strasbourg: Council of Europe.

Hossack, A., Playle, S., Spencer, A. and Carey, A. (2004) 'Helpline: accessible help inviting active or potential paedophiles', *Journal of Sexual Aggression*, **10(1)**, 123–32.

Howard League (1985) *Unlawful Sex: Offences, Victim and Offenders in England and Wales, 1996. Issue 3/97*. London: Waterlow Publishers.

Howarth, G. (1999) *Hansard. Written Answers for 10 May: Column 37 [On-line]*. http://www.publications.parliament.uk/pa/cm199899/cmhansrd/vo990510/text/90510w11.htm#90510w11.htm_sbhd5.

Howells, K. (1994) 'Child sexual abuse: Finkelhor's precondition model revisited', *Psychology, Crime and Law*, **1**, 201–13.

Howells, K., Day, A. and Wright, S. (2004) 'Affect, emotions and sex offending', *Psychology, Crime and Law*, **10(2)**, 179–95.

Howitt, D. (1995) 'Pornography and the paedophile: is it criminogenic?', *British Journal of Medical Psychology*, **68(1)**, 15–27.

Hudson, S.M. and Ward, T. (2000) 'Interpersonal competency in sex offenders', *Behavior Modification*, **24(4)**, 494–527.

Hudson, S.M., Wales, D.S. and Ward, T. (1998) 'Kia Marama: A Treatment Program for Child Molesters in New Zealand' in W.L. Marshall, Y.M. Fernandez, S.M. Hudson and T. Ward (eds) *Sourcebook of Treatment Programs for Sexual Offenders* (pp. 17–28). New York: Plenum Press.

Hudson, S.M., Ward, T. and McCormack, J.C. (1999) 'Offense pathways in sexual offenders', *Journal of Interpersonal Violence*, **14**, 779–98.

Hudson, S.M., Marshall, W.L., Wales, D. and McDonald, E. (1993) 'Emotional recognition skills of sex offenders', *Annals of Sex Research*, **6(3)**, 199–211.

Hudson, S.M., Wales, D.S., Bakker, L.W. and Ward, T. (2002) 'Dynamic risk factors: the Kia Marama evaluation', *Sexual Abuse: A Journal of Research and Treatment*, **14**, 103–19.

Hudson, S.M., Marshall, W.L., Ward, T., Johnston, P.W. and Jones, R.L. (1995) 'Kia Marama: a cognitive-behavioural program for incarcerated child molesters', *Behaviour Change*, **12(2)**, 69–80.

Hulme, P.A. (2004) 'Retrospective measurement of childhood sexual abuse: a review of instruments', *Child Maltreatment*, **9(2)**, 201–17.

Jennings, J.L. and Sawyer, S. (2003) 'Principles and techniques for maximizing the effectiveness of group therapy with sex offenders', *Sexual Abuse: A Journal of Research and Treatment*, **15(4)**, 251–67.

Jensen, S. and Jewell-Jensen, C. (1998) 'Why license sexual offender treatment providers? Because it's the responsible thing to do!', *Sexual Abuse: A Journal of Research and Treatment*, **10(3)**, 263–6.

John Howard Society of Alberta (1999) *Dangerous Offender Legislation around the World*. http://www.johnhoward.ab.ca/docs/dangrous/dangrcov.htm.

Kaul, A. (1993) 'Sex offenders – cure or management?', *Medicine, Science and the Law*, **33(3)**, 207–12.

Kear-Colwell, J. and Boer, D.P. (2000) 'The treatment of pedophiles: clinical experience and the implications of recent research', *International Journal of Offender Therapy and Comparative Criminology*, **44(5)**, 593–605.

Kear-Colwell, J. and Pollock, P. (1997) 'Motivation or confrontation: which approach to the child sex offender?', *Criminal Justice and Behavior*, **24(1)**, 20–33.

Kearns, B. (1995) 'Self-reflection in work with sex offenders: a process not just for therapists', *Journal of Child Sexual Abuse*, **4**, 107–10.

Kelly, L. (1995) *Tay Project: An Intervention for Convicted Adult Sex Offenders. Annual Report 1995–6*. Tayside Regional Council: Social Work Services to the Criminal Justice System.

Kelly, L., Regan, L. and Burton, S. (1991) *An Exploratory Study of the Prevalence of Sexual Abuse in a Sample of 16–21 Year-olds*. London: Child Abuse Studies Unit, Polytechnic of North London.

Kelly, R.J. (1982) 'Behavioral re-orientation of pedophiliacs: can it be done?', *Clinical Psychology Review*, **2**, 387–408.

Kempe, R.S. and Kempe, C.H. (1978) *Child Abuse*. London: Fontana/Open Books.

Kemshall, H., Mackenzie, G. and Wood, J. (2004) *Stop It Now! UK and Ireland: An Evaluation*. Leicester: De Monfort University.

Kershaw, C., Goodman, J. and White, S. (1999) *Reconvictions of Offenders Sentenced or Discharged from Prison in 1995, England and Wales*. Statistical Bulletin No. 19/99. London: HMSO.

Kitzinger, J. (1999) 'The Ultimate Neighbour from Hell? Stranger Danger and the Media Framing of Paedophiles' in B. Franklin (ed.) *Social Policy, The Media and Misrepresentation* (pp. 207–21). London: Routledge.

Knopp, F.H. (1982) *Remedial Intervention in Adolescent Sex Offenses: Nine Program Descriptions*. Orwell, VT: Safer Society Press.

Knopp, F.H. and Lackey, L.B. (1987) *Sexual Offenders Identified as Intellectually Disabled: A Summary of Data from Forty Treatment Providers*. Orwell, VT: Safer Society Press.

Knopp, F.H. and Stevenson, W.F. (1989) *Nationwide Survey of Juvenile and Adult Sex Offender Treatment Programs and Models: 1988*. Orwell, VT: Safer Society Press.

Knopp, F.H., Freeman-Longo, R.E. and Stevenson, W.F. (1992) *National Survey of Juvenile and Adult Sex Offender Treatment Programs and Models*. Orwell, VT: Safer Society Press.

Konopasky, R.J. (1996) 'Managing sex offenders: Some thoughts and suggestions', *Forum of Correction Research [On-Line]*, **8(2)**. http://198.103.98.138/text/pblct/forum/e082/082n_e.pdf.

Kosky, R.J. (1989). Should sex offenders be treated?', *Australian and New Zealand Journal of Psychiatry*, **23(2)**, 176–80.

Koss, M.P. (1993) 'Rape: scope, impact, interventions, and public policy responses', *American Psychologist*, **48(10)**, 1062–9.

Kroner, D.G. and Weekes, J.R. (1996) 'Balanced inventory of desirable responding: factor structure, reliability, and validity with an offender sample', *Personality and Individual Differences*, **21(3)**, 323–33.

Lambie, I.D. and Stewart, M.W. (2003) *Community Solutions for the Community's Problem: An Outcome Evaluation of Three New Zealand Community Child Sex Offender Treatment Programmes.* Wellington: New Zealand Department of Corrections.

Lancaster, E. (1996) 'Working with Men who Sexually Abuse Children: The Experience of the Probation Service', in B. Fawcett, B. Featherstone, J. Hearn and C. Toft (eds) *Violence and Gender Relations: Theories and Interventions* (pp. 130–46). London: SAGE.

Langevin, R., Wright, P. and Handy, L. (1988) 'Empathy, assertiveness, aggressiveness, and defensiveness among sex offenders', *Annals of Sex Research,* **1(4)**, 533–47.

Langton, C. and Marshall, W.L. (2000) 'The Role of Cognitive Distortions in Relapse Prevention Programs', in D.R. Laws, S.M. Hudson and T. Ward (eds) *Remaking Relapse Prevention with Sex Offenders* (pp. 167–86). New York: Guildford Press.

Lanyon, R. I. (1986) 'Theory and treatment in child molestation', *Journal of Consulting and Clinical Psychology,* **54(2)**, 176–82.

Larsen, J., Robertson, P., Hillman, D. and Hudson, S.M. (1998) 'Te Piriti: A Bicultural Model for Treating Child Molesters in Aotearoa/New Zealand', in W.L. Marshall, Y.M. Fernandez, S.M. Hudson and T. Ward (eds) *Sourcebook of Treatment Programs for Sexual Offenders* (pp. 385–98). New York: Plenum Press.

Larzelere, R.E., Kuhn, B.R. and Johnson, B. (2004) 'The intervention selection bias: an underrecognized confound in intervention research', *Psychological Bulletin,* **130(2)**, 289–303.

Launay, G. (2001) 'Relapse prevention with sex offenders: practice, theory and research', *Criminal Behaviour and Mental Health,* **11(1)**, 38–54.

Laws, D.R. (ed.). (1989) *Relapse Prevention with Sex Offenders.* New York: Guildford Press.

Laws, D.R. (1995) 'Central elements in relapse prevention procedures with sex offenders', *Psychology, Crime and Law,* **2(1)**, 41–53.

Laws, D.R. (1996) 'Relapse prevention or harm reduction?', *Sexual Abuse: A Journal of Research and Treatment,* **8(3)**, 243–7.

Laws, D.R. (1999) 'Relapse prevention: the state of the art', *Journal of Interpersonal Violence,* **14(3)**, 285–302.

Laws, D.R. (2000a) 'Relapse Prevention: Reconceptualization and Revision' in C.R. Hollin (ed.) *Handbook of Offender Assessment and Treatment.* Chichester: John Wiley & Sons.

Laws, D.R. (2000b) 'Sexual offending as a public health problem: a North American perspective', *Journal of Sexual Aggression,* **5(1)**, 30–44.

Laws, D.R. and Marshall, W.L. (1991) 'Masturbatory reconditioning with sexual deviates: An evaluative review', *Advances in Behaviour Research and Therapy,* **13(1)**, 13–25.

Laws, D.R. and Marshall, W.L. (2003) 'A brief history of behavioral and cognitive behavioral approaches to sexual offenders: Part 1. Early developments', *Sexual Abuse: A Journal of Research and Treatment,* **15(2)**, 75–92.

Laws, D.R. and O'Donohue, W. (eds) (1997) *Sexual Deviance: Theory, Assessment and Treatment.* New York: Guildford Press.

Lea, S., Auburn, T. and Kibblewhite, K. (1999) 'Working with sex offenders: the perceptions and experiences of professionals and paraprofessionals', *International Journal of Offender Therapy and Comparative Criminology*, **43(1)**, 103–19.

Lee, J.K.P., Proeve, M.J., Lancaster, M. and Jackson, H.J. (1996) 'An evaluation and 1-year follow-up study of a community-based treatment program for sex offenders', *Australian Psychologist*, **31(2)**, 147–52.

Lees, M. (2001) 'Indigenous sex offender treatment program', Paper presented at the *Best Practice Interventions in Corrections for Indigenous People Conference* convened by the Australian Institute of Criminology, Sydney, 8–9 October.

Lewis, C.F. and Stanley, C.R. (2000) 'Women accused of sexual offenses', *Behavioral Sciences and the Law*, **18(1)**, 73–81.

Lewis, P. and Perkins, D. (1996) 'Collaborative Strategies for Sex Offenders in Secure Settings' in C. Cordess and M. Cox (eds) *Forensic Psychotherapy: Crime, Psychodynamics and the Offender Patient*. London: Jessica Kingsley.

Lievore, D. (2004) *Recidivism of Sexual Assault Offenders: Rates, Risk Factors and Treatment Efficacy*. Canberra: Australian Institute of Criminology.

Lindsay, W.R. (2002) 'Research and literature on sex offenders with intellectual and developmental disabilities', *Journal of Intellectual Disability Research*, **46(1)**, 74–85.

Lindsay, W.R. and Smith, A.H. (1998) 'Responses to treatment for sex offenders with intellectual disability: a comparison of men with 1 and 2 year probation sentences', *Journal of Intellectual Disability Research*, **42(5)**, 346–53.

Lindsay, W.R., Marshall, I. and Neilson, C. (1998) 'The treatment of men with a learning disability convicted of exhibitionism', *Research in Developmental Disabilities*, **19(4)**, 295–316.

Lindsay, W.R., Neilson, C.Q., Morrison, F. and Smith, A.H. (1998) 'The treatment of six men with a learning disability convicted of sex offences with children', *British Journal of Clinical Psychology*, **37(1)**, 83–98.

Lindsay, W.R., Smith, A.H.W., Law, J., Quinn, K., Anderson, A., Smith, A., *et al.* (2002) 'A treatment service for sex offenders and abusers with intellectual disability: characteristics of referrals and evaluation', *Journal of Applied Research in Intellectual Disabilities*, **15**, 166–74.

Lipsey, M.W. (1989) 'The efficacy of intervention for juvenile delinquency: results from 400 studies', paper presented at the 41st *Annual Meeting of the American Society of Criminology*, Reno, NV, November.

Lipsey, M.W. (1995) 'What Do We Learn From 400 Research Studies on the Effectiveness of Treatment with Juvenile Delinquents?' in J. McGuire (ed.) *What Works: Reducing Reoffending* (pp. 63–78) The Wiley Series in Offender Rehabilitation. Chichester: John Wiley & Sons.

Lipton, D.N., Martinson, R. and Wilkes, J. (1975) *The Effectiveness of Correctional Treatment: A Survey of Treatment Evaluation Studies*. New York: Praeger.

Lloyd, C., Mair, G. and Hough, J.M. (1994) *Explaining Reconviction Rates: A Critical Analysis*. Home Office Research Study No. 136. London: HMSO.

Logan, C.H. (1972) 'Evaluation research in crime and delinquency: a reappraisal', *Journal of Criminal Law, Criminology and Police Science*, **63**, 378–87.

Looman, J., Abracen, J. and Nicholaichuk, T.P. (2000) 'Recidivism among treated sexual offenders and matched controls: data from the Regional Treatment Centre (Ontario)', *Journal of Interpersonal Violence*, **15(3)**, 279–90.

Lösel, F. (1995) 'The Efficacy of Correctional Treatment: A Review and Synthesis of Meta-evaluations' in J. McGuire (ed.) *What Works: Reducing Reoffending. Guidelines for Research and Practice* (pp. 79–111). The Wiley Series in Offender Rehailitation. Chichester: John Wiley & Sons.

Lund, C.A. (2000) 'Predictors of sexual recidivism: did meta-analysis clarify the role and relevance of denial?' *Sexual Abuse: A Journal of Research and Treatment*, **12(4)**, 275–87.

Lundström, F. (2002) *The Development of a New Multi-Disiplinary Sex Offender Rehabilitation Programme for the Irish Prison Service.* http://www.irishprisons. ie/pdf/sex_offerder_programme.pdf.

Mailloux, D.L., Abracen, J., Serin, R., Cousineau, C., Malcolm, B. and Looman, J. (2003) 'Dosage of treatment to sexual offenders: are we overprescribing?', *International Journal of Offender Therapy and Comparative Criminology*, **47(2)**, 171–84.

Malamuth, N.M. (1981) 'Rape proclivity among males', *Journal of Social Issues*, **37**, 138–57.

Malcolm, P.B. (1996) 'Millhaven's specialized sex offender intake assessment: a preliminary evaluation', *Forum of Correction Research [On-Line]*, **8(2)**. http:// www.csc-scc.gc.ca/text/pblct/forum/e082/082f_e.pdf.

Maletzky, B.M. (1991) *Treating the Sexual Offender.* Newbury Park, CA: SAGE.

Maletzky, B.M. (1993) 'Factors associated with success and failure in behavioural and cognitive treatment of sexual offenders', *Annals of Sex Research*, **6**, 241–58.

Maletzky, B.M. and Steinhauser, C. (2002) 'A 25 year follow up of cognitive/ behavioral therapy with 7,275 sexual offenders', *Behaviour Modification*, **26(2)**, 123–47.

Mann, R.E. and Thornton, D. (1998) 'The Evolution of a Multisite Sexual Offender Treatment Program' in W.L. Marshall, Y.M. Fernandez, S.M. Hudson and T. Ward (eds) *Sourcebook of Treatment Programs for Sexual Offenders.* New York: Plenum Press.

Marlatt, G.A. (1982) 'Relapse Prevention: A Self-control Program for the Treatment of Addictive Behaviors' in R. Stuart (ed.) *Adherence, Compliance and Generalization in Behavioral Medicine* (pp. 329–78). New York: Brunner/Mazel.

Marlatt, G.A. (2000) 'Foreword' in D.R. Laws, S.M. Hudson and T. Ward (eds) *Remaking Relapse Prevention with Sex Offenders* (pp. ix–xiv). New York: Guildford Press.

Marlatt, G.A. and Gordon, J.R. (1985) *Relapse Prevention: Maintenance Strategies in the Treatment of Addictive Behaviours.* New York: Guildford Press.

Marques, J.K. (1999) 'How to answer the question "Does sexual offender treatment work?"' *Journal of Interpersonal Violence*, **14(4)**, 437–51.

Marques, J.K. and Nelson, C. (1989) 'Understanding and Preventing Relapse in Sex Offenders' in M. Glossop (ed.) *Relapse and Addictive Behaviours* (pp. 96–106). London: Tavistock.

Marques, J.K., Day, D.M., Nelson, C. and Miner, M. (1989) *The Sex Offender Evaluation Project: Third Report to the State Legislature in Response to PC1365.* Sacramento: California Department of Mental Health.

Marques, J.K., Day, D.M., Nelson, C. and West, M.A. (1993) 'Findings and Recommendations from California's Experimental Treatment Program' in G.C.N. Hall, R. Hirschman, J.R. Graham and M.S. Zaragoza (eds) *Sexual*

Aggression: Issues in Etiology, Assessment and Treatment (pp. 197–214). Washington, DC: Taylor & Francis.

Marques, J.K., Day, D.M., Nelson, C. and West, M.A. (1994) 'Effects of cognitive-behavioural treatment on sex offender recidivism', *Criminal Justice and Behavior*, **21(1)**, 28–54.

Marques, J.K., Nelson, C., West, M.A. and Day, D.M. (1994) 'The relationship between treatment goals and recidivism among child molesters', *Behavior, Research and Therapy*, **32(5)**, 577–58.

Marques, J.K., Nelson, C., Alarcon, J.-M. and Day, D.M. (2000) 'Preventing Relapse in Sex Offenders: What We Learned From SOTEP's Experimental Treatment Program' in D.R. Laws, S.M. Hudson and T. Ward (eds) *Remaking Relapse Prevention with Sex Offenders: A Sourcebook* (pp. 321–40). London: SAGE.

Marshall, P. (1997) *The Prevalence of Convictions for Sexual Offending. Research Findings No. 55*. London: HMSO. http://www.homeoffice.gov.uk/rds/pdfs/r55.pdf.

Marshall, W.L. (1989) 'Intimacy, loneliness and sexual offenders', *Behaviour Research and Therapy*, **27(5)**, 491–503.

Marshall, W.L. (1992) 'The social value of treatment for sexual offenders', *The Canadian Journal of Human Sexuality*, **1(3)**, 109–14.

Marshall, W.L. (1993a) 'A Revised Approach to the Treatment of Men Who Sexually Assault Adult Females' in G.C.N. Hall, R. Hirschman, J.R. Graham and M.S. Zaragoza (eds) *Sexual Aggression: Issues in Etiology, Assessment and Treatment* (pp. 143–65). Washington, DC: Taylor & Francis.

Marshall, W.L. (1993b) 'The role of attachments, intimacy, and loneliness in the etiology and maintenance of sexual offending', *Sexual and Marital Therapy*, **8(2)**, 109–21.

Marshall, W.L. (1993c) 'The treatment of sex offenders: what does the outcome data tell us? A reply to Quinsey, Harris, Rice, and Lalumière', *Journal of Interpersonal Violence*, **8(4)**, 524–30.

Marshall, W.L. (1994) 'Treatment effects on denial and minimization in incarcerated sex offenders', *Behaviour Research and Therapy*, **32(5)**, 559–64.

Marshall, W.L. (1996a) 'Assessment, treatment, and theorizing about sex offenders: developments during the past twenty years and future directions', *Criminal Justice and Behavior*, **23(1)**, 162–99.

Marshall, W.L. (1996b) 'The sexual offender: monster, victim, or everyman?', *Sexual Abuse: A Journal of Research and Treatment*, **8(4)**, 317–35.

Marshall, W.L. (1997) 'The relationship between self-esteem and deviant sexual arousal in nonfamilial child molesters', *Behavior Modification*, **21(1)**, 86–96.

Marshall, W.L. and Anderson, D. (1996) 'An evaluation of the benefits of relapse prevention programs with sexual offenders', *Sexual Abuse: A Journal of Research and Treatment*, **8(3)**, 209–21.

Marshall, W.L. and Anderson, D. (2000) 'Do Relapse Prevention Components Enhance Treatment Effectiveness?' in D.R. Laws, S.M. Hudson and T. Ward (eds) *Remaking Relapse Prevention with Sex Offenders* (pp. 39–55). New York: Guildford Press.

Marshall, W.L. and Barbaree, H.E. (1988) 'The long-term evaluation of a behavioral treatment program for child molesters', *Behaviour Research and Therapy*, **26(6)**, 499–511.

Marshall, W.L. and Barbaree, H.E. (1989) 'Sexual Violence' in K. Howells and C.R. Hollin (eds) *Clinical Approaches to Violence*. Chichester: John Wiley & Sons.

Marshall, W.L. and Barbaree, H.E. (1990a) 'An Integrated Theory of the Etiology of Sexual Offending' in W.L. Marshall, D.R. Laws and H.E. Barbaree (eds) *Handbook of Sexual Assault: Issues, Theories, and Treatment of the Offender* (pp. 257–75). New York: Plenum Press.

Marshall, W.L. and Barbaree, H.E. (1990b) 'Outcome of Comprehensive Cognitive-behavioral Treatment Programs' in W.L. Marshall, D.R. Laws and H.E. Barbaree (eds) *Handbook of Sexual Assault: Issues, Theories, and Treatment of the Offender* (pp. 363–85). New York: Plenum Press.

Marshall, W.L. and Eccles, A. (1991) 'Issues in clinical practice with sex offenders', *Journal of Interpersonal Violence*, **6(1)**, 68–93.

Marshall, W.L. and Eccles, A. (1996) 'Cognitive-behavioral Treatment of Sex Offenders' in V.B. Van Hasselt and M. Hersen (eds) *Sourcebook of Psychological Treatment Manuals for Adult Disorders*. London: B.T. Batsford.

Marshall, W.L. and Hambley, L.S. (1996) 'Intimacy and loneliness, and their relationship to rape myth acceptance and hostility toward women among rapists', *Journal of Interpersonal Violence*, **11(4)**, 586–92.

Marshall, W.L. and Laws, D.R. (2003) 'A brief history of behavioral and cognitive behavioral approaches to sexual offender treatment: part 2. The modern era', *Sexual Abuse: A Journal of Research and Treatment*, **15(2)**, 93–120.

Marshall, W.L. and Mazzucco, A. (1995) 'Self-esteem and parental attachments in child molesters', *Sexual Abuse: A Journal of Research and Treatment*, **7(4)**, 279–85.

Marshall, W.L. and McGuire, J. (2003) 'Effect sizes in the treatment of sexual offenders', *International Journal of Offender Therapy and Comparative Criminology*, **47(6)**, 653–63.

Marshall, W.L. and Pithers, W.D. (1994) 'A reconsideration of treatment outcome with sex offenders', *Criminal Justice and Behavior*, **21(1)**, 10–27.

Marshall, W.L. and Serran, G.A. (2000) 'Improving the effectiveness of sexual offender treatment', *Trauma, Violence and Abuse*, **1(3)**, 203–22.

Marshall, W.L. and Williams, S. (1975) 'A behavioral approach to the modification of rape', *Quarterly Bulletin of the British Association for Behavioural Psychotherapy*, **4**, 78.

Marshall, W.L., Anderson, D. and Champagne, F. (1997) 'Self-esteem and its relationship to sexual offending', *Psychology, Crime and Law*, **3(3)**, 161–86.

Marshall, W.L., Anderson, D. and Fernandez, Y.M. (1999) *Cognitive Behavioural Treatment Programmes*. Chichester: John Wiley & Sons.

Marshall, W.L., Barbaree, H.E. and Eccles, A. (1991) 'Early onset and deviant sexuality in child molesters', *Journal of Interpersonal Violence*, **6(3)**, 323–35.

Marshall, W.L., Barbaree, H.E. and Fernandez, Y.M. (1995) 'Some aspects of social competence in sexual offenders', *Sexual Abuse: A Journal of Research and Treatment*, **7(2)**, 113–27.

Marshall, W.L., Eccles, A. and Barbaree, H.E. (1993) 'A three-tiered approach to the rehabilitation of incarcerated sex offenders', *Behavioral Sciences and the Law*, **11(4)**, 441–55.

Marshall, W.L., Hamilton, K. and Fernandez, Y. (2001) 'Empathy deficits and cognitive distortions in child molesters', *Sexual Abuse: A Journal of Research and Treatment*, **13(2)**, 123–30.

Marshall, W.L., Hudson, S.M. and Jones, R. (1994) 'Sexual Deviance' in P. H. Wilson (ed.) *Principles and Practice of Relapse Prevention*. New York: Guildford Press.

Marshall, W.L., Champagne, F., Brown, C. and Miller, S. (1997a) 'Empathy, loneliness, and self esteem in nonfamilial child molesters: a brief report', *Journal of Child Sexual Abuse*, **6(3)**, 87–98.

Marshall, W.L., Champagne, F., Sturgeon, C. and Bryce, P. (1997b) 'Increasing the self esteem of child molesters', *Sexual Abuse: A Journal of Research and Treatment*, **9(4)**, 321–33.

Marshall, W.L., Fernandez, Y.M., Hudson, S.M. and Ward, T. (1998) *Sourcebook of Treatment Programs for Sexual Offenders*. New York: Plenum Press.

Marshall, W.L., Jones, R., Ward, T. and Johnston, P. (1991) 'Treatment outcome with sex offenders', *Clinical Psychology Review*, **11(4)**, 465–85.

Marshall, W.L., Thornton, D., Marshall, L.E., Fernandez, Y.M. and Mann, R. (2001) 'Treatment of sexual offenders who are in categorical denial: a pilot project', *Sexual Abuse: A Journal of Research and Treatment*, **13(3)**, 205–15.

Marshall, W.L., Serran, G.A., Fernandez, Y.M., Mulloy, R.E., Mann, R.E. and Thornton, D. (2003) 'Therapist characteristics in the treatment of sexual offenders: tentative data on their relationship with indices of behaviour change', *Journal of Sexual Aggression*, **9(1)**, 25–30.

Marshall, W.L., Serran, G., Moulden, H., Mulloy, R., Fernandez, Y.M., Mann, R.E., et al. (2002) 'Therapist features in sexual offender treatment: their reliable identification and influence on behaviour change', *Clinical Psychology and Psychotherapy*, **9**, 395–405.

Marshall, W.L., Fernandez, Y.M., Serran, G.A., Mulloy, R., Thornton, D., Mann, R.E., *et al.* (2003) 'Process variables in the treatment of sexual offenders: a review of the relevant literature', *Aggression and Violent Behavior*, **8(2)**, 205–34.

Martinson, R. (1974) 'What works? Questions and answers about prison reform', *The Public Interest*, **35**, 22–54.

Martinson, R. (1979) 'New findings, new views: a note of caution regarding sentencing reform', *Hofstra Law Review*, **7**, 243–58.

Marx, B.P., Miranda, R. and Meyerson, L.A. (1999) 'Cognitive-behavioural treatment for rapists: can we do better?', *Clinical Psychology Review*, **19(7)**, 875–94.

Mayhew, P., Elliot, D. and Dowds, L. (1989) *The British Crime Survey*. Home Office Research Study No. 111. London: HMSO.

McAlinden, A.M. (1999) 'Panel: sex offenders in the community. Paper: tracking sex offenders', paper presented at the *British Criminology Conference*, Liverpool.

McCall, G.J. (1993) 'Risk factors and sexual assault prevention', *Journal of Interpersonal Violence*, **8(2)**, 227–95.

McConaghy, N. (1995) 'Are sex offenders ever "cured"?', *The Medical Journal of Australia*, **162(1)**, 397.

McConaghy, N. (1998) 'Neglect of evidence that relapse prevention is ineffective in treatment of incarcerated sexual offenders [letter to the editor]', *Sexual Abuse: Journal of Research and Treatment*, **10(2)**, 159–62.

McConaghy, N. (1999a) 'Methodological issues concerning evaluation of treatment for sexual offenders: randomization, treatment dropouts, untreated controls, and within-treatment studies', *Sexual Abuse: A Journal of Research and Treatment*, **11(3)**, 183–93.

McConaghy, N. (1999b) 'Unresolved issues in scientific sexology', *Archives of Sexual Behavior*, **28(4)**, 285–318.

McGrath, R.J. (1991) 'Sex offender risk assessment and disposition planning: a review of empirical and clinical findings', *International Journal of Offender Therapy and Comparative Criminology*, **35(4)**, 328–50.

McGrath, R.J. (1995) 'Sex offender treatment: does it work?', *Perspectives*, **19**, 24–6.

McGrath, R.J., Hoke, S.E. and Vojtisek, J.E. (1998) 'Cognitive-behavioral treatment of sex offenders: a treatment comparison and long term follow up study', *Criminal Justice and Behavior*, **25(2)**, 203–25.

McGrath, R.J., Cumming, G., Livingston, J.A. and Hoke, S.E. (2003) 'Outcome of a treatment program for adult sex offenders: from prison to community', *Journal of Interpersonal Violence*, **18(1)**, 3–18.

McGuire, J. (2000) *An Introduction to Theory and Research: Cognitive-Behavioural Approaches*. HM Inspectorate of Probation Report. London: HMSO.

McGuire, J. and Priestley, P. (1995) 'Reviewing "What Works": Past, Present and Future' in J. McGuire (ed.) *What Works: Reducing Reoffending. Guidelines from Research and Practice* (pp. 3–34) The Wiley Series in Offender Rehabilitation. Chichester: John Wiley & Sons.

McGuire, R.J., Carlisle, J.M. and Young, B.G. (1965) 'Sexual deviations as conditioned behaviour: a hypothesis', *Behaviour Research and Therapy*, **3**, 185–90.

McMahon, P.M. (2000) 'The public health approach to the prevention of sexual violence', *Sexual Abuse: A Journal of Research and Treatment*, **12(1)**, 27–36.

McMahon, P.M. and Puett, R.C. (1999) 'Child sexual abuse as a public health issue: recommendation of an expert panel', *Sexual Abuse: A Journal of Research and Treatment*, **11(4)**, 257–66.

McPherson, M., Chein, D., Van Maren, N. and Swenson, D. (1994). *Sex Offender Treatment Programs*. Program Evaluation Division Office of the Legislative Auditor State of Minnesota. Saint Paul, MN: Centennial Office Building.

Mehrabian, A. and Epstein, N. (1972) 'A measure of emotional empathy', *Journal of Personality*, **40**, 525–43.

Mercy, J.A. (1999) 'Having new eyes: viewing child sexual abuse as a public health problem', *Sexual Abuse: A Journal of Research and Treatment*, **11(4)**, 317–21.

Miner, M.H. (1997) 'How can we conduct treatment outcome research?', *Sexual Abuse: A Journal of Research and Treatment*, **9(2)**, 95–110.

Miner, M.H. and Dwyer, S.M. (1995) 'Analysis of dropouts from outpatient sex offender treatment', *Journal of Psychology and Human Sexuality*, **7(3)**, 77–93.

Miner, M.H., Marques, J.K., Day, D.M. and Nelson, C. (1990) 'Impact of relapse prevention in treating sex offenders: preliminary findings', *Annals of Sex Research*, **3(2)**, 165–85.

Morgan, R., Luborsky, L., Crits-Christoph, P., Curtis, H. and Solomon, J. (1982) 'Predicting the outcomes of psychotherapy by the Penn Helping Alliance Rating Method', *Archives of General Psychiatry*, **39(4)**, 397–402.

Motiuk, L.L. and Brown, S.L. (1996) 'Factors related to recidivism among released federal sex offenders', *Forum of Correction Research [On-Line]*. http://www.csc-scc.gc.ca/crd/reports/r49e/r49e.htm.

Muran, J.C., Gorman, B.S., Safran, J.D. and Twining, L. (1995) 'Linking in-session change to overall outcome in short-term cognitive therapy', *Journal of Consulting and Clinical Psychology*, **63(4)**, 651–7.

Murphy, P. (1998) 'A therapeutic programme for imprisoned sex offenders: progress to date and issues for the future', *Irish Journal of Psychology*, **19(1)**, 190–207.

Murphy, W.D. (1990) 'Assessment and Modification of Cognitive Distortions in Sex Offenders' in W.L. Marshall, D.R. Laws and H.E. Barbaree (eds) *Handbook of Sexual Assault: Issues, Theories and Treatment of the Offender* (pp. 331–42). New York: Plenum Press.

Murphy, W.D., Abel, G.G. and Becker, J.V. (1980) 'Future Research Issues' in D.J. Cox and R.J. Daitzman (eds) *Exhibitionism: Description, Assessment and Treatment* (pp. 339–92). New York: Garland STPM Press.

Murphy, W.D., Coleman, E.M. and Haynes, M.R. (1983) 'Treatment and Evaluation Issues with the Mentally Retarded Sex Offender' in J.G. Greer and I.R. Stuart (eds) *The Sexual Aggressor: Current Perspectives on Treatment* (pp. 22–41). New York: Van Nostrand Reinhold.

Myhill, A. and Allen, J. (2002) *Rape and Sexual Assault of Women: Findings from the British Crime Survey.* Research Findings No. 159. London: Home Office Research, Development and Statistics Directorate.

Nash, M. (1999) *Police, Probation and Protecting the Public.* London: Blackstone Press.

Nathan, L., Wilson, N.J. and Hillman, D. (2003) *Te Whakakotahitanga: An Evaluation of the Te Piriti Special Treatment Programme for Child Sex Offenders in New Zealand.* Wellington: New Zealand Department of Corrections.

Nathan, P. and Ward, T. (2002) 'Female sex offenders: clinical and demographic features', *Journal of Sexual Aggression*, **8(1)**, 5–21.

New Zealand Department of Corrections (2004a) *Kia Marama Special Treatment Unit.* http://www.corrections.govt.nz/public/aboutus/factsheets/special treatmentprogrammes/kiamaramastu.html.

New Zealand Department of Corrections (2004b) *Te Piriti Special Treatment Unit.* http://www.corrections.govt.nz/public/aboutus/factsheets/specialtreatmen-tprogrammes/tepiriti.html.

Nicholaichuk, T.P. (1996) 'Sex offender treatment priority: an illustration of the risk/need principle', *Forum of Correction Research [On-Line]*, **8(2)**. http://198.103.98.138/text/pblct/forum/e082/082ȷ_e.pdf.

Nicholaichuk, T.P., Gordon, A., Gu, D. and Wong, S. (2000) 'Outcome of an institutional sexual offender treatment program: a comparison between treated and matched untreated offenders', *Sexual Abuse: A Journal of Research and Treatment*, **12(2)**, 139–5.

Nugent, P.M. and Kroner, D.G. (1996) 'Denial, response styles, and admittance of offences among child molesters and rapists', *Journal of Interpersonal Violence*, **11(4)**, 475–86.

O'Donohue, W. and Letourneau, E. (1993) 'A brief group treatment for the modification of denial in child sexual abusers: outcome and follow up', *Child Abuse and Neglect*, **17(2)**, 299–304.

O'Donohue, W., Letourneau, E. and Dowling, H. (1997) 'Development and preliminary validation of a paraphilic sexual fantasy questionnaire', *Sexual Abuse: A Journal of Research and Treatment*, **9(3)**, 167–78.

Palmer, T. (1975) 'Martinson revisited', *Journal of Research in Crime and Delinquency*, **12**, 133–52.

Patel, K. and Lord, A. (2001) 'Ethnic minority sex offenders' experiences of treatment', *Journal of Sexual Aggression*, **7**, 40–51.

Pawson, R. and Tilley, N. (1994) 'What works in evaluation research?', *British Journal of Criminology*, **34(3)**, 291–306.

Peebles, J.E. (1999) 'Therapeutic jurisprudence and the sentencing of sexual offenders in Canada', *International Journal of Offender Therapy and Comparative Criminology*, **43(3)**, 275–90.

Percy, A. and Mayhew, P. (1997) 'Estimating sexual victimisation in a national crime survey: a new approach', *Studies on Crime and Crime Prevention*, **6(2)**, 125–50.

Perkins, D.E. (1987) 'A Psychological Treatment Programme for Sex Offenders' in B.J. McGurk, D.M. Thornton and M. Williams (eds) *Applying Psychology to Imprisonment: Theory and Practice* (pp. 192–217). London: HMSO.

Perkins, D.E. (1990) 'The Case for Treating Sex Offenders' in K. Howells and C. R. Hollin (eds) *Clinical Approaches to Working with Mentally Disordered and Sexual Offenders*. D.C.L.P. Issues in Criminological Psychology. Occasional Paper No. 16. Leicester: British Psychological Society.

Perkins, D.E. (1991) 'Clinical Work with Sex Offenders in Secure Settings' in C.R. Hollin and K. Howells (eds) *Clinical Approaches to Sex Offenders and their Victims*. Chichester: John Wiley & Sons.

Petrunik, M.G. (2002) 'Managing unacceptable risk: sex offenders, community response, and social policy in the United States and Canada', *International Journal of Offender Therapy and Comparative Criminology*, **46(4)**, 483–511.

Pithers, W.D. (1990) 'Relapse Prevention with Sexual Aggressors: A Method for Maintaining Therapeutic Gain and Enhancing External Supervision' in W.L. Marshall, D.R. Laws and H.E. Barbaree (eds) *Handbook of Sexual Assault: Issues, Theories and Treatment of the Offender*. New York: Plenum Press.

Pithers, W.D. (1991) 'Relapse prevention with sexual aggressors', *Forum of Correction Research [On-Line]*, **3(4)**. http://198.103.98.138/text/pblct/forum/e034/034f_e.pdf.

Pithers, W.D. (1994) 'Process evaluation of a group therapy component designed to enhance sex offenders' empathy for sexual abuse survivors', *Behaviour Research and Therapy*, **32(5)**, 565–70.

Pithers, W.D. (1997) 'Maintaining treatment integrity with sexual abusers', *Criminal Justice and Behavior*, **24(1)**, 34–51.

Pithers, W.D. (1999) 'Empathy: definition, enhancement, and relevance to the treatment of sexual abusers', *Journal of Interpersonal Violence*, **14(3)**, 257–84.

Pithers, W.D., Martin, G.R. and Cumming, G.F. (1989) 'Vermont Treatment Program for Sexual Aggressors' in D. R. Laws (ed.) *Relapse Prevention with Sex Offenders*. New York: Guildford Press.

Pithers, W.D., Beal, L.S., Armstrong, J. and Petty, J. (1989) 'Identification of Risk Factors Through Clinical Interviews and Analysis of Records' in D.R. Laws (ed.) *Relapse Prevention with Sex Offenders*. New York: Guildford Press.

Pithers, W.D., Kashima, K.M., Cumming, G.F. and Beal, L.S. (1988) 'Relapse Prevention: A Method of Enhancing Maintenance of Change in Sex Offenders' in A.C. Salter (ed.) *Treating Child Sex Offenders and Victims: A Practical Guide*. London: SAGE.

Pithers, W.D., Marques, J.K., Gibat, C.C. and Marlatt, G.A. (1983) 'Relapse Prevention with Sexual Aggressives: A Self-control Model of Treatment and Maintenance of Change' in J.G. Greer and I.R. Stuart (eds) *The Sexual Aggressor: Current Perspectives on Treatment*. New York: Van Nostrand Reinhold.

Plotnick, R.D. and Deppman, L. (1999) 'Using benefit-cost analysis to assess child abuse prevention and intervention programs', *Child Welfare*, **78(3)**, 381–407.

Polaschek, D.L.L. (2003) 'Relapse prevention, offense process models, and the treatment of sexual offenders', *Professional Psychology: Research and Practice*, **34(4)**, 361–7.

Polizzi, D.M., MacKenzie, D.L. and Hickman, L.J. (1999) 'What works in adult sex offender treatment? A review of prison- and non-prison-based treatment programs', *International Journal of Offender Therapy and Comparative Criminology*, **43(3)**, 357–74.

Proctor, E. (1994) 'Sex offender programmes: do they work?', *Probation Journal*, **41(1)**, 31–2.

Proctor, E. (1996) 'A five year outcome evaluation of a community-based treatment programme for convicted sexual offenders run by the probation service', *The Journal of Sexual Aggression*, **2(1)**, 3–16.

Proulx, J., Pellerin, B., Paradis, Y., McKibben, A., Aubut, J. and Ouimet, M. (1997) 'Static and dynamic predictors of recidivism in sexual aggressors', *Sexual Abuse: A Journal of Research and Treatment*, **9(1)**, 7–28.

Quay, H.C. (1977) 'The three faces of evaluation: what can be expected to work?', *Criminal Justice and Behavior*, **4**, 341–54.

Quinsey, V.L. and Earls, C.M. (1990) 'The Modification of Sexual Preferences' in W.L. Marshall, D.R. Laws and H.E. Barbaree (eds) *Handbook of Sexual Assault: Issues, Theories, and Treatment of the Offender*. New York: Plenum Press.

Quinsey, V.L., Harris, G.T., Rice, M.E. and Lalumière, M.L. (1993) 'Assessing the treatment efficacy in outcome studies of sex offenders', *Journal of Interpersonal Violence*, **8(4)**, 512–23.

Quinsey, V.L., Rice, M.E. and Harris, G.T. (1995) 'Actuarial prediction of sexual recidivism', *Journal of Interpersonal Violence*, **10(1)**, 85–105.

Quinsey, V.L., Khanna, A. and Malcolm, P.B. (1998) 'A retrospective evaluation of the Regional Treatment Centre sex offender treatment program', *Journal of Interpersonal Violence*, **13(5)**, 621–44.

Rapaport, K. and Burkhart, B.R. (1984) 'Personality and attitudinal characteristics of sexually coercive college males', *Journal of Abnormal Psychology*, **93(2)**, 216–21.

Renvoize, J. (1993) *Innocence Destroyed: A Study of Child Abuse*. London: Routledge.

Rice, M.E. and Harris, G.T. (1997) 'The Treatment of Adult Offenders' in D.M. Stoff, J. Breiling and J.D. Master (eds) *Handbook of Antisocial Behaviour* (pp. 425–35). Toronto: John Wiley & Sons.

Rice, M.E., Quinsey, V.L. and Harris, G.T. (1991) 'Sexual recidivism among child molesters released from a maximum security psychiatric institution', *Journal of Consulting and Clinical Psychology*, **59(3)**, 381–6.

Rice, M.E., Chaplin, T.C., Harris, G.T. and Coutts, J. (1994) 'Empathy for the victim and sexual arousal among rapists and nonrapists', *Journal of Interpersonal Violence*, **9(4)**, 435–49.

Rich, P. (2003) *Juvenile Sexual Offenders: Understanding, Assessing and Rehabilitating.* Hoboken, NJ: John Wiley & Sons.

Robinson, J. and Smith, G. (1971) 'The effectiveness of correctional programmes', *Crime and Delinquency,* **17**, 67–80.

Rogers, R. and Dickey, R. (1991) 'Denial and minimisation among sex offenders: a review of competing models of deception', *Annals of Sex Research,* **4**, 49–63.

Rose, P. and Wright, S. (1999) 'Sex monster free soon: Home Office powerless to prevent the release of this dangerous paedophile'. *Daily Mail,* 7 April.

Ross, R.R. and Gendreau, P. (1980) *Effective Correctional Treatment.* Toronto: Butterworth.

Roys, D.T. (1997) 'Empirical and theoretical considerations of empathy in sex offenders', *International Journal of Offender Therapy and Comparative Criminology,* **41(1)**, 53–64.

Sabor, M. (1992) 'The sex offender treatment programme in prisons', *Probation Journal,* **39(1)**, 14–18.

Salter, A.C. (ed.) (1988) *Treating Child Sex Offenders and Victims: A Practical Guide.* London: SAGE.

Sampson, A. (1994) *Acts of Abuse: Sex Offenders and the Criminal Justice System.* London: Routledge.

Saradjian, J. (1996) *Women Who Sexually Abuse Children: From Research to Clinical Practice.* London: John Wiley & Sons.

Scheela, R.A. (1995) 'Remodeling as metaphor: sex offenders' perceptions of the treatment process', *Issues in Mental Health Nursing,* **16(6)**, 493–504.

Scheela, R.A. (2001) 'Sex offender treatment: therapists' experiences and perceptions', *Issues in Mental Health Nursing,* **22**, 749–67.

Scheela, R.A. and Stern, P.N. (1994) 'Falling apart: a process integral to the remodeling of male incest offenders', *Archives of Psychiatric Nursing,* **8(2)**, 91–100.

Schlank, A. (1999) 'Guidelines for the Development of New Programs' in A. Schlank and F. Cohen (eds) *The Sexual Predator: Law, Policy, Evaluation and Treatment.* Kinston, NJ: Civic Research Institute.

Schlank, A. and Shaw, T.A. (1996) 'Treating sex offenders who deny their guilt: a pilot study', *Sexual Abuse: A Journal of Research and Treatment,* **8**, 17–23.

Schlank, A., Harry, R. and Farnsworth, M. (1999) 'The Minnesota Sex Offender Program' in A. Schlank and F. Cohen (eds) *The Sexual Predator: Law, Policy, Evaluation and Treatment.* Kinston, NJ: Civic Research Institute.

Schwartz, B.K. (1992) 'Effective treatment for sex offenders', *Psychiatric Annals,* **22(6)**, 315–19.

Schwartz, B.K. (1995) 'Theories of Sexual Offenders' in B.K. Schwartz and H.R. Cellini (eds) *The Sex Offender: Corrections, Treatment and Legal Practice.* Kingston, NJ: Civic Research Institute.

Scully, D. (1990) *Understanding Sexual Violence: A Study of Convicted Rapists.* Boston: Unwin Hyman.

Seidman, B.T., Marshall, W.L., Hudson, S.M. and Robertson, P.J. (1994) 'An examination of intimacy and loneliness in sex offenders', *Journal of Interpersonal Violence,* **9(4)**, 518–34.

Serran, G., Fernandez, Y., Marshall, W.L. and Mann, R.E. (2003) 'Process issues in treatment: application to sexual offender programs', *Professional Psychology: Research and Practice*, **34(4)**, 368–75.

Seto, M.C. and Barbaree, H.E. (1999) 'Psychopathy, treatment behavior, and sex offender recidivism', *Journal of Interpersonal Violence*, **14(12)**, 1235–48.

Seto, M.C., Maric, A. and Barbaree, H.E. (2001) 'The role of pornography in the etiology of sexual aggression', *Aggression and Violent Behavior*, **6(1)**, 35–53.

Shanahan, M. and Donato, R. (2001) 'Counting the cost: estimating the economic benefit of pedophile treatment programs', *Child Abuse and Neglect*, **25(4)**, 541–55.

Shaughnessy, J.T. and Zechmeister, E.B. (1997) *Research Methods in Psychology* (4th ed.). New York: McGraw-Hill International Editions.

Shaw, J.A., Lewis, J.E., Loeb, A., Rosado, J. and Rodriguez, R.A. (2000) 'Child on child sexual abuse: psychological perspectives', *Child Abuse and Neglect*, **24(12)**, 1591–600.

Shaw, T.A., Herkov, M.J. and Greer, R.A. (1995) 'Examination of treatment completion and predicted outcome among incarcerated sex offenders', *Bulletin of the American Academy of Psychiatry and the Law*, **23(1)**, 35–41.

Sheath, M. (1990) ' "Confrontative" work with sex offenders: legitimised nonce bashing?', *Probation Journal*, **37(4)**, 159–62.

Shelby, R.A., Stoddart, R.M. and Taylor, K.T. (2001) 'Factors contributing to levels of burnout amoung sex offender treatment providers', *Journal of Interpersonal Violence*, **16(11)**, 1205–17.

Silverman, J. and Wilson, D. (2002) *Innocence Betrayed: Paedophilia, the Media and Society*. Cambridge: Polity.

Simkins, L., Ward, W., Bowman, S. and Rinck, C.M. (1989) 'The multiphasic sex inventory: diagnosis and prediction of treatment response in child sexual abusers', *Annals of Sex Research*, **2**, 205–26.

Simon, L.M.J. (2000) 'An examination of the assumptions of specialization, mental disorder, and dangerousness in sex offenders', *Behavioral Sciences and the Law*, **18(2–3)**, 275–308.

Smallbone, S.W., Wheaton, J. and Hourigan, D. (2003) 'Trait empathy and criminal versatility in sexual offenders', *Sexual Abuse: A Journal of Research and Treatment*, **15(1)**, 49–60.

Smith, L. (1989) *Concerns about Rape. Home Office Research Study No. 106*. London: HMSO.

Snell, W.E., Belk, S.S., Papini, D.R. and Clark, S. (1989) 'Development and validation of the Sexual Self-Disclosure Scale', *Annals of Sex Research*, **2**, 307–34.

Soothill, K.L. and Gibbens, T.C.N. (1978) 'Recidivism of sex offenders: a re-appraisal', *British Journal of Criminology*, **18(3)**, 267–76.

Soothill, K.L. and Walby, J. (1991) *Sex Crime in the News*. London: Routledge.

Spencer, A. (1998) 'Peterhead Prison Program' in W.L. Marshall, Y.M. Fernandez, S.M. Hudson and T. Ward (eds) *Sourcebook of Treatment Programs for Sex Offenders*. New York: Plenum Press.

Spencer, A. (2002) *Report of the Review Group on the Future Management of Sex Offenders within Scottish Prisons*. http://www.sps.gov.uk/keydocs/sex_offenders/default.asp.

Startup, M. and Edmonds, J. (1994) 'Compliance with homework assignments in cognitive-behavioral psychotherapy for depression: relation to outcome and methods of enhancement. *Cognitive Therapy and Research*, **18(6)**, 567–79.

Stermac, L.E. and Segal, Z.V. (1989) 'Adult sexual contact with children: an examination of cognitive factors', *Behavior Therapy*, **20(4)**, 573–84.

Strathclyde Regional Council, Social Work Department and the Scottish Prison Service (1995) *P.E.T.E.O. (Profiling, Evaluating, Targeting and Educating Offenders) A Sex Offender Groupwork Programme within HM Prison Schotts: Discussion Document.* Glasgow: Strathclyde Regional Council.

Tabachnick, J. and Dawson, E. (2000) *Stop It Now! Vermont: Four Year Program Evaluation 1995–1999.* Haydenville and Brandon, VT: Stop It Now!.

Tarolla, S.M., Wagner, E.F., Rabinowitz, J. and Tubman, J.G. (2002) 'Understanding and treating juvenile offenders: a review of current knowledge and future directions', *Aggression and Violent Behavior*, **10(2)**, 125–44.

Taylor, B. (ed.). (1981) *Perspective on Paedophilia.* London: Batsford.

Teuma, R.T., Smith, D.I., Stewart, A.A. and Lee, J.K.P. (2003) 'Measurement of victim empathy in intrafamilial and extrafamilial child molesters using the Child Molester Empathy Measure (CMEM)', *International Journal of Forensic Psychology [On-line]*, **1(1)**, 120–32. http://ijfp.psyc.uow.edu.au/index2.html.

Thornton, D. (1987) 'Treatment Effects on Recidivism: A Reappraisal of the "Nothing Works" Doctrine' in B.J. McGurk, D.M. Thornton and M. Williams (eds) *Applying Psychology to Imprisonment: Theory and Practice.* London: HMSO.

Thornton, D. (1991) 'Treatment of Sexual Offenders in Prison: A Strategy' in *Treatment Programmes for Sex Offenders in Custody: A Strategy* (pp. 13–38). London: HM Prison Service.

Thornton, D. and Hogue, T. (1993) 'The large-scale provision of programmes for imprisoned sex offenders: issues, dilemmas and progress', *Criminal Behaviour and Mental Health*, **3(4)**, 371–80.

Tierney, D.W. and McCabe, M.P. (2001) 'An evaluation of self-report measures of cognitive distortions and empathy among Australian sex offenders', *Archives of Sexual Behavior*, **30(5)**, 495–519.

Tilley, N. (1992) 'Chapter 15' in W. Stainton, D. Rogers, D. Hevey, J. Roche and E. Ash (eds) *Child Abuse and Neglect: Facing the Challenge* (Revised 2nd ed.). London: B.T. Batsford.

Valliant, P.A. and Antonowicz, D.H. (1992) 'Rapists, incest offenders, and child molesters in treatment: cognitive and social skills training', *International Journal of Offender Therapy and Comparative Criminology*, **36(3)**, 221–30.

Vanhouche, W. and Vertommen, H. (1999) 'Assessing cognitive distortions in sex offenders: a review of commonly used versus recently developed instruments', *Psychologica Belgica*, **39(2–3)**, 163–87.

Vennard, J., Sugg, D. and Hedderman, C. (1997) *Changing Offenders' Attitudes and Behaviour: What Works?* Home Office Research Study No. 171. London: HMSO.

Walborn, F.S. (1996) *Process Variables: Four Common Elements of Counselling and Psychotherapy.* Belmont, CA: Brooks/Cole.

Ward, T. (2000) 'Sexual offenders' cognitive distortions as implicit theories', *Aggression and Violent Behavior*, **5(5)**, 491–507.

Ward, T. (2001) 'A critique of Hall and Hirschman's quadripartite model of child sexual abuse', *Psychology, Crime and Law*, **7(4)**, 333–50.

Ward, T. (2002a) 'Good lives and the rehabilitation of offenders: promises and problems', *Aggression and Violent Behavior*, **7(5)**, 513–28.

Ward, T. (2002b) 'Marshall and Barbaree's integrated theory of child sexual abuse: a critique', *Psychology, Crime and Law*, **8(3)**, 209–28.

Ward, T. and Hudson, S.M. (1998a) 'The construction and development of theory in the sexual offending area: a metatheoretical framework', *Sexual Abuse: A Journal of Research and Treatment*, **10(1)**, 47–63.

Ward, T. and Hudson, S.M. (1998b) 'A model of the relapse process in sexual offenders', *Journal of Interpersonal Violence*, **13**, 700–25.

Ward, T. and Hudson, S.M. (2000) 'Sexual offenders' implicit planning: a conceptual model', *Sexual Abuse: A Journal of Research and Treatment*, **12(3)**, 189–202.

Ward, T. and Hudson, S.M. (2001) 'Finkelhor's precondition model of child sexual abuse: a critique', *Psychology, Crime and Law*, **7(4)**, 291–307.

Ward, T. and Keenan, T. (1999) 'Child molesters' implicit theories', *Journal of Interpersonal Violence*, **14(8)**, 821–38.

Ward, T. and Siegert, R.J. (2002) 'Toward a comprehensive theory of child sexual abuse: a theory knitting perspective', *Psychology, Crime and Law*, **8(4)**, 319–51.

Ward, T. and Stewart, C.A. (2003) 'The treatment of sex offenders: risk management and good lives', *Professional Psychology: Research and Practice*, **34(4)**, 353–60.

Ward, T., Hudson, S.M. and Marshall, W.L. (1994) 'The abstinence violation effect in child molesters', *Behavior, Research and Therapy*, **32**, 431–7.

Ward, T., Hudson, S.M. and Marshall, W.L. (1995) 'Cognitive distortions and affective deficits in sex offenders: a cognitive deconstructionist interpretation', *Sexual Abuse: A Journal of Research and Treatment*, **7(1)**, 67–83.

Ward, T., Hudson, S.M., Marshall, W.L. and Siegert, R. (1995) 'Attachment style and intimacy deficits in sexual offenders: a theoretical framework', *Sexual Abuse: A Journal of Research and Treatment*, **7(4)**, 317–35.

Ward, T., Hudson, S.M. and Siegert, R.J. (1995) 'A critical comment on Pithers' relapse prevention model', *Sexual Abuse: A Journal of Research and Treatment*, **7(2)**, 167–75.

Ward, T., Louden, K., Hudson, S.M. and Marshall, W.L. (1995) 'A descriptive model of the offense chain for child molesters', *Journal of Interpersonal Violence*, **10(4)**, 452–72.

Ward, T., Hudson, S.M., Johnston, L. and Marshall, W.L. (1997) 'Cognitive distortions in sex offenders: an integrative review', *Clinical Psychology Review*, **17(5)**, 479–507.

Ward, T., Fon, C., Hudson, S.M. and McCormack, J. (1998) 'A descriptive model of dysfunctional cognitions in child molesters', *Journal of Interpersonal Violence*, **13(1)**, 129–55.

Ward, T., Keenan, T. and Hudson, S.M. (2000) 'Understanding cognitive, affective, and intimacy deficits in sexual offenders: a developmental perspective', *Aggression and Violent Behavior*, **5(1)**, 41–62.

Webster, S.D., Akhtar, S., Bowers, L.E., Mann, R.E., Rallings, M. and Marshall, W.L. (2004) 'The impact of the prison service sex offender treatment pro-

Index

accreditation *see under* programmes
Adapted Programme (AP) 56–7, 61, 62
addiction theory 88
adolescents 53, 56, 71, 75
    treatment 37, 50, 53, 56, 64, 77
American Psychological Association
    157
anger 23, 139
AP (Adapted Programme) 56–7, 61, 62
Arbour Hill Prison 65, 203
assessment *see under* programmes,
    risk
attitudes 23, 120–1, 242
augmented behavioural programmes
    23
Australia 71–5, 205, 218–19
    cognitive-behavioural treatment 205
    programmes 70–5

Bandura's model of self-efficacy 142
Bath Programme 49
behavioural programmes 20–3, 34, 35,
    209
    see also cognitive behavioural
        treatment
    augmented 23
    cognitive 23–4, 33–8, 47–50, 55,
        61–8, 71–7
    effectiveness 22–3, 196, 199–200, 212
    positive findings 193–6, 201–2,
        206–7, 211, 213–14
behavioural theory 21–2
best practice guidance 189
biological theory 22, 80, 90
Booster Programme 57, 62

burden of client's potential 104–5, 110

C-SOGP 65, 66–7
    evaluation 204–5, 226
California 158, 196–9, 229
Canada 18, 33–40, 45, 45–50, 95–102,
    193–5, 199–202, 218, 225–6
    community programmes 45–50
    treatment programmes 46–50
Capital Territory 71
characteristics *see under* offenders
characteristics, clinical 175
child abuse, of sex offenders 11
circles of support 245–6
client's potential 104–5, 110
clinical characteristics 175
coerced treatment 43, 57, 72, 97–8
cognitive behavioural programmes
    23–4, 33–8, 47–50, 55, 61–8, 71–7
cognitive behavioural treatment 33,
    95–102
    see also behavioural programmes
    Australia 205
    Canada 192–202
    confrontation 100–2
    effectiveness 191–216
    equivocal findings 191–2, 196–201,
        202–5, 207, 209–10
    ethos 87, 95–102
    groupwork 99–100, 116, 180, 230,
        240
    meta-analyses 208–14
    negative findings 191–2, 196–201,
        202–5, 207, 209–10
    New Zealand 206–8

no cure 98–9, 244
Republic of Ireland 202–5
techniques 116
therapeutic style 101–2, 230–2
United Kingdom 202–5
United States 192–202
cognitive distortions 120–3
restructuring 127, 237
effectiveness 34–5, 81, 85, 88, 91,
130–1, 149, 237
cognitive theory 33–4
deconstruction 132–3
implicit 123–6
community programmes 49–50, 58–60,
65–8, 71–5
Canada 45–50
New South Wales 72
New Zealand 207–8
Northern Ireland 68
Queensland 73
Republic of Ireland 68
Scotland 68
UK 54–5, 58–60, 65–6, 203–5
United States 52–3, 194–6, 200
Western Australia 74–5
comparison groups 161, 193–5, 200–2,
204–7, 210–14
construct choice 175–6
coordination failure 88
CORE (CUBIT outreach programme)
72
Core Programme (CP) 56–7, 62, 147
evaluation 202–3
Correctional Service of Canada (CSC)
45–50
cost-benefit analysis 165–6, 217–19
cost-effectiveness 42, 217–19
Kia Marama 218
crime rates 2, 8–9
criminal justice response 1, 12–14, 20,
45–6, 56, 60, 70, 75, 235
CUBIT outreach programme (CORE)
72
Curragh Prison 65, 203
currency of treatment 193–4, 196, 199,
200
custodial treatment 48–9, 56–8, 61–4,
71–7

Northern Ireland 65
Scotland 57–8
UK 56–8, 61, 62, 147, 202–3
staff 56
United States 51–2
Custody-Based Intensive Treatment
(CUBIT) 71–2

definitions 2–3
denial and minimisation 116–20, 149,
237, 238
development see under programmes
developmental theory 80
deviant arousal 22–3, 135–6, 138–9,
237
and fantasy 136–7
goals 35, 81, 85, 88, 91, 135–7, 239
drop outs 152, 183–5, 197–9, 205,
210–14, 220–1
dynamic risk factors 10–11, 152, 225–6,
238–9

emotional regulation 81, 85, 91, 135,
139, 239
empathy 134, 237
deficits 129–30
goals 23, 35, 128–35, 149, 229, 237–9
model 128–9, 129
EP (Extended Programme) 62–3
ESTOP (Extended Programme) 64
ethics 155–8
ethnicity 226–7
evaluation 151–2
effect size 24–5, 168–9, 186–7, 188,
209–14
experimental designs 153–63, 232–4,
241
follow-up period 153–4, 171–2,
199–200, 207
generalisation of findings 151–2, 178
internal validity 163
low base rates 172–3, 186–7, 202, 204
methodology 15, 19, 24, 191–2,
200–2, 209–15, 241
New Zealand 206–7
programmes 193, 194–5, 199, 200–2,
205
publication bias 26

qualitative methods 123, 129, 178, 182, 188, 226, 232–4
  reasons for 151–2
  sample sizes 24, 26, 173, 186–7, 198, 202, 204, 208
  selection bias 26, 160–1, 193
  validity 176–7, 238–9
evidence–based practice 32–4, 40, 46, 56, 61–2, 65, 70, 78
Extended Programme (EP) 62–3
Extended Programme (ESTOP) 64

family theory 89
female offenders 6–7, 38, 50, 53, 62, 75, 77
  relationships 64
  Scotland 57–8, 64
  UK 57, 59, 62, 66
feminist theory 23, 120, 242
Finkelhor's integrated theory 85–7, 89–90, 94
Florida 194

gender of staff 106
goals 79, 114–16, 149–50, 237–9
  non-offence specific 140, 237
Gracewell Clinic 55
group processes 181, 230
groupwork 99–100, 116, 180, 230, 240

Hall and Hirschman's quadripartite model 81–2, 89
hostility 23, 139

images in media 1–2, 5–6, 235–6
incidence 1, 4–5
Indigenous Medium Programme 74
indigenous populations 73–7
  Australia 73–4
  Canada 50
  New Zealand 77, 206–7
  United States 53
Indigenous Sex Offender Treatment Programme (ISOTP) 73–4
integrated theory 33, 80, 85–7, 89, 89–90, 94, 236
integrity, programmes 31–2, 56, 112, 239–40

Intellectually Disabled Programme 74
Intensive Programme 74
intimacy deficits 91, 139, 139–40, 140
Ireland, Republic of 61, 65, 68, 202–5
ISOTP (Indigenous Sex Offender Treatment Programme) 73–4

juveniles 56, 71, 75
  treatment 37, 50, 53, 56, 64, 77

Kia Marama
  cost-effectiveness 218
  custodial setting 75–7
  evaluation 206–7

learning disabilities 38, 50, 53, 71, 73–5, 77
  UK 62, 64, 66
legal definitions 3
legislation 17–19, 39
  Canada 18, 45
  United Kingdom 1, 12, 99
  United States 17–19, 51
licensing see under programmes
link theory 88
low self-esteem see self-esteem

management 46, 59, 60, 63, 65–6, 68
Marshall's model of empathy 128–9
media
  public education 236, 243–4, 245
  response 1–2, 5–6, 12, 235
Medium Programme 74
mental health treatment 47–8, 73
  regional secure units 69–70
mental illness 6
meta-analysis 24–7, 208–14
methodology 15, 19, 24, 191–2, 200–2, 209–15, 241
minimisation of denial 116–19, 237
model
  empathy 128–9, 129
  multi-factor 87–9, 94
  pathways 90–2, 93
  quadripartite 81–2, 89
  self-efficacy 142
  self-regulation 92–3, 147
mono-causal theory 22, 80, 89, 236

moral panic 1, 12
motive and releaser theory 84–5
multi-factor model 87–9, 94
multi-modal theory 33, 80, 89, 236

N-SOGP 65, 67, 68
National Offender Management
    System (NOMS) 60, 68
need and responsivity 29–31, 182–3,
    227–8, 240
New Jersey 200
New South Wales 71–2
New Zealand 75–7, 206–8, 218
    programmes 75–7
no cure 98–9, 244
Northern Ireland 61, 65, 68
Northern Territory 71
Nothing Works 19–20, 27–8, 42–3

offence cycles/chains 35, 87–9, 143,
    146, 148
offenders see sex offenders
Ontario 49–50
outcomes
    personal/clinical characteristics 175
    recidivism 166–71, 174

paedophilia 3
pathways model 90–2, 93
personal/clinical characteristics 175
Pithers's model of empathy 129
placebo intervention 153, 154–5
political response 1, 12–14, 20, 45–6,
    56, 60, 70, 75, 235
pornography users 136–7
Preparation for intervention
    Programme (PIP) 73
prevalence 1, 4–5
primary prevention 243
programmes 14
    see also evaluation
    accreditation 46, 51, 112, 229, 239–40
        Scotland 61
        UK 32–3, 60, 61, 65
        United States 51
    assessment 46, 71
        Scotland 63
        UK 59, 65, 66

attitudes 35, 91
    characteristics 179–80, 227–30
    compliance 221–2
    cost effectiveness 218–19
    description 179
    development 20–4, 33–40, 45, 70–1
        Scotland 57–8, 64
        UK 35, 54–7, 58–9
        United States 17–19, 20–4, 33–40
    differences 151, 162, 179, 181, 222–9,
        230–2
    drift 31, 112, 180, 229–30, 239–40
    early 18, 21
    effectiveness 15, 151, 191–2, 237–9,
        240–1
        Nothing Works 27–8, 42–3
        risk, need and responsivity 30–1
    evaluation 193, 194–5, 199, 200–2,
        205
    expansion 14–15, 36–8, 235, 246
        UK 56–7, 59
    implementation 180
    integrity 31–2, 56, 112, 239–40
    licensing 46, 51, 112, 229, 239–40
        UK 32–3, 60, 61, 65
    management 46
        Scotland 63
        UK 59, 65, 66
    manuals 32, 46, 94, 179–80, 229,
        239–40
    range 47–50, 51–3, 71–4
    reversal 31
    selection of offenders 57, 59, 66, 71
    staffing 46–7
psychodynamic programmes 18, 21
psychometric tests/scales 122–3, 129,
    164, 176, 177, 238–9
psychopathy 18
psychotherapy legislation 17–19, 39
public education 236, 243–4, 245
public health approach 242–5
publication bias 26

quadripartite model 81–2, 89
Queensland 73–4

random allocation 26, 153, 155–8,
    197–9

randomised control trial (RTC) 153–8
rapists 222–3, 240
recidivism 8–9, 152, 166–71, 172–3, 174
  measurement 170–1
  within-treatment studies 163–5
regional secure units 69–70
Regional Treatment Centre (RTCSOP)
  47–8
relapse prevention 142–7, 237
  goals 14, 35–6, 87–9, 94, 141, 163–4,
    229, 237–9
relationships
  female offenders 64
  staff 107–8
Republic of Ireland 61, 65, 68, 202–5
residential treatment 54–5, 68
responsivity 29–31, 182–3, 227, 240
risk 8–9, 238–9
  assessment 10–11, 39–40, 93, 238–9
  factors 10–11, 39, 152
    dynamic 10–11, 152, 225–6, 238–9
    static 10, 238–9
risk, need and responsivity 29–31,
  182–3, 227, 240
  effectiveness 30–1
  integrity 31–2, 56, 112, 239–40
Rolling Programme (RSTOP) 62, 64

sample sizes 24, 26, 173, 186–7, 198,
  202, 204, 208
Schwartz motive and releaser theory
  84–5
Scotland 57–8, 61–5, 68, 96
secondary prevention 243
secure units 47–8, 69–70, 73
selection of offenders 57, 59, 66, 71
self–efficacy model 142
self-esteem 23, 35, 87, 101, 139, 140
self-regulation model 92–3, 147
Sex Offender Awareness Programmes
  (SOAP) 64
Sex Offender Intervention Programme
  (SOIP) 74
Sex Offender Treatment and
  Evaluation Project (SOTEP)
  158, 196–9, 229
sex offenders
  abused as children 11

as adolescents 7
characteristics 6–11, 182, 220–7
in community 13–14, 42–4, 235
in custody 12–14, 42–4, 235
definitions 2–3
as juveniles 7
loneliness 140
numbers 5
reasons for treatment 41–4
selection 59, 66, 71
specialist 9–10
as strangers 7–8
typologies 81, 91–2
Sexual Offender Programme (SOTP)
  73
sexual psychotherapy legislation
  17–19, 39
SOAP (Sex Offender Awareness
  Programmes) 64
social skill 23, 91, 139, 140
social theory 23, 80
SOIP (Sex Offender Intervention
  Programme) 74
SOTEP (Sex Offender Treatment and
  Evaluation Project) 158, 196–9,
  229
Southern Australia 71
specialist offenders 9–10
staff
  burden of client's potential 104–5,
    110
  burnout 105, 109, 112
  colleagues' attitudes 103, 105, 110
  custodial treatment 56
  effect of work 103–13
  gender 106
  positive effects 110–11
  relationships 107–8
  Republic of Ireland 65
  society's attitudes 103, 105, 110
  stigma 103, 105
  stress 104–7, 111, 112
  support 105, 110
  therapeutic style 101–2, 107
  training 46–7, 56, 107, 108, 112
  victimisation issues 106
static risk factors 10, 238–9
statistics

power 185–7, 198, 202, 204, 208
  significance 164, 194
stigma 103, 105
Stop It Now! helpline 44, 243–4
STOP Programme 57–8, 63–4, 96
stress 104–7, 111, 112
support circles 245–6

Tasmania 71
Te Piriti
  custodial setting 77
  evaluation 206–7
tertiary prevention 243
tests
  psychometric 122–3, 129, 164, 176, 177, 238–9
  transparency 123, 129, 177, 238
theory
  knitting 90
  levels 89
therapist characteristics 101–2, 107, 181–2, 230–2
training 46–7, 56, 107, 108, 112
TV-SOGP 65, 67
  evaluation 205

United Kingdom 1, 12, 32–3, 54–68, 99, 202–6
United States 17–19, 20–4, 33–40, 51–4, 158, 194–200, 229

Vermont 195–6
victimisation, staff issues 106
Victoria 72–3
voluntary treatment 43, 57, 72, 97–8

Ward and Hudson's self-regulation model 92–3, 147
Ward and Siegert's pathways model 90–2, 93
Warkworth Programme 48–9
Western Australia 74–5
What Works literature 19–20, 24–33, 240
within-treatment studies 163–5
Wolf's multi-factor model 87–9, 94
women offenders *see* female offenders

Young Offender Programme (YSTOP) 64